Ezra Stiles Gannett.

KENNIKAT PRESS SCHOLARLY REPRINTS

Dr. Ralph Adams Brown, Senior Editor

Series on
LITERARY AMERICA IN THE NINETEENTH CENTURY
Under the General Editorial Supervision of
Dr. Walter Harding
University Professor, State University of New York

Ezra Stiles Gannett.

Unitarian Minister in Boston,

1824–1871.

A MEMOIR.

BY HIS SON

WILLIAM C. GANNETT.

KENNIKAT PRESS
Port Washington, N. Y./London

128553

EZRA STILES GANNETT

First published in 1875
Reissued in 1971 by Kennikat Press
Library of Congress Catalog Card No: 79-122654
ISBN 0-8046-1302-8

Manufactured by Taylor Publishing Company   Dallas, Texas

TO

K. B. T.,

MY MOTHER-AUNT.

THIS book has been written chiefly for old friends who loved Dr. Gannett. He would have entreated that it be not written, — that was his temper ever. The colors of the picture are largely his own as he left them in yearnings and confessions; but those old friends will make the colors brighter from their memories, — and I would that other readers might bear that in mind. It is a minister's story, with little unique, nothing eventful, in it. There was but little even of that biographical material which undramatic workmen have often left behind them; for he put but little of himself into letters or journals, and his talk ran seldom on by-gone days and deeds. In more than one sense he forgot himself. The seventeen hundred sermons that kept the tally of the earnest weeks, and the nameless acts and words that filled the days with kindness, — Ezra, "Helper," was his name, — these were his forms of self-expression. Such expression passed into other lives more easily than it now can pass into his own memoir. But, because the sermons were simply himself written out, they in a measure supply this autobiographical element. For that reason a few have been added at the end, less to show the preacher than the man. They are an essential part of the " Life," as is explained at greater length in the pages that introduce them.

Beyond his home and parish he so closely identified his interests with those of his denomination, that an account of the Unitarianism of New England makes the natural background throughout the story; but the sketch of its rise and growth and several phases has been purposely filled in with more detail than was strictly needed for that purpose. It may be welcomed by some readers, while others can easily skip Chapters III. and VII., and certain pages in Chapters V. and X. It is mainly a chronicle of facts. What little criticism there is upon the facts will probably be assented to by neither " side " as wholly truthful, which makes the hope not less strong that it may be truthful. Yet, as the impression is not in all respects that which Dr. Gannett would himself convey, I would call attention to his own statements on pages 128 and 222, and what follows in each place.

The portrait engraved by Mr. J. A. J. WILCOX is slightly altered from a crayon drawn by ROWSE, in 1863. The wood-cuts have been done by Mr. S. S. KILBURN.

Several friends will see that they have helped to write the book. One chapter is altogether a service of their love ; and, so far as a son may thank them for such loving help, I would most gratefully acknowledge it.

W. C. GANNETT.

BOSTON, January, 1875.

I WOULD like to make another acknowledgment of aid, although to make it may seem to exaggerate the importance of one part of the book: the materials for the sketch of Unitarianism were chiefly gathered from sermons, reports, biographies, and from the old magazines and controversial volumes mentioned in the text; but much aid has also been drawn from writers who have before described the same " flow of faith." Among works in regard to the earlier phases of the movement, I would specially refer to a series of letters, hostile, but full of facts, on the " Introduction and Progress of Unitarianism in New England," in the " Spirit of the Pilgrims," vols. ii.–iv., 1829–1831 ; to a pamphlet, fair and thorough, while unsympathetic, by Bishop Burgess of Maine, called " Pages from the Ecclesiastical History of New England," 1740–1840 ; and to a long, fair article by Professor E. H. Gillett, in the " Historical Magazine " for April, 1871, on the " History and Literature of the Unitarian Controversy," — a compilation helpful by its abundant quotations and a large, though incomplete, bibliography; also to Sprague's " Annals" of the Unitarian Pulpit, Rev. Dr. J. S. Clark's " Sketch of the Congregational Churches in Massachusetts," and Rev. Dr. George E. Ellis's " Half-Century of the Unitarian Controversy."

The later " Transcendental" phase has been described by John Weiss and O. B. Frothingham in their Lives of. Theodore Parker, and part of it lies reflected in Margaret Fuller's Memoirs. Such accounts were freely used; and here again there were the pamphlets of a controversy, and the Unitarian magazines and reports, to quarry in. But the history of those " Transcendental" years of Boston life has never been written out as it should be. There still live elders who were themselves a large part of that stirring time: may not we, born out of due time, hope to thank one of them some day for the full, true story?

W. C. G.

FEBRUARY, 1875.

CONTENTS.

I.

THE HOME AND THE BOY, 1801–1816.

II.

SEEKING AND FINDING, 1816–1820.

III.

THE RISE OF UNITARIANISM IN NEW ENGLAND.

From Calvinism to Arminianism, 1620–1740.

From Arminianism to Unitarianism, 1740–1815.

The Unitarian Controversy, 1815–1833.

IV.

THE GIRDING, 1821–1824.

V.

MORNING WORK, WITHOUT AND WITHIN: ESTABLISHING THE FAITH, 1824–1836.

Without: Parish Work and Problems.

CONTENTS.

Unitarian History (*continued*).

Establishing the Faith.

Within: Struggle.

VI.

REST IN EUROPE, 1836–1838.

VII.

THE TRANSCENDENTAL MOVEMENT IN NEW ENGLAND

VIII.

MID-DAY: KEEPING THE FAITH, 1838–1852.

Mid-day Work.

Keeping the Faith.

Mid-day Passing.

IX.

AFTERNOON: ANTI-SLAVERY AND WAR TIMES, 1852–1865.

The Home and the Man.

Anti-Slavery and War Times.

X.

A FATHER IN THE CHURCH, 1865–1871.

XI.

AFTER-GLOW.

Tributes of Friends.

XII.

SERMONS.

CALEB AND RUTH.

EZRA STILES GANNETT.

I.

THE HOME AND THE BOY.

1801–1816.

IT was a true New England home, such as homes
were in the New England of seventy years ago, — a
solemn spot for a little man to be born in. They were
homes with more reverence than grace in their life,
more duty than beauty, where strict disciplines and a
very present conscience took not only their own place,
but the place of humor and caresses and easy sympathies. Not that the sympathy and love were lacking,
but sense of the duty stiffened them. The boys and
girls sent "duty" instead of "love" to their elders.
Life was a responsibility in these homes, a "charge to

keep." The parents would fain transmit their own strong principles and earnest ways through set routines of thought and conduct. The Bible, the Sabbath, the Meeting-House and Minister, the fear of God and reverent behavior, — of these the children heard much on week-days as well as Sabbath-days.

Caleb, the father in this particular New England home, was a thick-set man, with a slow dignity in his face, and momentous manners; exact, not fluent; given to precepts; not to be imposed upon; intellectual by balance of faculties rather than by talents. His rounded judgment and thorough honesty and diligent, stable habits, made him a man for trusts. " He was always active," — thus his boy's journal describes him, — " and in the performance of duty ever calm and under self-control, steady in the pursuit of his high purpose of living, and always under the influence of a pure and sanctifying spirit of religion." For a few years in early life he had been a minister, rather liberal in thought for that day, for he styled himself a Baxterian rather than a Calvinist, and asked his teacher, Dr. Gay of Hingham, — sometimes called " the father of American Unitarianism," — to preach his ordination sermon. But judged by the funeral sermon, that came a full half-century afterward, " Mr. Gannett disliked the temerity of philosophizing theologians, and his religious principles were in strict accord with the churches of New England;" so it is probable that, after the first advance, he stood still, and let the age catch up with him. He was still young, however, — the war had not yet begun, — when he was already back at Harvard as mathematical tutor. There for nearly forty years, until his death, he was the Steward of the College. The Treasurer of Cambridge parish too; and now and then, to keep his mathematics above the level of the bills and ledgers, he sent a paper on Eclipses or the Aurora Borealis to the American Academy of Arts and Sciences, of which he was a founder.

Back of him lay four or five generations of Massachusetts farmer-life. The Gannetts were early settlers in the Old Colony, and Caleb was doubtless glad to count among his sixteen great-great-great-grandmothers one Mary Chilton, a "Mayflower" girl, and the first of woman-kind — so says the family tradition — to touch the Plymouth sands at the general landing of the Pilgrims. Common country-folk the Gannetts had been through all these years, and Caleb's generation was the first to win the good fortune of a Harvard education.

The first mother in this home had died, leaving two girls and two boys behind her. A year and a half passed by, and the second mother had come in and was conscientiously at work doing her best by the children. She was Ruth Stiles, daughter of the President of Yale College. Not much romance could there have been in this marriage between the Steward and the President's daughter. He was fifty-five and she was thirty-five years old. Perhaps they had learned to esteem each other at the house of their close neighbor, the Rev. Dr. Holmes, parish minister, who had married Ruth's elder sister. Perhaps her love of order and her religious habits tallied well with his. And yet she must have brought into the home a nature quite unlike the father's. His picture shows the face that could send the children supperless upstairs with a look and a silent finger-gesture, and make the students sober-minded at first sight. Her picture has the large sensitive features of a refined and clear-brained woman. Her father was one of the learned men of our Revolutionary time, a friend of Franklin and Jefferson and Washington and Adams, one who entertained foreigners, and carried on

a large correspondence with English scholars; so that
Ruth had enjoyed much more than a girl's usual chance
for culture. She was even literary herself, although her
verses, some left in print and some in manuscript, are as
bare of poetry as they are full of her religiousness.

For she was very deeply religious, with a real and
tender trust. In belief, she was the true daughter of
three generations of Calvinistic ministers. The fly-leaf
of her Bible contains the record of her readings in it.
Twenty-two times from cover to cover since she was
ten years old! Every eighteen months, on the average,
found her beginning Genesis anew. But she was growing wiser towards the end; of her last two years the
entry tells: "I have confined my reading principally
to the New Testament and Psalms, occasionally reading
the Prophets." In her hymn-book is a similar note of
" hymns read in the first part of what I now consider
my last sickness, several of which I committed to memory. Hymns marked otherwise were read with great
delight in a more advanced stage of my disorder."
Was it only her father's note-book habit strong in her;
or was she thinking of her boy, and hoping that
through this little record he might come to know his
dead mother? These favorite hymns are those of simple yearning trust. But there is a manuscript of Birthday Reflections, which shows her nature best; and it may
be interesting to those who loved her boy, as indicating
whence he derived some of his marked traits. Year by
year, she sets down her self-reproach, her thanksgiving,
and her prayers against besetting sins. A quick impatience seems to have cost her many regretful sighs.
Morbid introspection, with a deep sense of sinfulness,
darkens almost every page. "Another year, dreadful
thought! is to be given an account of." She is an ungrateful " cumberer of the ground," and trusts only to

the atoning blood of Christ. " I am continually prone
to doubt my own sincerity, so deeply has sin poisoned
every faculty of my soul. Known only unto Thee is
it, whether I am still in a state of nature and deluding
myself with a false hope of blessedness. . . . Yet it appears that I love Thee better than all things else, and
hope my love increases with my years." After her
marriage she grows more cheerful, being busied with
the charge of the children, and very thankful for the
birth of her own child. Here is her Birthday Psalm
after her little Stiles was born : —

" How great are the mercies that I have this day to record!
The past year has opened a new era of my life. I have been
carried through weakness and distress, pain and sorrow, and
at length have been made to feel the most exquisite of all
earthly pleasures, a joy which none but the mother can experience. What shall I render to the Lord for all his goodness ? Oh that I may be enabled to devote the life spared,
and the life saved, to Thee, my heavenly Father ! While I
meditate on Thy mercies, my heart overflows with gratitude
and praise ; but, alas, how transient is the remembrance,
how weak the impression ! When will this ungrateful heart
cease to be drawn off from Thee by the things of this vain
world ? "

And then she prays to be kept from showing " an
undue partiality to the dear child " which God has
given her, and for grace to bring him up in the nurture
and admonition of the Lord.

He was the only child of this marriage. At his advent the other children were already far away in years :
one, a boy in college ; and one, a boy studying his Latin
Grammar ; and one was a young maiden, who, soon after,
married a minister-husband ; and there was a little girl
ten years old. Stiles, as the stranger was called, was
" the baby " of the house. With all the decorum and

ordered ways of the home-life, and those silent finger-gestures, the letters show warm feelings, and a happy, cheerful intercourse, even some fun and sentiment. Ruth's sentiment ran into verse. Now there is a hymn for "Master Stiles Gannett," and now a rhyme wrapped round a bit of the boy's hair as he "sends duty to grand-mamma." Pleasant neighbors and relations lived close by; for the Gannetts belonged to the cultured, staid society that centred round the college-yard and college interests, and was eyed aloof by the towns-people, who murmured something about "exclusive aristocrats." Their house was on the notch at the corner of Kirkland Street and North Avenue, very nearly on the spot where the Dining Hall now stands. From the door one looked out on the "Common," festive and crowded, and covered with booths on the great Commencement Days; while a moment's walk brought one to the old brick buildings set in the sacred green.

Such were the parent-moulds, and such the home of the boy who was born on the fourth of May, 1801, and named after his grandfather, Ezra Stiles. If we may venture to trace back the characteristics that later life displayed, it is probable that his energy, his enthusiasm, his constant sense of dissatisfaction with himself, and his warm, impulsive speech, were mainly due to the mother; and that to his father he owed more largely the exactness of his conscience, his sense of justice, and the steady, conservative clinch on convictions that had once been formed. The practical, unspeculating intellect that saw points so acutely, and kept so logically on the way to them, came to him, perhaps, from both.

Not very long did "the life spared" last to care for "the life given." The boy was barely seven when his mother died. His conscious memories of her were very slight, but she had had time to give him some of those

strong impressions about God and duty that underlay
all his subsequent purpose. A trivial incident may
as well be told, though only one of those little child-
pictures that happen to print themselves off on a mind,
and, after lying buried for years, so oddly come to light
from an old friend's memory. Once the mother tested
him. They were making plum-puddings in the kitchen.
"Sally, take these raisins into the parlor, and offer
them to Stiles, and *urge* him to take them," she said.
The girl played her part faithfully. " I don't want
them, Sally." " Why, don't you love raisins ? " " Yes,
but don't you know that my dear mother does not wish
me to eat them? " " Oh, nonsense! she won't know
any thing about it; take them!" He looked his Eve in
the face solemnly, and said, " Sally, I am *astonished* at
you! Do you think I would do any thing that I knew
my dear mother did not wish me to do, because she did
not know it? I am astonished at you!" It sounds a
little "goody" for the boy, and not quite so good as
might be for the mother; but it gives the key-note of
the whole after-life, and gives it chiming true to the
mother's anxious touch. A few relics of her tenderness
were treasured all through that life. Among them is a
small brown book inscribed, " The mother's gift to her
little boy," which contains in her handwriting some
childish prayers and hymns, and a tiny, trusting catechism that she herself composed for him. It suggests a
pleasant picture of the earnest, clear-faced mother, and
" her black-eyed urchin," as she calls him, by her side,
catching her smile and the reverence of her tones. His
grave child-face appearing with her in the meeting-
house is still remembered. " Nothing around disturbed
his eye or ear from the preacher," writes one, then a
little maid, who sat in the next pew watching him.
And it seems as if her hand guided the boy to his future

profession, when, in his chronicle of Sunday sermons, we read back through an era of long abstracts, and another of short " heads," into a still earlier one of bare texts, and find that this primitive stage begins inside his mother's life-time, that the first few texts are recorded for him by the mother's hand.

Her latter years were years of pain, and the " Birth-day Reflections " show her looking at death afar off, patient, but waiting, and wondering why the life so use-less is still prolonged.

" Is it to give me time to fill up the measure of my iniquity, and to ripen for destruction ? I dare not admit so awful a supposition ! Is it that I am still in an unregenerate state, and that my will has not yet been subdued, nor my soul bowed to the sceptre of Jesus, that a merciful God is waiting to be gracious; that light may yet arise out of darkness, and the wanderer be restored to his father's home ? Or is it (delightful thought!) to complete a work of grace already begun in the soul, and to perfect that holiness without which none shall see the Lord ? Is this the case, welcome sufferings and trials, afflictions and sorrows; for, though the feeble body shall shrink from them, the soul shall be purified and made meet to be partaker with the saints in light."

This last was her real thought, and its delight made her sick-room the resort of all her friends, and even of strangers desirous to see a person so happy in full view of death. Once, among the pilgrims, came the young Mr. Channing, recently settled in Boston ; and there by the mother's death-bed he, perhaps, saw for the first time the little boy who was to be his colleague and successor.

Very quietly and systematically she made herself ready for the vanishing. For a whole year now, another little book had held a few memorials of her own father and mother : " copied May, 1807, by Ruth Gannett, for the use and benefit of her *only child*, to whom they are

devoutly recommended by his affectionate Mother."
She knew she would never read them to him. She
had set down, in lists, her worldly goods, directing how
" the white cotton countapain with pink stars," and " the
quilted peticoat that was my mother's," and " the large
green fan," and " the best white fan," and " the black
fan," and all the rest of the wifely furnishing, should
be disposed of. Relatives would come riding from a
distance to the funeral, so she had the hard gingerbread
made up ready for them. And now — in a different,
trembling hand — she added to the list, " To Stiles," —
her boy, — " globe, books, writing-desk, green glasses,
trunk of papers, white hair-trunk, family hair-ring,
brooch," — there her hand seems to have suddenly
failed, the word is hardly legible; perhaps the mother's
heart broke down.

Before long he was sent away to Rev. Mr. Williams,
the minister at Lexington, to be housed and taught for
a year; and his first letters date from this country-
home. They tell his progress in big, grave words, with
bigger interlined by the minister. " Besides the common
studies and beginning Latin, I recite in the catechism
and Dr. Doddridge's ' Education of Children.' " Evidently he was a good boy, — a trying one. He copies
and recopies his letter, sends " duty," and seems very
solemn. He reads the Bible daily, and receives his first
own Bible from the father; " and not so much from
you as from God," as the father had written him he
ought to receive it. Twice on Sundays he is in the
pew, earnest to take down the text of the discourse.

Six months more at home, and the boy starts again
into the world, — this time for Phillips Academy, at
Andover. Well charged with precepts come the father's
letters : " Obsta principiis," " omnia vincit labor," are
the maxims for the young Latinist. He is to centre

himself in religion; "go straight forward and avoid by-paths," as well as awkwardness and shy manners and loud talk; and to get music, if he can, but is cautioned against "too much." "Psalmody is the best." He never could get any. "We take Emerson's Catechism in place of grammar;" and the little book, with "Ezra S. Gannett, ejus liber, 1812," on the cover, was kept as long as he lived. A row of New England pastors testifies that it will tend to "guard the rising generation against the fatal errors which are so zealously propagated at the present day by the enemies of truth," — which means the then unchristened Unitarians. A queer, grim book to rear children on! First come inch-square barbarous wood-cuts, beginning with Cain standing over Abel with a club; Abraham poises his big knife over Isaac; Jael drives her nail; David holds the giant's head; Joab spears Absalom; and Solomon's soldier brandishes the baby; and Nebuchadnezzar creeps on all fours, bristling like a hedgehog. A "Minor Doctrinal Catechism" follows, from which the boys learned of what God made all things; viz., "Of nothing, Heb. xi. 3." "For whom did God make all things? For himself." — "What do you deserve? I deserve everlasting destruction in hell." — "If you should go to hell, how long must you continue there? For ever and ever, as long as God shall exist, Matt. xxv. 46." Then the "Minor Historical Catechism" gives a synopsis of Biblical events, and the "Shorter Westminster Catechism" ends the course, well bulwarked with texts and comments by Dr. Watts. This last "has probably done ten times more good than any volume written by man uninspired, and is undoubtedly the best catechism in existence;" so an appended note declares. Perhaps this unstrained milk for babes gave Stiles his first distaste for the faith that he so soon outgrew.

The second Thanksgiving found him at home again, and there he passed four more quick years in the good times that an earnest boy has when preparing for college. College looks like a little career in itself to a Cambridge boy of the inner circle, offering a whole set of life-aims and motives in miniature. By his bits of journals there must have been hard work done in the studies, but it was mixed with fun. The man's habits are in germ ; for here are curious lists of his " Books, Clothes, and Other Things," of the school-mates, and the cycle of school-games, and of expenses. The outlays were not extravagant for one almost a Freshman : one dollar and sixty-seven cents is the amount of pocket-money received from " D. F." (Dear Father) between January and September, 1816. These seem to fore-shadow his ways of careful registry, and the struggle to balance the week's accounts on the Saturday nights long afterwards. Perhaps that clothes-journal — in which the " soling of boots," and the epoch of the " shirts not white " and the " new jacket," are so minutely dated — prophesied the punctilious linen, the thrifty endur-ance of well-brushed coats, and the frequent hand-bathings of older days. Nicely copied, there remains a set of conundrums, in which St. Ives, and the frog climbing the well, and the river-puzzle of fox, goose, and corn, and the three travellers at the cara-vansary, with other venerable problems, appear, besides a few religious extracts and elect statistics, — such as the middle verse of the Bible, how often the word " and " occurs in it, &c. In January, 1814, the boy projected a monthly literary and political newspaper, named allegorically " The Stile." " The circulation is to be limited to twelve subscribers, as the editor has not time to make more than twelve copies of his issue, and the subscribers are to pay one cent on subscription and

one on receipt of each paper." It contained one other
original feature also, — the first number was redated to
become the second. And then, apparently, it died, —
even of that issue three copies remaining on the projector's
hands to tell the tale. The book-list reveals a strong
predominance of sober elements. Rasselas, The Idler,
Pleasures of Hope, Telemachus, Aphorisms on Man,
Trials of Temper, Watts's Divine Songs, Wonders of
Nature and Art, and Harris's Encyclopædia, seem to
have thus far made much of his lighter reading.

But the most characteristic " remains " of this period
are those sermon-abstracts which run back to the
mother's suggestion, and grow longer and longer as he
grows older. There are few Sundays on which the pew
does not hold him twice. The habit must have done
much to educate his quickness in getting the points of
a book, and the tendency to treat his own subjects in
the logical, divided way. When he chanced — it was
but rarely — to hear a sermon in after-life, he always
enjoyed setting up its frame-work at the tea-table talk.
Dr. Holmes's doctrine accorded, though not too precisely, with the catechism. There was open exchange,
however, in those days ; and Cambridge pulpit was often
occupied by pastors of the neighborhood more liberal
than himself. Unitarianism had not yet been driven
to the break with Orthodoxy ; but opinions were fast
ripening to distinctness, and most of the men who a
little later took part in the controversy were already in
their places. Besides " Uncle Holmes," as Stiles called
him, and the other conservative preachers, the boy was
reporting Kirkland and Ware and Pierce and Porter
and Lowell and Channing.

Dr. Hedge's recollection of his schoolmate will fitly
end the sketch of these young days : —

"We were pupils together for a few months — I just entering on my classical studies, he far advanced in his preparation for college — in a private school, taught by Dr. John G. Palfrey, former minister of Brattle Street Church, then a resident graduate and student of theology in Cambridge. I recall looking up to this older school-fellow then with the mingled awe and admiration with which a boy of nine years is apt to regard a superior youth of fourteen; his brilliant recitations from the Latin text-book, his flowing speech, his maturity and choice of diction, the fascination of which to my boyish ear was such that I could not choose but listen in the single rude school-room where all the lessons were audible to all, neglecting my own tasks at the risk of the penalty which, under Dr. Palfrey's wholesome rule, awaited such neglect. I well remember how his schoolmates looked upon him then as quite an exceptional youth. 'Stiles Gannett,' it was whispered among us, 'is very religious;' and anecdotes were current of his exceptional piety. Boys are not usually charmed with that quality in a schoolmate, and boyish criticism is apt to cavil at whatever seems a damper on boyish mirth ; but no ridicule ever attached to young Gannett's serious ways."

THE CAMBRIDGE HOMESTEAD.

II.

SEEKING AND FINDING.

1816–1821.

"AUGUST 31, 1816. Was accepted upon examination, having studied, besides the Grammars and smaller books, part of the first volume of Morse's Universal Geography; Cummings' Geography; Webber's Arithmetic; Webber's Mathematics, as far as Equations in Algebra; Euclid's Geometry, two books; Bibliothèque Portative, 147 pages; Virgil; Cicero; Sallust; Greek Testament; Græca Minora; Livy, three books; Terence, one play and part of another; Decerpta Ovidii; Homer, three books; and considerable writing Latin."

That is the little chronicle with which he sums up the burden of his boyhood. Now the boyhood was over. He was a Freshman at Harvard, a bright lad of fifteen years, eager for the College friendships and prizes and pleasures; at the same time, gradually coming to himself, and saddening by the way.

Halfway through the course, his father died, and the home was broken up. The two had never been intimately acquainted. On the son's side, the relation was one of reverence rather than of childlike love. In after-life, his strongest recollections of the father were associated with serious conversations, with the Sunday window-seat where the boy sat ensconced, listening to the weekly instruction, and the Saturday nights when the family sat around the fire in the office and quieted themselves in preparation for the Sabbath, — the weary boy now and then devising an escape to the kitchen. Still he felt the loss deeply. Life, henceforth, meant life by and for himself, and he was not by nature very self-reliant. To the end, he always longed for an arm of love with the right to rest upon it.

The next winter (1818–19) brought an odd experience. The scene was Bedford, a tiny village a dozen miles away, where he attempted teaching "district-school." On the scrap of paper on which the shy teacher enrolled the names of his twenty-four boys and girls, the letters are all shaken from their forms. A note, added later, explains: "These names were written on the first day of my entering the school at Bedford. The paper is worth preserving as a proof of my fear, which was so great as to cause such trembling of my hand as prevented my writing intelligibly." He must have bravely conquered first-morning fears, however; for the Bedford career was shortened by his speedily winning a reputation for quite the opposite quality. Undue severity, and incapacity, were the two specifications of the charge brought against him, at a meeting of the school committee called at his request. The committee, after hearing the witnesses, rebuked the district, and fully exonerated the young teacher.

But the teacher had withdrawn, and was back at Cambridge, no doubt feeling dismal and indignant.

Dismal and despondent, at least; for the mother's self-reproaching habit was strong in the son already. The orphan-feeling brooded over him. He is wondering what he shall be, and his dreams are tinted by the thought: —

"How foolish does it appear to waste one's time in endeavors to gain distinction, or even happiness, when we look at the close of life, and consider that the grave closes alike upon all. . . . I sometimes think I should prefer to devote my time to study and science, that I should glory in distinction; but at others I say to myself, how much better it were, if possible, to settle down the pastor of some retired and obscure village, and, forsaking and forgot by the world, to devote myself solely to the cause of religion and virtue, to be the friend as well as the minister of my people, and if old age should spread its wrinkles on my brow, to descend to my grave after devoting my life to the cause of my God and Saviour!"

This was in June, 1819. A little later the gloom had settled more deeply, and he wrote: —

"Why am I discontented? It is, it must be, because I want religion. I know it, I dare not tell myself how sinful, how neglectful, I have been and am. Religion and I are strangers: I know it only from report. Its real influence, its sanctifying power, I never felt. I have neglected its duties; I have wasted its privileges. Uneasy, discontented, and fickle must I continue, till I know more of its power, till I become a disciple of the Saviour, till I have repented for past sins, and feel that to do good is my desire, to be good my object." . . .

. . . "I believe there is a God; for there is such evidence of him in *nature* that I must believe it. But there I stop

As for Christianity, what is it? Why is not Mahometanism as good? I have no faith in the religion of Jesus. As a moralist I follow no standard, have no rules. There are some sentiments of honor, some notions of right and good, which I suppose are natural. I owe them not to cultivation. I am passionate; I govern not my anger excepting from policy, for withal I am politic. Perhaps by policy I mean nothing but selfishness, — a feeling which leads one to impose upon others for his own benefit, to make himself the great object of all his care, all his actions."

Such expressions half refute themselves. They tell the story of the morbidly self-conscious temperament, and betray that struggle with himself, beginning then, which went on to the last day of his life. It was primarily due to inheritance. Had the mother lived to train the steady counter-habits, he might have conquered this laming of his birth. The father's colder touch never made good her loss. Or the necessity so often imposed by inferior talents might have saved him; but he was too bright, and worked too successfully in emergencies, to get help in that way. He had pride; he had ambition; above all, he had a conscience haunted by a sense of duty stronger than his will, and therefore by a constant self-reproach. The will was of the pushing rather than the pressing kind. It prompted much; but time would slip away, and opportunities be forfeited, and plans abandoned, leaving the feeling of an ideal thwarted by a want of worth. All this made him suffer; but as these same qualities drove him also into action, and the activity always took the form of helpfulness to others, he led, more than most men do, two lives, — an inner one unusually sad, self-questioning, and struggling, an outer one of unselfish energy and rare enthusiasm. Throughout our story we shall have

to turn from one man to the other in him; and the
chief good in writing out the life will lie in showing
what rich success in character and service can be won
under these circumstances.   Although he never gained
the clear victory over temperament, in the striving he
accomplished such brave living that the seventy years
were filled with uses large and glad to all eyes save his
own.   But, to show this truly, the life must be written
truly and the sadness told.

In college, the fact of the two selves was already
known by those who saw most of him.   The weeks,
however, were by no means all so gloomy as those extracts might portend.   Gannett enjoyed the pleasant
college times; was popular with his fellows; and, with
the two or three best friends who used to laugh him out
of the moods, was merry enough.   Of the Hasty Pudding
Club, which in that day made real its name, he was
chosen President: and an address before the "S.S."
faintly echoes a Bacchanalian ring; so sermon-like,
however, that it hints the good boy's difficulty.   These
mild revelries were well remembered; and always afterwards he loved an abstemious "treat," and fondly
appreciated the physical basis of geniality.   In the ex-
pense-book of his vacation journeys by the Greenfield
and New Haven stage, it is odd, in contrast with his
later strictness, to see how often the "drink" comes in
at the change of horses.   At that time both drinks and
lottery-tickets were within the lines of righteousness in
Massachusetts.

He learned the lessons too quickly for his own good.
"Four hours a day," writes his chum Kent, gave him
the first honors at graduation.   Nor does he seem to
have spent his leisure very usefully.   A journal of the
last college vacation shows him rising late, which doubtless implies late sittings-up, — riding and going to the

theatre, and reading " Gil Blas," and Petrarch, and
" Thalaba," and " Decision." Possibly it was out of
his own experience that he chose for the subject of the
Class Oration " The Influence of Literature on the Character of Individuals and Society," and emphasized especially its dangers. The first part at Commencement was
also his, and in this he considered " The Revolutionary
Spirit of Modern Times." It was 1820; Napoleon's fate
was near enough to point the moral; while the benefactors of Harvard supplied contrast to the Emperor, and,
according to the college rule, turned off the peroration
nicely. The " Master's Oration," three years later,
was assigned him, but by his request was transferred
to a classmate whose sickness during the course had
possibly cost him the first rank. The " parts " and his
college themes are written in a very careful style, and
filled with sober, just reflections; but they lack humor,
dash, and poetry. Harvard pruning is severe on young
exuberance, and this lad was grave by nature. The
coming sermons cast their shadows before.

Between the college days and the first texts lay a few
months of doubt, however. What should the life-path
be? A high purpose and religious feeling, literary tastes,
a gift of ready speech, and the attraction of a " cause,"
called him towards the ministry. But he went slowly,
with misgivings; and the misgivings lasted long. A
good aunt in Greenfield remembered the orphan exposed to the perils of Harvard's liberality, and did her
best to dissuade him from yielding to them. " It is a
wise son that looketh betimes to his launching in the
business of life. In counsel safety is found; and, dear
youth, you shall have it from me. Enter your Uncle
Leavitt's office, a student at law and one of his family." He seriously thought of choosing law for his profession.

Meanwhile a tour might benefit him. Or hurt him,
thought his aunt, who sent him counsel in reference to
travel. " I now say for a young man to take a circui-
tous, lengthy Journey amongst Strangers, ignorant of
public Inns, not well acquainted with Men and Rogues,
such as infest our land at this day, without much prospect of retaining or obtaining much for his trouble,
expense, fatigue, and time, — in my opinion, I say, the
experience hereafter with the company of some experienced friend would be best." But he, having inherited
a little money, felt prodigal, and took his journey. It
lasted a month, cost him $109.72, and his far country
embraced New Haven, New York, Brunswick, Albany,
Schoodick, Northampton, and Brattleboro'.

Then he was back in Cambridge, restless and un-
decided. Another bit of teaching — this time a " Private Grammar School " at Cambridgeport — gave a few
months more to think the matter over. There came a
last appeal from the aunt : —

" Shall I once more endeavor to lead you in the path of wisdom? The blessed Immanuel expounded the Law at twelve
years old ; his knowledge was perfect then ; it was divine exposition : but are you fully endued with knowledge, mental
powers, perception equal to discern the divine scheme, the
most momentous subject which is held up to mortal view ? I
would tenderly caution you against your Opinion upon God
and upon Man, untill you have given yourself to prayer, to
searching the Scriptures, to examining the fact, — are all
your ancestors' lives of diligence, search, faith, piety, works,
perseverance, knowledge, to be set down as vagaries ? No,
my Nephew, the Influences of the Divinity you disbelieve
were as the Sun in mid-day lighting their way through the
lives of labor, sickness, perplexities within and without, up to
the realms where possibly They may now be interceding in
your behalf."

Her earnest pleading did not keep him from entering the Divinity School at Cambridge. His three nearest friends among the classmates — Calvin Lincoln, Benjamin Kent, and William Henry Furness — were already there. He joined them, but with a mind not all made up. Gloomy hours were frequent. He was wont to filially observe the anniversary of his father's death: but this time — it was in April, 1821 — the thought of his own future intruded to darken all the memories: —

"I considered that I was going into the world without any fixed principles of conduct or belief, with habits of indolence and procrastination, and that I was now pursuing a course without determinate end, and thus had not even foundation on which I might build hope, for I never would preach with such unsettled views, and could never become a minister, as I never could perform that important part of a minister's duty, — visiting."

Still he had resolved to study. None thought so poorly of him as himself. Where the heart felt faint showed where the ideal was highest. He became, above all else, the "pastor" of his people; and, as to principles and views, they were not even then unsettled.

According to a Commencement custom then in vogue, the young men graduating dedicated sets of Latin theses to the officials of the State and University, the reverend pastors of the churches, and " in short to all friends of education on the earth, all patrons of the cause of letters in the Republic," — summary theses on Logic, Rhetoric, Metaphysics, and the like; and, among the rest, a miniature system of Theology, Natural and Revealed. The duty of preparing the last fell, in his class, to Gannett, — which suggests that the sermon-shadows were recognized by friends and teachers in spite of his own sad doubts. The theses, as printed, keep the discreet silence on disputed points becoming to a college Senior in a professor's eyes; but they, and still better his rough draft of them, from which we quote some fragments, reveal the position in religious thought which his mind had reached. He had already outgrown the doctrines held by the father and mother, and was in full sympathy with the radicalism and heresy of his day. But this radicalism had the sanction of many of the most prominent clergymen in and near Boston, and was favored by the prevailing influence at Harvard. The sentences show also how little his thought changed afterwards. Like his father before him, he saw his vision early, and none other ever seemed so true.

"The seat of religion is the heart. Its object is to amend the life by regulating the passions and affections. Love is the great principle which it demands, sincerity the duty which it requires, and a good life the test which it establishes of profession.

"The objects of the last revelation from heaven were to give clearer views of the character of God, to add to the motives for a good life the high sanction of a future state of rewards and punishments, to show a way of salvation for offending sinners through Christ, and to give in his life a perfect example for our imitation.

"The evidence furnished by miracles is the highest which can be brought in proof of any system.

"The sacred Scriptures being the only rule of faith, the right of private judgment, in matters of religion, can be denied to no one.

"In interpreting Scripture, we should always be guided by this rule, that no article of the Christian faith, delivered in the sacred Scriptures, is contrary to right reason; for revelation is only a more complete reason.

"Nor are we to suppose that God would give man a revelation to be the guide of his conduct, both for this and for an eternal world, which he could not understand, but which lies involved in mystery.

"During the dark ages of religion many errors crept into the Christian system, that, handed down by education and supported by the great causes of prejudice, authority, and credulity, have been allowed to corrupt the simplicity of the gospel.

"Thus we find supported, at the present day, the doctrines of a Trinity of persons in the Deity, and of absolute election : the first of which is not only unintelligible, but involves the idea of three Gods; and the latter is alike repugnant to reason and the divine attributes, and is highly dangerous in its consequences, as authorizing a life of sin without repentance.

"The doctrine that infinite sin requires an infinite punishment or an infinite redemption rests upon the idea that sin is an infinite evil, because committed against an infinite being: now this is giving an infinite attribute to a finite being; and if sin be infinite because it is disobedience to the law of an infinite being, then virtue is infinite because it is obedience to the same law ; hence, man is infinitely sinful and infinitely virtuous at the same time, which is absurd.

"Bigotry and intolerance are contrary to the spirit and declarations of the gospel. Love to God and love to man are the two great commandments. 'Faith, hope, charity; but the greatest of these is charity.'"

CHANNING.

FREEMAN.

WORCESTER.

III.

THE RISE OF UNITARIANISM IN NEW ENGLAND.

How came the college Senior, home-bred in Orthodoxy, albeit a moderate Orthodoxy, to worship the God
of his fathers thus distinctly after the manner which
they called heresy? His life was to be so closely connected with the young denomination then just getting
the name " Unitarianism," that in order to know him
we must understand it. We will glance back, and
trace with some detail the gradual change that had
come over religious thought in the old homesteads of
the Puritans. It was the slow embryonic growth of a
hundred and fifty years that was at last emerging to
recognition and a name.

The "Mayflower" band, and those who settled
Massachusetts Bay, were men who felt themselves to
be in personal covenant with God, like Israel of old.
Their "conversation was in heaven." In their log-
houses they "endured, as seeing Him who is invisible."
They framed their state as a temple, and invited the

Eternal to reign there over them. Their state-assembly was likewise a church-council. The voters were all church-members, only voters because members, only citizens because " saints." The first constitution was " Moses his judicials; " the second was drawn up by a minister and bulwarked with Bible texts ; the third, made by another minister, still aimed to shape a strict theocracy. The Bible was a book full to them of God's own literal language, Old Testament as well as New ; and every " Thus saith the Lord " therein gave a pattern by which the General Court was to model its enactments. The meeting-house was supported like the school, and before the school or any thing else, by public tax ; and attendance was enforced by a five-shillings fine for absence. The week days were illumined like planets from the Sunday. The minister was the chief man in the town, and next to him the deacons. And members, ministers, Bible, Church, and State, all represented the purest Calvinism. Not for free religion, by any means, had the colonists of Massachusetts Bay come into the wilderness ; only for freedom to be religious themselves in their own elected way. To that end they had spent their estates, ventured their lives, left their country ; and therefore they felt they had a right to say on what conditions new men should come into their Canaan, and who should be kept out, lest it be involved in the religious wreck they saw impending in the mother land. That land was full of vagrant religions begging and gesticulating for followers. No sects and schisms here ! The settlers of New England held in holy horror all claims of private inspiration and " inner lights." Antinomians, Anabaptists, Quakers, suffered exile from the exiles.

8

But the age was too vital for them.   This rigid Puritanism hardly outlasted their own gray heads and
dauntless hearts.

First the ordinances crumbled.   As early as the
Synod of 1662, baptism was granted on a "half-way covenant," and from the civil government the impress of
Moses and the ministers began to wear away.   Before
a second fifty years had passed " the venerable Stod-
dard," of Northampton, was arguing that, properly
regarded, the Lord's Supper was a means to regeneration, not a sign of grace attained ; and the unconverted,
welcoming the idea, were pressing into full church-mem-
bership.

Then the beliefs began to lose their sharp outlines,
while sturdy men like the Mathers raised sad laments
over the decay of piety.   By the time that Whitefield's revival flashed through the land, startling the
torpid parishes to " the Great Awakening," the doctrines had undergone much quiet change.   Just as
the Pilgrims were leaving their Netherland retreat,
their hearts had been cheered by the decisions of Dort ;
the Westminster, and, later still, the Savoy Confession,
had been heartily accepted in their turn.   And now, —
it was but 1740, — in the very landing-places and
first settlements, the children's children, nor those
among them who were least in intellect and station,
found themselves turning away from the views so often
and so solemnly proclaimed.

" The Great Awakening " partly made, in part it
only marked, the crisis in the New England Church.
It had most earnest advocates.   The venerable dogmas,
galvanized into young vigor, suddenly became as real
to multitudes as ever they had been to the forefathers.
The churches filled and glowed with new-born **mem**

bers. Every household had a man or woman in it who had felt the touch of God, and could tell the story of that wondrous touch. Not a few ministers confessed that for the first time they knew what religion meant. But, after a while, the revival had earnest opponents also. If Jonathan Edwards harvested half its fruits by leading many churches back to the strict terms of membership, in other minds Calvinism died the speedier death at sight of the old creed freshly wielded and the itinerant enthusiasts, whose preaching split the parishes and produced strange physical excesses in their hearers. These Protestants discovered that their thought had almost given place to what had long borne that name of dread, — Arminianism! Yea, a word of far deeper horror even had been pronounced, — Socinianism! The religious genius of New England, in quiet exile among the Stockbridge Indians, began to write his famous books to stem the rising tide of rationalism. "Within seven years the dangerous doctrines have made vastly more progress than ever before in the same space," he says; and, while Edwards was thus writing, some New Hampshire ministers improved the Catechism by leaving out the Calvinism.

The new names, however, were very vaguely used. "Arminianism" covered the whole growing emphasis in behalf of man's free-will and moral responsibility and power to win salvation, and of God's impartial love. It covered therefore many degrees of dissent from Calvinism. No division in the Church was dreamed of yet. Only, from the mid-century onward, two parties were recognized in Orthodoxy, and they were felt to be diverging more and more from one another.

The Calvinists made one party. But they within themselves were not long one. While some remained

loyal to the old meanings of the creed, a more moderate
class, the " Hopkinsian Calvinists," appeared under the
impulse of Edwards's somewhat novel teaching and
that of his disciples Bellamy and Hopkins ; and these
grew numerous, as the latter half of the century went
by.   Abiding by the substance of the creed, they insisted that they had bettered its interpretation.   The
bolder features of Imputation — actual transfer of
Adam's guilt and of Christ's righteousness to the sinner — were disclaimed.   Yet Total Depravity was still
total and innate, though man by nature was only " morally," not "physically," unable to will holiness, — whatever that may really mean.   The Vicarious Atonement,
still vicarious, was explained no longer as a mere ran-
som of war, a bare exchange of victims.   The honor of
God's moral government, it now was said, required that
penalty should surely follow sin, but not that it should
necessarily fall upon the sinner.   Christ bore the penalty
for us, and thus made a universal forgiveness morally
possible to God.   Election and Reprobation were Election and Reprobation still, but had shifted their place
from before to after, this Atonement : God, in using his
opportunity of mercy, elected to salvation only whom
he pleased, and, calling these by his Holy Spirit, left
the rest to that native inability which simply made
their eternal agony sure.

Meanwhile, the other party, the Arminians, were
definitely giving up the historic " points " of Calvinism ; nor these alone, — they had begun to doubt the
Vicarious Atonement and even the Divinity of Christ.
Their movement was very quiet and gradual.   Not
every year, but every ten years, marked the progress
of their minds.   Now and then, some thinker in advance
of his brethren broke the stillness with a slighting word ;

now and then, some clear-sighted old believer raised a
cry of warning. But, in general, the sceptics hardly
knew what they did think so well as what they did
not think. Their thought was plainly not the fathers'
thought, — but what did the Bible really say? That
was the great question now. Were the venerated doctrines there, after all? Many a Massachusetts minister,
in the quiet of his study, bent over the holy book with
his ten fingers between the leaves, drawing up lists of
texts on this side and on that, trying to focus the rays
of Bible light into one clear word.

Slowly two special emphases grew louder. The first
was, *Few fundamentals in religion.* The second, *No
human creed, — only Bible words are fit to phrase the
Bible mysteries.* Could man improve on God's own
language? it was asked. No human explanations of
that language should be deemed essential to Christianity. On these grounds the seekers took their stand
with increasing boldness against the use of creeds as
tests of Orthodoxy, and this stand began to mark them
off as "Liberals" in opposition to the "Evangelicals;"
such presently became the party names.

Jonathan Mayhew, pastor of the "West Church,"
was the freest preacher in Boston. The city ministers
had declined to assist at his ordination, and he did not
join their "Association," but set up his own week-day
"Lecture." His thought was more precise, and his
words more clearly matched his thought, than was common at that time in the pulpits. Where his brethren
disapproved, he denounced, creed-making; where they
practised the right of private judgment in religion, he
strenuously urged the duty; where they disbelieved, he
boldly denied, the doctrines of total depravity and justification by mere faith. His rashest thing he did in

1755, — in a volume of sermons he ventured to insert a
fine-print note that slurred the doctrine of the Trinity.
At the unprecedented act a little breeze of rejoinders
sprang up among the Boston clergy. But Mayhew was
not quite alone. Two older men, Dr. Chauncy of "First
Church" — he had led the onset against Whitefield —
and Dr. Gay of Hingham — the one spoken of above as
having preached Caleb Gannett's ordination sermon —
were also recognized as leaders of the Liberal movement.
President John Adams, when an old man, declared that
several ministers besides them, and many laymen in all
ranks of life, were Unitarians as early as 1750. But in
1750 that was a secret probably unrealized even to themselves. The chief outward sign of the changing thought
was the silent withdrawal of the doubted doctrines from
the pulpit, or, when they did appear there, their careful
retreat into Bible phrases. Another sign was that broad
toleration was distinctly advocated in ordination and
convention sermons; another, that, at ordinations in
and around Boston, the ministers often abstained from
examining a candidate about his Orthodoxy; another,
that the books of Emlyn, Clarke, and Taylor, three English Unitarian leaders, were in circulation; and still
another, that the Evangelicals were alarmed, and grew
more definite themselves, and already began to charge
the Liberals with evasion.

The first church that was willing to bear the open
reproach of Unitarianism was, after all, not Congregational, but Episcopalian, — an alien in New England, —
"the King's Chapel" in Boston ; perhaps, because it
was an alien. The position of dissent from an established church naturally makes men bold, and here Episcopalianism was the Dissent. Moreover, the war for
Independence was not yet over, and the ties to the

mother-church were somewhat loosened when James
Freeman was invited to become reader at the Chapel.
He felt himself to be in perfect sympathy with the
Liberal sentiments around him; but while the Congregational ministers could quietly change their Trinitarian
doxologies to a Bible phrase, and leave out all the Atha-
nasianism from their sermons, and be ordained without
subscribing any creed, he found his conscience tripped
by the dogmas in the Prayer Book which he was expected to read. The revolutionary spirit was abroad, and
the Chapel proprietors, Liberals as well as he, promptly
authorized him to purge the Liturgy of what he disbelieved. And then, as they loved him, and as no
bishop would lay ordaining hand on the young heretic,
they themselves gave him a Bible instead, and thereby
made him the first avowedly Unitarian minister, and
their church the first Unitarian Church, in America.
This ordination happened in 1787. There were other
Episcopalian congregations in the States at this time
not very far behind in Liberal idèas; "but, with the exception of King's Chapel, which had been hasty in its
honesty, the body relapsed into quietude."

Across the sea in London, Mr. Lindsey had lately
tried a similar experiment. To him, as to a sympathetic
listener, Freeman tells his whole story : that he did not
venture to alter quite as much as he would have liked
to, and that the public at first were shy, but soon approved the change ; that Priestley's and Lindsey's books
were being read, and many ministers had lately given
up the Trinitarian doxology; that there was only one [1]
minister in New England who openly preached "the
Socinian scheme," although "there are many churches
in which the worship is strictly Unitarian," and some of
New England's most eminent laymen did not hesitate to

---

[1] That one was Freeman's classmate, Rev. Wm. Bentley, of Salem, a very
learned man and very bold, of whom Edward Everett said in the sermon at his
funeral, "He dared to *speak* what others did not dare to *think*." As a " Human-

avow their creed. A little later, in 1796, he writes: " There are a number of ministers who avow and preach their sentiments, while there are others, more cautious, who content themselves with leading their hearers, by a course of rational but prudent sermons, gradually and insensibly to embrace it. Though the latter mode is not what I entirely approve, yet it produces good effects."

Opinion was plainly ripening. When the year 1800 came, the First Church at Plymouth, the very church of the " Mayflower " men, was just about to break in two, because a Liberal was to be settled. There were nine Congregational churches in Boston, and in every one minister and people were deeply infected with the heresy. The Old South was probably the most Orthodox, yet even Joseph Eckley, its pastor, " hesitated to affirm the entire equality of the Father and the Son." The two most important features of Boston thought at this time were the certainty of the decay, not only of Calvinism, but of Trinitarianism, and the vagueness of the new growth that was emerging. " He was classed with Liberals ; " " he avoided controversial subjects in the pulpit ; " " the type of his Unitarianism was unknown ; " " he was probably an Arian : " such expressions abound in Sprague's Annals of the early Unitarian worthies of Massachusetts, — the elders who passed away, while their younger brethren were accepting the new name and defining their heresy. And, in this on-growth from the faith of the fathers, Boston was by no means alone. The other large towns of the State, first-born of Puritanism, showed a similar spectacle. Of two hundred Congregational churches east of Worcester County, at this time, not more than two in five were under Evangelical ministry, says the Orthodox historian of those churches.

itarian," his welcome was restricted even among the Liberal pulpits. But, as in Freeman's case. his own people stood by him : in 1785, two years after his ordination, the church and society unanimously voted to make him their sole preacher, — his elder colleague, who was an ultra-Calvinist, retiring with a pension.

This cultured Liberalism of Massachusetts was the most important, but was not the only, phase of the revolt from Calvinism. It was not even the most distinct. In periods of changing thought the vigor of outspoken dissent is seldom found in the cultured classes and the regular churches. Wholly outside of college influence a much more uncompromising heresy upstarted in three different forms during the last years of the century.

Ever since the Revolution there had been rough-and-ready thinkers in the land, who, over a work-bench perhaps, or after farm-chores were done, talked sharp common-sense about the current faith, — men who welcomed bits from Voltaire, and presently were reading Tom Paine's " Age of Reason " with keen relish. At the opposite extreme also of society, there were a few suspected Free-thinkers who thought to some good purpose. To their lack of Orthodoxy the National Constitution largely owes its principle of religious liberty. But, all told, these village infidels and their high-bred cousins were not many ; and indignant neighbors could afford to shrug their shoulders at them and pass by.

Other critics, more enthusiastic, and therefore more exasperating, were abroad. Here and there a Baptist " member " broke out in condemnation of Election and Eternal Punishment, and forced a hearing about his county for the gospel of Universal Salvation. No Deists or Free-thinkers these. Rather they out-evangelized the Evangelicals. It was text against text between the two. The bright promise was only promise because most literally spelled out from words of Revelation. At first their revolt was purely of the heart, not of the head. English Mr. Murray founded " Universalism " on the doctrine of vicarious atonement ;

and next to him in fame among the early preachers was
Winchester.   Both were Trinitarian and Orthodox
enough, save on the point that the Bible pledged salvation unto all.   In the enthusiasm of this one discovery,
a few itinerants went about, mainly through the country-
side and among the common people, gathering little
groups of open dissenters.   These Universalists were
men of a different stamp from the Boston Liberals, —
less cultured, more direct.   Murray came to New England just before the war; and before the end of the
century the scattered country-groups had met time and
again in General Convention, had assumed a name, and
publicly organized themselves as a new sect.   Nor was
this all.   Under their eager scanning, more truth broke
out from the Bible Word.   Their faith in the doctrines
of the Trinity and the Atonement speedily began to
waver; and, soon after 1800, at the impulse of a few
outspoken men, both ideas were discarded by the
majority of the denomination.

The story of the " Christians " runs back to the same
time, and repeats that of the Universalists.   Theirs
was another rebellion of the common-sense of country
people against the arbitrary dogmatism and violence
of the ruling Orthodoxy, — another going forth of un-
taught missionaries to preach a purer, tenderer Bible
faith.   They originated independently among the
Baptists in New England, among Presbyterians in
the Middle States, among Methodists in the South.
" Christian " was the simple name they took.   Opposition to sectarianism was their reason for existence.
Scripture, and individual liberty to interpret Scripture,
were their two fundamentals.   When they first broke
away, they also were still the Trinitarians they had
been ; but search in the Book with eyes unsealed again
led to a rejection of the Trinity and all the cognate

thought. They differed from the Universalists only by failing to find and insist on the doctrine of final restitution, and from the Boston Liberals by being more evangelical, less rationalistic, in their tendency.

Here, then, were the Liberals, the Free-thinkers, the Universalists, the " Christians," — no band of brethren, yet all companions in revolt. If we recall the popularity of the Hopkinsian views among the Orthodox themselves, it would be true to say that, at the meeting of the centuries, a very large part of New England's faith was undergoing change, and change in one direction. For even the Hopkinsian modifications, though comparatively slight, showed a degree of yielding to the same rationalistic spirit. They certainly rounded the sharp points of Calvinism, and softened them into that mystic state which renders spring-growth again possible in long rigid dogmas. Their effect was, therefore, partly good for Orthodoxy, because they served to keep some of the restless in the old allegiance. But only in part ; for, like the Great Revival in which they had their origin, they inspired preachers to urge home with all the ardor of a new conviction those general ideas which now, in any form, were foolishness to many minds and horror to so many hearts. At the close of the Revolution three parties were well marked off from one another, — Old Calvinists, these Moderate Calvinists, and the Liberals. But as the Liberal tendencies, in one form and another, grew more pronounced, the two schools of Orthodoxy tended to join forces again, and the Hopkinsian theories gradually prevailed. A little later, a home was built for them at Andover. Eventually they became what is known to-day as the " New England Theology." The stronghold of the older, stricter Calvinism was the Presbyterian Church

outside of New England. With it the change was
always most unpopular, and the New York and New
Jersey clergy hurled many of the same hard words at
New England Orthodoxy which the New England
Orthodox lavished on the rising Unitarians. "The
new Hopkinsian light," they said, was darkness; its
"improvements" of Calvinism were nonsense, were
impiety, — they led to infidelity and atheism; the New
England Evangelicals taught "another gospel," whereas
"the way of salvation was one," and that of course was
the *old* Calvinistic path.

And now the time drew near when the hard words
were to be hurled. Young Channing had just come to
Boston, and scarcely made his second round of parish calls,
when certain Orthodox men leaped to their feet with
indignation. Not at Channing yet, but because Harvard College had appointed Henry Ware to the vacant
professorship of Divinity. Harvard College, — founded
by the fathers "for Christ and the Church"! Henry
Ware, known to be Arminian, suspected of being Arian!
And in a chair established by the terms of the old
bequest for a teacher "sound or Orthodox"! It was
too true. The Liberals had already firm possession of
the College; and this was one of those cases that
always must seem unjust to the neighbors who inherit the old faith in its pristine purity, or, rather,
least unchanged from pristine purity, — one of those
cases that must arise until people believe in evolution
in religion, and in their bequests allow for nature's
fact of growth. The Liberals had possession of the
College, but they had obtained it by no intrigue. From
the first the College had descended in trust along the
line of Massachusetts culture. By that title of culture,
at the beginning of the century, the Liberals held it

fast. Both in the Corporation and among the Overseers they now were in majority, — no new-comers, but men who bore old names familiar in the State for generations. Only a few years after Ware's election they called Kirkland from a Boston pulpit to be the President, and Kirkland was one of the most advanced of the silent brotherhood. Yet, after all, as to theological position, Willard, Webber, Kirkland, made a not unnatural succession. For Willard (1781–1804) was, "on the whole, a moderate Evangelical," and Webber (1806–1810) was "probably Unitarian." Dr. Kirkland's friends soon took steps to organize at Cambridge a Liberal Divinity School.

From Ware's appointment onwards, the magazines afford best tracking-ground for those who care to follow the movement of thought. There was a club then in Boston in which much of the younger Liberal intellect was concentrated, — the "Anthology Club." William Emerson, father of the son ; Buckminster, the wondrous pulpit boy, whose eloquence and novel passion for Bible criticism gave him more than a grown man's use ; Thacher, the Harry Percy of the band ; Tuckerman, with his skilled philanthropy yet to ripen ; and Kirkland ; Gardiner, too, of Trinity Church, — were among its minister members. With them were joined certain lawyers and physicians, then before their fame, whose names have long been reverent memories to us ; and two whose time-worn faces have hardly ceased to bless the Boston streets. Choice spirits were they all, so choice that the ladies of Boston village did not invite company on the Anthology evening, because the Club meeting had their rarest gentlemen. The Club had a literary magazine (1804–1811), the beginning of the five-linked chain of Liberal magazines of which " Old and New " is the last

link. Its theological attitude was definite as to **Anti-**
Calvinism, but non-committal about the Trinity. Now
and then a sharp article against the Orthodox appeared;
as when young Thacher wrote about the Andover School
just established with a creed skilfully drawn up to
smooth over the differences between the old and the new
Calvinism, — a creed which " it is solemnly enjoined
shall for ever remain entirely and identically the same,
without the least alteration, addition, or diminution,"
and be repeated anew by the professors every five years.
He retorted the charge of evasion which the Evangelicals were now loudly pressing against the Liberals
" This we believe," he said, " to be the first instance on
record of a creed being originally formed with a designed
ambiguity of meaning, with the express intention of per-
mitting men òf different opinions to sign it." Presently
he made an earnest plea for Liberal propagandism, because he saw that " a theological combat was preparing,
with fanaticism, ignorance, and credulity hurrying to
the fight." Then he renewed the attack upon the creed-
makers, urging the point of Dr. Porter's startling Convention sermon, — that the sole fundamental of Christian
belief laid down in the New Testament was the confession, " Jesus is the Christ." Kirkland also threw some
closely packed sentences of satire against the weak spots
of Calvinism, and even ventured to sketch the argument
against the doctrine of Christ's divinity. All this, however, was anonymous. The circle, not the individuals,
appeared in the " Anthology."

A bolder Review succeeded it, the " General Repository " (1812–1813), edited by Andrews Norton, then a
young man, who was born to be a " defender of the
faith." Taking " *Nec temere, nec timide*," for his motto,
he boldly wrote for his first article a " Defence of

Liberal Christianity." A small but able band of scholars helped him, Buckminster and Edward Everett among them. By one or another, the common-sense, the historical, and the Scriptural arguments against the dogma of the Trinity were set plainly forth. Like all radical magazines, however, the " Anthology " and " Repository" were " caviare to the general." Each New Year's Day the editors, in a fresh preface, gallantly hugged each other before the public over the quality, which, they said, made good the lacking quantity, of favor.

Channing and some of his friends desired a different tone from Norton's, and the " Christian Disciple " (1813–1823) was next born. " Speaking the truth in love " was its motto ; and Noah Worcester, the author of " Bible News," but soon to win his title of " Apostle of Peace," was editor. It was so very peaceful that from its pages one would never divine that the great disclosure of Unitarianism occurred just after its advent. The little controversy it contained was with Calvinism, and its worst offence in this direction was simply to note the mutations within Orthodoxy itself, as shown by the dispute between the Old-School and the New-School Calvinists, — a dispute so bitter in New York about this time that there was " some reason for saying that Boston is the temperate, and New York the torrid, zone of ecclesiastical controversy." The subject of the Trinity was scarcely mentioned by the " Disciple," and the name " Unitarianism " as rarely. Its one constant emphasis was for practical religion and Christian charity and the open mind, and against the use of creeds and sectarian exclusiveness. But the magazine was too tame for the stirring times after " the controversy " began ; and it languished until it changed its editor and

tone, and stood distinctly for ideas as well as a holy
spirit.

In other ways the heresy was taking shape and size,
— taking every thing except a name.   Books were written: notably, Ballou's Universalist "Treatise on the
Atonement," in 1805; "probably the first book published in this country that advocated the strict unity of
God, and views accordant therewith,"— and Worcester's
" Bible News of Father, Son, and Holy Ghost," which
a little later startled all New England, and ruffled
circles where reasons against the Trinity had never
broken in before.   Emerson and Buckminster printed a
hymn-book which had Pope's " Universal Prayer " in
it.   Still worse, an improved version of the New Testament, garnished with Unitarian notes by its English
editors, was reprinted here.   The Orthodox saw in its
welcome the worst of omens; and Dr. Mason, a Presbyterian divine of New York, described it as "the
amended Bible which the Iscariot bands of professed
Christianity are laboring to thrust into the hands of the
simple, — straining into the cup of salvation the venom
of Socinian blasphemy."   Through the Annual Convention sermons, also, the heresy flowed and ebbed, according to the preacher's theological position.   One year the
"few fundamentals" would be pointed out to the assembled ministers; by the next, the sea of charity had
shrunk away, and *all* the old rocks stood bare again.

Meanwhile, in these dozen years of rapid Liberal
growth, the Orthodox were far from idle.   Eyes were
open to the danger; troops were marching; the muster
before the onset had begun.   Dr. Morse of Charlestown, he of the Geography, was the first Orthodox
champion to take the field and strive to rally the Puritan
feeling around " the faith once delivered to the saints."

He set up a magazine, the " Panoplist," that proved a
doughty man-at-arms, confronting each Liberal en-
croachment, watching on the walls of Zion, and chal-
lenging the suspected heretics to declare themselves.
In long reviews of the condition of the New England
Church, it laid bare the secret decay that was eating
away the old discipline and doctrine. The Andover
School in 1808 made another strong barrier ; and the
next year Park Street Church was built, professedly to
give asylum to high Orthodoxy in the midst of the
enemy. In Connecticut and New Hampshire, where
the hand of Orthodoxy was stronger than in Massachusetts, two or three country ministers lost their pulpits
for the heresy. Certain Evangelicals near Boston began
to decline exchanges with their Liberal brethren, caus-
ing much hurt feeling thereby. Church-breaks occurred
in New Bedford, Sandwich, and Dorchester. Then
came a proposition which filled the Boston men with
indignation. Connecticut had crushed out the germ
of heresy by her Consociations, and the Presbyterians
beyond New England by their Synods and Assembly.
And now a plan was strenuously urged by Dr. Morse
and his friends to set up similar ecclesiastical tribunals
in Massachusetts ; but for that our Congregationalists
were not ready. Massachusetts owes much to the
escape.

The crisis was close at hand. No name but " Liberal
or Rational Christianity " was acknowledged by the
Boston ministers ; but it was known through the city
and the State that they thought things they did not
preach, and had no objection to each other's parlor
heresies. " It is the prevailing idea, all over the United
States, that the clergy of Boston are little better than
deists," writes Buckminster, one of their number, in

4

1809. Country parsons and strangers visiting Boston
would attend the churches, or listen at the "Association meetings," or the "Thursday lecture," or the College Commencement, with ears wary for the ambushed
heresy; and sometimes compared notes afterwards, or
told at country firesides that they had heard a service
with no word of Christ's divinity or his atonement in
it. But it was seldom or never possible to say that they
had heard denial of these doctrines.

The refusal of the Unitarian name was one thing:
this silence was another. For refusing that name there
was a special and good reason. It was already so appropriated by the English Unitarians as to be commonly
identified with their Socinian, *i.e. humanitarian,* view of
Christ, — a view which few in New England had at
that time reached. The great majority here were of the
Arian type: Christ to them was a being between God
and man, higher than all archangels. And they felt it
was a great injustice and untruth to confound them
with the followers of Priestley. Therefore, when the
Orthodox called Dr. Ware at his election a Unitarian,
his friends could truly say it was a calumny; and five
years later Thacher could call that name "a flower of
rhetoric." No doubt, too, many still were Liberal by
tendency rather than by clear decision. But, when all
such allowance has been made, there can be as little
doubt that from 1800 there was a conscious silence on
the part of Liberals about their thought *after* that
thought was pretty definite in their own minds. The
quick side-taking when the issue was forced showed the
real ripeness of opinion. Channing and Thacher then
expressly admitted the previous silence, and defended
it. Other Liberals admitted and excused it. Still
others admitted and rebuked it. It was the universal

impression of the Orthodox, the theme of common talk among them. Their charge of "concealment" was afterwards denied; but, when the Orthodox for ten years were restlessly questioning, silence practically was concealment. The motives for it were, and may be, variously construed. It was attributed to self-denial, Christian charity, intellectual humility, prudence, policy, temporizing, cowardice, hypocrisy. Individuals — Channing and Thacher, for instance — were most certainly free from stain of cowardice or hypocrisy. All perhaps were not. Channing's principle of avoiding controversy because the points denied seemed to be of little moment to real religion, while religious controversy was most direful in its consequences, — this was doubtless the deepest motive with them all. The older men especially would feel that motive strongly. They saw that clear statement on certain points would make a bitter schism in the dear, old Church of the forefathers; and they could not bear that thought. So that a curious phenomenon was seen in the religious world : these rationalizers, even more than the Orthodox with their plenary inspiration, were the men seen clinging to the letter, and calling loudly *they* were the Bible men! These freer thinkers were standing as the advocates of vague thinking and dim speech, while the Orthodox were the defenders of the right to think, and the duty of speaking, distinctly in religion! — a curious but not a rare phenomenon wherever a Liberal party is moving forward. The world is still so little used to free inquiry in religion, that it has not fully learned the ethics of the process; and this was seventy years ago. The Orthodox were right to some extent in their charge of concealment. Our fathers, the Unitarians before Unitarianism, chose the double, the esoteric and exoteric,

way; and the choice exposed them to the pain of a
sudden crisis of disclosure.

An indignant friend and an indignant foe joined
hands in bringing on the crisis. The friend lived across
the water, — Belsham, a London Unitarian of the extreme Priestley school, and vexed in his soul that the
American brethren were so slow of tongue. In writing
the Life of Lindsey, James Freeman's friend, he accordingly put in a long chapter citing Freeman's old letters
about them, and adding fresh ones just received from
Boston, all courteously betraying the non-commital
policy. Dr. Morse rubbed his hands. That was what
he wanted. Out came that chapter in a pamphlet; and
straightway his "Panoplist" hailed it as the most important publication of the day. That it was. It was a fire-
brand, and the Review was wind to it. The churches
started up and watched to see what would happen.
The Review had made three points: the New England
heretics shared Belsham's low views of Christ and muti-
lated the New Testament as he did; the ministers who
led the way in this apostasy were systematic hypocrites;
all Christian fellowship must be denied them.

The Liberals could not keep silence now. But who
should be their spokesman?

Channing was thirty-five years old. The beautiful
face in Allston's portrait shows him as he then was,
with the light of his great thought dawning on him,
before the eyes gazed widely and the lips were set. He
had been a quiet minister, making his calls, preaching
his twice a day, not often going to the Anthology Club,
but becoming known as one who made men feel religious. Sad and indignant, Channing answered the attack. He admitted the Unitarianism, using that word
in its broad sense, unconfined to Belsham's view of

Christ. Opinions differed among them as to Christ, he said. "To think with Belsham was no crime." But, as a fact, few did. For himself he had always scrupu‹ lously avoided every expression that might seem to acknowledge the Trinity; and, when asked in conversation, had explicitly avowed dissent. As to the *pulpit* silence about the Unitarianism, he admitted, justified, glorified it. The charge of hypocrisy was a slander. "We preach precisely as if no such doctrine as the Trinity had ever been known." No doctrine was more abstract or perplexing, so apt to gender strife. "We all of us think it best to preach what we esteem to be the truth, and to say very little about (speculative) error." About Calvinism had they not been also silent? Yet they were well known Anti-Calvinists, and no preaching was more easy or more popular than attack upon its dogmas, and they deemed its errors far more injurious than any about Christ's person. "Yet the name Calvinist has never, I presume, been uttered by us in the pulpit." Not hypocrisy, but self-denial rather. And then, with all his heart and soul and mind and strength, he deprecated the threatened break in the Church.

To answer him, a second champion now stepped forward in behalf of Orthodoxy, Samuel Worcester, brother of the one who wrote the "Bible News" and now was editing the "Disciple" for the Liberals. To and fro the letters went till each had three in print. This was the first set debate in the Unitarian controversy. As such, it turned less on the proof and disproof of the doctrines (that came later) than on the importance of the doctrines doubted as a ground for denying Christian fellowship. Must the sacred old New England Church now break in two? Were the Liberals "un-Christian" be‑

cause un-Trinitarian?   " A solemn, infinitely important
question," Channing calls it.   He insisted that the differences were like the differences between the two
schools of Calvinism, not fundamental.   Worcester insisted that they were fundamental.   That was all; but
that was final.   Channing said the Bible was vague
about the *nature* of Christ and the *way* of the Atonement, and that therefore the Liberals were vague, " because we are faithful."   By that Holy Word only one
belief was needful for the Christian name, — that " Jesus
is the Christ."   The Bible vague about Christ's essential divinity and the propitiatory sacrifice! cried Worcester.   The Liberals indifferent about these things!
Why, " set these aside, and what but Natural Religion
is left?"

At last, then, the heresy was out!   Its veil was torn
off; a name was forced upon it; and the schism had
begun.   It was the year 1815.   The long, slow process, that had quietly gone on since the Arminian crisis
two generations before, had reached a second crisis.
Sides were quickly taken, though not without protests
against the new name and the necessity of schism.   The
reluctance was felt chiefly by the elders, who were
hurried along in the Liberal movement in advance of
their sympathies, — men who had out-thought, but not
outgrown, the old faith that yet had power over them,
and who still, perhaps, distrusted their own minds in
presence of the wise and good and great majority of the
Church to whom the new ideas gave contradiction.   But
the Orthodox were peremptory.   They claimed the
right — surely they had it — to gather what they
thought plain Bible meanings into plainer words, those
" human creeds" so-called; the right to say to the
Liberals, Since for us the essential basis of salvation is

what you deny as even fact, since in your eyes we hold monstrosities of belief and in our eyes you hold monstrosities of unbelief, you must go by yourselves and be a church apart from us. Surely they had the right to say so. They went far beyond this, however, and to being peremptory added being arbitrary and presumptuous where they had no right. Identifying their church-fellowship with Christian fellowship, they denied the name " Christian " to those who appealed as conscientiously as themselves to a common Bible. " Are you of the Boston religion or of the Christian religion? " was a common question, while a pamphlet from a layman on the other side — such a slur from that side was exceptional — retorted, " Are you a Christian or a Calvinist? " In spite of all reluctance, therefore, the two churches, no longer now two parties of one church, drew off from one another.

Twenty stormy years followed the acceptance of the Unitarian name, the years from 1815 to 1835, before the new sect fairly won its claimed position inside the Christian Church. They were years of controversy with the Orthodox and of inward organization.

Channing kept the leader's place; and once, twice, thrice again his plain, strong words served to draw fresh attacks. But he left the defence to other hands. His own main work was to be constructive, — to unfold the doctrine of the divinity of human nature. Nothing that he wrote of a controversial nature remains unpublished, no single sermon, says his biographer; which shows how very little of a controversialist he was, in spite of his fame of leadership. He soon recognized that the break was necessary, whatever were the consequences; and in 1819, at the ordination of Jared Sparks in Baltimore, he preached a sermon defining Unitarianism. It made a sensation greater probably than any other sermon ever preached in America before or since. Two articles in the " Disciple " quickly followed. In one he considered the objections to Unitarian Christianity, and in the other urged the moral argument against Calvinism. In his vestry the next spring, the first Unitarian organization, the " Berry Street Conference of Ministers," was formed. His opening address held up as the real question at issue between the Liberals and the Orthodox, " How far is Reason to be used in explaining Revelation ? " A great question, he said, because the advancing intelligence of the age must choose between a rational Christianity and infidelity, and the choice would affect all practical morality and piety.

When they heard the echoes of the Baltimore sermon, three Orthodox professors buckled on their armor, — Dr. Miller of Princeton, Stuart and Woods at Andover. The young man whom the sermon had ordained boldly faced the first, while the two professors at the Harvard Divinity School stood forth to meet the others, — Norton against Stuart on the dogma of the Trinity, Ware against Woods on the dogmas of Calvinism. The two latter debates are the classics of the Unitarian controversy.

Channing had truly stated the question at issue. Both parties appealed to the Bible ; but, in their exegesis, the champions from Andover refused to admit as elements of knowledge " the known character of God " and " the state of the writer." They simply studied till they got the writer's meaning. There they reached an ultimate authority and rested, however contrary the meaning seemed to common-sense and common morality. Was it not to be expected that Revelation would teach something which Natural Religion could not; and how

can we measure inspiration? they asked. The Uni
tarians went further: they ventured to criticise the
writer's meaning at the bar of their own reason and
conscience, — not very severely, indeed, but enough so
to reject what seemed to them self-contradictory and
cruel.

Stuart granted that he could not explain the distinction of the Three Persons in the Trinity, nor that of the
Two Natures in Christ; but, since Revelation gave
Christ's deity as a *fact*, the mystery was to be accepted.
Nor was it more a mystery, after all, he urged, than
God's self-existence or man's own double nature, — mind
and body, — both of which mysteries reason admitted to
belief. Norton met him with that able argument and
text-array which afterwards grew into his volume, the
" Statement of Reasons for Not Believing the Doctrines
of Trinitarians."

Professor Woods had the harder task, for he defended
views that shocked not reason only, but the moral sense.
The facts of Revelation for him were man's entire native
depravity, Christ's vicarious atonement for sin, God's
particular election and irresistible calling. Like his
friend, he owned the difficulty of his " facts," constantly
pointed to the equal mystery shrouding the problem of
evil on the plane of reason, and claimed that, strictly
speaking, his inquiry had nothing to do with reconciling
the doctrines with the Divine Perfection. *There* in the
Bible they stood. As to their true interpretation, he
disavowed the early Calvinism as crude exaggeration,
and fortified himself upon Hopkinsian ground. His
best success was in showing that " depravity " was
"native." He failed to prove it " total ; " and completely failed to show how this and the cognate doctrines could consist with moral responsibility, although

he strenuously insisted that they did. His defence of
" election " is a wondrous sacrifice of logic to loyalty.
Throughout the argument he treats his innate depravity of the human constitution as identical with "sin."
" Nothing can be more groundless than the notion that
man cannot be culpable for any thing which is not the
consequence of his own choice ; " " the propensity to sin
is the very essence of sin ; " " the distinction between the
character born and that which is acquired has no concern with this subject." Around this point circled much
of the debate; for " the grand fundamental error of the
Unitarians is this: they overlook the ruined state of
man." With this point all the other doctrines were
necessarily connected ; and the heart's revulsion from
these doctrines — vicarious atonement, election, total
depravity — was itself due to man's depravity. So
pleaded Andover.

Where Andover was strong in the metaphysics of
necessity, Dr. Ware was weak. He simply cut the
knot by assuming pure choice as the ultimate cause of
sin ; speaks as if saint and sinner, Adam and each one
of Adam's offspring, were all endowed at birth with the
same moral nature, and misses the fact of inherited
tendencies, — not " sin," — in which he might have
touched a reconciling truth. And where Professor
Woods was weak, — in the *morals* of necessity, — Dr.
Ware was comparatively strong; for, on this assumption of a pure will-power, he could keep intact man's
responsibility and the goodness of God.

Channing had spoken a fruitful word at Baltimore.
From the sermon itself and the discussions that followed
it, men at last saw plainly what Unitarianism was: that
its stand was taken squarely on the Bible, and its weapons
were very largely Bible texts. God's Unity against the

Trinity, human ability against Calvinism, were established on that basis. Revelation, miracles, apostolic
authority, the Christ, not only were allowed, they were
emphasized. But the Revelation was interpreted with a
strangely daring reason, which insisted that itself also was
from God ; and that the Christ, whatever his rank, or
whatever his death accomplished, was not God, was not
God-man. They saw, too, — for here the emphasis
grew yet stronger, — that no shred of Calvinism was
left; that Unitarians could not see how a little lovable
child was " totally depraved ; " how moral responsibility
could consist with " born depravity " of any sort, or
" election " with God's impartial goodness, or " vicarious
atonement " with God's justice, or " irresistible " grace
with man's free will. The negations were now made
very clear by Unitarianism. Its affirmations were whatever was left in revelation and religion when these were
taken away. It was a Bible faith : yet, within certain
Bible limits, it was a protest of reason against unreason ;
of the moral sense against inhumanity in doctrine ; of
common-sense against strange practices that still prevailed as modes of religious influence and action, — in
short, a protest of the mind and heart of the early nineteenth century against the mind and heart of the past.
Words henceforth were hardly strong enough to express
the differences which four years before had seemed to
Liberals " not fundamental."

Now that these beliefs and disbeliefs were openly
declared, Unitarian societies soon sprang up in Philadelphia, Washington, Charleston, and New York; but
they were as tiny islands in the broad main of Orthodoxy. Only in New England, and of New England
only in Massachusetts, and of Massachusetts only in the
eastern counties, did the new faith win large following.

The country population as a whole remained loyal to the old faith. But towards the sea-board the church-breaks began to multiply. The growth of religious thought had been so much a part of the general intellectual growth of the day, that, when the crisis came, a large portion of the culture of the State was already pledged to the heresy. It almost seemed like a social movement, beginning at the top and working down. Distinguished laymen even more than distinguished ministers gave it character. Near Boston it was even fashionable.

But wherever it appeared, each parish, each neighborhood, sometimes each family, was divided against itself. Up to this time a whole township had often used but a single meeting-house. Now the second steeple rose in many a village, and signalized a bitter controversy going on below, the opening of an important question that the courts only could decide, and not even the courts could close.

By ecclesiastic usage in New England there had always been a church within a church. The communicants, or " members " proper, composed the inner body, to whom by courtesy belonged the privilege of leading in all church matters. Outside of these was the rest of the parish, the towns-people, who filled up the congregation on the Sunday, and who, by civil law, were obliged to support the minister, as they had to pay the town's school-master or its constable. As right belief had generally been one condition of admission to the inner circle, it often proved, when the break occurred, that the majority of the " members " were Orthodox in faith, while the majority of the parish as a whole had become Liberal. The deacons were the legal trustees of the church property ; but now, for the first time, the question rose, For whom did the deacons hold it. — for the " church-members " or for the " whole parish " ? Which of the two bodies really made *the* church ? In 1820, just as the professors' letters were going to and fro, the Supreme Court of the State, in a famous test-case at Dedham, gave judgment in favor of the parish. By this decision, in case of separation, the meeting-house, the church-funds, the ancient name, even the communion-plate, remained with the heretics where they were in majority in the town ; while the lot of exile and poverty fell to the doctrinally faithful Orthodox. No wonder that the feeling grew more and more bitter through the next few years.

The new party now had its name, its definite doctrines, its leader. For older chiefs, it had most of the pastors of the Boston churches and of many "First Churches" in the towns near by; some of them, however, still reluctant chiefs. For bolder champions, it had the young preachers just coming forward, eager to bear its reproach and turn it into glory. It had its Divinity School and able professors there, and its ministerial conferences. For literary organs, it had the " Christian Disciple," edited now by the younger Ware ; the " Unitarian Miscellany," issued at Baltimore by Jared Sparks; and the weekly " Christian Register." The College was largely under its control, and many of the best minds in the State were its helpers.

Still the Liberals had not yet organized themselves into a *sect*.

WARE.

NORTON.

IV.

THE GIRDING.

1821–1824.

THE Commencement theses of the college Senior are therefore amply explained. He grew up in the very centre of the Liberal influences. The time, the place, the society of which his home was part, laid strong hands on him. His college years came just after the opening controversy that followed Channing's acceptance of the Unitarian name. The Liberal Divinity School was organized in his Freshman year, and he graduated when the Baltimore sermon and the Dedham decision were fresh themes for indignation and applause. The father, shy in his old age of the pushing thought, died while two years yet remained in which the boy's mind was turning towards the ministry. Close by, in Cambridgeport, an older brother preached in sympathy with the advanced theology. There was a stir of battle all around him. The pure gospel was to be rescued from its hurters, the cause of religious liberty was to be defended, the faith and the reason of the age were to be brought into harmony : all this, besides the ever-existing call to help men's souls. What wonder that amid such circumstances the feet straying along the sermon-path should find their way into the new Theological School? The spell of the lectures in Professor Norton's library drew them on.

So the pleasant student-life continued nearly three years longer, growing pleasanter as the purpose deepened through the lingering doubts of fitness. Professor Ware taught the evidences and the doctrines of religion, the way to write the sermons and to be true ministers. A sheet of notes taken at the lectures on Ministerial Duties still lies among the pupil's papers, and would serve well as a sketch of his principles of pastorship, so closely was the ideal there held up embodied in his after-practice. In between the lectures, Ware was writing his replies to Andover. But less on him than on Professor Norton fell the burden of supporting the reputation of the School ; for Norton taught Biblical Exegesis, and Unitarianism had to make good its claim to be a Bible faith against a host of challengers. The outspoken editor of the early " Repository " had trained himself into the ripest scholar of the land in Scripture lore. Sacred criticism was zealously pursued by the young men under his inspiration. " Michaelis and Rosenmüller were names as familiar then as Mill and Spencer now, and were pronounced with as great respect. He who could buy nothing else bought a Griesbach, and he who owned a Wetstein was rich, indeed." The taste for Bible work now caught lasted through life with Mr. Gannett. It was his favorite form of literary labor. Years afterwards, when, a patriarch in the denomination, he gave the address that celebrated a finished half cen-

tury of the School's existence, he thus praised those
who moulded him and so many of his fellows : —

"They who came under Dr. Ware's influence can never
forget the calm dignity, the practical wisdom, the judicial fairness, or the friendly interest which secured for him more
than respect, — it was veneration which we felt. That clear,
strong mind abhorred double-dealing with truth or with
man. As candid as he was firm, as little blinded by self-
esteem as by sophistry, he taught us to hold in just regard
alike the privileges and the limitations of human thought."

"It may not be easy for those who cannot recall evenings
spent in that well-furnished library, which he converted into
the most attractive of recitation-rooms, to believe that Mr.
Norton inspired an enthusiasm which still glows in hearts no
longer young. Yet they who came nearest to him might
tell us how admiration for the scholar melted into grateful
esteem for the friend. A leader among those who were then
taunted as infidels, his religious faith was 'as Mount Zion,
which cannot be removed.' Standing between Orthodoxy
and Rationalism, he dealt heavy blows on either hand. Too
individual to be sectarian, as the champion of an unpopular
cause his single arm vindicated its right to respectful consideration. Mr. Norton erred through want of sympathy
with the multitude. He had little respect for the associations
which, if they sometimes conceal mental poverty, more often
uphold a trembling heart. That any one should wish to
retain a doubtful word in the common version of the Scriptures, because it had grown dear to the experience of generations, seemed to him an offence against truth. Severe as a
critic, and pungent in rebuke of personal fault ; when his class
trusted him, how he took them into his embrace, and bore
them into the storehouses of his great learning ! "

Of a part of his life in the School he kept a record.
It would not be his journal, were it not one of omissions
and failings rather than of performance.

"I have spent none of this vacation in studying, but my time has been quite as well employed as it usually is in vacation, and perhaps better. Experience has taught me that it is useless for me to arrange any system of study or reading for a vacation. I am indolent, unless I am forced by the recurrence of exercises, or something of the kind, to apply myself."

"Sat up all Wednesday night to finish dissertation, from 10 P.M. to 6 A.M.; wrote steadily without once closing my eyes."

"Came home, and after 11 o'clock Friday night began a sermon, wrote till 3 in the morning. Saturday, writing sermon; preached at 8 o'clock in the evening. The sermon seemed to give satisfaction, and I have felt some little vanity in the rapidity of its composition."

Against the impression given by such extracts must be put his reputation for scholarship and high purpose, and the expectations he excited among his friends, for which there must have been some basis in achievement. "Exceeding thorough," Dr. Ware used to say to his dissertations. He probably travelled too far among the books in preparing to write, then had to execute too fast. The sermons were usually a solid argument astir with religious earnestness and practical in aim. First sermons are apt to contain the life-long emphasis and the germs of half one's later thought. Mr. Gannett's first subject was Personal Love of Jesus Christ. Among the other early choices were Prayer, Repentance, Sins of the Tongue, Practical Infidelity, Conversion, the Scene of our Saviour's Crucifixion, Mercies of God, Universal Influence of Religion on Character, — a favorite this, for it was preached sixteen times. "He preached from the outset very fervently, and his prayers were most simple and devotional," says one who remembers the school-days well. In thought he ranked among his classmates as a conservative. They used to preach in turn before each other. When his first turn came, he prayed : " We beseech Thee to forgive us for the sake of Jesus Christ." Dr. Ware spoke of it, and Gannett replied : " I used the words purposely, with meaning." The Doctor said, " You will change." But it was a long while into the second term before the meaning grew untrue to him.

The young man was no bigot, one way or the other. He could see the fault in views he held, and the good in those which he rejected. Although the ideas of religion were of much account to him, religion was something greater and deeper than the doctrines.

Sept. 23, 1821. " Last week I returned from a journey to Greenfield. I have always found my mind, after a visit to this place or to Connecticut, in a very different state from what is usual at home. My thoughts are more directed to the subject of religion, of vital and internal piety. Going among those whose religious sentiments are different from mine, I hear remarks unlike those to which I am accustomed. Conferences and religious meetings are common, and religion seems more an every-day thing than it is with us. It cannot be denied that, whatever may be the tendencies of Unitarianism, its effect is to produce less apparent attention to religion. We may discuss doctrinal points, or we may talk of social or relative duties ; but piety, devotion, our connection with God and a future world, are less the subjects of conversation, and I never feel my own guilt and utter want of holiness so much as during one of these visits. I am almost frightened into the belief of their speculative articles. I am confident, when I think calmly, that their views are erroneous ; yet, certainly, the fruit looks fairer and more abundant. I do not see the necessity of this. If we would feel as we believe, that there is a future world of reward and punishment, that life is uncertain, and yet on this depends eternity ; that religion is a thing of supreme importance that should engross every affection and, I would say, every thought, — we should not be so inert and lifeless in our devotion and our piety."

March 2, 1822. "Yesterday I went to the President and signed the church-covenant of the College. Furness and Lincoln went the day before, and Kent yesterday morning. We had conversed much on the subject. When our class first came here, Dr. Ware mentioned it. I saw the President and conversed a little with him, and he gave me a copy of the covenant some months since. We deferred the profession from motives of doubt concerning the nature of the ordinance, and our own fitness. I had early imbibed reverential and awful notions of the Lord's Supper, considering it something to which only the true and high Christian could be admitted, — without any distinct ideas of its nature and obligation, viewing it with apprehension and awe. These ideas I was bound to define and examine, and I was thus led to see their fallacy. I found the Supper an ordinance binding upon all who call themselves Christians, but not implying any greater degree of virtue and holiness than was obligatory before, being simply a memorial of the Saviour, and a means of improving our Christian characters and dispositions. I knew also that I was too much attached to the world. My resolutions and my endeavors have effected but little, but I would look to the divine grace for strength. Certainly, because I fall infinitely short of Christian holiness is no reason for my neglecting an obvious duty of the disciple of Christ, especially when that may aid me in the observance of others."

June 26, 1822. "I had something like a dispute with Dr. Ware on the example set us by Jesus Christ. It is represented in the New Testament as being a perfect example, and yet is proposed for our imitation. Now, if Jesus Christ was a being of superior order to man, his conduct cannot be an example to us, because, his powers being superior to ours, the circumstances of life could not affect him as they affect us; if he were a simple man, he could not have been perfect and sinless without a supernatural, miraculous, moral influence operating from God on his mind, and which we can never partake. Dr. Ware said this was an unfounded supposition: that, when he believed in the pre-existence and superior nature of Jesus Christ, his being plainly and constantly presented as an example was the greatest difficulty with which he had to contend; that now, considering our Saviour a man, this was removed; and he thought this perfection of character was attainable without a miraculous influence, as we find great differences of moral excellence at present, for which we cannot account, but which we refer to circumstances beyond our knowledge."

The studies at the School were over in the summer of 1823. But before the first candidating came the " Approbation." Shall we look in upon the scene?

" On Monday, November 10, I was approved by the Boston Association. I sent at the preceding meeting for a subject. The text assigned was 1 Cor. xv. 10 : 'By the grace of God I am what I am.' The Association met at Mr. Frothingham's in Boston. Present: . . . all excepting Dr. Harris. My dissertation took twenty-nine minutes in reading. Henry Ware then asked me some questions from the manuscript book; such as, What attribute of God must we suppose before we examine the truth of a revelation pretending to come from him? (To which I answered, His goodness: the correct answer would have been, His veracity.) What are the fundamental doctrines of Christianity? What is meant by the internal evidence in favor of Christianity? What is meant by the doctrine of satisfaction? Does this doctrine necessarily imply that of imputation? What other views of the atonement are held by Christians? Are you willing to state your own views on this subject? (To this

I answered that I was not fully decided; that many passages of the Scripture seem to ascribe some peculiar merit to the death of Christ, and the doctrine must therefore in a great measure depend on their interpretation; that the last mentioned view of the atonement, that which supposed some efficacy in his death without in any degree attempting to explain that efficacy, seemed to me a nugatory representation.) All the questions amounted to between a dozen or so, entirely on the evidences and doctrines of religion, none on Biblical criticism, interpretation, or ecclesiastical history. After he had concluded, no other gentleman putting any question, I went into another room for five minutes. On returning to the Association, Dr. Porter, moderator, told me they had voted to approve me, and wished me success, &c. I drank tea, and stayed till about 7, — and brought out a text for Kent."

The Journal continues : —

" On a Saturday morning in October, I called on Dr. Channing with Upham, in consequence of a repeated request from U., he assuring me that Dr. C. had desired him to bring me to his house. We found Dr. C. at home. I was introduced to him, I believe, for the first time in my life, and sat perhaps half an hour. A few days afterwards (October 15), I was surprised by a visit from Dr. C. He told me, in consequence of what he had heard from my friends, and the interview with me a few mornings before, he came to request me to preach for him half the time. He was very particular in impressing upon me that I was not to preach as a candidate, but merely to relieve him. I consented, partly because I had not time to hesitate, and engaged to commence on the second Sabbath after approbation. On reflection, and mentioning it to Thomas, I found the engagement was a very loose one. I called on Dr. C., conversed with him, and fixed the time during which I was to preach at eight Sundays, he preaching alternately in the A.M. and P.M. Nothing was

said of pay, and the engagement was entirely a private one
between him and me."

Nov. 16, 1823. " Preached for the first time at Mr. Walker's,
Charlestown. I was not so much fatigued as I expected;
had a good audience and performed all the services."

Nov. 23. " Preached at Dr. Channing's, Federal Street,
for the first time. Did not find it a difficult house for speaking, but was disappointed; saw many inattentive, and felt
little excitement."

Dec. 21. " Enjoyed preaching to-day for the first time.
I did not like my prayers; am afraid I shall be compelled to
write them."

Jan. 11, 1824. " This day ends my engagement with
Dr. C. I have found it rather a pleasant engagement, have
become acquainted with Dr. C., and been pretty completely
broken in to preaching, but have experienced considerable
inconvenience from the uncertainty in which I was continually placed with regard to the extent of my services on
the coming Sabbath, whether for the whole or part only of
the day. I have most shamefully neglected to write, having finished but one sermon in eight weeks, and have thus
been compelled to preach sermons which I never meant to
deliver. Dr. C. spoke to me to-day in terms of great kindness, expressed his satisfaction with my services, and his
belief that his people were also satisfied with them. He had
told them he should be satisfied with whatever they might
do. I engaged last week to preach four Sundays at the
New South."

In that day the New England custom, by which pastor
and parish entered into a life-long connection with each
other, was but beginning to wane. It was still considered rather dishonorable for a church to seek a preacher
already settled over another church. Young men,
therefore, fresh from their study, were looked to as
the natural colleagues or successors of the most distin-

guished fathers, were watched with interest by city and country parishes, and taken at once into warm fellowship by the older brethren. The minister's relation to his people was a more affectional, less an intellectual, relation than it now is. The good pastor was sought even more than the good preacher; and a young man could rely on being tested not by his Sunday efforts merely, but by the outcome of his whole strength and life.

Dr. Channing had possibly first seen his colleague as a little fellow in his mother's chamber. Now the young man, in turn, meets a little fellow who was to be his successor; and he begins to be aware that he is fairly leaving the quiet Cambridge shelter, and entering the world: —

April 4, 1824. "Preached at Rev. Mr. Ware's in Boston. I dined with Mr. W. and two beautiful children, the eldest of whom, a boy, is between five and six.

April 8. Called on Mrs. — I fear that I shall never learn the etiquette and manners of fashionable society. This is the first instance in which I ever felt the misery of patronage."

April 19. "Messrs. C. and W., of Boston, called on me. They introduced themselves, and stated that their object was to see me, as there would be a meeting of Dr. Channing's society on Wednesday evening, on the subject of giving me a call. The conversation was partly on the subject of our Saviour's pre-existence, which Mr. W. defended and seemed to consider of great importance, which I told him appeared to me not an essential point of faith, and one which I did not believe, though I was not satisfied on either side of the question. They stated very expressly that their visit was entirely in their private capacity, and had in it nothing official."

The private questioners, however, were heralds. Very soon he wrote: —

June 27. "Did not preach. Attended meeting in morning at College Chapel, and in afternoon at Cambridgeport, this being the last Sabbath of freedom that I should have."

He had been preaching again for Dr. Channing. " Dr. C. wished me to preach as much as I could, but he did not think a young man ought to write more than one sermon a week." In all, he had been heard fifteen times before the invitation came to be colleague pastor of the Federal Street Church. The vote was not unanimous ; and the young man demurred, as well he might, for many reasons. Mr. Lewis Tappan gave him courage : —

" I learn with much pleasure that Dr. Channing expresses to his parishioners the most unqualified approbation of their invitation to you to be colleague pastor. I fear, from what is said and what I observed, that the circumstance of two deacons being in the minority, and a few other highly respectable gentlemen being cool or partially opposed, depresses you. The opposition is *feeble* in every thing except the personal characters of the opponents. One fears your religious views may not be perfectly satisfactory ; two decline voting, because those in their confidence are not in the affirmative ; two or three are not so well satisfied with your pulpit services as they could wish ; and a few are not taken with the preacher's style of reading, speaking, &c. I feel persuaded that most, if not all, the persons will in a short time be satisfied and cordial. Perhaps no greater unanimity has occurred in this city in settling a pastor, and it is hardly possible that it should be greater. It is not expected that a single individual will leave if you are settled with us ; and, if you are not, there is no doubt many will, in their dissatisfaction that a colleague is not settled. You see, sir, I argue as if *you* were an opponent. The fact is, ninety proprietors out of one hundred and fourteen (in town, scat-

tered, sick, &c.) are decidedly and warmly and anxiously
desirous of your settlement, and will be greatly disappointed
if you decline it."

This was reassuring. But then to be a colleague
with Dr. Channing! To stand by the side of the first
preacher of Boston, the man whom the citizens revered,
whom the "brethren" hailed as chief, whom strangers
sought out on the Sundays! To rise in that pulpit and
meet the disappointed faces of the audience, hoping to
hear his elder; not to know perhaps, till the church-
hour, in consequence of the frail minister's uncertain
health, whether his own Saturday night's sermon was
to be read or not; to have the youthful sermons and
services contrasted week by week with the other's deep
thought, his chastened words, his wondrous manner, —
all this might make even a young and bold heart shrink.
Shrink no doubt his did, but the heart *was* bold and
ardent, and the ambition noble, in spite of his self-
reproaching and distrustful habits. He could resolve
mightily, and hope, at all events. He was full of feeling about the greatness of the minister's work. That
work which he called " an office that his Saviour held,
a work together with God," was in itself vastly more
responsible than the special place of service, wherever
this might be.

The young man pondered seriously, took counsel
with his brother, and sent acceptance: —

CHRISTIAN FRIENDS, — After much deliberation, I have
resolved to comply with your invitation, trusting in the sincerity of my desire to be useful as a minister of Christ, and
relying on your candor and on the grace of God. To Him I
look for light and assistance. I have been chiefly deterred
from entering on this connection by a consciousness of my
own imperfections, and a fear that I might not benefit you

nor secure my own happiness. My acceptance of your proposal is accompanied by distrust of myself and a hope of
your indulgence for my involuntary errors. I would devote
myself to the office and to your good, praying that the connection may be a means of improvement to us both, and that
the blessing of God our Father may attend my exertions.

Your friend and brother,

EZRA STILES GANNETT

CAMBRIDGE, May 27, 1824.

The ordination followed speedily, on June 30 ; but
in between there came a " Gown and seven pair of
Bands," — yea, and a suit of clothes, and cravats and
hose and handkerchiefs and gloves, — a first present from
the parish ladies to their young, motherless pastor-elect.

An ordination was an important ceremony in days
when not once in a generation, perhaps, did the worshippers meet to welcome a new minister. Moreover,
this ordination was in Boston, and in Dr. Channing's
church.   Five " church-members " and five " proprietors " were chosen to superintend the arrangements.
A chief-marshal and aids were appointed.   " The
Reverend Clergy of the Ordaining Council " assembled
hard by to give formal sanction to the candidate, who
seems to have read a declaration of belief and purpose,
after which, heading a procession of the " male members," they marched into church. It had been voted,
after full discussion, to " invite all the clergy of the city
other than those of the Methodists." So, besides the
Congregationalists of both wings, the Liberal and the
Evangelical, Episcopalians, Baptists, Universalists, a
Presbyterian and a Catholic, were specially provided for,
with a score or more of other ministers, candidates, and
students in divinity, " the University under the care of
Rev. Dr. Kirkland," and a few honored lay-guests, —

Chief-Justice Parker, General Simon Eliot, Hon. William Phillips, and Baron de Wallenstein, Secretary of the Russian Legation. The services were those that still are common, save that no Scripture then was read. Dr. Channing preached a sermon upon the ministry demanded by the age : it must be enlightened, fervent, strong to controvert scepticism and false views of religion, and filled with the spirit of practical reform. " We had a most delightful ordination," wrote Henry Ware to a friend. " It is not possible for you to conceive the excitement produced by Dr. Channing. I never have seen the enthusiasm equalled. To hear such a sermon is one of the memorable things in a man's life. It forms an epoch in his existence." A dinner " very sumptuous " was waiting at the Marlboro' Hotel, at which the young man, now " Reverend," sat between his colleague and the Head of the University. Rev. Dr. Gardiner (of Trinity Church) asked the blessing at the table. " No man who witnessed the general prevalence of catholicism and good-will through the day could go away without catching something more of the affectionate spirit of our blessed religion."

And what were the feelings of the man thus welcomed to his life-work, — the slender, dark-eyed stripling, twenty-three years old, with the strong, fresh face, and serious yet eager look ? His graduating essay at the School was on the " Means of a General Revival of Practical Religion." That tells somewhat. The sermon with which he met his people on the first Sunday — it was July 4, 1824 — tells more. Paul's yearning words gave the text : " Receive us ; . . . for I have said before that ye are in our hearts to die and live with you." He pictured his ideal of the relation of pastor and people, and the duties of each : asking from them confidence,

sympathy, indulgence, attention, religious co-operation ;
hoping, on his part, to be their teacher, friend, and comforter, and their example he knows he should be.   Let
us listen to the pleading and the vow : —

"My friends, my destiny for this life is determined.   I
have consecrated myself to God and the Church.   I have
connected my happiness with yours ; and I, who, a few days
since, was almost without a home, cast on the waters of a
wide world, am now fixed among many friends, and made the
associate of one of whom I had heard, and to whom I had
listened, with admiration. . . . Be indulgent to me.   Consider the novelty of my situation ; the character of its duties,
so different from those to which I have been accustomed ;
the early age at which I am to undertake them.   Do not
compare my instructions with those which you have so long
heard from this pulpit.   Consider only whether they are the
words of truth and soberness ; and though, when you have
listened to eloquence and thought poured forth from the
lips of one whom you venerate, there shall be little intellectual gratification or little fervor in my ministrations, remember that they are offered in sincerity, and that they are meant
for your improvement.   The inspiration of genius I cannot
bring to you, but the services of a devoted heart shall be
yours.

" . . . The salvation of his people is the minister's business,
his vocation, his employment, with which nothing else may
interfere, but to which he must give his powers, his affections,
and his time.   And he must feel a holy interest in its success.
His thoughts, his words, and his actions must all tend to this.
He must not come to its denials and its pains with a reluctant
heart, and, while the words of humility are flowing from his
lips, let a worldly ambition be torturing his soul.   He must
not come to it as an easy resting-place for life, or an honorable condition.   It is not an easy service.   It requires a
sacrifice of self-love and self-indulgence ; and he who enters

the temple of God to be a priest, consecrated to the ministry of Jesus, must lay down at its threshold every sinful passion, every indulgent habit. He takes up the cross of his Master; and he must bear it with him in all places, though the scoffs of men be heaped upon him. It is an honorable service, but only when it is maintained in its true spirit, when it is performed as in the sight of God and without hypocrisy or sloth. Then, indeed, it is a noble and a pleasant service. The trial has its rewards. The minister is the servant of God for the purposes of His benevolence, and angels are no more. He fills an office which his Saviour held on earth, and he works together with God in the regeneration of man.

" . . . Brethren, to God and to the guidance of His grace I commend you, and I commend myself; and, as it is in my heart to die and live with you, may our lives be those of friends, and our death be that of the righteous."

FEDERAL STREET PULPIT.

FEDERAL STREET CHURCH.

V.

MORNING WORK, WITHOUT AND WITHIN;
ESTABLISHING THE FAITH.

1824–1836.

HE had found his place to stand: now with both
hands he grasped his lever. " One thing I do," became
the motto of his life. He felt himself to be a Unitarian minister; nothing more, but all of that, — pastor,
preacher of religion, and champion of certain ideas in
religion, then much spoken against. No study, no literary taste, no " philanthropy," no politics, no overstrain
of mind, no maimings of the body, were to draw him
from the chosen task. As other duties came, they were
attended to, but all turned into ministerial plan and ministerial performance at his hands. In the place where
the work began, it ended, forty-seven years later, — with
the life.

First of all, the young pastor must learn to call each
of the flock by name. So round and round the parish
he went, diligently eying the strange faces, noting the
voices, and fastening all in memory and in his chronicle ;
for, fresh from the School, he was very systematic with
his note-books. There were a hundred and fifty homes
to visit. Before the first six months had gone, he was well
advanced in the third circuit. This was the very part
of the work that, from the college point of view, had
looked insuperable. And, doubtless, it cost his inbred
shyness many a doorstep struggle to ring at the homes of
the fine families that attended Dr. Channing's church.
At the fashionable parties, according to confession afterwards, his hands were too much for him, and the grace
of small talk sadly failed, and he yearned then for the
doorsteps. Yet traditions linger that the bending earnestness of tone and manner was winsome even in such
society ; and a certain " Book Club " was quite famous
for its happy times. With those not rich and fashionable he felt more at home, and probably those saw him
oftenest. He may have been a serious caller, but that
would be expected from " our minister." Of course he
had to solve over again for himself all the inevitable problems. How could he be social, not official, in the calls,
and turn, not thrust, the conversation towards religious
topics ? Sometimes he came away after a long visit
with a feeling of spiritual unfaithfulness in not having
spoken, and sometimes feeling regret for a faithful,
awkward homily. In his young strength he sometimes
wished he could be sick a little, to better understand and
sympathize with pain and weakness. Above all, what
could a boy of twenty-three say to gray-haired sorrow-
ers ? Perhaps others besides Mr. Lovering, who heard it
first, and tells it, may take courage from this story : —

"There had been sickness and death in my parish. I was
called to my first duty as a minister in the sick-room and by
the death-bed. I went to our brother, Dr. Gannett, for the advice and encouragement which I needed and he was so ready
to give. I told him my utter agony of mind, — how I went
from my home with heavy feet; how I stood upon the doorstep, recalling this phrase and another in Holy Scripture, and
praying for God's help all the time. He heard me through.
Then he told me how he had passed through the same struggle. He told me how, at the very commencement of his
ministry, he had been oppressed with the sense of the better
confidence his parishioners had in Dr. Channing; and yet
there seemed a sacred duty laid upon himself. He told me
that one died in a family of much refinement and wealth, but
having no very earnest religious faith. He visited them; was
received politely, but coolly; spoke of the affliction that had
befallen them, and of the solace of Christian trust. He was
not interrupted; no attempt was made to relieve him from
any embarrassment he might have. All were somewhat
moved, excepting, apparently, the father. At last he rose to
leave; and, as he did so, the father said courteously, with no
expression of feeling, 'Mr. Gannett, you have doubtless done
what you thought to be your duty, and I thank you.' Dr.
Gannett told me he went home thoroughly disheartened.
He felt that he had somehow been an intruder, and had, with
the best of motives, made an egregious mistake. To his surprise, he learned, some time afterward, that he had won the
hearty esteem of the whole family, and that his words were
bearing fruit in a thoroughly consecrated Christian life. As
my interview with him closed, he said, in effect, 'Go wherever
your duty calls you, and always go with a prayer in your
heart.'"

Before the faces were well learned, the "meetings"
began, and these also fell to the new colleague's share
of duty.

Dec. 21, 1824. " Had our first vestry meeting. Explained Rom. x., and made some extempore remarks on verse 25, about fifteen minutes, — my virgin effort at extemporaneous delivery. Did quite well, — altogether beyond my expectation. Had also singing and devotional exercises."

Year after year, save during the city's summer thinning, or when the monthly lecture before the communion service took its place, this quiet vestry-hour returned each week. The elaborate " plans " attest Professor Norton's trained disciple, and laid the ground-work for the many hundred Bible hours that were spent with men and women not then born. At first, the subjects fluttered here and there in the beginner's way; then gradually drew together in courses. One course was on Mosaic history ; one on the nature of Christ ; two or three on practical religion ; another on the parables ; and two winters were given to the facts of Jesus' life. By and by, when his thought had filled out connections and rounded to a system, he aspired to treat the " History of Revealed Religion," which included, according to his division, the history of the Natural, the Patriarchal, the Mosaic, and the Christian Revelations, and gave room to discuss large themes like Prophecy and Miracles and Inspiration and the Sufficiency of Christianity. Of all the week, the vestry-talk was probably to him the richest hour in good. It gave him his inner circle of friends, obliged him to keep up Bible studies, and hid him during the painful early practice in extempore speaking. And it must have been pleasant to others, to have left this picture in an old friend's memory : —

" I valued those meetings even more than the Sunday services. He seemed to be then peculiarly on his *own ground ;* and his manner, less vehement than when in the pulpit, was tender, impressive, very sweet in voice and look, penetrating

6

the heart. 'For our conversation is in heaven,' — that was one of his subjects that I remember best, and it hints the tone of all. I think he felt happy at such gatherings as at those of our Book Club, because he knew he was with true friends who all loved and welcomed him gladly, and he saw how much he interested them. There was no restraint. All were very social, the conversation free; and, for a time at least, it was quite a parish meeting."

Not by any means of all the tryings could he write so buoyantly, "Beyond my expectations." On the contrary, "I have made one more attempt to hold religious meetings of ladies, and am convinced that I cannot succeed. For the present, I had far better attend to other parts of ministerial duty." The courage returned, however, with the need; but that seems not to have come until Mr. Kirk's zeal set some of his young people to searching the Scriptures anxiously. The pastor's study then became the natural resort for help in the things hard to understand in Gospel and Epistle, and gradually the Bible class also grew into a part of the week's regular work and pleasure and success. The same friend says : —

"The lessons were invaluable to us. His admiration of St. Paul was great; and when he expressed it, as he often did very warmly at such times, it caused us ladies to smile at one another sometimes to hear how, in expressing it, he was unconsciously praising himself."

The children were the next care : what should he do for them? Sunday schools were still a novelty in Boston churches. At first he tried the old way of catechisms on a week-day. Before long, however, the teachers of the "Franklin and Chauncy Schools" were meeting to discuss the best methods of instruction, and he was with them seeking light. For him, at least, the problem

went unsolved. Sunday school never ceased to be a
burden, bringing the consciousness of constant strain and
poor performance. Not but that he did far better than
he thought ; but his ideals of behavior and instruction
were too serious to be very taking in the eyes of little
ones. Once rather grimly he ventured again upon the
play-hours. " My object is personal," he writes to Dr.
Channing, who was consulted on all projects : " the
children will gain little direct good and will enjoy little
pleasure, but I am willing to appropriate this portion
of their time for my own sake. On the attachment of
these children to me as a friend, I build almost all my
hopes of usefulness to my parish." Now and then he
wrote special sermons for them. Very solemnly they
read to-day ; then they were deemed admirable, some
of them finding their way to print and English reprint. The fiftieth anniversary of Robert Raikes's experiment he celebrated with an address before the new
" Sunday School Society : " that also made one of his
earliest pamphlets. And in the spring of 1835, at the request of the same Society, he gave a course of lectures
on " Christian Morals as a Branch of Sunday School
Instruction." Four lectures only had been asked for :
they grew to seven, and his trouble was to hold them
there. It was a case of duty : —

" I have consented to deliver them, from a belief that one
of the plainest dictates of morality is obeyed when we undertake to do the best we can in a good work to which we are
invited. I could give no reason for declining a compliance
with this request but the consciousness of my inability to prepare such lectures as I should wish you might hear. But, if I
yielded to the sense of my own deficiencies, with what face —
when, upon soliciting a friend to become a Sunday school
teacher, I should be met with the frequent objection, ' I do

not feel that I am competent'— could I reply, as I have so
often done, 'Try, do as well as you can, this is all that is
expected of you'?"

No Sunday in those days went by without two
services, nor was there then a summer resting-time
when the church-doors were shut. The " Thursday
Lecture " came round in turn; the " Anniversary Sermons," too, then preached in behalf of the various
city charities ; and frequent summons to take part at
ordinations. One winter (1828–29) he stirred up the
brethren to join him in holding a Sunday *evening* service, — a great innovation. "Head and hands full,"
says a letter : " I am tired, and have an indistinct view
of two monsters called sermons, neither of which has
shape or beauty, — they must be caught and prepared
for exhibition before Sunday." But that must have
been one more than usual. Dr. Channing preached
when he was able, — sometimes ten times a year, sometimes twice as often ; and, as exchanges then were
frequent, — the chronicle shows three a month out of
the eight services, — only forty or fifty new sermons,
after all, were born within a twelvemonth. Hardly one
written during the first eight years was ever preached a
second time at home. For the most part, they were sermons not of " mere morality," but of practical piety,
presenting religion as the consciousness of spiritual relations and the culture of a spiritual life. In 1835, at the
end of his eleventh year, he summed up the five points
of his preaching, " repeated this morning in your hearing for perhaps the thousandth time," as —

" Filial reverence for God, brotherly love for man, a grateful faith in Christ, receiving him as the revelation of divine
and the model of human character; the reality of the spiritual

world; and regeneration, consisting in such a change of the
temper and way of life as may be wrought by one's own will
and effort, and shall issue in the establishment of the sentiments and habits just described. . . . Let a man observe
these five principles, and he will be saved here and hereafter.
. . . And if you are not saved, oh, consider you must be
lost! Ask ye the meaning of that word? Who can tell its
fearful import? Self-reproach, exclusion from the happiness
of heaven, removal from the favor of God; to live but to
suffer; to be surrounded by proofs of the Divine Majesty,
only to be tormented by the sight; to be conscious of power,
affections, and wants, craving and pining and raging for
satisfaction; and to feel one's self at variance with all that is
true and good and beautiful in the universe, — this it is, in
part, to be lost through one's own folly. What more it is,
eternity will disclose. . . .

"So I preach, brethren, for such it seems to me is the instruction of Scripture, confirmed by all which the study of
our own souls and of God's providence can collect of light
on the most important subjects of human inquiry. So, as I
conceive, have you been taught by other lips than mine, to
which the inspiration of a deeper acquaintance with these
subjects has given a far more persuasive force. So ought I
to preach with the convictions that now fill my mind in the
pulpit and from house to house. So by God's help would I,
and will I, preach more earnestly and more effectively than
I have done, both by the audible voice and by the silent
example. Brethren, let the prayer of your faith and your
sympathy help the endeavors that may be made for your
instruction in righteousness."

That the tone was fervent and "evangelical," the extract shows. Underneath his religious thought lay the
philosophy common to the early Unitarian thinkers of
this country and of England, although not here, as in
England, had Locke's analysis been carried out to doc-

trines of materialism and philosophical necessity. In
theory there was nothing mystic, nothing transcendental. "Faith" was common intellectual belief applied
to the specific truths of religion. Like all belief, it was
based on evidence; and the evidence sufficed to make
him a most assured supernaturalist. First, the historic
reality of the Gospel incidents must be and was established beyond all doubt. Next, the prophecies fulfilled
in Christ, his miracles and resurrection, fully proved the
special divine commission that he claimed; and, were
still more proof needed, the depravity and spiritual
ignorance of the classic world afforded it, — so fair a
form as Christianity appearing at so foul a time *must*
have been a Heaven-sent interposition. The Revelation,
thus proved genuine by Reason, then became the source
of man's highest knowledge on the most momentous
themes; as such, it was incomparably the great event
of human history. Reason again was called on as its
interpreter; and not even where the deepest longings
cried for light was the meaning of the sacred message
hastily assumed. The nature of Christ, for instance, was
a confessed secret to him. "I have often heard him
lament the Orthodox exaltation of Christ's influence,
because it obscured 'the Father.' The rank of Christ
personally, he said, we were not shown, but the divinity
of his mission was clear, — that was enough for us."
The future punishment of the wicked, the reunion of
friends beyond the grave, were other secrets: the New
Testament disclosed nothing definite about them. But
the glorious news that God is our "Father," that forgiveness of sins is possible, that there *is* a future life, —
these were truths disclosed there, and for him they were
truths which depended wholly on that Revelation for
their *certainty*. Natural Religion only furnished a "per-

haps." No wonder, therefore, that around " Christianity," in the specific sense, much of his thought and
gratitude centred. In this early time he preached sermons on its evidences, even a course of lectures once or
twice. Very often he spoke of the Revealer, his character, his influence on the life of the world and in the
individual soul; and always the fact of Christ's mission
was the ground from which he urged his most earnest
appeal for love and trust and loyalty towards God.

A clear-cut system this. His mind demanded such.
Had he been a pure " Rationalist," had the Revelation
failed to warrant itself as authentic event, he would
probably have been sceptical in regard to much that
many minds easily accept from Reason, — a sceptic on
the ground that there was no sufficing proof. But, as
it was, the clear-cut system was any thing but a cold,
unworshipful system. The piety, which some need
mystery to beget, in him sprang from the intenseness
of a definite conception. Belief must needs be fixed by
an intellectual process first: then his feeling rose and
gathered round it, until the two became one in a fervent
religious experience, as genuinely " transcendental," as
truly a " Christian consciousness," as any thing that
claims those mystic names. And, as applied to duty,
the faith showed itself a very strong, persistent motive-
force. Yet the religious feeling thus generated bore
signs of its origin. The associations of his childhood
and his ancestry abode with him. It reveals the character and the realness of his faith, that he could not
bear to hear Christ called simply " Jesus," and in some
moods shrunk from calling God " our Father." The
one address was too familiar: the other was privilege so
mighty, such infinite condescension on the Father's part,
that it seemed like self-forgetful daring in man to use it

freely. Fear was not cast out of the love. The gratitude was oftener the man's self-conscious duty than
the child's spontaneous thanksgiving. The trust was
the trust of an awed dependence rather than of sympathy. To quote a word addressed to his friend, Mr.
Kent: —

" I wish I had as clear and strong a faith in the goodness
of God as —— has. It reconciles him to every thing, and
makes him always calm and cheerful. I cannot divest myself of early impressions, and I am in continual fear lest I
should think *too mildly* of God and should not sufficiently
reverence His justice and holiness. He resolves every thing
into Love. I am afraid to do so. And yet I believe that
God is infinitely good, but we are miserable sinners who
deserve His displeasure."

All this gave way at other times to completely self-
forgetting " fellowship with the Father ; " and the
movement of his mind was towards, not away from,
such experience. Here is another letter to Kent, with
a passage from a sermon of 1834 : —

"FEB. 3, 1832.

" ... How wonderfully God has arranged the circumstances
of affliction ! There never was a bereavement, there is no form
of trial, to which do not belong peculiar topics of consolation. Oh! if we would only believe that all things are right,
and that divine love watches over us with infinite skill of
tenderness (if I may use so strange an expression), what a
blessed life we might lead! I thank God that His discipline
has taught me that, till I have learned to give myself up to
Him in practical trust, submission, faith, I shall never be at
peace. Outward circumstances could not make me happy.
I have been prospered and been disappointed, have had
blessings and troubles; but I believe I can say, with conviction and understanding of its truth, that I never had one

trouble which I did not bring on myself, or in which I did not see that God was *anxious* for my good. I have had some hard rubs in the experience of life, and there are some tender places in my heart now. But I am as thoroughly convinced as that I live that just the experience which I have had was what I needed, and that any thing less severe would have been mischievous. Now if I can only make the light of this faith rest upon the future as well as on the past! Ah, there's the difficulty. We must try, Kent. That's the law, — try, pray, watch, and God will help us."

In the sermon, the words seem to pant and struggle to utter the feeling : —

"Fellowship with the Father and His Son, Jesus Christ: fellowship, — friendship, sympathy, communion, yea, more, — consciousness of unity between the creature and His Maker!

"Fellowship with the Father and His Son, Jesus Christ: it is promised and given to satisfy the wants of man's spiritual nature, it is what the soul sighs after, seeks for, struggles for!

"Fellowship with the Father and His Son, Jesus Christ: it is given unto us to live in fellowship, to hold communion, *to be one*, with that Great Being whose home is the *everywhere of existence, whose life is Eternity, whose essence is Thought, whose action is Love*, — Love revealed through Christ Jesus, our Lord!"

In *style* the sermons were what would be expected from a vigorous, logical mind, not widely trained by literary culture. They always had a "plan." The hearer, even if he missed the text, could tell to what subject he had listened for the forty minutes, and could easily carry home the ideas, if he would, in their well-ordered sequence. But no epigram, no anecdote, had drawn his wandering eyes up to the pulpit. Judged by the feeling of to-day, there was nothing brilliant, nothing subtle, little poetry, little play of imagination or vivid picturesqueness ; few illustrations came straying in from books ; more came from Nature and from common life, but even these were wont to enter somewhat formally as analogues and parallels. In general, the language, left to itself, went soberly straightforward to the meaning. The purpose was too grave for the expression to be other than simple and direct ; but through the gravity there always glowed a force of moral feeling, which oft-times kindled into real eloquence.

This chastened sobriety was the usual style of good discourses then. The thought, also, he shared with others. But the utterance was his own, and unique. It disclosed his inmost self to those who looked and listened. Not the lips alone, the whole man spoke. As he warmed, the deep-set eyes shone, the face was lighted, the head trembled, the voice almost shouted, and the hands fitted all the words with free, abounding gesture. All this habitually, even when reading written sermons. To some the fervor proved displeasing. A friend warns him that he ranted : " Your manner was so impassioned, you betrayed so much want of self-control, as quite to take off the mind from the subject and fix it on the speaker." Both Henry Ware and Dr. Channing hasten to tell him that in his absorption he is not aware how long he makes his prayers. And the sermons too : " You have always leaned to the danger of too great length," writes Dr. Channing. And again : " Some of our friends spoke to me of your having preached a *long* sermon on a hot summer afternoon. I was sorry for you and your hearers. Will you not spare yourself ? " He never learned that kind of frugality and philanthropy. But the long sermons were

very apt to rise at the end to a sweep and power of eloquence that sent the hearers away well repaid for the
middle spaces of their patience.

In the moral feeling thus fused with every word lay
the main secret of his rare success as an extemporaneous speaker. Such speech was a kind of action, and
in action he at once forgot himself. Another secret
was the might of his base-convictions, and the logical
habit of his mind in working from them. Standing on
the firm-set premises, he sighted his points clearly, and
on the way towards them in argument was not to be
drawn off into vagueness or side-issues. The success
was not achieved, however, without struggle. Once,
while still a boy at preaching so that each Sunday
brought a fresh experience to be noted, the honest
record reads : —

Feb. 15, 1824. " Preached at Cambridge. The associations connected with the place, and my situation, embarrassed
me ; and I delivered my sermon very badly, with too much
haste, in some passages with mere declamation. As I had
not been accustomed to the short prayers at the commencement of the service, I found them very difficult ; and in the
afternoon hesitated and paused in the midst of a sentence for
a minute, — a most dreadful minute, — a dead silence that
must be broken by me, and I knowing not what to say."

The first time he *preached* extempore was at the
House of Correction, and on the Sunday after his
" virgin effort " in the vestry had made him bold : —

Dec. 26, 1824. " Fifty or sixty females present. Trusted
entirely to extempore address, and made wretched work.
Spoke only about ten minutes, on the evil of sin, from Titus ii.
11–18. It was a complete failure. Did not hesitate, because,
as soon as I found my stock of ideas and words exhausted,

I closed; but it consisted of the merest commonplaces. I was abundantly mortified and frightened."

Not for four or five years does he seem to have trusted himself again; and then, when he ventured, it was oftener at Dr. Tuckerman's or Mr. Barnard's mission-chapel than in the pulpit which he called "home." The first time at Federal Street, "it failed." A Fast Day gave him courage to try once more, for Fast Day was not quite a Sunday. The fifth time is still marked "miserable. Never extemporize in church again." But the seventh time — it did not come till September, 1832 — was "better than ever before in extempore preaching in church. Had no notes before me, and found it an advantage to be free from them." The consciousness of power must now have been near dawning; for soon afterwards he was delivering lectures in course, using only notes. The vestry-talks had brought him through to victory.

Whether written or extemporaneous, friends called the sermons fine productions for a man of his few years. Not so thought he. Now and then, but rarely, a discovery brightened him about them. "I can see his glowing face as I told him that his sermon on Family Prayer had led to the beginning of the habit in some of his families." He wrote that friend that she had done more than she could well imagine for his happiness. Another message from the helper who told him that he ranted: —

"I cannot see you under such discouragement, and refrain from remonstrating against it. I know you would be grieved, were you aware that you rendered ingratitude for your best gifts; and when you repine, what else is it? You may depend upon it you estimate your powers at too low a rate.

The day you preached on ' Guarding our Religious Liberties,' I walked home with Dr. Channing, and asked him what he thought of the sermon. He approved of it, and added that it was a remarkable production for so young a man. On the day when you preached before the Society for Indigent Boys, Dr. Tuckerman sat in the same pew: I asked him the same question. He was warmer yet in your praise, and approved every part of it except the apologies in the beginning; and those, he said, he *could not bear.* He thought those unacquainted with the singular humility of your character could not believe them spoken with sincerity. But it seems that you gave such satisfaction to the public in the former address before the Female Orphan Asylum that you were chosen for this also. . . . We all, from the first, admired the Christian humility which could consent to place yourself in comparison with Dr. Channing; and, believe me, we think your sermons fully as useful."

His relations with the elder pastor were most pleasant; but they were wholly different men. Dr. Channing was a recluse in habits, a still and careful thinker, searching far for higher views of man and God, and applying them to theories of social reform : the other was impetuous, directly practical in aim, enthusiastic in action, more given to define and organize and spread abroad the truth already fitted to his mind and tongue than to seek farther truth. One, too, was in the zenith of his fame, the man whom all in and out of the denomination thought of when they mentioned Unitarianism : the other was but a beginner by his side, and a beginner strangely humble-minded for one so eager and ambitious. Their intercourse was unequal. Perhaps they never could have come into close sympathy. The young man's manner expressed the reverence he felt, — too great for intimacy. Dr. Channing, from his side, looked out kindly for his colleague's comfort, and delicately avoided interfering in the work: indeed, there could have been little need of offering advice where consultation was so sure and deferential. He once had an opportunity to tell their people : " Of the faithfulness of our friend to this congregation I need not speak. He toiled day and night for the cause to which he had given himself. Of his connection with myself, let me say that it has never for a moment been disturbed by a word, I may add by a thought, which friendship would wish to recall. Mutual confidence, a disposition in each to concede to the other unrestricted freedom of opinion and operation, and, I trust, a disposition to rejoice in one another's success, have given us the benefits of this relation, unmixed with the evils to which it is thought to be liable." Few letters passed between them, for only during Dr. Channing's long Newport summers was correspondence held. But one caution was oft repeated in these few. A few days after the ordination, he wrote from the Island : —

" Many young ministers, whose heart is in their work, suffer from an excess of excitement and cares at the beginning of their labors. I have every motive for urging on you a wise moderation. You have expressed so earnest a desire to afford me relief that I ought to say that I never left my people with so light and unburdened a spirit as at present. I have a strong confidence that you will be a blessing to them."

In 1830 he writes again from Newport: —

" My life passes almost unvaried by incidents. One day repeats the last. This way of life is not best for all, perhaps not for many. To some it is a necessity. You, my dear sir, were made for action almost without intermission; and you and your class fill a most important place in the church and the world."

Between these messages, as we shall see, had come much stronger warnings against overwork and despondency, given in a friendly, outspoken way. The state of his health obliged him to throw on the helper so much of the parish care, that he tried at once to make him accept a part of his own salary, — but in vain: he found that he could approach his purpose only indirectly, by accepting less himself from the parish.

To that parish, first and last and always, the young man felt that he owed himself. The keenest sense of justice to the people's rights ruled all the busy action. To their preferences, all preferences of his own must bend. The feeling showed itself in delicate concern to meet their wishes in little things, in reverence for the usage of the church, in loyalty to Dr. Channing. Was any church-custom to be altered, there would be long pondering and questioning. Such a letter as the following reveals him in a very natural light: —

1831. " I am anxious for a change in respect to the admission of members to our church. When I was settled, and for some years after that time, I sincerely preferred the use of a covenant; but for several months I have been receding from that ground, and now think the use of any creed or public profession unscriptural and wrong. Where, however, the people from opinion or habit are attached to the form, and more harm than good would come from laying it aside, I would not urge its sudden relinquishment. But I do wish the minister was authorized to admit any one whom he pleased, on the simple expression of a desire to communicate. I could then say, and *feel*, that we have a covenant which those may acknowledge who like such a form, but no impediment is raised before those who think the table should be free to

all Christians. You will remember that the committee on
one branch of this subject have never reported. I hope on
your return you will consent to the discussion of the whole
subject, and I shall rejoice if your views should accord with
mine. I need not add I should not propose any change without your approbation."

Twice in the course of these first twelve years Mr.
Gannett was asked to leave his people. To both offers
he listened against his wishes, till he felt sure that duty
bade him stay, not go. The first asking was in 1827, —
a unanimous call from the new " Second " Society in
New York City to become their pastor. When it was
known that he had received it, the men with one voice
passed a vote begging him to " relieve their solicitude
by giving an early answer declining the invitation ; "
while the ladies hurried from house to house signing a
long paper with their names. He suffered a good deal
while in doubt. " Give me your advice frankly, as the
friend you have always been," he writes his old chum,
Kent. " If I look at personal happiness, I shall stay in
Boston ; but usefulness and duty, — these are the points
on which the decision should rest, and on these I am in
the dark. I shall be guided by the advice of others."
Finally he sent word, No. But that did not prevent the
New York friends from hoping for awhile and waiting
for a second word. Their new society was regarded as
very important to the Unitarian cause ; and they believed,
with reason, that loyalty to that cause would overcome
all preferences.

Five years later, in 1832, the American Unitarian
Association, which had by that time fairly won its way
to favor and was preparing to enter on larger work,
wished him to take the field as their General Agent. It
was a new office, and he was the first one chosen to fill

it, — chosen unanimously. It would require a man's
entire time and energy. Again he earnestly considered
the question of duty, and again his people turned the
scale.

Such invitations suggest that the young minister in
Federal Street had won some reputation in his denomination. As we turn from the parish to watch him in
extra-parochial relations, we find ourselves again in face
of Unitarian history, and pause awhile to fill in the
background with that history.

When Mr. Gannett came to Boston, he found, as has
been said, the elements of the new denomination all
present, — a name, definite doctrines, a body of conscious believers ready to give reasons for their faith, outspoken teachers, a recognized leader, a newspaper, and
a review ; but the elements had not yet assumed organic
form as a sect. He came just in time to lend his touch
at the shaping moment.

Long afterwards, in 1860, he thus describes the brotherhood of which he then became a member : —

"Thirty-six years ago I met in this ministerial circle Dr.
Porter, of Roxbury, wise, calm, sententious, from whose remark in one of our discussions I have tried to draw comfort
ever since, — ' A minister should feel that he does no small
amount of good in preventing the evil which would show
itself, if he were not in his place ; ' Dr. Freeman, sensibly
feeling the infirmities of age, but with a mind that years had
only ripened, and a heart that never grew old ; Dr. Harris,
of Dorchester, the faithful pastor and diligent student, sensitive, tender, and devout ; Dr. Pierce, of Brookline, always
laden with facts, and always prompt with kind greetings ;
Dr. Gray, who never dreaded the truth, but who loved harmony more than controversy ; Dr. Tuckerman, then minister

7

at Chelsea, where he was preparing himself for the work that has spread his name through Christendom; Dr. Richmond, gentle, urbane, modest; Dr. Channing, who came to the meetings but seldom, but when present showed his interest in our purposes; Dr. Lowell, always genial, always faithful, whose affectionate notes from his retirement at Elmwood show an interest which he has never lost in us. Of the men whom I accounted venerable as I looked on their grave faces and mature forms, he alone remains. Of those who stood on a lower plane of age, but were regarded with little less of timid respect, one still gives us the light of his benignant countenance and the warmth of his cordial sympathy (Dr. Frothingham), though he has chosen to withdraw himself from our professional labors. Parkman was with us, full of terse sayings, and often disturbing me by a quotation from Scripture so apt that its pertinency made its irreverence; Mr. Pierpont, earnest, ready, eloquent; Henry Ware, whose place in our hearts is indicated by the constancy with which we spoke of him under his Christian name, and who could always be relied on for co-operation in every measure that aimed at personal or social improvement; Palfrey, then as industrious in his clerical service, and as upright in his purposes, as he has been laborious and consistent ever since; Greenwood, delicate in health, sweet in temper, spiritual in his tastes, refined in his habits; Walker, sturdy in mind, as true as steel, and as fraternal as he was honest, — he who is now the candid hearer where he was once the careful preacher; and others who took a less frequent or less earnest part in our meetings.

"These meetings were held then, as now, twice every month, at our several houses. We were more punctual in attendance than of late years, and came together, as it seemed to me, rather for friendly conversation than for deliberate discussion. Dr. Lowell and Dr. Pierce were the first to appear; and more of ecclesiastical news and more of the results of our professional experience were exchanged between us than at present. The older members preferred the agreeable

and desultory talk which was a refreshment after the exertions of Sunday ; while the younger brethren made successive
— and successful — attempts to turn the afternoon to a more
profitable use. . . .

" The most distinct among the impressions which I retain
of the years in which I was one of the younger members of
this body relates to the character of our intercourse with one
another. It was free, frank, cordial, and healthy to a most
remarkable degree. Difference of age, of opinion, of taste,
of situation, produced no estrangement nor coolness. Discussions in which we maintained opposite views caused no heart-
burning or ungenerous criticism. The playful remark, often
bearing a sharp point, or the severe dissent honestly expressed,
if it inflicted a momentary pain, only became the occasion of
a more hearty confidence. Perhaps distance throws a false
light over those days ; but I love to look back on the mutual
respect and bold trust which marked our social relations at
that time as almost without a parallel among ecclesiastical
men ; and I well remember the surprise created twenty years
ago, at a meeting of ministers in England, when I described
to them the harmony which reigned over all our diversities
of thought and feeling, and the unction of which was then
fresh on my heart. . . .

" If I were called to lay down a rule for every meeting, it
should be moved to give this rule precedence over every
other, — that every one present should say something.   I
know I express the wish of the older part of the Association
when I entreat the younger brethren to enter into the discussion as promptly and as fully as the oldest or the wisest
in the room.   There is a wisdom of youth as well as of
age : we want them both. The modesty which keeps the
younger portion of our circle silent is of comparatively recent
date. It did not close the lips of the junior members of our
body thirty years ago, — as I have occasion to remember,
with a sense of personal presumption indeed, yet not without
a feeling of approval for those who threw themselves upon

the privileges of an occasion, even at some risk of incurring a gentle rebuke. Such rebuke, however, if it ever came, was very gentle."

Many of the names in the list above are those of the Fathers of Unitarianism, whose ministries began while the Puritan Church of New England was yet unbroken, and who, from being Liberals and Arians then, found themselves compelled to side with the heretics as events ripened to the schism. Not far off in the country, shar-- ing with these the fathership, were Drs. Bancroft at Worcester, Ripley at Concord, Thayer at Lancaster, Prince at Salem, Abbot at Beverly, Parker at Portsmouth, and Kendall at Plymouth, — all men of weight, whose impress lingers yet upon their towns. The elder Ware, Dr. Kirkland, and Professor Norton were connected with the College; and Worcester, the "apostle of peace," lived close by at Brighton. Dr. Channing was among the younger of these elders. His two most brilliant contemporaries, Buckminster and Thacher, had died young, leaving him as an intellect comparatively alone in a midway position between the white-haired and the dark-haired men, — a fact which had something to do with his leadership in the movement. The younger ministers — those whose active life began about the year of crisis, 1815, and who were to do champions' work for their faith in New England — were Walker, Palfrey, Pierpont, Henry Ware the son, and Dewey. William Ware and Gilman had gone to outpost duty at New York and Charleston respectively. Jared Sparks had just left Baltimore, after valiant service there. At Philadelphia, a little group of Liberals were soon to welcome Gannett's classmate, Furness, as their minister; and at Washington still another handful were wont to greet each other at a Sunday service.

The Liberal Churches were slow to organize themselves into a distinct party; but the subject of organization was growing in thought and on the lips. The
elder ministers, those who had resisted the break with
Orthodoxy, continued, as a body, lukewarm or opposed.
Did they not know the evils of sectarianism? Were
they not exiles from their homestead of faith through
its malignity? Had they not for twenty years past
been protesting against exclusion in religion? and
now should they draw lines around themselves? To
the end of their long ministries, — and some of these
Fathers died after fifty years' connection with a single
parish, — such men preferred the name of Liberal or
Catholic Christians to that of Unitarians. Norton also,
though in favor of outspoken literature, pointing to
Grotius, LeClerc, and Locke as exemplars of the true
method of influence, was strongly opposed to any formal
name-taking and combination ; yet he and Channing
were among the number who thought that some slight
bond of association, if that were possible, might be
useful. But the younger men, believing that the time
was fulfilled, were eager to press forward. They knew
the danger, but meant to escape it. They *did* hope
to make a sect without sectarianism. They thought
lines *could* be safely drawn ; for had they not the
" fundamentals " common to all sects? and did not
Professor Norton's principles of Bible criticism cover
all possible advance? Could there be any thing beyond
Unitarianism claiming to be Christian? And certainly
they could not hope to do effective work without organization. Mr. Gannett at once threw in his heart and
hand and voice with these.

In January, 1825, an invitation was issued to certain
prominent ministers and laymen to meet in Dr. Chan-

ning's vestry, and " confer together on the expediency
of appointing an annual meeting for the purpose of
union, sympathy, and co-operation in the cause of Christian truth and Christian charity." Of some thirty gentlemen who responded to the call in person or by letter,
most, but not all, liked the suggestion, and the minority
was probably large enough to make the others hesitate.

Four months passed by. " Anniversary Week " came
round, bringing to Boston, as usual, many ministers
and earnest church-men from the country. It was
suddenly decided by those most deeply interested to use
the opportunity for action. A meeting was called, and
the proposal made to form some bond of co-operation
between the Unitarian Christians of the United States.
The discussion now showed a heartier welcome for
the measure. On the next day a Constitution was
adopted, officers were chosen, and the American Unitarian Association came into being. Dr. Bancroft, one
of the elders, was willing to accept the Presidency ;
influential laymen appeared as Vice-Presidents ; and
with them, as Executive Committee to do the work,
were joined young men earnest in the cause, — James
Walker and Henry Ware, Jr., who had both been
prominent in the preliminary movement, Samuel Barrett, Lewis Tappan, and Ezra S. Gannett. The last
was chosen Secretary ; and it is said that he drew up
the simple Constitution. " His whole soul is in it," wrote
Henry Ware just after the event.

Some twenty years later, Mr. Gannett thus describes
the motive of the founders : —

" The American Unitarian Association had its origin, not
in a sectarian purpose, but in a desire to promote the increase
of religion in the land. Other denominations had their societies, to which the pecuniary contributions of Unitarians

might be paid, but in the management of which they were allowed to have no voice. The officers of these societies connected the propagation of tenets, which we account false, with whatever measures of general utility they might adopt. We found ourselves placed under the painful necessity of contributing our assistance to the diffusion of such views, or of forming an Association through which we might address the great truths of religion to our fellow-men, without the adulteration of erroneous dogmas. To take one of these two courses, or to do nothing in the way of Christian beneficence, was the only alternative permitted us. The name which was adopted has a sectarian sound. But it was chosen to avoid equivocation on the one hand, and misapprehension on the other."

He surprised Dr. Channing, summering at Newport, with the news. The answer came : —

"I was a little disappointed at learning that the General Unitarian Association is to commence its operations imme diately. I conversed with Mr. Norton on the subject before leaving Boston, and found him so indisposed to engage in it that I imagined it would be let alone for the present. The office which in your kindness you have assigned to me I must beg to decline. As you have made a beginning, I truly rejoice in your success."

Funds did not overflow the treasury. The first year s income amounted to not quite $1300. In Boston itself only sixty-five friends offered the annual subscription. All was tentative. Such definite action was contrary to Liberal precedents. The officers could attempt little more than the publishing of a few tracts, a commission to a solitary scout to go into the back parts of Pennsylvania and Ohio, and report "the demand for Unitarianism in the West," the partial adoption of a missionary to the city poor, and a vigorous anniversary

meeting in the grand muster-week of spring, when all
the ecclesiasticism of the State appeared upon parade
in Boston.   The Unitarians were outcasts, and the casting out was still in process.   Dr. Channing could congratulate them at their third anniversary on the cheering
sight of so many persons not ashamed to assemble on
such an occasion and for such purposes.   Judge Story
thrice appeared in as many years to make the plea for
religious liberty, and to reiterate that the Association
had its highest claim to favor, not as a powerful means
of diffusing a certain set of religious opinions, but as an
instrument for maintaining the rights of conscience,
freedom of inquiry, and the common principles of Protestantism.   For a time of such hot attack, compelling
self-defence, much good temper was displayed at these
early meetings ; but great determination too.   A positive,
practical spirit appeared.   They faced the future, and
were not to be put down by outcry.   How could they
spread the truth ? was the main question.

The process of organization went on.   The " Christian
Disciple " had just given place to the " Christian Examiner," which began its examinations with a boldness that made good the name.   Within the .next few
years the " Liberal Preacher," the " Christian Teacher's
Manual," the " Unitarian," the " Unitarian Advocate,"
the " Unitarian Essayist," the " Unitarian Christian,"
the " Philanthropist," still another " Unitarian," and the
" Scriptural Interpreter," started up and spent short
lives of zeal, as one man after another felt a call upon
him.   Young men in Boston formed a " Christian Book
and Pamphlet Society ˙ to circulate gratuitously the
Unitarian publications.   The Sunday School Society
followed.   A building for the Divinity School at Harvard College was erected in 1826 ; and in the same year,

at the dedication of the Second Unitarian Church in
New York, Dr. Channing preached another famous sermon on the new faith, — this time to vindicate it as
" the system most favorable to piety." His plain, strong
words contrasted its tendencies with those of Trinitarian
Calvinism in a way that startled friends and shocked and
angered all opponents. The latter have never yet forgiven him his reference to " the central gallows of the
universe."

In spite of these signs of progress, Unitarianism began
to feel a check. The formation of the American Unitarian Association may be said to nearly mark the end
of that rapid advance which had seemed at first like
actual triumph, and flushed the talk of the Boston ministers with hope.

The chief cause of the check lay, doubtless, in the
simple fact that, during the decade now gone by since
the year of crisis, almost all the Liberal sentiment ac-
cumulated through two long generations, that could be
appropriated by this special movement, had already been
appropriated ; and cultured Rationalism, by its very
nature, can never quickly generate fresh material. The
blossoming had been rapid, because the blossom-moment
had been so long deferred. But Unitarianism, it proved,
was to spread in no wide-flashing spring. It was intellectual, it made public-spirited citizens, dutiful lives, wise
philanthropy, common-sense preaching. It was found
not rarely with true spirituality of mind. But it was
seldom found with warm expressive feelings, and what
excited little apparent enthusiasm even among its own
followers would fail, of course, to touch the general
heart. As a system of thought, it was *too* intelligible.
It lacked the mysticism which the religious imagination
commonly demands as room to play in. Its negations

were very distinct; and its positive ideas, in spite of Dr. Channing's showing that they ought not to, must needs seem meagre and cold to those who were wont to gaze on a God that once stood in the midst of men, and bore their nature with them, and suffered for them in that great love-spectacle set between the earth and heavens. For such believers, Election, Total Depravity, Eternal Punishment, were swallowed up in the glory of the Incarnation and the almighty love of the Atonement. If Unitarianism were shorn of unreason for the few, it was also shorn of power for the multitude. Because more than other systems it embodied reason, its presence was henceforth to influence, like reason, as a leaven, — not begetting Unitarians so much as modifying Orthodoxy. There still was open growth indeed, but from this time forward slow growth. In the back counties of Massachusetts it was hardship long after 1825 to bear the name, and outside of New England to take it was to court social ostracism. Even in its native haunt, it soon became evident that Unitarianism, relatively to the neighbor-sects, was losing influence. The country population came flocking towards the city in greater crowds each year, bringing with them ever fresh supplies of the home-bred Puritanic faith; and the dozen old city churches that had given up that faith were speedily outnumbered by the new ones that retained it.

What now happened on a small scale in New England recalls what happened on a large scale in the early days of Protestantism, — save that not now, as then, was much ground lost that had once been won. Protestant worship then proved less satisfying, and the doctrines less inspiring, than their advocates had hoped. Thus it was, as we have just said, with New England Unitarianism. The Roman Catholics partially reformed themselves at Trent: thus, too, the New England Calvinists. They had already a little improved their dogmas, and now began more openly to avow the improvements; yet not without something that looked like evasion in regard to past interpretation. Fifteen years before it had been hard to discover what " Liberalism " really was: now what was " Calvinism " ?   " The term Calvinistic for this party," said Mr. Gannett, in his Fast-day sermon of 1828, " is objectionable, because it conveys no definite idea.   There is Calvinism of every hue, from consistent Hopkinsianism to the chameleon-like Calvinism of some living preachers. If the Genevan reformer could appear among us, he might rejoice at the inroads which common-sense and good feeling have made upon his system ; but he would, methinks, be not a little amazed at the constancy with which his name attended this changeable faith."   Unitarians refuting the old " points " were liable to be complained of in one breath for misrepresenting, and perhaps were told that this or that dogma never had existed ; in the next, the time-honored creed was reasserted " true for substance." Thrice they had to prove to their reluctant neighbors that, according to Calvin and his apostles, the creeds *did* mean, in spite of all denial, certain horrors which many in New England now were willing to repudiate. The change in meaning was admirable, but it did not seem fair to appeal to the familiar phrases and ignore it.

And finally, in the sixteenth century, a great flame of zeal burst forth in the new order of Jesuits. So now the zeal of the Orthodox rekindled, and Lyman Beecher was their Loyola. A revival began in Boston as early as 1822–23, and was eagerly watched by friends outside, who hoped to see it absorb the strength of the schism. Lyman Beecher watched from Connecticut till he could

stand no longer a mere looker-on. He came to Boston,
first as helper, then in 1826 to live, and his presence
meant fire and fight. The shattered ranks closed up.
Church-bells rang out of hours for novel meetings.
Neighborhood conferences met from house to house.
Sunday schools and Bible classes were put in training
to educate hostility to heresy. Beecher brought the
" Spirit of the Pilgrims " in his heart, and soon threw
it into a magazine thus christened, which far excelled
the early " Panoplist," in unremitting vigor of attack.
" The Boston Recorder " by its side also bristled with
denunciation. A fierce revival raged in Central New
York, — raged until even Beecher, who at first had
hailed it as the Lord's presence in the land, led the
warning against its coarse excesses. Only against such
excesses : against Unitarianism in its stronghold the
siege was as hotly urged as ever. Its preachers were
now debarred from taking their usual turn in the Annual
Convention Sermon. Its members were charged, from
one quarter, with usurping an undue share of the offices of State, and from another with altering the constitution of the Harvard Theological School so as to seal
it to their sect. A form of trust-deed was devised to
secure church-property against future perversion by
heresy. All the while church-breaks were going on in
one village or another ; and now and then a fiercer feud
than usual, like the one at Groton and that in the First
Cambridge Parish, drove gusts of angry feeling far and
wide.

" The Unitarian controversy " lasted about ten years
after the American Unitarian Association was formed,
and the first half of this period held the bitterest years
of all. What Ware and Woods, what Norton and
Stuart wrote, was little and mild compared to what had

since been written or was written now. Boston, New
York, Baltimore, and Princeton, — city ministers, country parsons, and laymen, —editors, pamphleteers, and
correspondents, even children, took public part in it.
Both sides were sadly violent ; for each felt outraged
by the other, and each believed itself to have a sacred
cause in charge, — the one, salvation by the atoning
blood ; the other, liberty for reason in religion. For a
while the Unitarians repelled the attack. Besides their
energy in print, the ministers in many a village meeting-
house, like Dr. Channing in his famous sermons, were
busied in refuting Orthodoxy, discussing the nature of
" heresy,"defending the rights of reason in religion, and
setting forth the excellence of the Unitarian system.
As the quarrel grew more personal and angry, there
came a feeling of revulsion. *This* was not Christianity
at any rate. The " Examiner " and the " Register "
sighed for peace, and both gave notice that thenceforth
they should try to keep it. Sermons against controversy were preached and published. But there was no
peace. It was not possible so soon. Personalities more
gross, insinuations more libellous, and " coalitions "
more dangerous and determined than ever before to put
down Unitarianism, were indignantly denounced in the
Unitarian Association's Report for 1829. The next
year Dr. Channing for a fourth time roused ire. His
Election Sermon spoke of modern forms of " Inqui-
sition ; " and the preface to his volume of sermons, the
first volume he ever printed, held other words as strong.
Professor Stuart from Andover addressed him an earnest
" Letter on Religious Liberty," and turned upon the
Unitarians themselves their favorite weapon, accusing
them of violating religious liberty by their flagrant
misrepresentations of Orthodoxy, and these reiterated

charges of bigotry and superstition and dark designs to
put down free inquiry.   Bernard Whitman sharply answered the Letter.   A number of the "Spirit of the Pilgrims" was devoted to refuting him; to which he wrote a
second thick answer to present the proofs, and dared denial, — he could furnish more.   Whitman's two pamphlets
contain a Unitarian chronicle of the Orthodox misdeeds
throughout the whole long controversy.   It is arranged
in a systematic indictment, each head giving details of
the parish scandals, and altogether makes no pleasant
reading.   Dr. Channing wrote from Santa Cruz to Mr.
Gannett: "I am humbled when I think that such a book
is needed, — if indeed it be. . . . I may carry my aversion to personal warfare too far.   Certainly it is not
my element. . . . I can fight for or against *opinions*,
but I wish to detach them from the men who hold
them.   Others must judge for themselves; but my own
love of truth and capacity for discovering it are not
aided by mixing up private friendship or enmity with
the matter under discussion."

But now the end was near.   Only one more shot of
consequence was fired, — "Cheever's Vituperations,"
which blazed out from Salem in 1833.

By that time church-breaking had nearly ceased, the
exiles were settling down in their new meeting-houses,
and local bitterness began to subside.   In all, about one
hundred and twenty-five parishes changed faith and
name.   As the two parties became organically distinct,
and Unitarianism lost proselyting power, while its zeal
in home-philanthropy could not be denied, its neighbors
grew more silent, — perhaps in sign of settled pity
rather than of reconciliation.   Under the pity, however,
the term "Christian" began to take on that slow en-
largement of its meaning by which right life comes to

receive more stress than right belief. Each party, too, discerned fresh divergences appearing within itself to occupy attention. The long controversy had, meanwhile, helped to enlighten public opinion as to the relations of Church and State: in 1833, when the Constitution of Massachusetts was amended, the civil and the ecclesiastical affairs were separated as they never yet had been among these children of the Puritans. The church-tax levied on all voters was given up, the support of ministers became henceforth wholly voluntary, and " First Parishes " lost their old-time prerogatives.

All this time the two sister-sects of Unitarianism, the Universalists and the " Christians," were also winning way ; in New England, chiefly the former of the two. The voice of its champions in press and pulpit, and of sturdy village-propagandists, gave forth no uncertain sound. But its literary field still lay apart from that of Unitarians. It maintained its evangelical and democratic character, making appeal to a class that would only have been offended by the high cold rationalism of the Boston set. And the Boston set from its side was little disposed to fraternize. The peculiar Universalist doctrine had now assumed two forms. According to one form, all of earth's sinners were sure of final bliss, but only after due discipline of future retribution. According to the other, — and thus believed most Universalists in 1830, — sin knew no penalty beyond the grave; death brought immediate happiness. The Unitarians held that the Scriptures kept a silence about " restoration," which they were therefore bound to imitate ; or, if, on any ground, they avowed disbelief in eternal torture, they felt no special enthusiasm over the denial. But the more popular doctrine — salvation instantaneous as well as universal, they held was not unscriptural

only, but irrational and dangerously immoral. Against
that some of the leading ministers were moved to send
to print their formal protest.

The last ten stormy years of the Unitarian controversy very nearly cover the opening portion of Mr.
Gannett's ministry, — the years with which this chapter
deals. He was, of course, too young to take a prominent part in the literature of the controversy, but he
had all the young man's enthusiasm to defend and extend the faith. The letters to Kent read like those of
a young bishop in training, — he is so interested in the
parishes and the candidates, and how to get the right
man introduced to the right place. His zeal in helping
to form the Association has been mentioned. A goodly
share of its early work fell to him as Secretary. To his
own parish he presented its cause very modestly, owing
perhaps to Dr. Channing's minor interest in it. But
before long he was going about organizing auxiliary
societies in the neighboring towns.

"I don't like to preach before the ministers, but if it will
help the Unitarian Association I will do it; otherwise, No."

Sept. 16, 1827. "At Waltham, in Whitman's church, to
form auxiliary of American Unitarian Association; made an
address of more than an hour. Thirty-six members. $52.00
subscribed this evening."

And thus at Dedham, Lexington, Medford, and elsewhere. One of Dr. Channing's letters in answer to the
request for tract-material deserves remembrance, because it shows from what conscientiousness of intellect
his words got that rare temper which keeps them strong
so long : —

"Aug. 8, 1826.

"You gratify me by proposing to publish the Dudleian lecture as a tract. I have not looked yet at the sermon on intemperance. I am afraid you do not quite understand /my feelings about publishing my sermons. In most of them are some positions which I wish to consider more thoroughly before giving them to the press, — some doctrines stated without proper limitations, perhaps some great truths very superficially stated. My objection to publishing is that I have not that conviction of the *truth* of every part which is to me the *essential requisite.* This is the case with the sermon on intemperance. Some objections have been made to it, which I have not had time or disposition to weigh. As to the Dudleian lecture, though written rather rapidly, it was the fruit of a good deal of thought. I have had assurances of its doing good, and I shall be glad to have it spread."

During the first few years the Secretary hardly ever ventured into print himself, save to serve apprenticeship for a while as one of the editors of the " Christian Register." He was ready to do his part in any thing. " My strong-hearted coadjutor " Henry Ware called him in 1826, as the tired man rode off in quest of the health lost in his own over-strains of labor, leaving " the drudgery of the paper " to younger hands. A similar arrangement was again adopted a little later. The co-editors had their own good times. Long afterwards, over the dinner-table where the " Register " was celebrating its semi-centennial, and Dr. Gannett as a father in the denomination was speaking of its day of small things, he referred to this editorial experience :

" I remember another period, when there was a sort of combination editorship, which I am afraid was rather poor; but we had pleasant times. There were four or five of us,

8

among whom were Dr. Barrett and George Ripley, who
undertook to edit the paper by holding a weekly meeting.
We met together, and spent one evening a week in laying
out the matter for the next week's paper; and if our work
was not as sacred as that of another committee, which at
the present time holds its meeting in England for the revi-
sion of the Bible, I think we did our work as conscientiously;
and this I know, that neither heresy nor bigotry ever disturbed our intercourse."

In Mr. Gannett's eyes there was a right and necessary
sectarianism as well as a wrong and dangerous kind.
He believed in charity; but that " truth is the only
sure basis of charity," and that ideas as ideas carried
force for good and ill. Since his own ideas were clear
and to himself momentous, he expected other thinkers
to value theirs as much and shape them as precisely;
and he showed his intellectual sympathy with such
thinkers, not by vague half-way accommodation of his
thought to theirs, but in hearty recognition of their
intelligence and sincerity across the gulfs of difference.
Negations came squarely from him, — especially denial
of the Trinity, a doctrine which affected him as " idolatry " affects most Christians; but it was part of his own
case, both in public and in private, to state an adversary's case at its best. If his indignation were deliberate and deep, it summoned all the more his truthfulness
and justice into action. Personal denunciation very
rarely escaped his lips, sarcasm or ridicule towards
religious opinions perhaps never. He was somewhat
shielded indeed from the last temptation by having little
sense of humor; but that was not the only reason why
he abstained. In the presence of earnest feeling, it
seemed to him contempt; and contempt was not ungenerous only, but unjust and irreverent to the spirit of
truthfulness.

Far more than any denials, the Unitarian affirmations received his emphasis. He loved to glorify the faith. It was the beauty of holiness to him. To draw its doctrines out in systematic order, and describe them operating on the heart and life, was his delight, — a work, too, for which he was well fitted by the fervor and logical cast of his mind. Time and again he re·turned to it, as the years went by. The love was born in these early days, when such work was essential to the organization of the new sect.

In this spirit he used to preach a set sermon upon Unitarianism once or twice a year; and at the vestry-talks, in one aspect or another, it much oftener furnished themes. Sometimes there would be a stout defence all along the line, then an argument for or against some special point, and presently a stirring appeal to its advocates to feel and live out its high demands. In August, 1826, at the dedication of the church in Purchase Street, the young man preached an admirable sermon, long and strong, on " Unitarian Christianity Favorable to Religious Zeal," — nearly the same subject which the elder colleague made famous a few months later in New York. His first published ordination sermon (1831) was on " Unitarian Christianity Suited to Make Men Holy." The first published dedication sermon (1833) aimed to prove " Unitarianism Not a Negative System." And, by that time waxing bold in extempore speech, he gave a course of lectures, elaborately discussing those Orthodox doctrines which the Unitarians reject or modify. The vestry overflowed with listeners at once : the speaker had to lead them first into a hall, at last into the large church.

Some extracts from such sermons are inserted. They show the eager young champion committed, heart,

mind, and voice, to the cause; and they also serve to
indicate through him the beliefs of the founders of the
denomination, the spirit in which they worked, the
sense of duty and necessity which drove them forward
under the attacks which they had to meet.   The Fast
Day words of 1828 come out of a very heated moment
of the controversy, and probably hold his most indignant
public utterance.   The sermon written in 1857 to defend the early Unitarians against two common charges,
contentiousness and coldness, gives a general view of
these stirring years, as he looked back on them long
afterwards.

1827.   *The Name " Unitarian Christianity."* — " This
appellation — till within a few years as strange as it was
odious even in this part of our country, but now gladly borne
by many sincere and humble Christians, — seems to me preferable to any other, as it expresses the two chief points of our
faith, — the unity of God and the divine mission of Christ;
since it is less liable to the charge of arrogance than some other
terms that have been adopted by the advocates of this system,
and is at the same time less capable of perversion; and since
it cannot be denied that the friends of this faith hold to the
divine unity in a more strict sense than other classes of Christians.   Names in themselves are nothing; but as in the intercourse of life they are made to be of great importance, and as
in the divisions that have rent the church of Christ it is
almost necessary that we should assume some distinctive title,
I wish that we might take this, which those who differ from us
are willing we should have, and that we should honor it by
our lips and glorify it by our lives.   I rejoice to appropriate
it to the faith which I have embraced; for it represents to
my mind the simple, genuine religion of the Son of God, —
the system of doctrines, precepts, sanctions, and hopes which
are unfolded in the gospel, the collection of facts and truths

which are embodied in the New Testament, what an apostle
called 'the glorious gospel of the blessed God,' what Jesus
Christ declared to be 'the true bread from heaven,' — 'the
words that are spirit and life.'"

1829. *Religious Controversy.* — "Among the means of
ascertaining Christian truth, religious controversy must be
regarded as important, if not essential. There is a sensitiveness on this subject in the minds of many excellent Christians,
with which I cannot sympathize. They dread the name,
the aspect, the tone, of controversy. They are supremely
anxious to preserve peace, candor, charity. Their spirit is
a good spirit, the spirit of love; but they seem to me to
misunderstand its instructions. Their argument is a poor
one: Because 'love is the fulfilling of the law,' therefore
cultivate love at all sacrifices. I reply, No, never sacrifice
truth, nor betray its interests. Truth is the only sure basis
of charity. Do not, for the sake of quiet, withhold your aid
from the suppression of error. It is better that one generation should be involved in the heat and smoke of religious
dissensions, than that subsequent ages should be enveloped in
the darkness of a false theology. Let the light in upon society; and if it startle, nay, if it provoke the passions and prejudices of men, so be it. For the blessed truth's sake, and
for man's sake who needs it, in the name of God who sent it,
let it have free course. Let it run and be glorified. The
evil will be temporary, the good will be permanent, and the
present evil will be exceeded by the present good. . . . One
has no more right to lock up the truth in his breast than
to confine his charity there. Truth will always be found
the best friend to whose protection charity can trust itself.
Strike from the tablets of history the effects which may be
traced to controversy, and you will efface many stains from
the annals of mankind, but you will remove likewise the
marks and evidences of progress. It is controversy which
has kept the wheels of improvement in motion, and has dis-
engaged them when they have become fixed among the

prejudices and creeds of the age.   But men need not forget
for a moment the obligations under which they lie to cultivate peace and good-will.   They may secure each other's
esteem by the exhibition of a Christian temper at the times
when their difference of opinion is most prominent.   The
gospel does not desire a peace which is the result of silence
or apathy, but a peace which is the fruit of self-discipline."

1826.   *Unitarians   should   assert   their   Rights.* — "My
dear Friend, . . . The prospects of a Unitarian society's
being gathered immediately in Woodstock must be very
small, but the effect of a few Sabbaths' preaching may be
seen months hence.   It is desirable that the Liberal part
of the community should show their determination to assert
their rights, and should have the opportunity of hearing
such prayers and discourses as may benefit them.   Every
day confirms my conviction of the duty and the necessity
under which Unitarians are placed of defending their claims
to Christian treatment.   If they choose to be trampled to
the dust, they deserve not their privileges.   Oh! it makes
me indignant, alike, when I see Orthodox men, frail and accountable as we are, spurn us from the church of Christ, and
outrage truth and decency in their efforts to crush the energies of a growing community, and when I see Unitarians
succumbing, and trembling before the breath of falsehood.
It is a shame that they who have received God's most glorious gift in a less perverted form than any of their fellow-men
should be afraid to hold it forth to public admiration or
public scorn, — I care not which, since it is in itself invaluable, — or should be indifferent to the means by which others
may be brought to feel its hallowed influences.   Yet there
are such men.   Are they not 'ashamed of Christ and his
name'?"

Fast Day, 1828.   *The Unitarian Controversy.* — "Two
great religious parties exist among us.   Let us disguise or
soften it as we may, this is the fact.   The last year has disclosed this fact more clearly than it was seen before.   Every

week is rendering it more distinct and prominent. . . . The adherents of the old school are unwearied in their efforts to control popular sentiment, to bring the many into a slavish submission to the few, and to direct the energies of public opinion against the new theology. Observe the tone of arrogance, that would not disgrace the papal palace; and of exultation at presumed success, that would not be out of place if a victory had been achieved over the enemies of God and man. See how jealously the received translation of our Bible is guarded from any imputation upon its purity. Observe, too, with what a sanctity the opinions of former times are invested, and what an outcry is raised against innovation. This reverence for the past or for existing abuses has, more than any other circumstance, suggested the appellation of 'old school.' The spirit of the new school is diverse from this. It is a spirit of progress, of improvement. It respects nothing merely for its antiquity, and is not afraid to lay aside whatever is unworthy of preservation. Above all, the cardinal doctrine of the new theology is that every man should read, think, and judge for himself.

The probable result of the contest I scarcely dare to anticipate. I trust in the Protestant spirit which the people drew in with their first breath, in the genius of the American character, which is appreciated by every freeman; and I trust also in the extremities to which the opponents of free inquiry are pressing matters. More caution might have effected plans which an unwise zeal may defeat. In the ultimate success of that which I have denominated the new school of theology, because, though as old as the time of Jesus Christ and his apostles, it is of recent growth in New England, — in the ultimate success of these opinions I have the same confidence that I have in their truth. How speedily and by what instruments they will be spread through the community, it requires a prophet's eye to foresee. If they should for a season be overwhelmed, and not only arrested in their progress, but banished from the land, it would not surprise

me; nor would it furnish any evidence against their divinity.
The signs of the times do not encourage sanguine hopes.
On the one side are seen talent busy in behalf of what it
deems the truth of God, experience employing its treasures
to the same end, zeal that will compass heaven and earth to
make one proselyte, confidence that an immediate revelation
in its favor could not increase, a policy organized by the
most sagacious ingenuity, and an expenditure of money that
promises soon to outstrip the profusion of the Catholic Prop-
agandists. On the other side are found an indisposition to
active labors, an unwillingness to contribute the means of
diffusing light, an insensibility to the evils of comparative
darkness, a dread of fanaticism that is equivalent to indifference about the progress of truth, a distrust of the justice or
worth of those tenets which are the distinctive marks of a
system, and a dislike to concert that almost amounts to a
distaste for religious sympathy. If this be a correct exhibition of the parties which divide the community, we ought to
feel no surprise at the diffusion of those opinions which are
most cordially embraced and most earnestly inculcated. God
will not work a miracle to perpetuate or extend the glory
that beams from the gospel of His Son. His providence
teaches us our duty: if we will not understand its precepts, or
if, understanding, we will not obey them, what are we to
expect but that He will suffer us to reap the fruits of our
folly? We shall go to our graves, or, if conscience do not
speak here, we shall rise to our judgment, with the conviction that we have neglected a most holy office. Others will
do what it is our privilege to undertake and should be our
ambition to perform, the service of enlightening the world
on the most important subjects that can interest human
beings."

1830. *The Unitarian Belief.* — " By Unitarian Christianity I understand, negatively, a faith that rejects every
form of the Trinity, and all the peculiar tenets of Calvinism,
of whatever period, be it that which was taught by the semi-

reformer in Geneva, or that which is taught by those who are willing to bear his name in America; be it the Calvinism of New England or New York, of Massachusetts or Connecticut, of one school or another . . . But now, to present its positive character, it declares that there is one God, supreme and perfect, of spotless holiness, of everlasting justice, of universal benevolence; an Infinite Spirit, who alone is God. It affirms that He exercises a moral government over His creatures; that, while He regards sin with abhorrence, He is rich in mercy ; that, according to His mercy, He hath saved and is saving men by sending His Son, Jesus Christ, to be a teacher of righteousness, and a mediator to reconcile the disobedient to himself through repentance; that, in the execution of this office, Jesus Christ, being filled with the spirit of God, proclaimed certain truths, demanded obedience to his precepts, and enjoined imitation of his own example; that, having discharged this ministry, he closed it by giving his life as a sacrifice, that he might establish the truth and show the value of his words, and make the atonement, or effect the reconciliation of sinners to God ; and that he rose from the dead to triumph over scepticism and wickedness, through this attestation to the divinity of his instructions. It receives as the only record of these instructions the New Testament, written by men who were supernaturally inspired with the truth which they communicated. It avers that, according to the teaching of this volume, men are placed in this world in a state of moral discipline; that, if by patient continuance in well-doing they seek after a glorious immortality, they will inherit eternal happiness, but that they who are disobedient and impenitent must expect tribulation and anguish in a future life; that God sent his Son to save men by turning them from their iniquities to piety and virtue, and that in their endeavors to do his will they will receive the aid of his spiritual influence; that there is one salvation, and but one salvation, for all men, — salvation from sin by the acquisition of a holy character; and that, of this charac-

ter, love to God and love to man are the principles, and
devotion and benevolence, humility and purity, the manifestations. . . .

"The Unitarian Christian beholds in God his Father, the
Author of all his powers, the Source of all his blessings, the
Giver of all his hopes, whose love no words can describe,
and to whom the least return he can make for unceasing
tenderness is the entire devotion of his heart. He believes,
too, that God will accept this devotion, and that he shall find
in it a happiness to which all earthly pleasure is as a drop to
the ocean. It is not fear which drives him to the throne of
the Most High, or keeps him in trembling abasement at His
footstool; for he does not believe that such a prostration of
his nature is desired. He appears before God as His child,
with the confidence of filial sentiment tempering the awe
inspired by divine majesty . . . Unitarians cannot love Jesus
Christ, it is said. God forgive them who utter the falsehood! Cannot love him? What! are not reverence,
gratitude, admiration, and sympathy, occasions of love?
Is it in human hearts to be insensible to his character and
services, as they are described by us? Is it possible that
such virtues and sufferings and benefits, as are connected
with our remembrance of him, should be estimated justly,
and not fill the soul with a love almost passionate in its
ardor? . . .

"This is Unitarian Christianity, as I understand it. A
faith whose topics are the mercy of God, the love of Christ,
the duty and immortality of man; a faith which beholds a
ladder reaching from earth to heaven, as in the patriarch's
dream, along which the influences of the divine compassion and the prayers of human hearts are continually ascending and descending; a faith which links time to eternity
by a chain of moral causes and effects; a faith which utters
its woe against impenitence with a heart-thrilling pity, which
wins souls to Christ with a melting tenderness; a faith which
sanctifies and blesses the relations of daily life, which takes

from death its terror and its power, and supports the soul
on the arms of its hope, till it is borne into the society of the
angels."

1830. *Unitarianism fitted to convert Sinners.* — " It is
said that Unitarian Christianity, if it be suited to encourage progress in excellence, is not adapted to the conversion of sinners; if it make the good better, it does net
make the bad good.   Unfortunately for this theory, it is con-
tradicted by facts.   Examples enough there are to put this
charge for ever to silence, of men in different stations, among
the rich and poor, who have been brought by the power of
this faith to newness of life. . . . But, putting aside facts,
what support has it in the nature of the faith?   Are not the
truths which we have seen to belong to Unitarian Christianity as well adapted to startle a slumbering, as to quicken an
active, conscience?   A God looking from heaven with parental
pity, a Saviour expiring on the cross, a destiny reaching
through the illimitable future, ability, duty, responsibleness,
retribution, such as they have been described, — faintly, indeed, in comparison even with the images which exist in our
minds, yet such as they have been described, — are not these
themes suited to awaken the careless, and to reclaim the
profligate?   What are there of mightier efficacy?   What
that will pierce the soul with deeper anguish, or move it to
a more godly sorrow?   Hell, do you say, with its everlasting
flames?   We have a hell in our picture of woe, — the hell
which an impenitent spirit creates for itself from the elements of its own nature, where the flames of passion and
remorse feed on its immortal substance.   Is there a fire more
torturing, a worm more gnawing, than this?   The evil of
sin, do you say?   Who paints this evil in darker colors than
we?   Do we not declare it to be a rebellion against the
Ruler of the universe, ingratitude to the best of Benefactors,
the destruction of the soul's peace and hope?   Do we not
implore men, by all the love they bear themselves, to shun
the paths of disobedience?   Do we not mourn over a corrupt

mind as over the most sad spectacle on earth? Do we not
tell the sinner that he is in the most abject slavery, that he
is a blot on the fair face of the creation, that he is treading
the path to spiritual death? Have you stronger appeals than
these to make? So have we. We beseech him by the mercies of God, we remind him of the goodness and long-suffer-
ing which are meant to lead him to repentance, we call upon
the unextinguished capacities of virtue of which he is conscious, we entreat him by the compassion of his Heavenly
Father, by the promise of His forgiveness and spirit, by the
blood and intercession of Jesus, by the joy of the angels over
one sinner that repenteth, by the glories of heaven, — we
urge him, we adjure him, to become a new creature; and
when we leave him, we bear his wants on our prayers to the
mercy-seat of the Divine Presence, and make supplication
for him to the God who heareth prayer. This we do, because our faith requires us to do it. Is not this a faith for
the conversion of sinners?" . . .

"This is the faith which its friends are called to vindicate
from the charge of contemplating with an unfriendly eye,
and of helping with a feeble hand, the cause of righteousness.
This is the faith of which it is said that it is a lax, speculative, worldly religion! It is sounded through the land, from
the pulpit and the press, that Unitarianism is an easy religion, that says little about sin and less about holiness, and
lulls its disciple in a dream of carnal security; while from
first to last, in its doctrines and its precepts and its spirit, it
enjoins the acquisition of a holy character as the one thing
needful."

1830. *Unitarianism no "Half-way House" to Infidelity.* —
"Its tendency is said to be towards scepticism. It has been
pronounced, with a pert sarcasm, the half-way house to infidelity. If this be true, I am ready to admit that our
opinions cannot be very fruitful in holiness; for I have little
confidence in a character that is not founded on faith in
divine revelation. But what reason is there for thinking it

true ?   What presumptive evidence is there to sustain the
insinuation ?   Do we find it in the fact that some of the
ablest defences that have been furnished of the divine origin
of Christianity have come from Unitarians, — defences that,
for depth of research and cogency of argument, can hardly
be surpassed in any future age ?   Do we find it in another
fact, that many who have embraced our opinions in the place
of deism have acknowledged that, if they had been sooner
made acquainted with them, they should have escaped the
gloom of unbelief ?   Or in yet another fact, that many intelligent minds reject the Christian revelation, because they
cannot receive the contradictions and absurdities which have
been blended with it, and which they suppose are essential
to it ?   Or in yet another fact, that almost all the sneers and
arguments of infidelity are levelled against what we deem
corruptions of the gospel ?   In which of these *facts* do we
discover the needed proof ?   If in none of them, shall we
look for it in the nature of the system, which, according to
the definition which I gave of its name, presents as its two
cardinal doctrines the being of a God and the divine legation of Jesus Christ ? or in any of those other doctrines
which I have shown to belong to it ?   Look, brethren, at the
doctrines I have laid before you.   I have not learned to
estimate the amount or the value of a man's faith by the
length of his creed ; but, if there is not enough in our belief
to distinguish us from those who deny that God has made a
supernatural revelation of his will, or that Jesus Christ was a
divine messenger, you may construct creeds, or covenants,
or systems of theology, till the words of John should be
literally accomplished, — that 'the world could not contain
the books that should be written,' — without proving that
there is a Christian on earth. . . . Is it not apparent, from
the simple exhibition of our tenets, that we believe in that
Saviour whose love the apostles celebrated, even God our
Father, and in him who, under God, is the Saviour of all who
come to him ?   It is said that Unitarians do not reverence the

Bible; and yet from this book alone, and from no human formularies, they draw their hope of forgiveness and their faith in
immortality. . . . Where shall we meet with the evidence that
Unitarian Christianity promotes scepticism and infidelity?
This is a question which it is beyond my power to answer.
It encourages freedom of inquiry, open discussion, fearless
avowal of opinion, and independence of human authority;
but by this encouragement it takes the surest method of
making men firm believers, by leading them to examine the
impregnable foundations of the Christian faith."

1833. *Unitarianism not a Negative System.* — "A curious and instructive volume might be prepared from the writings of Catholic controversialists against Protestants, and
the replies which they have called forth, having for its object
to collect the evidence that almost every reproach which
Orthodoxy has brought against Unitarianism has been urged
against Protestantism, and been repelled by the same arguments with which Unitarianism is defended. . . . The fact
that we deny some popular doctrines has given plausibility
to the remark that our ' belief consists in unbelief.' So may
the Catholic say to the Protestant of any denomination: You
deny the infallibility of the Church, the authority of tradition,
the doctrines of transubstantiation and purgatory, the validity of some of the sacraments, the value of the religious
service which we pay to the saints, and, above all, the everlasting perdition of them who die out of the pale of the one
Catholic Apostolic Church. You Protestants deny all these
essential articles of a Christian's faith. Yours is nothing but
a system of negations. How does the Protestant reply? By
showing that he believes much that the Catholic takes into
his creed, and rejects nothing which the New Testament
makes essential to a Christian's faith. Look now at this
same Protestant turning round upon another, who, like him,
has renounced the supremacy of the Pope, and upbraiding
him with holding a negative system, because he disbelieves
the doctrines of the Trinity, total depravity, vicarious sacri-

fice, immediate conversion, and the endless torment of them who die not in the true faith, and persisting in the reproach, though his brother show him that he believes much which he takes into his own creed, and rejects nothing which the New Testament makes essential to a Christian's faith! What an example of consistency does this conduct of the Orthodox Protestant present!

"The fact that we consider many of the articles of the popular belief unscriptural and unsound is not, however, the only circumstance that has induced the charge which we are examining. It has so happened, or rather it has been a necessary consequence of our situation, that we have been much occupied in proving the unsound and unscriptural character of these prevalent opinions. The difference between us and the majority of Christians consists indeed in our rejection of dogmas which they esteem sacred; that is, in disbelief on our part. Such dissent we have been compelled to justify. The great truths of the gospel it has not been our immediate object to defend; for these truths other bodies of Christians profess to hold in equal regard with ourselves, although, as we contend, they mingle with them tenets which impair their value and often change their character. The Trinitarian, for example, believes in the infinite perfection of God, and the Calvinist in the immortality and accountableness of man. It is not therefore to establish these points that we have labored; but, taking them for granted, we have endeavored to show that the infinite perfection of the Deity is inconsistent with a tri-personal existence, — and that accountableness cannot be predicated of a being who, by nature wholly corrupt, could be made capable of holiness only by an irresistible action of the Divine Spirit, — and, still farther, that the doctrines of the Trinity and of total depravity and supernatural conversion have no support in Scripture. Now I confess that if one should judge from some writings of Unitarians, regardless of the circumstances under which they have been placed, he might suppose that the overthrow of a

false theology was the object which they had most at heart;
for persons situated as they have been could act on the de-
fensive only by taking the position of assailants.   We have
had enough — too much, perhaps — of this sort of warfare.
I rejoice that a different kind of writing is becoming more
common among us.   I would not have Unitarian Christianity always wear a belligerent aspect.   It is not natural to
it.   Our dissent from Orthodoxy has been fully vindicated.
What has been done will remain.   Let the materials that
have been collected be used.   But let us cease to give our
principal attention to the errors that prevail around us.   Let
our writings show, by the diligence with which they unfold
the great truths of Christianity, and the earnestness with
which they press them on the conscience and the heart, that
we desire yet more to make men feel the power of the truths
which we believe, than to disabuse their minds of the opinions which we condemn."

1857.   *Charges brought against the Early Unitarianism
of New England considered.* — " It is affirmed that these
men were too fond of controversy, and have earned an unen-
viable reputation for theological pugnacity.   In point of fact,
as is well known, the early preachers in this country were
accused of concealing their belief or unbelief beneath a style
of discourse cautiously silent in regard to doctrine.   They
were challenged to break this alleged silence, that their real
opinions might be understood.   Such an accusation is inconsistent with the supposition of an eagerness for controversy
or a prevalence of doctrinal discussion in the pulpit, and suggests the thought that they were forced into a departure
from the method which they had from choice pursued.   As
another historical fact, we know that they were drawn into
the field of theological debate by statements boldly made
and diligently circulated, which they could not let pass
unheeded without a loss of self-respect and disloyalty to the
truth which they cherished.

" Next let us observe that when they took the unpleasant

attitude of combatants, and blows were returned for blows, which had long been borne in silence, they were moved by three considerations of the gravest character.

"First, they found not only their own faith in the Bible denied, but the interpretation of this sacred volume grossly misconducted. The use of reason, not as a superior teacher, but as a divinely appointed guide through the teachings of the Bible, was maintained by those who saw that any other position than their own exposed its pages to the cavil and refutation of infidelity. It should be kept in mind, if we would do simple justice to the champions of a liberal faith in New England, forty years ago, that their vindications of their own belief were eminently Scriptural. The service which they rendered in bringing to light the true character and proper use of the Bible cannot be overrated. By insisting on an accurate text, instead of that of which the errors were undeniable; by showing that the language of Scripture, like all human language, is subject to certain laws of interpretation, a neglect of which can only make Scripture responsible for heresies of the greatest variety and enormity; and by examining difficult or important passages by the test of these laws, — they effected a revolution in the habits of the religious community, as much needed as it was earnestly resisted. A blind reverence was displaced by an intelligent respect, and both the meaning and the value of the Bible were presented in a clear light. What has been the consequence, not only among those who openly adopt the views which were then pronounced false and unsafe? One after another of the old errors has been relinquished, and the principles of Scriptural interpretation, which were pronounced dangerous when broached by Ware and Norton, are now taught in theological seminaries, and defended in periodical publications of the great Protestant sects of the country.

"Another consideration which had weight with the advocates of Unitarian Christianity, in the days when it is thought to have assumed a particularly pugilistic attitude, was the

practical influence of the popular conceptions of religious
truth.   The attacks which Channing, Noah Worcester,
Sparks, and others made on the citadel of self-styled Orthodoxy, were not directed against speculative tenets, — that is,
against theories which one might hold without their affecting his religious life ; on the contrary, the views of the
divine character, of human nature, of the atonement, and of
Christ's dignity, which prevailed, interwove themselves with
the texture of a man's religious character.   They were, of
necessity, either held only as verbal propositions, the force of
which was not felt, — in which case faith became one form, and
a very dangerous form, of hypocrisy ; or they were heartily
believed, — in which case, unless their influence was neutral-
ized by the sounder views with which they might be combined, they produced judgments, feelings, associations, and
conduct very unlike those which the gospel was meant to
encourage.   It was the moral influence of Calvinism which
excited **Dr.** Channing's special abhorrence, — a word which
could not have been used in connection with his name, except in relation to such an exciting cause.   It was the influence of a belief in the doctrine of the Trinity upon the
simplicity and enjoyment of worship, which made its opponents strenuous in their resistance to its propagation.   So
long as theological error remains purely speculative, it does
no harm, and hardly needs exposure.   It is as if a man should
believe that the sun actually moves round the earth, yet
pursues his agricultural labors with a constant recognition of
the effects of the earth's revolution round the sun.   But
when one entertains false ideas of his own ability or responsibleness, of the nature of guilt or the means of moral relief,
of the character of the Supreme Being or of the laws of
divine government, he is placed under such great disadvantage in respect to a good life, that it is no more than kindness, and no less than duty, to convince him, if possible,
of his mistake.   It was a perception and anticipation of the
evils which must flow from accrediting the commonly re-

ceived opinions, that caused the doctrinal preaching among Unitarians at one period to assume so much of a controversial tone.

"A third constraining motive was the denial, on the part of those from whose theological dogmas the Unitarian confessors dissented, of any saving grace in the doctrines which they drew from the study of the Holy Scriptures. It was necessary to defend and justify the position which they took, when it was asserted on every hand that these positions involved a loss to the soul. It was the assumption, and the reiteration of the assumption, and the warning founded on the assumption, that no one could be saved who rejected the common theories of salvation, which dragged those writers into a controversy as for life. It was this exclusiveness, this injustice, this worst of all forms of sectarian arrogance or ecclesiastical persecution, that left the Unitarians of Massachusetts no alternative. They were compelled by every sentiment of propriety or duty, by a desire to retain their good name as Christians instead of being classed with reprobates and scoffers, by an appreciation of the truth which was so recklessly vilified, by a regard for their fellow-men whom such language — not of calm remonstrance, or careful argument, but of the boldest denunciation — was suited to deter from an examination of the new tendencies of thought, and by their gratitude for the light which they had found, disclosing to them an interpretation of the gospel more worthy of Him from whom it came, and more fit to obtain the confidence of those to whom it was sent, — by these and other stringent inducements, they were bound to speak out in behalf of their traduced faith. If sometimes they were betrayed into a severity of recrimination that we may regret, who will not pardon their error, when remembering the magnitude of their provocation? . . .

"A more serious charge even than that which we have already examined is brought against them. Their religion is said to have been cold, intellectual, negative, — or, at best,

moral. If we had time at our command, we might analyze
this accusation, — for such it really is, — and the result might
convince us that its force lies morè in the sound of the words
in which it is conveyed, than in the strength of the facts
which it suggests. Cold if they seem to have been, a comparison with the enthusiasm which has often wrought such
mischief to private character and to social order might incline us to impute to them a less dangerous extreme. Negative they were, only in respect to the errors which they
repudiated. They had a positive faith and a substantial
excellence. Who of us shall call either in question? Intellectual were they, because they brought their minds to
the study of religion, and exemplified the benefit, while they
exercised the privilege, of free inquiry? Then let us all bear
the same opprobrium, for only as men keep earnest and free
minds can the service of God be more than an hereditary
faith or a mechanical obedience. Moral were they? If by
this epithet it be meant that they ignored the offices of spiritual communion, or did not allow the need of the closet or the
worth of the cross, we pronounce the insinuation a slander;
but if it be meant that they insisted on the virtues of social
life, — integrity, kindness, industry, content, — and the graces
which sweeten home and adorn society, then they shall bear
that imputation, for well and nobly did they deserve it.

They were not so spiritual, however, we are told, as are
their children: the discourses of that day dwelt less on
themes of the inner life, the prayers were less fervent, and
the religious sympathies less lively than now. If this commendation of our ways over our fathers' be proper, it is only
saying that under different circumstances, and with the
advantage of their history to guide and to warn us, we have
gone farther in the right direction than they. And, if on
such progress we may congratulate ourselves, we need not
doubt that, if they were here, they would rejoice with us.

"But, in regard to the justice of the allegation, let me
briefly notice three points of defence, which are open to the

use of every one who honors their memory.   There are
three tests by which we may try the characters of men in
our own or in a former generation.   First, by their writings;
secondly, by their behavior; and, thirdly, by their influence.
Now, of the Unitarian ministers and laymen of twenty,
thirty, forty years ago, with whose writings we are familiar,
can it be justly said that they are deficient in a true Christian spirituality; that there is no 'life' in their sermons or
their essays; that the 'light' was clear, but cold?   Who
were the preachers of that time?   Buckminster, Channing,
Parker, or, a little later, Ware, Palfrey, Greenwood, — were
they mere moral preachers?   It is worthy of notice that the
Unitarian literature includes a larger number of printed
volumes of sermons, in proportion to the whole amount of
matter, than probably the religious literature of any other
denomination.   And of those volumes, I venture to say, an
impartial reader will pronounce the greater part to consist
of good, serious, Christian sermons.

" The personal life of the Unitarians of this neighborhood,
at the period of which we are speaking, was not marked by
asceticism or any affectation of piety.   They were cheerful
in their temper and social in their habits.   But were they
not good men?   Has any one ever dared to say they were
not, as a body, virtuous and even exemplary?   Were they
not, too, devout?   Was not Priestley, that much-abused
man since his death as well as before, — was not he devout?
Who can read his biography, and hesitate as to the answer
that should be given?   Were not those whom we have
known, and others whose names only we may have heard as
household words, spiritually minded?   Riper, richer, sweeter
examples of the Christian character the world has never
seen, than were set before the community in the lives of some
of its members, professors of the Christian faith, men and
women, during that season of religious languor and mere
intellectual belief, — as it has sometimes been described, even
by their own children.

"Of the influence which they exerted, the annals of this city and the memories of some whom I address furnish sufficient proof. The healthiest period in the moral life of Boston and its vicinity was during the quarter of a century between the years 1810 and 1835. Witness the benevolent institutions that were then founded, the philanthropic societies that were organized, the places of public worship that were built, the general quiet of the town, the kindly feelings and the friendly intercourse that prevailed, the refinement of manners and the tone of cultivated and pure thought which were cherished. And to whom did our metropolis owe these characteristics, for which it certainly does not deserve a higher reputation now than then? To the Unitarians, in whose hands the chief social influence resided. To them, I say; for I speak only what every one acquainted with our history knows.

"I dismiss, then, the charge of want of life in the Unitarianism of thirty years ago, as not sustained by facts. Different phases of spiritual interest, and different forms of religious activity, arise with the changing circumstances of each generation. I do not mean to claim for our ecclesiastical fathers that they had that fulness of a divine life, after which we all should be aspiring. They had their defects, — who has not? They committed mistakes, — who are exempt from the same liability? But they were not only intelligent and honest believers, they were true-hearted and consistent Christians. They had the 'light of life,' and it was in them both light and life." . . .

When, in 1831, after six years' service, Mr. Gannett resigned the secretaryship of the Unitarian Association, — still to remain on its Board of Directors, — what way of using his new leisure in the cause so natural as the way of print? Two or three tracts appeared " by E. S. Gannett," several sermons were given to the " Liberal Preacher" and the " Unitarian Advocate," one or two little volumes by Harriet Martineau were reprinted, and he began to publish a small bi-monthly magazine called the " Scriptural Interpreter." Unitarianism was a Bible-faith, and his taste for exegesis has been already spoken of. " It has long seemed to me," he says, " that such a work as I hope this will be is needed. The Bible is imperfectly understood ; and its meaning must often be misconstrued or remain obscure, unless *popular* instruction is furnished and is brought within the reach of common readers." From the best expository books, and with the help of his friends, Furness, Young, Hall, Dewey, Dabney, and others, it was not hard to fill the forty-eight pages. A large part, however, was his own. For four or five years (1831–1835) the mag-- azine was in his hands, — and now and then was tardy in leaving them on the due first-days of the month. By and by, as his work deepened into lectures, and at the same time strength began to fail, three young men in the Divinity School, Theodore Parker, George E. Ellis, and William Silsbee, for a while took charge of it, and gave it honorable ending. It is chiefly notice-able for the unconscious prophecies it contained : each number contained a section that was an early type of the Sunday-school manuals on the one-lesson system that has lately come in vogue ; and if we would trace the first " evidential " discoveries, among the old fa-miliar texts, that have given Dr. Furness fame as a photographer of the Gospel incidents, or would watch the first faint germs of Parker's pushing thought, we must turn to the pages of the little " Interpreter."

When the " Association " had been some ten years in existence, the Unitarians of Boston, more ready always for benevolent than intellectual alliances, clasped hands to form another society. The stir of the mid-century

was beginning. The town was fast swelling to the
large city, and with the change new social problems
rose to face its people. Better provision must be made
for the poorer classes. The various town-societies for
"Indigent Boys," "for Widows," &c., no longer held
the want and evil in control; and heads and hearts
were already at work devising new methods of relief.
Henry Ware and a few kindred spirits had long before
carried their gospel on Sunday evenings to room-meet-
ings in the neglected districts; and since 1826 Dr.
Tuckerman with his heart of Christ had "been about
the Father's business," as he always called it, among
the city's poor. Two young men, Charles Barnard and
Frederic Gray, caught his fire, and joined themselves
with him. The three "ministers-at-large" did so much
good, and yet so little of the good that needed to be
done, that the Unitarian Association, being indirectly
charged with their support, had discussed from time to
time plans for extending their work and putting it on
an independent and permanent basis. In 1832 Mr.
Gannett laid before the Association "a sketch of his
plan in relation to the Mission to the Poor in Boston;"
and Henry Ware, Jr., and he were appointed to prepare
a circular, with a list of persons to whom it should be
sent. Their report was received, but action lingered.
At last, in the spring of 1834, he addressed this letter
to the Executive Committee: —

BRETHREN,— . . . We have had before us for months
a plan of organization of our city ministry, but have done
nothing about it. We received last summer a communication from a respected friend on the propriety of entering
with more spirit upon philanthropic exertions, which we received with the regard to which it was entitled. Still the

suggestions which it offered have not been adopted, nor much considered by us. Meanwhile infidelity has been counting its proselytes and securing its victims among the lower classes in our city. Licentiousness is corrupting and ruining many. And we scarce give a thought to their condition. Our Christian brethren of other denominations have anticipated us in the very movement which we were last summer meditating, and have just formed an association which may be exceedingly useful. We cannot expect that our friends generally will act together with that association, on account of the peculiar religious tenets to the spread of which it will be made subservient. Yet what an amount of talent, industry, benevolent feeling, and wealth, is there among our friends, which might be, and ought to be, brought into exercise for the improvement of the ignorant, the degraded, and sinful! It seems to me that we ought no longer to defer at least incipient measures towards the accomplishment of some permanent result, — the establishment of some instrumentality which shall have within itself resources for its own activity and continuance. It is a bad time to ask for money. But we do not want money till we have matured plans. . . . I would propose that the subject of moral reform among the poor and vicious in the city of Boston receive our immediate attention, . . . and that a committee be appointed, to whom the following questions shall be submitted : —

1. Is it important that the Ministry-at-large, which has been under the patronage of the American Unitarian Association, should be placed on a permanent foundation ?

2. If yes, how can this object be effected ?

3. Is it important that the ministers should be able to give their principal attention to the moral state — the reformation and improvement — of those whom they visit ?

4. Is it expedient that a more active sympathy and a more effective co-operation be secured towards the rescue of the lower classes of our population from irreligion and guilt ?

5. Is it best that a society should be formed for securing the ends intimated in the preceding questions ?

Let me hope that you will neither blame me for pressing this subject on your notice, nor suffer these hints to lie on the table, to be called up any time or never.

Yours respectfully and affectionately,

E. S. GANNETT.

MARCH 27, 1834.

Now the matter was vigorously pressed. Friends met at once: a committee was appointed, with the letter-writer for its chairman, " to digest a plan for a systematic organization for the moral and religious improvement of the poor in this city ; " and nine parishes decided to form themselves into a " Benevolent Fraternity of Churches for the Support of the Ministry-at-large," according to the plan sketched in the committee's report. " The sole object was to provide instruction and solace for souls, not to add another to the eleemosynary institutions of the city." As before, in the American Unitarian Association, Mr. Gannett accepted the workman's office of Secretary of the Central Board.

It was quite in character both that the philanthropic work should be thus practical and constructive, and that it should thus connect itself with his profession and his Unitarianism. This, of course, was not the first work of the kind in which the minister had taken part. But that kind left little separate record. By signs here and there among his papers, we find him in Deacon Grant's parlor, discussing prison-reform ; on his way to Worcester to attend the General Temperance Convention ; serving on the School Committee ; writing arguments against imprisonment for debt. The two causes nearest his heart were those of Temperance and Peace. He

thought that reason, religion, the whole spirit as well as
the letter of the gospel, united in forbidding war. Probably he was " non-resistant " up *to*, rather than *in*, the
absolutely last extremity; although he writes that an
English book, which Dr. Channing lent him as the best
he knew upon the subject, "has made me a *thorough
peace man*." Often, in the sermons, he urged the practicability of universal peace; and his strong conviction
on this point had much to do with his reluctance in Anti-
Slavery procedure. On Thanksgiving and Fast Day,
when the men in pulpits had an undisputed right to look
broadly off in the direction of politics, Mr. Gannett used
his chance from time to time in a way that showed the
interest with which he watched public measures. The
printed Thanksgiving sermon for 1830 was on the importance of diffusing a just moral sentiment, in view of
the vital dangers then rising before the country in the
midst of its prosperity. The warnings about the office-
seeker, and "the popularity of unprincipled talent,"
sound strangely familiar to-day. For certain other
words the time is overpast, but by the fulfilment of
their prophecy, not by the granting of their prayer: —

" The greatest evil under which our nation labors is the
existence of slavery. It is the only vicious part in the body-
politic; but this is a deep and disgusting sore, weakening the
parts which it immediately affects, and sending inflammation
through the whole system. It must be treated with the
utmost judgment and skill. A rash hand is on no account to
be preferred to an eye blind to its character. But that it
must be at no very distant time a subject of thorough examination, and, if possible, of cure, no man of calm mind, it
seems to me, can doubt. We have unequivocal indications
to warn us how any attempt to examine it will be received.
When the hour comes, the influence of all good citizens will

be needed to prevent scenes that would disgrace our annals,
if they should not end our national existence.   In that crisis
may Heaven save us from civil discord!   A most rare union
of firmness and moderation alone can avert bloodshed.   We
are approaching that crisis.   The foul plague permitted by
our fathers to enter among our institutions will not be suffered to remain without an effort for its removal.   I tremble
when I think on what a precipice we may be standing!   May
integrity and wisdom guide us along its brink!   Is it not
clear that our only safety lies in a moral sentiment which
shall restrain the passions and teach men to judge impartially
and act uprightly?   Without this protector, what is to prevent bitterness, strife, and hostility?"

The Anti-Slavery movement was just beginning then,
beginning with a very few men, — "fanatics."   So Mr.
Gannett also judged them.   He was alive to the outrage
at the South.   With the Colonization Society he had
been connected from its formation; not believing that
its influence in diminishing slavery here would be great,
but that it might be made the instrument of destroying
the slave-trade in Africa, and possibly of beginning the
regeneration of that continent.   But, with his views and
temperament, he could never join the Anti-Slavery Society.   The violence of the Abolitionists offended both
his sense of justice and his sense of practicality.   To
press first principles by open attack, he said "would
snap the bonds of union, and then what could we do?
Nothing next year, and perhaps nothing for a century."
Proceed, but proceed slowly by moderate and gradual
measures, with forbearance towards the master as well
as sympathy for the slave, — and he "doubted not
that every year would see a decrease of the evil and
a multiplication of the facilities for the deliverance of
the South from this burthen and the country from its

disgrace." But to this subject we are to return in a later chapter.

We have been watching one who was by nature an organizer, not a seeker, of material; and the labors for parish and denomination, so abundantly performed, strengthened each year the disposition. Not much time had he for study or the quiet meditation which keeps the roots of great ideas in growth. One who lived in the home with him recalls the whirl and hurry of the week; the people coming and going; the many meetings; the tea-pot and the long-lit lamp at night. The sermons used to gather and shape themselves in the streets, as the then quick feet pressed on from house to house. In between the calls there would be an appointment with some committee, and in the late evening a Bible lesson to prepare for the next day's class, and in the morning proofs to read while the boy waited in the entry. So Friday, even Saturday, passed. Saturday night arrived, when at last the sermon came forth, beginning with a struggle probably, — by and by, in the small hours, flashing over the pages. Then the Sunday's strain, with its two services, brought him again in face of another similar week.

From the outside all seemed bright enough in the busy life. Parish success as pastor and as preacher, pleasant relations with Dr. Channing, unusual repute in the denomination as a stirring young champion of the faith, — this was his. His homes, too, were real homes: much of the time he lived in the " parsonage " with one of his most motherly parishioners. Choice intimacies were growing up among his welcomers and listeners; and the ministers, as we have seen, were real " brethren " in

those days. The old college friendships with the four
or five were, meanwhile, kept very warm. " Who was
ever richer in friends than I ? " he says to Kent. " I
have seen three classmates marry, and, instead of losing
their affection, have obtained three sisters. If I were
one hundredth part as good as I ought to be, when our
Father in heaven has bestowed so many blessings on me,
how good and happy I should be ! " The salary was
ample. Before many years the fifteen hundred dollars
were increased, after one or two refusals on his part,
to two thousand. Ample, at least, such allowance
would have been, had there been none but himself to
care for ; but, as affairs were, the money fled too rapidly. He had to borrow more, and even sell some
books.

But " Morning Work, Without *and Within,*" the
chapter is called. In spite of all this outside brightness, when we look in, behind the works, upon the workman's inward life, the contrast startles. Of course, as in
college, happy hours were many, and happy days lasted
on into happy weeks, when the letters show him laughing over his business. " Sometimes," says a friend, " he
would come in gleeful like a child, with merry eyes ; but
often he was overshadowed, and he seemed like a man
overworking all the time." Overworking and wrongly
working he was. Few men live out a more minute
conscientiousness in duty due to others : few good men
have had less conscientiousness in duty due themselves.
There was much of the old ascetic in him, — the ascetic's
self-devotion as well as his thriftless ignorance and disregard of Nature's laws of flesh. In a word, the old depression, his by birth, preyed on him more deeply year
by year, as the incessant, reckless strain went on. There
were certain secret struggles also, of which no story can

be told, besides the ever-wearing comparison of himself
with the man at whose side he stood before the public,
— all this to increase the gloom.   Self-distrust darkened
every prospect.   Not distrust of God's goodness, nor of
friends' sincerity, but of his own use and goodness.   He
longed for others' good opinion, and constantly fell short
of his own.   He had no ability, no fitness for the ministry ; was both fool and hypocrite ; people saw it, and
were treating him accordingly, — such was too often the
vision of himself!   Little slights among his families
were thus justified to them, while their kindness was
" pity," and Dr. Channing's was " forbearance."   The
mood made him very sensitive and exacting with those
few friends who knew his feelings best ; and their words
rebuking, cheering, jesting, reasoning with him, are sad
to read.   Underneath the weakness lay all that deep unselfishness, that active loyalty to justice and to duty, for
which friends clung to him, and from which he habitually worked.   Out from the depths he would go forth,
meet men, and labor in his calling, and labored best
under pressures of emergency by those late night-efforts
and sharp concentrations of the mind ; then, as the spent
nerves rested, the sense of failure came again.

So the young minister's life was really a kind of
tragedy, — in part, but only in part, his fault.   This
book, we say again, would be no true " life," if it lacked
full reference to the contrast between the " without "
and this " within."   It makes the life a warning.   It
makes it also an encouragement.   The best and strongest things in him are appreciated only when these are
known.   That busy, self-forgetting energy shows out
the more strikingly against the dark background of
self-remembering despondency.

The final break-down was sure to come.   His very

first year in Federal Street prophesied it. A few sentences of his own, and some friendly answers from wise helpers, shall hint the story. He had just been telling Mr. Kent that he wrote " six things — for the honor of the ministry don't call them sermons — in three weeks," and continues: —

Nov. 9, 1824. "You are right in speaking of my situation as very difficult to me, but it would not be to a man of decent ability and industry a more laborious place than many others, because the feeling of responsibleness for the improvement of the society is thrown in good measure upon another; for it seems to me I can do little good or hurt. But I know so little of books, of men, or of religion, and am so abominably and almost insuperably lazy, that I encounter mortification and toil every step of my way. It's hard work to be good, and it's monstrously hard to be a good minister."

One Saturday in the next spring he writes again to him: —

"I am very well in body, but am ready to scream, Who is sufficient for these things? I am sufficient in no way. What shall I do? When I have neither talents nor virtues proper for such a place, ought I not to quit it directly? I would be a day-laborer, (that I am now,) I would be a brick-maker, to secure peace of mind and consciousness of virtue. I would give or do any thing, if I could only cherish that spirit of devotion without which a minister sins every time he is forced to pray; and this I do day after day, and it is registered against me. Ought I not to be miserable? Can I help inquiring what shall I do?"

A true Saturday afternoon letter, when " the sermon is not half done." Kent makes answer: —

"Are you a settled, incorrigible, thorough Hopkinsian, — totally depraved? Do you mean to tell me that you have no reverence for God and religion, and are making only a show of worship in the church? Is it true, Gannett, that you have no talents? How, then, — I am going to be plain, for you are uselessly tormenting yourself, — how, then, were the Government of College such fools as to rank you first of fifty-four, whom I know to have studied not more than four hours in a day while there? You received an almost, if not quite, unanimous call from Dr. Channing's society, although you differed from them on a question which they considered of great importance. You were invited by Professor Norton to unite with him and others in what he intended should be an important work. You preached at Philadelphia, Baltimore, and Washington: at the first place I was told by Mr. Ware that you chained the attention of the whole audience, and in the second by Mr. Appleton, 'How happy should we be, could we always hear such preaching!' *It is not true* that you have no qualifications for the ministry, or I have lived months and years with a person more artful than any other human being. You ingeniously magnify every little defect of your own character, and are merciless in self-condemnation. You are unhappy because you have imagined a perfection to which few, if any, can attain. . . .

" 'A bricklayer'? Do you imagine that this would make you *virtuous?* Suppose we should set up a pair of trucks, and with our whips and frocks drive through the streets of Boston, or Alexandria in Egypt if you please, what do you suppose our conversation would relate to at the close of the day? . . . O Gannett, what a pang of misery would every stroke of a bell carry to our souls, if we relinquished the most holy cause and the service of a most benevolent Master, for no other reason than because we were wicked! Be satisfied with doing as much good as the most active who are toiling with you. You may still plead your sinfulness, I will no more believe you than I did my good deacon, who said he was more wicked and abominable in the sight of God than the greatest sinner living, than the liar, thief, or murderer!

I know you will not be angry with me for plainness. You will not accuse me of abusing that confidence, by impertinence, for which I feel very grateful.

                    "Your sincere friend,
                              "B. KENT."

That was before one year of work was over. Four months later, only fourteen from ordination, he wrote his first letter of resignation. It was not sent to the parish, but something like it was sent, and more than once sent, to Dr. Channing; and other letters still linger in the files whence, perhaps, some brighter mood, some parishioner's kind greeting, or some clench of resolve, kept them from ever escaping. Amid all his success and the people's increasing love, he must have known days of almost despair. Twice, at least, Dr. Channing sent words of help, that may help others besides him: —

                                   "MAY 20, 1825.

"MY DEAR SIR, — I was truly grieved to receive your letter from Portland, and yet I am glad you wrote it. Not a suspicion of the feelings you express had ever crossed my mind; and, believing that you had grounds for encouragement, I took it for granted that you were encouraged. But it seems I erred; and it is well that I am undeceived, for I hope to be useful to you. I know by experience more of your state of mind than you imagine. In truth, many, if not most, ministers pass through the trial of misgivings and fear; and, were these yielded to, our profession would lose its most conscientious and useful members. In the present case, these fears have no foundation; and I entreat you to cast them out, or at least to resist them. Depression is the palsy of the mind, of the moral as well as intellectual nature; and, in a world overrun with obstacles and difficulties, we must gird ourselves with courage, if we hope to make progress or do much good. . . . Brace your spirit by all the means of reason and religion. Take care of your health, for despondence is half the time a bodily disease. I know not where you can look for a more promising field of labor than where you are. You would injure yourself and the church by any step which would weaken your connection with it. I beg you not to express your feelings except to me; for they are exaggerated and misrepresented, when communicated freely or even to a *few* friends. For myself, I should be exceedingly grieved by your persevering in your present views. I have felt entire satisfaction in our connection, and should esteem a dissolution of it a personal calamity. As to the future, I can give you no promise. I promise myself nothing. Such are the fluctuations of opinion, that a minister should prepare himself for the worst. He must do his best, and leave the future, which he may not live to see, to the All-wise Disposer. True submission has as much of resolution as of patience, and armed with this spirit you have nothing to fear. . . .

"Very affectionately your friend,

"W. E. C."

"RHODE ISLAND, August 12, 1829.

"MY DEAR SIR, — You were right in thinking that you should grieve me, and yet I am truly grateful to you for writing. I shall rejoice if I can aid you in your struggle, — a struggle to which no minister, I suppose, is wholly a stranger, though some suffer under it peculiarly. It is difficult for one to understand fully another's mind; and I well know that we may do injury by striving to allay in a friend apprehensions which we ought rather to strengthen, by ascribing to innocent infirmity what ought to be reproved as crime. I have, however, a very strong conviction — and I am bound to express it — that you suffer now from a morbid state of mind. That you have cause for humiliation, I doubt not; but I have nearly as undoubting a belief that, could you shake off most of your apprehensions and anxieties, you would be a better Christian; that they are trials to be overcome, not intima-

tions to be obeyed. I found my belief at once on what I
know of you and what I know of human nature. Human
nature is ever more prone to groundless solicitude than to
groundless hope. This is a general principle, which we are
to apply in the treatment of others, and, what is much more
difficult, in managing our own minds. The fact that others
abandon themselves without cause to desponding views of
themselves, that spiritual gloom enters largely into the experience of excellent individuals, is so often witnessed, that
we may properly suspect the influence of the same principle
in ourselves. The cause we may not be able to explain. It
seems to reside in our physical system; for every man ob-
servant of himself — especially a dyspeptic — is conscious,
under certain states of the body, of a tendency to utter
despair, and of entire distrust of his own powers. May I say
to you that a person, accustomed to read the signs of the
physical and mental temperament, could hardly see you,
without suspecting some tendency to excessive sensitiveness? In one particular I have seen this infirmity. You have
imagined yourself undervalued by those who have high impressions of your powers. Your letter shows what, I confess,
I thought to be subdued, — a distrust of my sentiments
towards you. Ever since your settlement, I have had a
growing conviction of your fitness for your work, I have
been struck with the activity and resources of your mind, I
have felt more and more as if you were becoming more than
I have been to my people, and as if my removal from them
would hardly be a calamity; yet, in the midst of these cheering anticipations, I learn that you consider me as needing
much patience to endure my relation to you. My respect
for your character, my belief that you were working out for
yourself a better course than I could prescribe, my unwillingness to interfere with or shackle an independent mind, and,
let me add, much self-distrust, have led me to be sparing of
counsel; and now I apprehend that the conduct which has
been prompted by sentiments of peculiar regard has been

wholly misinterpreted. But I will write no more. . . . Why
will you not get a supply, and come here next Sunday and
preach to my flock in Portsmouth? I should be glad of rest.
"Believe me, most truly,
"Your sincere and affectionate friend,
"W. E. CHANNING."

If this young minister had an ideal before him as
a working-model, it was that same consecrated Henry
Ware who had called him "my strong-hearted coadjutor." He was older than himself by only seven years;
and in spirit and purpose and ways of work the two
were so much alike, that the thought of one called up
the thought of the other to their friends. The sickness
long due had at last fallen on Henry Ware; and he sent
testimony, in hopes of saving his younger brother: —

1828. "The long letter which I proposed writing was
chiefly to be a lecture on health, with personal application to
the younger bishop of Federal Street. But I will give you
two sentences, instead of an epistle. I have long been concerned at your mode of life, which appears to be a careless,
reckless throwing away of a chance for longevity. And, since
I have been suddenly cut off in the midst of a similar career,
I have thought of you much, and been anxious, like Dives,
to send you a message, lest you also come into this place of
torment. I refer not to work, but to imprudence; for it is
nonsense to suppose that either of us work too much, whatever friends may say. Other men there have been who do
more. But we work imprudently, and, I think, very much
alike. Want of method, late and irregular hours, neglect of
regular exercise of body to balance every day the fatigue of
the mind, and sometimes violent exercise, as if to do up the
thing by the job, — no constitutions can stand such a life. . . .
For me, it is too late: for you, it is not. And I am deeply
anxious that you should do prudently from my experience, and

not wait for your own. It is not health only, it is the power of usefulness, and the sin which weighs upon the mind and depresses it, and takes away the consolations of a sick-bed; embittering the heart with the thought that we are suffering the just punishment of our folly and neglect of duty. And there is no little sting added to the mortification, if, meantime, friends are attributing the evil to undue earnestness in duty. . . . I beg you to think on this subject, and *act.* You are endowed with powers of doing good which not many possess, and which you ought not to trifle with. In these days they are needed."

Six years later, Mr. Gannett, who had actually ventured to remonstrate with his friend against what seemed like new imprudence, got this word back : —

". . . Let me ask you to reflect whether the *beam*, as big and as violently worked as a battering-ram, ought not to be plucked out of your eye, now that you have got the mote out of mine. There is no doubt that you are fast overthrowing yourself, and are soon to be numbered among the crippled. It ought not to be so. The company of invalid pensioners is large enough; and the Church cannot afford to have you taken from its active service and thrown into its hospital. I know that you will think and act for yourself; but if the four last years of my *bitter, bitter* experience could but warn and move you, and save you from premature decrepitude, I should have one more reason to bless God for having allowed me to do some good.

"Yours in all truth and love,

"H. WARE, Jr."

The warnings were little heeded : only his own experience, if any, was to serve him. Deeper and deeper in work each year, how could he change, amid the pressures, habits that were even older than himself ?

But there came a season's beautiful uplifting. In the

spring of 1835 friends noticed that his face was brighter. There fell "a day that to me was the beginning of a new life." He now was nearly thirty-five years old. Anna Tilden was twenty-five, — a shy, gentle woman, having hidden strengths of thought and character, a conscientiousness as certain as his own, and deep religious feeling. She was one of the family with whom he had long found a home ; and a struggle with religious doubts, in which he had been her only confidant, had brought their two minds close together. During a journey to Niagara and Lake George, the summer previous, her secret dawned on her. His secret broke on him, like a revelation, amid the winter-work. On the last day of the winter they owned it to each other. The next October saw Dr. Channing coming up from Newport on purpose for the wedding, and the parish furnishing a home with comforts for them. Now all outward things seemed bright indeed ; and how bright the world could look to him in happy moments, a letter written to a dear friend on the Niagara journey shall show : —

> "Sunrise, on Lake George, opposite Diamond Island, half-past five o'clock, Friday, Aug. 22, 1834.

"My dear Mrs. Torrey, — It is one of the most splendid mornings that ever shone on the eyes of mortals. We are seated on deck, enjoying the glorious light, the cool breeze, and the beautiful scenery. The sun has just gained the ascent of the hills. The vapor which clung to their feet has received the radiance that is poured over their summits, and, after reflecting it in various hues, has slowly melted away, as if, when its adoration of the glorious orb was paid by silent sympathy, its work was done, and its existence might be closed. How natural was the idolatry of the sun! I wonder not that men, in their blindness, — nay, was it not rather the unconscious spirituality of their souls? — worshipped that object which rises in splendor to enlighten and bless the earth. And yet the sunset is to me, and always has been, far more beautiful. It speaks to my heart: sunrise only demands my admiration. Anna, to whom I was just making this remark, gave a most poetical as well as kind solution. The sunrise, said she, has too much of promise to be touching to you. There was more of rebuke than of compliment, I fear, in her words, despite her love.

" . . . By our long visit at Niagara Falls I was enabled to bring away a distinct impression of their *meaning*, and a clear picture of their appearance. To me they spoke of beauty, and of beauty only. I could not obtain the feeling of sublimity, and to connect ideas of terror and passion with the scene appears to me almost like sacrilege. There is beauty in the rapids as they hasten along as if rejoicing to plunge into the abyss, in the deep white of the foam, in the innumerable crystals, sparkling and joyous, which crown the fall and cover the upper half of its descent; and beauty, surpassing beauty, in the light vapor that plàys over the bed of the chasm, and seems like ethereal loveliness softening the majesty of the spot. And there is beauty in the slow and tranquil passage of the waters over the centre of the Horseshoe Fall, where the observer beholds that almost solid, yet living and, as it were, conscious green, to which as there is no resemblance in nature, so are there no terms in language to represent. Strange as it may seem to you, strange as it certainly was to me, *slow* and *tranquil* describe the passage of the water over the bosom of the great Fall, where the river has its greatest depth and wears its deepest color. The water never has the amber hue except after a storm, when, as Mr. Ingraham tells us, the stream is rendered turbid above the rapids, and rushes towards the Falls, bearing its muddy current, which, under the glancing sunbeams, assumes a rich amber color, — and the very impurities of the river are converted into beauty. . . .

" We have seen and enjoyed much at Niagara and Trenton. Of course we have thought and felt as well as seen. One impression has prevailed over every other in my mind, — this is a *beautiful* world in which we live. There is beauty everywhere, — above us, around us, in the perishable forms and the more durable aspects of nature. The creation is a vast storehouse of beauty, or rather a mirror reflecting continually the Infinite Beauty in which it had its source. For all this variety of the beautiful reveals an Author, intelligent and loving, of His creatures. There is a spirituality in this beauty of the material world that I cannot resist. It addresses the spiritual in man. It awakens in him the consciousness of a nature born to enjoy the lovely. This nature cannot be doomed to decay. My faith in immortality has gained strength amidst God's glorious works. I have learned, too, — I need not, indeed, have left home to learn it, — that our sense of the beautiful depends upon ourselves. If we are in a state to enjoy, we find enjoyment everywhere: the clouds feed the sentiment of delight within us. If we are not in harmony with the beautiful, which the Creator has diffused over all things, even Niagara loses its charm. . . .

" The intelligence which your letter and the newspapers have given us of the burning of the Catholic nunnery at Charlestown by the mob makes me, for the first time in my life, ashamed of my home. I know of nothing so atrocious within my recollection, and scarcely within the history of our land. I do not wonder that you have been kept in great excitement at Boston. Nothing can be done to erase the reproach. It must remain upon us so long as there shall be tongues to tell of the deed.

" Your account of the preaching gratified me much. I knew our people could not but be delighted with Mr. Furness. . . .

" Yours gratefully and affectionately,

" Ezra S. Gannett."

But all through the glad six months of the betrothal.
the tired brain gave omens ; and the letters that go to
and fro are sad as well as tender.   Only a few weeks
before the wedding-day he wrote to Mrs. Tilden, "It
seems to me that I am worn out;" and doubts whether
he ought not to delay the marriage a few months, and seek
some other employment.   Yet, "if I could only believe
I were a good minister, I should be as happy as mortal
man ought to be in this world."

The new home began.   Barely a half-year had they
been in it, darkened not seldom by his sad mood, when
the hour so long delayed arrived.   All the regular work
was driving on; a volume of selections, called "Religious Consolation," had just been compiled and edited ;
and a course of lectures on grander themes than ever —
that already mentioned on the "History of Revealed
Religions" — was half-way through, when, by the wife's
urgency, a doctor was at last consulted.   And suddenly
words appeared in the "preaching-book" that had
never appeared there before since he had been in Boston : Sunday, March 27, 1836. "Stayed at home all
day."   Then : "March 31. I went to Roxbury, and
did not return to Boston to remain till — ".

The doctor's sentence of banishment was instant.
"Mr. Gannett, from excessive and long-continued exertion of mind, has fallen into a state of great nervous
weakness : " work of every kind must be stopped, and
a month or two would decide what next.   Mr. and Mrs.
Clapp, two friends very dear to him, received the sick
man into their country home at Leicester.   There he
waited, overcome with sorrow at having forfeited his
opportunity of work, and longing for just one trial
more, when he would be so very wise and careful.
They wanted preaching at Peoria in Illinois, the paper

said : could he not commute his sentence to a few weeks of missionary-service in prairie-land ? Every thing seemed to him to point fingers at his idleness. Did he read a good article in the " Examiner," it only made him heart-sick, recalling his inability to do what his brethren were doing. One month, at most two months, of rest, — then, surely, he would be well enough to be again among them ! But the friends knew better. The young wife took down the curtains, laid the manuscripts reverently in the study-table drawers, packed the furniture, and gave up the six-months' home to strangers ; he, the while, appealing to her to be slow, and to forgive him for " the fraud he had committed on her happiness ; " she in all tenderness consulting him in nightly letters, but firmly, sadly doing the thing that must be done. Then, when that broken hope was all sealed into the past, she joined her husband, to comfort and strengthen him.

No comfort and no strength could reach him. The doctor soon decreed new grief, — a voyage to Europe ; and, to make the change from home-associations as complete as possible, it was thought best that he should go alone. The parish had promptly voted to relieve him of all care for a year, supply the pulpit, and continue his full salary. That again was bitter, bitter trial, — to be their object of expense at the very moment he was failing them. Their kindness seemed to him unparalleled. But all was gradually yielded to the inevitable. The lonely man went on board the vessel in New York, and still another sum of money was put into his hands. " When I think how small, how less than nothing, — for such they seem to me, — are my claims to the love of these friends, when I consider how much more I might have done, I wonder at them and I wonder at myself." He left for them a letter of the most grateful, tenderest good-by. The benediction of Dr. Channing followed him : —

" I can only express my gratitude to God for your faithfulness to the people and your kindness to me. You carry with you my sympathy, esteem, affection. May God restore you to be a blessing to us ! "

VI.

REST IN EUROPE.

1836–1838.

As the husband and wife parted, their promise to each other was " to be cheerful for one another's sake." No task so impossible as that to the half-despairing exile, lonely with a loneliness that defied all the kind attentions of the friend who shared the state-room. He felt able to converse with no one. " Oh that I had more accomplishment or more impudence!" The ocean smote him with a sense of limitation, not of vastness. No day so solemn as the Sabbath day at sea, in his ideal, — how sadly disappointing the reality! All around him the conversation trifled, with no word, no look, of awe: " And yet I ought to acknowledge the greater quiet that prevailed. We were in a Christian vessel, every one must have felt, — so powerful an influence does Christianity exert indirectly upon the habits of men. It

controls where it does not sanctify." Of course, he
held a service, reading one of Dewey's sermons.

Now and then the dreaded feelings returned : —

"What a strange experience mine is! It must be in a
measure, at least, disease; for when I am overcome by these
sensations or emotions, whichever they be, I am equally distressed and helpless. I am but experiencing the just punishment of years of negligence and folly, of indolence and
self-indulgence. It is right. I do not complain. I am only
ashamed and discouraged. Still I have promised to try, and
I will."

The sight of land brought back strong longings for
his work, and the rhythm of the sermons still flows in
the Journal, as he words it : —

"If I return to my ministry, I must be more diligent in
my study, and more active out of it, than I have ever been.
Regular and ceaseless labor should be the Christian minister's rule.   Labor, — for he has an immense work to perform.
Ceaseless, — for his responsibilities are various and useful.
Regular, — because it is the want of method, not the excess
of toil, that breaks down a clergyman."

This visit to Europe fell in the days when old styles
of locomotion were giving way to new. A sailing-
vessel bore him out : the "Great Western," pioneer
of ocean steamships, brought him back. It was the
birthday of the telegraph : "They can communicate
by telegraph from Portsmouth to London in eight and
a half minutes ! " The railways, also, had begun to be ;
but none yet stretched over the southern downs. So the
"Regulator" stage-coach carried the sea-travellers, in a
long day, up to the great city ; and their earliest London "sight" was a glimpse of the mail-coaches starting
forth from the Post-Office, each with a guard, and each
guard with his trumpet.

Mr. Gannett's tour differed little from that of the thousand travellers of every day. Its sole peculiarity was that he looked on all things with ministerial eyes. Everywhere he goes, he records the Sunday ways, the churchly practices. A somewhat detailed picture of English Unitarianism and its clergy of forty years could be drawn from the sketches in his diary. We shall cite little but a passage here and there which thus reflects himself rather than his sight-seeing.

On the first Sunday the New England minister found his way into five services ! He notes " the persons who read, or rather chanted, (*nefandum !*) the prayers." Among the others, William J. Fox and Sydney Smith had that day's preaching reported; and one of the latter's sentences struck home to a sensitive heart, — " she who has agreed to share half her husband's joys, and, God knows, has agreed to share more than half his sorrows."

Wretched days these first ones must have been. " The vastness and loneliness of the great metropolis have overwhelmed me. . . . I stayed at the London Coffee-House till I was almost heart-broken." Then kind friends took him home ; but still no peace. One new friend, however, had power to soothe ; and the charm of his goodness is attested in many grateful praises : —

"Dr. Boott is one of the most delightful men on earth. Such true friendship I have scarce ever seen, and such a fine religious spirit. He is a Christian in the highest sense of the word, one who has known trial of the sharper sort, and learned the lessons of firmness, submission, and hope. Such a man is a rare gift of God to the world. ' I give only one invitation,' said Dr. B. at dinner. ' Come at all times, — morning, noon, or night, — and use us as your friends.' One could not distrust the sincerity of the invitation. I felt at home at once; and it was a relief to feel myself among friends in this new world. Dr. B. had much to say about Mr. Phillips, Tuckerman, Dewey, and Rammohun Roy. Of the last he could not speak without emotion, so great is his reverence for him. He says Boston has sent an influence across the ocean, which is felt in England, in the Establishment even. While English society indicates a higher refinement, there is an order of mind, of which Mr. Phillips is a representative, existing in America, that cannot be found in England. His views of the religious state of England are sad. Religion he believes to be a form, not understood or valued in its true character. . . . Dr. B. seemed to understand my case perfectly, and said I must be willing to have entire repose of mind. With patience and hope, he has no doubt I shall be as strong as ever."

But the wise doctor had seen more than he told ; and straightway a wondering letter sped across the Atlantic, declaring that the wife must come at once. In two days she was on the way, alone and anxious, through the long mid-winter voyage. " I dare not think how I may find my dear husband : he will have a glorious futurity, — that I am sure of," — was the thought that kept her company.

Meanwhile, the first home-words had come : —

"Nov. 7, 1836. Went to Baring & Co.'s, and found letters from home, — one from my own Anna. Oh, how welcome they were! I sat down in the counting-room, and cried as I read them. It is strange to read of such kindness as these letters express and announce, — strange that people should think so much better of me than I deserve."

There were trustful words from the mother and sisters, who tried to make the sufferer believe the faith and pride they had in him, in spite of the sad life to which he seemed to have led one so dear to them. And the parish sent its true love to him. "You can scarcely imagine the sensation which the arrival of news from you has created. It has been a complete levee morning," writes the wife. " If you could have heard Dr. Channing yesterday at the communion-table return thanks to our Father for the 'good tidings,' you would have been almost tempted to exclaim, Behold how he loved him!" But plainly salvation did not lie in London for him : three weeks of the life had brought nothing but fatigue and excitement. So he crossed the Channel, still cared for by the good companion of his voyage. They roved through the cities of Holland and Belgium towards Paris, where again friends gave warm welcome to their home. A Sunday in Rotterdam left its longing in the Journal : —

"Why does not the truth of His presence who is never absent prevent this oppression of solitude, and why do I not hold communion with the Invisible? Why is not the Infinite real to my imagination and my heart? Alas! these questions go to the root of my difficulty. God help me to correct myself, and to profit by His gracious discipline. Oh that I might learn in foreign lands how to use and enjoy my Sundays at home!"

"Jan. 1, 1837. Paris, at Mr. Lane's. What thoughts crowd upon me, — recollections of home, of past mercies, of past scenes of anxiety and perplexity! How wonderful has been the loving kindness of God, how remarkable the kindness of my fellow-men! Never was one so blessed, never one so unthankful. Constant experience of divine and human goodness seems only to have hardened my heart alike against the sense of God's beneficence and man's regard. This is the thought that has recurred with most force to day. I would make some good and effectual resolutions for the future; resolutions of self-denial, of mortification of bodily appetite, — my besetting sin; of trust in God; patience under disappointment; gratitude for the countless gifts of every hour; penitence for past sins, and fidelity henceforth in my social relations. Oh, may I keep them! Dear Anna, God be with us both! If I can only come to feel His presence, I shall be at peace."

He kept an interesting memorandum of conversations with M. Coquerel, the elder, then the leading Protestant minister in France : —

"I went to call on Rev. Athanase Coquerel to-day with John Parkman, and found him altogether agreeable. Our conversation related almost wholly to the state and prospects of religion in France. He says that Catholicism in France is prostrate, and 'can never revive.' The priests of the Catholic Church he represented as extremely ignorant, and as taken from the lower classes of the people. 'The French people are Theists, — believers in God, providence, the immortality of the soul, and a future life of retribution; but not Christians, — believers in the divine mission of Jesus Christ.' In reply to a question expressing a doubt on this point, he reiterated his conviction that the French, with few exceptions, were believers in these doctrines of God and immortality. The tendency, he says, is towards religion, not from it. But there is a sad want of the means by which this tendency may be encouraged and fulfilled. Methodism in France, by which he meant what is called the Evangelical party in England (and Orthodoxy with us), has done great harm to Protestantism. The efforts of Methodism have all mistaken the French mind. Religion must be presented to the French as an element of progress in every thing, — in the arts, in science, in politics. The French read nothing but newspapers, and read these to excess. He avowed himself neither a Trinitarian nor a Unitarian; but when I said he could not use the latter term in our sense, which meant an unbeliever in the Trinity, he replied that he was, then, decidedly a Unitarian. His views of the rank of the Saviour he said he could express in two words, — viz., 'Christ above all, and God above Christ.' He will not take names; neither does he seem to care because they are applied to him. He did not appear to have read Dr. Channing's books, nor to know much of Unitarianism in the United States.

"M. Coquerel was evidently aware of the importance of his situation, which he probably exaggerates a little. His study is continually visited by persons who come to consult him on domestic as well as religious subjects. One effect of the Catholic religion upon those who have thrown off its authority, is seen in the habit of his people of making him the depository of their secret history and the history of their families. They treat him as their confessor. He knows the private affairs of many a family, some of them in high life, as well as of his own. Parents come to him to provide husbands for their daughters. As a proof of the disposition of the people towards an enlightened and liberal Protestantism, he stated that this morning a lady, herself Catholic, had been to him to beg him to instruct her three children in the Protestant faith. A Catholic priest, too, had been to talk with him. He seemed to entertain sanguine hopes of the progress of correct religious views in France; and yet, when I asked what means existed in Paris for their diffusion, beside his preaching and the personal influence of those who accorded with him, he said *none*, and represented the Protestant Church and the theological schools as in a most sad condition, partly at least in consequence of the mismanagement of the Government."

Once or twice with his home-made French he made an odd mistake, as when he mistook an *abbatoir* "wonderfully neat and sweet" for the Hospice de la Salpetrière; and when he obtained admission at the Hôtel Dieu, where entrance was refused, by innocently insisting, "Je suis un étranger, un Americain ministre." He did not know what honors he had claimed till the laughing friends at home assured him he was only " un pasteur."

Then back to London to finish the waiting. One night, sadly disappointed at the empty stage, he returned to his lodgings — to find her there!

"Oh, what a blessed meeting. God be thanked for His goodness to me! Had tea, and talked, because we could not sleep, till 3 or 4 o'clock. Strength and hope have gained the victory over discouragement, and all this improvement I owe to her through whom I should most desire to receive it, my wife, my own Anna."

"LONDON, Feb. 10, 1837.

"MY DEAR MRS. TILDEN, — My first letter after Anna's arrival is due to you, for from you I received the treasure which every day has more and more proved her to be. Have we not both reason to be proud, you of such a daughter and I of such a wife? What affection and what energy has she shown! Just think of the same being, who, eighteen months ago, shrunk, with the timidity that her habits of seclusion had nourished, from exposure to new faces and strange scenes, now leaving her home at two days' notice, travelling in mid-winter to New York, and thence coming across the ocean alone, to meet a husband who had given her only anxiety and disappointment almost ever since their marriage. . . . You do not know what a difference has been wrought in my feelings. . . . For the first time during many weeks I have within the last two days cherished the thought that I may return to my ministry. It has seemed to me impossible, but now I hope I may go home to live among those who have done so much for me."

The ill turns were by no means over, but in between them now the pleasant time began for both. Hastening through Paris and Marseilles, they reached Rome, and a third time found home with Boston friends; for

Mr. Ticknor welcomed them to "the upper story of one of the best houses in Rome, where they have given us a nice chamber and made us members of their family. What kindness we meet with everywhere!" After a few weeks among the churches and pictures and ruins, they turned northwards. More than once a word like this occurs among their notes : —

"At the Tuscan border, the custom-house men proposed to let our baggage pass without examination, for a fee. I refused, but it was paid for me by the others."

May 7, Sunday at Verona. "Here I did very wrong. It was Sunday. I felt it was not right to travel; yet the inn was noisy, and the town full of people apparently engaged in their usual pursuits. After some hesitation, I decided to go on. This, perhaps, was not very wrong, — but then I wished to see the amphitheatre, and we set out by ourselves to find it; by mistake went to another part of the town, and spent an hour and a half walking about and sight-seeing, — then came on. The ride was wretched by my consciousness of sin. I ought to have made so much distinction between Sunday and the other days as to have rested."

It spoiled three days for the travellers, for on Tuesday there is record, "We have been made very unhappy to-day by the recollection of our fault at Verona." Some time later, in the Journal, while speaking of notions confirmed and notions altered by his travel, he writes: "My ideas respecting the proper method of spending the Sabbath have undergone a great change." Yet to the end of his life that Saturday evening silence and the Sabbath window-seat in the old home fixed his feeling on this point.

Florence, Venice, Milan, were much enjoyed.

"Every thing we saw in Italy was a lesson. Painting and statuary became to us revelations of unknown truths and unimagined feelings. Rome alone is worth ten voyages across the Atlantic. At Venice I can say we learned to love Titian, as before we had acquired almost an affection for Raphael. Now do not laugh. This is all true."

By the time they reached Switzerland, the Journal blossomed with thanksgivings and delight. Geneva afforded ground for studying Unitarianism as a "National Church." Stranger yet it seemed to Unitarian eyes that the one place on earth where this sight could be seen should be John Calvin's city. Here the "Separatists" were the Trinitarians. He made acquaintance with M. Chenevière, M. Cellerier, the Comte Sellon, and others, and found out from their conversation that his own faith as an Established Church shared the faults of all "Establishments."

"The Unitarians here are all Arians, and on the subject of the eternity of future punishment they say nothing. M. Capt says there are in the National Church a great many who agree with the Separatists in sentiment, are Trinitarians and moderate Calvinists, but do not think it right or best to withdraw from the Church. There are many who think that the Trinity is a subject so mysterious that they will neither deny nor assert it. This class he believes is increasing. The ministers of the Established Church write and commit their sermons. When chosen, they swear to observe the rules of the Council of State, therefore cannot separate the Church from the State; but there are Orthodox ministers as well as laymen in the National Church.

"The religious aspect of affairs does not gratify me. I doubt if Unitarianism be progressive here at present; or rather, while Unitarianism is stationary, Orthodoxy, I suspect, gradually spreads. The Unitarians, I am afraid, are not as active, zealous, or religious as they should be. The instruction of the young does not seem to me thorough, and the exercises of the pulpit are not so frequent as with us. Only four churches, served by fifteen ministers, preaching only once a day on Sunday. I have been very often reminded of home by what I have seen. The history and present state of Unitarianism seem to me very similar here and with us."

A lingering drift by row-boat down the Rhine made the heart of June beautiful; and thence they came again to Paris. What next? A question which only the doctors could answer. Dr. Louis said, "Return now to work, and you will soon be prostrate where you were." Yet delay seemed impossible. In lieu of longer absence, then, the Baths of Vichy were recommended as a speedy wonder-worker. The stirs of fashion had hardly yet disturbed the natives in their hay-fields. There they stayed six weeks, enjoying the hour-long baths, the drinkings, and the donkey-rides, and restful idle days, — immured by their language from the other visitors. The peasants' life, their farming and their festivals, the dancing and the Sunday worship, the odd dress and pleasant, courteous manners, all went into their chronicle. The waters seemed to give new life, and he wrote that he was "perfectly well." Once he made a donkey-expedition to Gannat, a little town eleven miles eastward, hoping to find some traces of his ancestry. But the editor of the village paper assured him that the Romans called the place *Gannatum*, which, if true, proved too much, and he returned from his donkey-ride as sireless as he went.

On the way back to Paris, they stopped at Moulins on an errand of Unitarian sympathy. Channing's brilliant young ally in the early movement out from Orthodoxy had sickened and died here among strangers, twenty years before. In a corner of the old graveyard

they found the cracked and moss-grown stone, " Memo-
riæ sacrum Reverendi Samuel Cooper Thacher," and
made arrangements by which its preservation might be
secured by friends at home.

Just where or when another story, not unlike, belongs,
does not appear from the Journal; but it may come in
here for us as Dr. Hedge tells it: —

" Travelling in Europe many years since, Mr. Gannett
chanced upon a fellow-countryman, unknown to him before,
journeyed with him for one or two days, then parted from
him in some continental town, leaving him not dangerously
ill, but too indisposed to continue his journey, and needing
longer rest. At the end of the second day this traveller,
from whose own lips I had the story, saw to his great surprise Mr. Gannett return, having retraced his steps many
miles, irresistibly drawn by the thought that a stranger in a
strange land might need a compatriot's aid."

At Paris a letter came " from the committee of our
church, giving me leave to stay till next July. Written,
too, before they knew of my intention of going to
Vichy. Was there ever such kindness ? I declare, I
do doubt if the world can furnish another such instance." His society had indeed been generous. It
had been a most disastrous season to the business men
at home, yet it was voted unanimously that their pastor's term of absence be extended another year, and
that his salary be continued as hitherto, the society
supplying the desk at its own charge.

He hesitated long before accepting the kindness.
They were very homesick: he longed for his pulpit and
the faces and the homes. Yet perplexity, or long continued effort of any kind, brought the old symptoms
back. The inward warnings were too plain to be
ignored, and the physicians consulted in Paris and Lon-

don with one voice declared the danger of resuming work.

"I cannot take up again the engagements of my profession gradually," he writes Mr. Savage. "I should be compelled, alike by feelings and by circumstances, to enter upon them all at once; and, until I am stronger than at present, I should dread the effect of such a change in my habits. Every week makes me feel more ability as well as more desire to resume my occupations; and I trust that my wish will yet be realized, of doing something for the cause of truth among those to whom the only return I can make for their long and patient tenderness towards me will be the exertion of all my powers in their behalf."

So to England again, where they were to spend their new year, and form many pleasant friendships. Wherever acquaintance led to friendship, he writes home that he found "the best qualities of mind and heart;" yet our democratic travellers felt the absence of geniality in the general tone of society, — "a sort of national self-complacency in one form or another pervading all classes, and giving a tincture even to their manners towards each other."

They paused in London long enough for him to give thanks, — "how different am I to-day from what I was just a year ago!"—and then, although nearly winter, set out for the Lakes of Westmoreland and the Scottish Highlands. Everywhere the ministers were hospitable to the Boston brother. Crossing from Glasgow, he made friends with those of Dublin and Belfast also.

TROSACHS, Dec. 15, 1837. "We may have lost much from the lateness of our visit, but we have gained no inconsiderable advantage in the hues which the mountains wear at this season; rich and various beyond any thing I had imagined that herbage could produce, and giving, when seen in the perfect reflection of the still lake, one of the most beautiful pictures that even Nature can furnish. Such a sight we had on Wednesday, in passing Loch Lubnaig, where the vast hill that rises from the water's edge on its western side was seen as distinctly below the surface as in the upper air, with each tint of earth and stone and heath clearly defined. One lesson I have learned, not to take any individual's opinion of particular scenery, so much depends on the circumstances and the feelings that distinguish each visit. I do not wonder now when my experience in visiting a place is totally different from that which other travellers had led me to expect. . . .

"We arrived at Taymouth just at sunset; and, as we crossed the bridge which spans the river at its departure from the lake, we stopped to gaze on a spectacle unlike any other I ever saw. On our left the sun had sunk beneath the clouds which filled the whole space across the head of the lake, bounded as it there is on either hand by hills, but these clouds were actually burning with the deepest colors. But when we looked to our right, directly opposite this magnificence of the western sky, the full moon was pouring forth her light and throwing her beams into the Tay, as if in rivalry of the orb that had just disappeared. It was, too, but 4 P.M., when we seemed to be at once in the midst of day and night. Though we are between 56° and 57° north latitude, the roses are in bud and bloom at the corner of the house."

December, 1837. "I hope that the rest of my life will not be fruitless. I never can do as I have done, but I have learned some wisdom and formed some resolutions the last year; and I hope I may live to be useful, at least by an example of *calm*, steady, and cheerful duty. I am a good deal older than I was a year ago; with more quiet faith and less ardent expectation."

Sunday, Jan. 14, 1838. "I have once more preached, the first time for more than sixteen months. How much occasion for gratitude! It seems to me that every day brings fresh reason for repeating this exclamation. I preached extemporaneously, and did not feel any embarrassment except when I suffered my mind to think, not of what I was saying, but how I should say it; and in the morning I did as well as I expected for the first time, but in the afternoon was far from satisfying myself. Still I have learned that I can preach without writing to a strange congregation, and I have little fear now that preaching with due moderation will hurt me."

In a sermon that he listened to at Edinboro', he saw himself reflected, — a vision most rare for him to see in any thing that he liked even moderately well: —

" The discourse was an hour long, and in all respects good ; not original nor very powerful, but clear, definite, and earnest, and was delivered with animation ; considerable gesture, though not much variety of it. The style, both of writing and preaching, seemed to me to resemble my own very much ; not remarkable in any way, but having that sort of genuineness about it that would induce people to listen, because the preacher seems to be persuaded that they ought to think as he does."

Genuineness was a quality which he was quick to recognize : —

" Dr. Chalmers has a thick voice ; a bad pronunciation, amounting almost to brogue ; and a manner that, though not awkward, is certainly not graceful. But there is an earnestness, a *straightforwardness* of delivery, as if his sole object were to communicate a conviction with which his own mind were charged. I saw little to remind me of Dr. Channing, with whom he has been compared. Each impresses you with the idea of strong sincerity, but the fervor of the one is marked by gentleness, while the other is rough, without, however, being coarse. Dr. C.'s lecture this morning was on the

Trinity. He made a memorable concession. Besides affirm-
ing that 'the moral influence,' 'the religious use' of the doctrine of the Trinity (so we may examine this dogma by the
test of moral import) 'lies in the separate propositions, and not
in the complex and comprehensive proposition,' he directly
asserted that 'its importance consists in the relations which
each of the three sustains to the others.' He then stated
the four propositions, each of which, he said, was perfectly
intelligible: '1. The Father is God; 2. The Son is God;
3. The Holy Spirit is God; 4. God is one. If you ask me
to reconcile the four, I answer, I cannot.' 'We require no one
to reconcile the personality of each with the unity of God.'
The words in quotation are, I believe, exactly his own."

A month's quiet at an emptied watering-place, Har-
rogate at mid-winter, followed this busy jaunting.
Here they found in his Patmos a cordial old sufferer for
righteousness' sake, — the Captain Thrush, of the Brit-
ish Navy, who first resigned his commission, and, though
poor, refused his half-pay because converted to peace-
principles, and then forfeited the sympathy of his
fellow-reformers because converted by Bible studies to
Unitarianism. "He is always busy, and employs himself very much with printing, by the help of a little
boy, Johnny, the tracts which he writes."

At last back to London, and into snug lodgings near
the good friend, Dr. Boott, where presently, —

"Out from the everywhere into here,"

a little girl came unto them. With double joy, for the
health restored and for their child, the grateful parents
now made ready for return to home. In the Unitarian
circle they met, meantime, with many a pleasant greeting, — from Miss Aikin and Mrs. Joanna Baillie, Lady
Byron, Dr. and Mary Somerville, and others. To the

well man London was as full of charm as to the sick
man it had been full of gloom.   It was a round of calls
and cosey breakfasts.   He was much among the ministers,
in their homes on week-days, and on Sundays preaching
from one chapel to another.   He always preached extemporaneously, taking themes of the spiritual life with
which his thought and feeling were most familiar, and
letting the full heart speak.   Such enthusiastic utterance
was in marked contrast to that common in the English
pulpits.   " The effect produced by your discourses was
very great," wrote Rev. Mr. Madge, — " greater than I
have observed from any other person for many years.
You are not, and you will not be quickly, forgotten."
Old letters that have recently passed into biography
speak warmly of him.   Rev. J. J. Tayler says : —

" I went in the morning to Carter Lane to hear our friend,
Dr. Gannett, who has been producing a great sensation in
the London pulpits.   Carter Lane was crowded, galleries
and all.   Lady Byron, we are told, follows the preacher from
place to place, and takes notes of all the sermons. . . . He
will do us a great deal of good.   We sadly want rousing."

And Miss Aikin writes to Dr. Channing : —

" Of his powers as a preacher I have not enabled myself
to judge, but I can bear strong testimony to the perfect
modesty and simplicity with which he receives tokens of a
success which would be sufficient to turn most heads.   Mrs.
Joanna Baillie told him truly, that he had been talked of
at a time when we had scarcely leisure to talk of any one,
so full were all heads with our grand coronation ; and I never
saw any thing more beautiful than the unaffected, modest
dignity with which he received the compliment, — it would
have delighted you to witness.   He carries back with him
the esteem and good wishes of all whose testimony is worth
having."

The English ministers were already discussing among themselves the subjects which were about to startle their brethren beyond the sea, and their visitor heard rehearsal of what he was to hear and take part in on his return : —

Oct. 2, 1837. " Mr. Tayler (Rev. J. J.) invited us last evening to breakfast with him this morning. An ample but simple breakfast was prepared, and, in the midst of agreeable conversation, the morning passed as if on wings. We sat around the table till almost one o'clock. Our topics were principally the religious nature of man, whether he might be termed a religious being in the same sense as he is styled a moral being, and the importance of external or miraculous testimony to Christianity. Mr. Tayler expressly avowed his belief in the miracles ; but they are not, to his mind, a ground of faith, — they tend to confirm, but not to produce, faith. Their reality he is compelled to admit, but why they were wrought he hardly seemed to know, and is willing to leave undetermined. He regards man as naturally adapted and prone to religion ; that is, there are phenomena which can only be ascribed to an ultimate law of his being, — his tendency to faith in a superior intelligence cannot be explained as the result of reasoning. It is the result of our own deep consciousness. We transfer the agency of which we are conscious in our own minds to a superior mind. The argument from design may be of use after this feeling is developed, but it will not, in the first instance, establish faith. Faith, Scripture faith, is the affinity between the soul and the Divine Being, — the acknowledgment of God through the force of our instinctive or intuitive sentiment. A manifestation of God by revelation will be accredited so far as it corresponds to this affinity of the soul. Hence, if I am convinced of the moral manifestation of God in a peculiar manner, I can believe in a miraculous agency exerted in connection, but the miracles will not produce the faith. Mr. T. speaks, as I love to hear one, of the spiritual life, and of sympathy with the character of Christ. In his views of the foundation of the spiritual life, he seems to me to accord with George Ripley. He admires Germany and the Germans, and thinks them religious. I like him better than any other minister whom I have met. He is inquisitive, but candid, clear and pleasant, about thirty-seven years old, a delightful man of true modesty. We bid him good-by, after a day of most pleasant intercourse, which I shall long remember."

W. J. Fox, of London, the Radical minister, is thus described : —

" Mr. Fox is rather short and thick-set, has nothing professional in his dress or manner, but a face which prepossesses by its expression of calm power. When we entered, the organ and choir were performing. A prayer followed, — short and, to me, novel, more a declaration respecting God as the object of worship and source of blessing than an address to Him, but clothed in choice language and uttered with reverence. A hymn was sung; then the discourse or lecture, — wholly extemporaneously, no notes even, an hour in length. I was more than satisfied, he went beyond my expectations. He was fluent, correct, graceful, and often rich in his use of language. His manner easy, and with a continual check whenever he found himself approaching declamation. No gesture except of the finger, slightly elevated or depressed. There was little direct use of the imagination, but constant proof that it was an active power of his mind. It was a philosophical rather than a poetical performance, showing acuteness of discrimination and depth of remark."

He heard him more than once, — sometimes with less pleasure : —

"The service seemed less congenial with religious worship. What Fox says is almost always sound, — you only regret its inappropriateness to place and time; still his mind is so comprehensive and fertile, his remarks spread themselves out so

clearly among the very foundations of truth and duty, and
his intellectual power is so manifest, that I could not but
listen with interest and profit."

" Mr. Thom called and went with us to Mr. Blanco White's,
where we had a most interesting visit.   Mr. White is rather
short, with stiff hair, and a face that might not displease, but
would not prepossess.   He has been confined to the house for
months by a loss of muscular energy.   His conversation was
clear and rich.   He considers the prospects of Spain most
gloomy: superstition and despotism have ruined her.   The
progress of society is very slow, and, if a man take his own
observation as the ground of judgment, there is little to be
hoped, — but faith in Providence justifies hope and confidence
for the future.   The oppression and mischief of an Establishment are intolerable.   Christians are still idolaters, paying
homage, not to a visible object, but to a false image of the Deity
which they have erected in their own minds.   God must be
known within us.   There He is, — in the conscience.   But
the most instructive part of Mr. W.'s conversation was his
mention of himself.   He told us how much he had suffered
from the Catholic religion, where two sisters had fallen victims to the severities of conventual life : and then remarked
that, in looking over his life, he was not able to put his finger
on a single circumstance that could have been better ordered
for him, — he did not see how any thing could have been better
for himself.   What an example of religious faith and trust ! "

" Called on Miss Harriet Martineau, in her little parlor
surrounded by her comforts, with her pile of American books
in the corner.   Her own book is half-written.   She speaks
of it as an easy and delightful employment, and says nothing
has yet been written so favorable to the Americans as this
work will be.   Furness's book she is delighted with.   Carlyle
says F. has shown Jesus as the dove, some one must now
present him as the eagle.   Carlyle's book on the French
Revolution will be published on the first of March.   Anti-

slavery is said to be flourishing in the United States. Miss M. full of hope."

English Unitarianism, as a whole, seemed to him cold, unspiritual, inactive, not co-operative and not prosperous. The general opinion as collected from one and another was that, at best, it was only holding its own, save perhaps in Ireland, where it might be gaining. Sometimes the word was, that, although Unitarianism was decreasing, liberal religious thought was spreading. The Sunday services appeared to lack fervor. Often all was read, even the prayers, and the feeling prompted little or no gesture. But great care was given to the composition of a sermon. "Mr. —— writes every sermon which he preaches three times." He heard that the York tutors discountenanced fervor and extemporaneous speaking; and thought it natural, therefore, to hear also that young men from Scotland and Ireland, with little or no theological education, were preferred by the congregations to the York students, and that poor children brought up in Unitarian chapels generally deserted the chapels for others as they grew up.

Most of the English Unitarians had passed from Arian to Humanitarian views of Christ. "There are only three or four Arian societies in England, and little is now said on the subject. Controversy is less preached than formerly." In Ireland thought was moving in the same direction, but was not so far advanced: the majority were Arian still. The doctrine of regeneration was just appearing, German philosophy was winning readers, and discussion was turning to questions of revelation *versus* faith.

"Mr. —— said, 'There are two tendencies here, one towards high views of the Saviour's offices, and one towards

12

rationalistic views of inspiration and miracle. The young
ministers are more inclined to the latter.' — The remarks at
the commencement of the Communion Service were upon
the degree of doubt that must mingle with Christian faith.
Is it not singular that the ministers should say so much about
the necessity of a *partial* confidence in Christianity? The
wine was poured from common bottles, — a little thing, but it
was in keeping with the characteristics given to the service.
— The word 'Christian' I think was never introduced into
the sermon, 'the good man' was used in preference: the
terms 'sin' and 'sinful' were also avoided."

" Mr. —— has that moderate tone of religious feeling and
Christian energy and hope which distinguishes the English
Unitarians, and is partly at least the result of their situation.
For theirs is a difficult as well as unpleasant position, and
one that exposes them to unhappy influences. Despised by
the Church and abhorred by the Orthodox Dissenters, they
feel themselves excluded from their proper place in society,
while their dread of bigotry, under which they have suffered
so much, and their dislike of the extravagance of the Evangelical party, incline them towards the opposite error of coldness and sluggishness; and their observation of the mischiefs
wrought by an excessive regard to forms in the Establishment leads them to reject or distrust the use even of profitable services. No one can estimate the embarrassments of
their situation till he has been among them."

To the ministers themselves he grew warmly attached.
To Rev. Lant Carpenter, one of his kindest hosts, he
writes: —

"I had not imagined that I should feel so much the pain
of separation as it is now realized by me. The tears came
involuntarily to my eyes to-day, glad as I was to be on my
way home, when I was mindful of the truth that the ocean
would soon spread its whole breadth, a space that I should
never repass, between my daily walks and the spots con-

nected with so many delightful recollections. Bristol, you
may be sure, is one of these spots. I have everywhere
experienced fraternal kindness at the hands of Unitarian
ministers in Great Britain. Wherever I have sought their
acquaintance, whether with or without letter of introduction,
— and I have availed myself of every opportunity of forming
such acquaintance, — I have been cordially welcomed, and
found the possession of a common faith a sufficient title to
their hospitality. I shall rejoice if I may ever return a part
of the kindness I have received."

More than two years had passed by since the sick
man left that abrupt blank in the "preaching-book."
Now he was able to send home as herald of return the
message : —

"I have more occasion for gratitude than words can
express. My health is perfectly restored; and, though I have
not the strength of former days, I am anticipating the re-
sumption of my professional engagements with full confidence in my physical ability to discharge them. . . . Never
was a human being more blessed than I have been. Every
circumstance in the last two years has not only been, but
has *seemed* propitious. Gratitude and duty be ours for
ever."

A very glad father and mother took passage with
their little child in the "Great Western," in July, 1838.
The voyage of fourteen days seemed short to those who
were making only the third voyage by steam that had
ever been made across the Atlantic. A day or two in
New York, — one little journey more, — and then " our
carriage bore us to Bumstead Place, where we were
welcomed amidst smiles and tears."

As his tribute of gratitude to friends, some of whom
are still living to receive it, shall we print the dedica-

tion to a volume which he planned to express the gratitude? The volume, in truth, never got far beyond its title-page, its modest preface, and the table of contents; but the heart's intent shall be preserved: —

To the Members of the Federal Street Congregation,

Whose kindness proposed, and whose generosity enabled me to make, the visit, in which I gathered the materials for this volume, and for whose patience and liberality towards me I desire to make the only return in my power, that of faithful service so long as Providence shall permit, these volumes are affectionately inscribed.

EMERSON.

RIPLEY.

PARKER.

VII.

THE TRANSCENDENTAL MOVEMENT IN NEW ENGLAND.

WHEN Mr. Gannett returned to his work in 1838, the Unitarian world at home wore a new aspect. Thus far, no one had been more eager in the party of advance then he: henceforward he found himself in the party that conserved. We must explain the change of aspect to do justice to his change of attitude.

The first stage of the Liberal movement showed Calvinism giving way to Arminianism. In the second, the Calvinism vanished, the doctrines of the Trinity and Vicarious Atonement slowly followed, reason grew bolder and bolder, and at last the Liberals became Unitarians and organized themselves as a new sect. They were still sincere Bible men: Reason and Revelation were their equal watchwords. The worth of the Bible to them, it is true, lay largely in its vagueness, its multiplicity of meaning, the room they thereby got **for**

thinking far and freely without fear. It lay much more
largely in this vagueness than they knew. They were
conscious and were very proud of their distinctive principle, — Free Inquiry in matters of religion, — but did
not see whither it would lead them. Now the hour
was near that was to show. By the time that the
Unitarian controversy was fairly over, and the church-
breaks had ceased, and the amended Constitution had
brought in the voluntary system of church-support, —
while the Unitarian Association, at last becoming popular, was rapidly increasing its membership and energy,
and just as the younger Ware was writing to his fellow-
believers (1835), " Now that we are a community by
ourselves, it behooves us to consider what we shall do,"
— even then the Liberal movement was passing into its
third stage. The little band of allies, that for twenty
years past had stood side by side in a common cause,
was already separating. The larger and elder part was
in its turn settling down on the ground already won
and made dear by their brave struggle for it. A few —
most of them young men and women — with a look of
enthusiasm in their faces, had begun to move on, seeking fresh fields of thought. Never before and never
since has the brain of Massachusetts felt such stimulus
as it received during the next few years. It was an
age of wide awakening, of general quickening in mind
and conscience; but in early and intense form the life-
stir seized on Boston as on material prepared for it.
And, of all who felt its influence, the Unitarians and
their ministers were the thinkers most affected.

Nor was this strange. If one should seek the causes
of " the Transcendental movement" as we knew it here,
the early Unitarian rationalism just spoken of would,
first and foremost, meet his eye with the burden of the

futu̧re in it. The characteristic principle of Free Inquiry in religion, of Reason in Revelation, was sure
to carry some minds beyond " the Revelation." The
Orthodox professors were true prophets, when they
said that Unitarianism would necessarily result in Natural Religion. The seeker would note also the results
to which this principle had already led a few even of
the elders, some, too, who were acknowledged teachers.
It is hard to tell how many of our fathers were Arians,
or of Arian type; how many were Humanitarian.
Stuart said to Channing, as early as 1819, " The
younger men are nearly all outstripping you." Even
Professor Ware, in his lectures at the Divinity School,
was, soon after, teaching that to him Christ seemed a
man: the protesting note-books of the students show it.
There were doubtless several like him, and more every
year. Probably few who were over forty years old at
the time of the disclosure in 1815 died other than
Arians. Probably there were few under forty then,
who did not at least grow doubtful, if not certain, the
other way.

Channing never gave up belief in miracles, and perhaps never said distinctly that Christ was a mere man.
While some of his later friends thus read his thought,
others, Mr. Gannett among them, were sure that he
always believed in Christ's pre-existence. At all events,
he never liked the " mere " way of putting any greatness. What is called " Channing Unitarianism " rightly
enough includes belief in a supernatural revelation confirmed by miracle and in a Christ of superhuman nature.
But that belief emphasized by itself would be a very
superficial measure of the faith that Channing held and
furthered. His mind had always dwelt above the sphere
of sectarian logic and proof-texts, and his influence told

strongly for the new advance. He lacked the method of historic criticism which gave rise to the negations of the Transcendentalists, but by his affirmations he might almost be counted in their band. For Channing's greatness lay in his noble insistance on *the worth of human nature.* This was the idea which has made him a star in the American firmament. It is his own word: " My one sublime idea, which has given me unity of mind, — the greatness, the divinity of the soul." Hence all his love of liberty. Hence all his plans for social regeneration. Hence the meanest man to him was an immortal, and brought thoughts of grandeur. " All minds are of one family," he said, thinking of men and Christ and God. " Yes, Christ, though so far above us, is still one of us; is only an illustration of the capacity which we all possess." " The minister is a fellow-worker with Christ and angels," was a favorite thought. " Each man should feel the greatness of his own spirit, — that it is so great as to justify all the mighty operations of Christianity, were there no other spirit which needed redemption." " The noblest use of travelling is to discern more of the godlike in the human." " The truths I have insisted on are written not from tradition, but from deep conviction, — may I not say from *inspiration?* I mean nothing miraculous. Does not God speak in us all ? " And he scrupled not to say of Reason in Revelation: " The truth is, and it ought not to be denied, that our ultimate reliance is and must be on our own reason. I am surer that my rational nature is from God than that any book is an expression of his will." These were the characteristic, not the exceptional, emphases in all the latter part of Channing's life, while his interest in the mere sect "Unitarianism" was waning, and his influence was sinking deep and spreading far.

Who can doubt the "flow of faith," or wonder from what unknown skies Transcendentalism lit in Boston brains? It climbed there from the soil.

Not but that alien skies sent mighty help. The new Idealism of Europe was beginning to be read. The spirits of Plato and Spinoza had arisen from the tomb. Kant's voice had called them forth by accrediting the human mind with higher structure than it of late had claimed, with innate forms of thought transcending all experience. Soon Schelling followed, founding his system on a faculty of intellectual intuition "that gave immediate knowledge of the Absolute;" and Jacobi, telling of an "inward sense" that gazed on spiritual realities. Then Schleiermacher, his heart inspired by the light and warmth of these new views, strove to win back to faith in an ennobled Christianity the unbelieving culture of his nation. To that end he carefully mapped out a broad psychology as the basis of religion: he found in man a conscious feeling of dependence on the Infinite, besides a conscious power that gave room for free-will and conscience; while, on the side of intellect, he found a direct intuition of God and truth, together with the reason which elaborates to full conceptions the ideas thus perceived. Inspiration he pronounced generic to the race; the worth of miracles as its evidence was slighted; the Bible unclothed of the historic garb shone with the eternal truths that lay beneath; all the Christian dogmas were enlarged and spiritualized, and religion became the vision of God in all things, and all things in God.

From Germany this stirring impulse circled far and wide, setting in activity new centres of "Transcendental" radiation. The one thought got many names. Cousin, after haunting the German shrines awhile, went back to France to explain what he called the "impersonal reason" that perceives the True, the Beautiful, the Good, in absolute essence. In England two men caught the secret, and startled their plain-thinking countrymen with strange oracles, — Coleridge, in mystic soliloquies about the "higher reason," the Logos in man by which we share in things eternal; and Carlyle, who thundered forth against the hollow mechanisms of society the gospel of irrevocable, instamped, spiritual laws.

The fame of other writers, too, was in the air: Goethe and Schiller, still unfamiliar in America; De Wette's Bible criticism, sufficiently advanced, but more exciting yet the book which Strauss published in 1835; Constant and Jouffroi; St. Simon, too, and Fourier. There were as yet few German students here, but, through translations and reviews and reprints, strains of the foreign thought gradually found their way across the ocean into the New England studies; and the deep, broad-viewed, intoxicating words came like wind and sunshine to the Transcendental growth already sprouting there. They were most important to that growth; but, by furnishing ready-made forms of thought and phraseology, and even of social life, they seemed to be still more important to it than they were, and made it easy for the scorners to dub it "German infidelity" and "French atheism."

Now these four influences (three coming through Unitarianism itself, its early principle of Free Inquiry, the growing recognition that Christ was a brother-man, and Channing's "dignity of human nature") joined to make the Unitarian mind diverge within itself. Two tendencies of thought were manifest, — one starting as of old from Locke's philosophy, the other representing

Kant's. Two schools of Bible criticism attached themselves respectively to these contrasted systems. One
accepted the external revelation, although nothing in
it that strained Reason overmuch. The other scanned
first the Old Testament and then the New with growing scepticism. The miracles faded from the pages or
seemed to blur them. Inconsistencies and immoralities
multiplied along the chapters. Moses could not have
written the Pentateuch. The prophets did not mean
the babe of Bethlehem. Those wondrous deeds of
Jesus, — were they or were they not a fact? and what
followed, if they were not? That was the question
which the Boston ministers were pondering and the
Boston maidens were discussing about 1840. It seemed
as if Strauss would blow out the whole Gospel in puffing
away its myths.

In 1836 it was still too early to read aright the signs of
the time. Two signs, however, were before men's eyes.
One was Ralph Waldo Emerson's withdrawal from the
Hanover Street pulpit, because he could no longer with
sincerity offer the Communion Service. Mr. Gannett
differed widely from his neighbor's view of the ordinance; but so admired his purity and integrity that,
when an Orthodox magazine misrepresented the frank
avowal, he had instantly stepped forward, and in print
pronounced its statement ungenerous and false. The
other, a kindred omen of discontent with the Church,
but in a very different stratum of society and thought,
was the rise of Abner Kneeland's company of Free-
thinkers, and his newspaper, the " Investigator." — Two
years later, when our traveller returned, the staid Unitarian circle was lively with excitement.

For people had by that time read a thin book by Mr.
Emerson, called " Nature," and some had sat half-mazed,

half-raptured, listening to his lectures. At the Harvard
Divinity School he had just given the startling "Address:" the old demurred and knit their brows, the
young were thrilled by its naked beauty. Here, too,
was a plea for Nature. The man self-exiled from the
pulpit came back to tell the pulpit-boys what wonders
of religion lay close by in that Nazareth, the Human
Soul. In contrast with its ever fresh divinity, he pointed
to the Church based on things external and the tradition
of another's vision. " The essence of all religion is the
sentiment of virtue. That is the embalmer of the world.
The silent song of the stars is in it. If a man is at heart
just, then in so far is he God: the safety of God, the
immortality of God, the majesty of God, do enter into
that man with justice. Yet miracles, prophecy, poetry,
the ideal life, the holy life, — they exist to-day as ancient
history merely. Men have come to speak of the Revelation as if God were dead. The Christian Church pro-
nounces Miracle as if it were Monster, not one with
the blowing clover and the falling rain. It dwells with
noxious exaggeration about the *person* of Jesus, till this
friend of man, this only soul in history who has appreciated the worth of man, is made the injurer of man.
The Moral Nature lies unexplored. In how many
churches, by how many prophets, tell me, is man made
sensible that he is an infinite Soul, that the earth and
heavens are passing into his mind; that he is drinking
for ever the soul of God?" The remedy for all these
deformities of the Church is, "first, Soul, and second,
Soul, and evermore, Soul." " I look for the Teacher
that shall see the world to be the mirror of the Soul;
shall see the identity of the law of gravitation with
purity of heart; and shall show that the Ought, that
Duty, is one thing with Science, with Beauty, and with

Joy." — It seemed like an echo of Channing's thought
attuned to a vaster rhythm, — the music of the spheres.

Evidently this teacher was himself no common seer.
But he was not alone. George Ripley, another Unitarian minister not yet withdrawn from pulpit-work,
was busy, with a few friends, translating for New England readers the fresh foreign thought. In a short time
a dozen works appeared in Boston libraries, — as if some
Cortes-band from the New World, discovering in the Old
World an El Dorado of the mind, had come back with
spoil. Dr. Channing used to meet some "Friends of
Progress," and discuss with them the theological and
social problems of the day. There was a "Transcendental Club," of which Dr. Francis was first president,
and its pilgrim-members met on the road to Concord.
Margaret Fuller presided at "Conversations." Certain
drawing-rooms became holy places, where rapt ones
chatted in oracles and watched for intuitions. Alcott's
school had already unfolded strange wealth of spirit-lore
in children's minds. Dr. Follen lectured on Pantheism
and Infidelity; Dr. Walker on Philosophy, and taught
an unfamiliar doctrine. Mr. Furness's first book was
out, picturing with reverent touch a Jesus of the new
faith. Orestes Brownson set up a Quarterly on purpose
to teach "New Views;" and soon, in the hands of
Margaret Fuller, Ripley, and Emerson, the "Dial," lit
by "the light that never was on sea or land," began to
tell the hours of eternity. Some country-folk and fisher-
men, who never had sat in drawing-rooms, gathered in
convention, and showed that they too, Come-outers from
all churches, knew the secrets of the Soul; among them,
"rough-looking men, whose countenances were full of
the divine." Their city brethren next, unruly Radicals of
every fibre, fine and coarse, passed sharp criticism on all

the established institutions of religion. The Philanthropies, moreover, were astir : the Temperance movement, of which Pierpont was to be the pulpit-martyr; the Anti-Slavery movement, which had already entered on its martyr era ; and the Education movement, with Horace Mann for chief. The plea for Woman's Rights began, and the Non-Resistants held convention. Combe's work was circulating ; phrenology, mesmerism, homœopathy, hydropathy, were themes of eager talk and experiment, besides a brood of smaller unnamed *isms*, — agitations against the use of flesh for food, of yeast in making bread, of animal manures in agriculture, and so on. Presently a cultured company of Socialists took counsel together to make real their dream. In the true society seeming opposites would be perfectly reconciled, — the rights of labor and the convenience of property, fineness of brain and hardness of hands, individuality and close co-operation : but why should not the marriage begin in 1841 ? In all glad hope the banns were published, and the home was formed. and the world's people gazed with smiles on the wondrous family in West Roxbury, to see what poets and Plato's kindred knew about farming. This also was George Ripley's project. Proud now are the gray-haired men and matrons scattered through the States who say, " We, too, were at Brook Farm ! " Nor were Brook Farm and its fate unique. It was only one of several similar experiments at this time tried in Massachusetts.

Of course, tumult such as this could not occur without reaction and remonstrance. To say nothing of issues practical, it at least seemed plain that, among the issues speculative, belief in Christianity as a special revelation, and even the belief in God, were in danger. Abner Kneeland's name will live as that of the last man imprisoned for blasphemy in Massachusetts: he had said in his newspaper that God was nothing but a chimera of the imagination. He barely saved the fame, however; for Professor Noyes, of the Harvard Divinity School, had proved that the Old Testament prophecies did not refer to Christ, and was threatened with prosecution for the news. This was not Unitarian procedure; but the Unitarians were, perhaps, even more troubled than the Orthodox. Were not these Transcendental vagaries, these Infidel enormities, the consequence of their own principle of Free Inquiry in religion? Henry Ware the son was now engaged in training the young ministers; and, as antidote to Emerson's address to them, — once Emerson had been ordained his colleague, — he preached and printed a sermon on the personality of God. As antidote; but there was no arguing with Emerson: " I could not possibly give you one of the ' arguments' you cruelly hint at, on which any doctrine of mine stands. For I do not know what arguments mean in reference to any expression of a thought. I delight in telling what I think; but, if you ask me how I dare say so, or why it is so, I am the most helpless of mortal men. " So answered our Transcendentalist. Next year the learned Norton, the veteran of the former advance, roused himself against this new departure. Twice already had he warned. Now he formally indicted it before the assembled Alumni of the School as the " latest form of Infidelity." The German philosophers were pronounced Atheists and Pantheists, senseless mystics; and the home-bred Transcendentalists of New England were disciples of their folly. At this a pamphlet-debate sprang up; for George Ripley, who *could* argue, published Letters to defend Spinoza, Schleiermacher, and De Wette from the charges, and rebuke the exclusiveness that would set up among Unitarians a standard of essentials for the Christian name, and thus abandon the very ground of their existence as a body.

The Boston ministers, also, were discussing whether Emerson were a " Christian," and whether difference of opinion about the value of miracles ought to sunder fellowship. On miracles the question turned, they being commonly regarded, as by Norton, the specific and only sure credential of a revelation. And some, with puzzled brows, kept asking, " What *is* an ' Intuition '? What *is* this ' Higher Reason '? Have you a faculty which we have not? *Verify* your sky-born visions." The soul could not be exactly controverted, — Over-Soul or soul within ; and yet it could not babble very plainly in its own defence. Not that it was unwilling to speak. There seem to have been a few silent brethren, radical in the study, conservative in the pulpit ; but thought had ripened so very quickly this time that it is easy to accredit their hesitation to still lingering doubts. It marks the really great advance that free thought had made within the generation, that, at least, the apostles of the new heresy were at once perfectly outspoken. The word came out as soon as the thought went in, — sometimes before, and made men wonder what the would-be sky-born might portend. This gave the men of miracles and logic laughter, — or it would have given laughter, had they not been so earnest in their own reverence that the whole tendency gave them fear. Of the men mentioned above as contributing, in one way or another, to the movement, — though not all would by any means have been numbered with the Transcendentalists, — Emerson, Ripley, Francis, Follen, Walker, Furness, Brownson, Pierpont, Noyes, were, or had been, Unitarian ministers. Many bright young thinkers in pulpit and in pew, readers and non-readers, both men and women, accepted impulses from the strange thought where they could not greet it heartily. But, as a denomination, the Unitarians said mostly, No, — an impatient, superior No.

Channing, as has been said, was not of the heretics, yet he was much disappointed with his brethren ; and this should be remembered when people speak of " Channing Unitarianism." Emerson's remedy for the Church — " first, Soul, and second, Soul, and evermore, Soul " — recalls Channing's " one sublime idea, the divinity of the soul." Ripley called himself " the child of Dr. Channing." Parker wrote to a friend in 1839 : " It is evident there are now two parties among the Unitarians : one is for progress; the other says, ' Our strength is to stand still.' Dr. Channing is the real head of the first party, the other has no head." His life just covered the early phase of the new growth, and in the last two or three years he often wrote : " I am little of a Unitarian," none at all as a sectarian. " The Unitarian body seems to be forsaking its first love, its liberality, its respect for the rights of individual judgment, its separation of the essential from the unessential in Christianity. I have felt for years that it must undergo important developments. It began as a protest against the rejection of reason. It pledged itself to progress as its life and end ; but it has gradually grown stationary, and now we have a Unitarian Orthodoxy." " Perhaps," he added, " this is not to be wondered at or deplored ; for all reforming bodies seem doomed to stop, in order to keep the ground which they have gained. They become conservative ; and out of them must spring new reformers, to be persecuted generally by the old."

It was a kind of prophecy. Emerson, Ripley, had spoken. Soon another bold, strong voice was heard. Theodore Parker, known as a young and breezy country-parson and many-tongued devourer of books, had already been forfeiting his exchanges, because he read those Germans, while there was a taint of heresy in what he wrote. In 1841 he preached at a South Boston ordination a sermon on "The Transient and the Permanent in Christianity." Among things transient were the Christian rites and doctrines; among such doctrines, the belief that the two Testaments contained a special revelation, and that Christ's nature and offices were unique in history. The ordaining brethren sat by with small if any protest. It was offensive bluntness; but no one knew that any thing momentous had occurred, until some Orthodox listeners who were present suddenly demanded in public, Did those other brethren endorse this as Unitarianism? Then came recoil fast and far. And this was really *not* the Unitarianism which had so hardly won its place among the Christian sects. It grieved the old defenders much to have to bear the scandal of its shelter. Parker's sermon made an epoch somewhat like Channing's Baltimore sermon, twenty-two years before. Not that the thought was novel, though it seldom rushed in such clear swift words as these; but the occasion and the hour gave effect. It was no quiet Sunday discourse in a little village meeting-house, but the public ordination sermon of a Unitarian minister, and delivered at a moment when it revealed the half-formed thoughts of many hearts, the half-formed fears of many others. The usual fate awaited the revealer. Parker became a sign spoken against in churches and in newspapers, — " The Infidel! Blasphemer! Atheist!"

He stood his ground, having felt already dimly conscious that he was sent to stand this ground. That autumn he gave lectures in the city to unfold his views, while the "Boston Association of Ministers" in meeting after meeting discussed the case. Could they exchange with him? they asked each other. Most of them thought not. Were there not limits to a minister's liberty of expressing opinions in the pulpit? That was a question that had much significance for some of them. Parker had a *church-right* membership in their brotherhood; and besides that, by their principle of Free Inquiry, they could not bid him go. Should they not go themselves, however, — dissolve the fellowship? The plan was very seriously mooted, for the whole body was held responsible by a hostile public for all vagaries covered by its name. A kind of revival was going on at this time in their parishes, — another expression of the general ferment. It was a year of unsettling in the churches. The ministers and laymen held meetings, that they might confer together on religious themes; and there, too, the subject came uppermost, mingling in much earnest talk about the relations of Unitarian pastors to their people. In this same year, 1841, Ripley resigned his pulpit to take Brook Farm; Pierpont was cited, by malcontents of his flock, before an ecclesiastical council; and James Freeman Clarke began to gather his "free church."

Parker's lectures soon appeared in print, the "Discourse of Matters pertaining to Religion." Here at last was Transcendentalism cleared up: plain in its denials, plain in affirmations; the vision caught and fixed as a theology, with much show of learning, and with many a psalm singing through the statement. When thus reduced, it proved to be simple and easy enough to understand ; not new in the main, rather shallow and one-sided in its psychology, — but right-sided for that time, — searching as a criticism of the current theologies, and, above all, mighty and fervent in its affirmation of one grand truth. The religious element Parker declared to be the strongest, deepest element in human nature, manifesting itself first in a dim sense of something unbounded and of our dependence thereon, then in Reason's direct intuitions of God, Immortality, and Duty, — primal instincts, facts not of demonstration, but of consciousness. He significantly called his system " Spiritualism," or " the Natural Religious View," as distinguished from " Rationalistic Naturalism," founded on the philosophy of sensation and experience, which viewed God as separate from man and nature, and tried to reach him by unsufficing " arguments ; " as distinguished also from the " Anti-Rationalistic Supernaturalism," founded on the same philosophy, but which viewed God as bridging the great gulf between himself and man by miracle and mediation.

Parker's " Spiritualism " affirmed, as the grand truth of religion, the *immanence of an infinitely perfect God in matter and mind*, and His constant activity in both spheres. The laws of nature are but His modes of action, phenomena His manifestations. Providence everywhere and always provides for every natural want its natural supply. Inspiration corresponds to the soul's want. " As God fills all space, so all spirit," inspiring men " by means of a law, certain, regular, and universal as the laws of gravitation." " Inspiration is the income of God to the soul, in the form of Truth through the reason, of Right through the conscience, of Love and Faith through the affections and religious element. Like vision, it must be everywhere the same thing in kind, however it differs in degree from race to race, from man to man," according to endowment and obedience. "All actual religion is revealed in us, or it could not be felt; all revealed religion is natural, or it would be of no use." "Religion is one, theologies are many." "Religion is the universal term, Christianity a particular form under this universal term." Yet true Christianity, the pure essence of what Jesus taught, divested of the gross errors of the Churches and the slight errors of the Teacher himself, he identified with Absolute Religion, — "the Christianity of Christ, the one only religion, everlasting, ever blest." Jesus was "the profoundest religious genius God has raised up, whose words and works help us to form and develop the idea of a complete religious man." Miracle as transcending law was self-contradiction ; as itself instance of transcendent law, wholly possible, but hard to authenticate in history. The Bible was "the greatest of books," the Church "the greatest of Human Institutions ;" but taken at the popular estimate they were idols too, and as idols received his scathing criticism. — Such were Parker's emphases, recalling closely those of Schleiermacher.

Viewed as a school of philosophy, the Transcendentalists were simply the little New England quota in the great return of thinkers to Idealism, after the long captivity to Sensationalism. Returns almost inevitably have the exaggeration and one-sidedness of reaction. The new king usurps entire allegiance, whereas allegiance seems due to one who rules at once both kingdoms, Intuition and Experience. As a school of critics, they were the earliest here who boldly used the modern historic method in the study of the Bible. As a school of theology, they dispensed with Mediation, in order to

claim for the soul access direct to its Father. They
have been credited with bringing the doctrine of the
Holy Spirit into the Unitarian "common sense in religion." But more than the common doctrine of the
Holy Spirit, and more than Orthodoxy compassed by
its faith in Incarnation and the Helping Grace, their
thought really implied. It implied a universal *law* of
access and communion. It affirmed abiding contact of
the finite and the Infinite in virtue of the very nature
of the soul and Over-Soul. Inspiration fresh as well
as old; Revelation constant; Miracle but the human
spirit's pinnacle of action; God the living God, not a
deity then and there announcing himself with evidence
of authenticity, but indwelling here and now in every
presence, — this was "Transcendentalism."

His brethren presently invited Mr. Parker to a conference where the point at issue became very distinct.
"The difference between Trinitarianism and Unitarianism is a difference in Christianity," it was said: "the
difference between Mr. Parker and the Association is
a difference between no Christianity and Christianity."
To him "Christianity" meant Natural Religion: to
them it meant Natural Religion *plus* Christ's specific
revelation and authority *plus* miracles. Could these
additions be denied, and "Christian" fellowship maintained? They doubted. These at least seemed to be
part of the "fundamentals," to use the old term. In
view of the difference, would not Mr. Parker withdraw
from the Association, and save it from his compromising
presence? "Not while the world standeth!" They
might vote him out, and he would not complain; but
they had identified him in a measure with freedom in
religion, with rights of conscience, and therefore it was
his duty to remain, he said. So remain he did, for

neither would they banish; but his exchanges now were narrowed down to three or four.

The persistent brother went to Europe for a while, and there was peace. Two years passed. Then it came his turn once more to give the " Thursday Lecture." The little handful of the faithful usually in attendance on such occasions suddenly became a throng that filled the meeting-house. They heard a glowing tribute to the greatness of Jesus, but a clearer denial of that which made him "the Christ" than "First Church" had ever heard before. "Or ever should again at Thursday Lecture," said the Boston Association, consulting with the pastor. They remembered that in primitive times the Lecture had belonged to "First Church" only. What simpler than for the ministers, who had long been wont to serve the Lecture in regular rotation, to surrender its control to its ancient manager, the pastor, — he to invite whom he would to give it? The act was understood. They thus before the public freed themselves in a degree from Parker, without official excommunication and without defining "Christianity." The ministers-at-large employed by the "Benevolent Fraternity of Churches" had already been requested by its directors to withhold exchange from him. One of the number, John T. Sargent, as conscientious as themselves, preferred to yield them up their pulpit rather than his liberality. James Freeman Clarke's young "free church" lost some of its best men and women for similar independence on his part. Those who did not then deny the heretic to-day are "named and known by that hour's feat." Mr. Parker accepted the situation by publicly serving a catechism on the Association, and begging it to answer and tell the world what Unitarian Orthodoxy was. Meanwhile a few

friends had resolved " that Mr. Parker have a chance to
be heard in Boston." The chance was made. For nearly
fifteen years he was heard there, and his word went
forth in books freeing and freshening multitudes, until
the new thought grew familiar, and the name " Transcendental " was forgotten, and the old issues broadened
into larger ones, and the little Boston eddy was lost
in the current of the age. The Unitarians who refused
his presence felt his influence. As they went forward
in this, the third, stage of their history, they found his
footsteps where they passed, and many of them came to
feel that he had been their rough-mannered pioneer and
broken paths for them.

Again, as thirty years before at the crisis of the
second stage, the question rises, Was this rejection of
fellowship right or wrong?

It is true the Unitarians were doing somewhat as the
Orthodox had done to them against their protest; for,
although the heretic had not been formally excluded
from Unitarianism, he had been effectually disowned by
Unitarians, and on the score of opinions. True, it was
a limitation of their cherished principle of Free Inquiry,
of their old objection to creeds, of their constant stress
that character rather than belief gave title to the Christian name: all this is true. But then they had always
sincerely *meant* that limitation, without believing it to
be a limitation. The men of 1825 really founded their
Association not on one, but on two bases: (1) the method,
—Free Inquiry in Religion; and (2) the belief in a
supernatural revelation, to which the method led them.
At that time the former of the two received the emphasis, because therein, with reference to neighbor sects,
lay their chief reason for existence; but they were
associated by their Constitution to uphold and further

" Unitarian Christianity," and each and all of them, however else they might have defined " Unitarian Christianity," would have insisted that it was a system of revealed religion in the usual meaning of that term. In all sorts of ways, in lectures, sermons, prayers, in elaborate statements of their views, in pointed replies to Orthodox insinuations, they over and over reasserted this to be their faith. They certainly did not intend to associate themselves with Deists or with Theists. They did not in set phrase exclude, because no one ever thought of including, such men. Their two bases appeared to them as one. They deemed Unitarianism identical with Reason-in-Religion, because they believed that reason established past all doubt the revelation. And for some fifteen years the two continued to appear as one. Then came a man, who, following out their method, had been gradually led by it to give up their belief; and still he claimed to be like them, Christian and Unitarian. For the first time the fact of duality was forced upon their consciousness with the question, Which of the two, the method or the belief, was *the* fundamental ?

Neither party faced the question squarely. Parker distinctly maintained the method ; but he also tried to retain the names he loved, " Christian " and " Unitarian," by ignoring the belief and thus changing the meanings of those names. They who rejected him as distinctly maintained the second ; while by refusing to state this belief as the creed of their denomination, or to pass formal excommunication, they also tried, in turn, to be loyal to the principle they loved.

Was it possible for Parker's brethren to have accepted off-hand the new meanings, — on the moment to have shorn away the supernatural Messianic significance that

" Christianity " had always borne to the world and to themselves, brought all down to the simple moral essence of the Gospel, and, calling this at once Christianity and Absolute Religion as he did, have thus unified the two bases and avoided the difficulty? Such changes in meaning grow, they cannot be made in a twinkling or a year. That reconciliation might be sincerely effected — sincerely, that is, if openly avowed — by men thirty years later than they in reading and in thought, men like their children of to-day, or like Parker himself, as compared with most of them, in their own day; but not by them. It was no shibboleth-difference, — they were still on intellectual ground. There was a real conflict of ideas under the names, and they could not have said " Christian " with Parker or to him, and been honest.

Therefore they did right to disclaim his fellowship. Their mistake lay in thinking that men can associate on the method of Free Inquiry in religion *and* on some belief to which inquiry conducts them, — on both together, the one in its fulness, the other in its finality. A mistake it would seem, because the first is illimitable, while the other is professedly its limit. It is natural, inevitable, that beliefs, *i.e.* the results of truth-seeking, should contradistinguish and give names; but, as inevitably, Free Inquiry stays by no beliefs and of course by no names, as final, until the perfect truth be reached, — which who shall formulate? That principle, that method taken by itself furnishes no basis for a religious association of the common kind; but it suggests a new kind of religious association, a wide brotherhood, hardly to be understood at first by men used only to sects based on the beliefs.

Whether Parker, on the other hand, decided well or

ill, no " Broad-Churchman " ought to blame him save
for violence. The Broad-Churchman is found in all
denominations ; and everywhere his characteristic is to
keep connection with the past, as Parker tried to do, by
vesting old terms with new significance. But, where
earnest majorities protest, it may be doubted whether
this will always seem as noble or as needful a procedure
as it has hitherto been judged by Liberals. Some day
the principle of Free Inquiry will widely, genuinely,
permeate religious thinking : and then the dissenter will
not taunt old allies for not following him to his results,
nor will they charge him with setting up *autochthony ;*
and fresh names will probably fit themselves to fresh
growths of thought without involving wide severance of
fellowship, — that common principle uniting all. Until
that day, new thought brings, presently, the practical
disfellowship in spite of all reluctance. The process,
painful as it is, is nature's process to keep thought clear
and speech sincere. Thus it was in the previous phase
of Unitarianism. Now again a separation was beginning ; and, through the recognition of its need by the
clear-headed conservatives, growth was probably hastened.

With this new background to our picture, we turn
again to Mr. Gannett's life.

4 BUMSTEAD PLACE.

VIII.

MID-DAY: KEEPING THE FAITH.

1838–1852.

COUNTRY-NOOKS still nestled between brick walls in the heart of Boston in 1838. Near where the Music Hall now stands, a narrow niche set in from the noisy street, gate-guarded from it, whose one whole side was lined with vines and trees, while a deep recess at the end held a large garden. This was " Bumstead Place." Of the four or five houses thus sequestered, one was a strange rambling building of four links, half of it hidden in a great grape-vine. It was but one room deep, — but then it had three front doors, and one door had a knocker! Inside, it had a quaint and old-time aspect, too. High-perched on the staircase wall, an arched and cur-tained window opened into darkness: what mortal knew

that secret ? Above, a long dim garret stretched ; down-
stairs the best rooms kept the carved mantel-piece and
shining brasses round the fire-place.

Here Mr. Gannett made the new home, and found
the next few years the brightest, happiest, of his life.
For he was noting for the first time baby-chronicles ;
the community already knew and trusted him ; and he
had brought home health and that praise for eloquence
in London pulpits, — besides a large stock of brave resolves. No man more wise than he looks forward from
the ship : —

" I must observe some general principles, *e. g.* : —
 " To sleep seven or eight hours in every twenty-four.
 " To go to bed as soon after ten o'clock as possible.
 " To begin my sermon on Tuesday or Wednesday,
   and finish it before Friday night, so as —
 " To have Saturday for rest.
 " To take Thursday for recreation, lecture, riding, &c.
 " To make cheerfulness and enjoyment of life essen-
   tial duties.
 " To avoid anxiety and excitement."

How could he but be hopeful ? Only thirty-seven
years old, with the best working-years yet to come. The
restlessness of other minds made his religious thought
seem doubly clear and fixed, and this stability just then,
being matched with the gift of utterance, was still another element of influence. His pulse did not beat in
sympathy with the general fever of the time. In every
way he was steadying himself.

Feb. 26, 1839. " Offered prayer at the sixth Simultaneous
Meeting of Friends of Temperance in Marlboro' Chapel. On
the whole, my distrust of the value of such meetings was
confirmed. They nourish, as well as grow out of, a system

of *agitation;* they excite rather than inform the people.
There is more or less of deception and machinery about
them.   They belong to an artificial mode of sustaining truth
and virtue.   One is tempted to say things that he would not
utter in calmer scenes because his convictions do not support them; but here he is led away by his sympathies.   I
used language respecting the laws of the Commonwealth
which I very much regret, because, although abstractly true,
yet it must have been immediately applied to the late legislation on this subject, and would seem to express my approbation of a law and of measures the wisdom of which I
doubt."

Sept. 10, 1840. " Great Whig procession to Bunker Hill.
I felt less sympathy than before with the whole movement.
A great political question settled by excitement.   I did not
go to the Fair for the Monument, as I cannot approve of this
attempt to perpetuate the remembrance of bloodshed and
civil strife."

Suddenly, from out the clear sky fell a stroke !   Was
he a doomed man, after all ?   All the work had been
renewed ; but what meant the strange uneasiness, this
inability to write ?   The tell-tale Journal reveals the
fate of those " general principles : " —

" Wrote till one o'clock; slept in chair till three, then wrote
till six, Sunday, A.M., when I went to bed.   I am sorry, but
could hardly help it. . . . This writing sermons is slow
martyrdom, and extempore preaching now is almost as bad."

At last, in the summer, — the very first summer after
the return, — there came " the longest night I think I
ever passed ; " and the next entry, a fortnight later,
was written when he was rising from a shock of par-
alysis : —

" Dr. Bigelow thinks it had been slowly and secretly coming on, that my constitution does not seem to be injured by

it, and that the limb will probably recover its usual strength in the course of time. . . . I must be patient. It is such a discipline as I needed, full of trial for my character and instruction for my soul. . . . I certainly have abundant reason for gratitude, both that I have suffered so little, and that I am recovering so soon. People have sent and called continually."

Not till October could he write : —

" Yesterday was a red-letter day in my life, — the anniversary of my marriage, and the day of my resuming my ministerial duties, after an absence of eight Sundays from church."

But the escape was not so complete as he had hoped. The power of the right leg, except to suffer, was for ever gone. Henceforth a pair of canes, two short hand-crutches, were his life-companions. Their advent is recorded, and that is almost the only time they appear in the Journal. They became a part of him, the signal to eye and ear, by which every one knew " Dr. Gannett " in Boston streets. When in a hurry for the cars, and he always was, — or belated for the church service, as he often was, — his quick leaps between them, as he fled clicking along the sidewalks, used to make the boys turn and shout ; a tribute that he never seemed to notice. When he was at home, the canes were always in the corner: the empty corner told his absence. As a fixed condition of his life, the infirmity was far past complaint, or even thought. He would join the party up the mountain, or guide an English friend to the State House cupola, or follow the streets as long as most men and as fast. In truth, it seemed to have given him, rather than almost robbed him of, a limb.

The arrangement of a hymn-book for his Sunday School was one fruit of the confinement. On recovery,

the first deed was to reprint a little volume, that he
liked, on Woman's Mission. Then came an elaborate
tract on Atonement, which Nehemiah Adams courteously
answered in behalf of the Orthodox. " I should be glad
to reply to your letter, if it were only to show by my
example in concurrence with your own that Christian
ministers can discuss subjects of the deepest interest in
good temper," Mr. Gannett wrote to him.

That an unwonted life thrilled through the Unitarian
Churches about this time, has been already mentioned.
Plans were mooted to increase the number of professors
at the Divinity School, and send out missionaries to help
the feeble parishes. Not seldom, in the Ministers' Association, or the " Berry Street Conference," or on the
special committees, Mr. Gannett was the one to suggest,
always he was one to urge forward, such measures, and
sometimes with an eagerness that brought repentance.
" An earnest discussion, and I at last spoke with a freedom and warmth that I rather regret: it was not wise."
Often comes that confession. His own Bible classes
grew more interesting, new members joined the church,
there were weekly conversation-meetings among the
people, and in his vestry the ministers and laymen discussed together the questions, which now, as twenty
years before, moved others besides the theologians.

But his more special contribution to the revival was
the " Monthly Miscellany of Religion and Letters," and
courses of Sunday evening lectures on Unitarian and
Scriptural Christianity. By January, 1840, in his first
limping days, he had undertaken the care of the magazine, — an infant that had been orphaned of its father
after one year of existence. It was designed to furnish
religious reading for the people, treat Unitarian opinions
in their practical bearings, and show their power to pro-

duce holiness of life ; and by weight of contents to
come between the weekly " Register" and the " Christian Examiner." Besides writing his articles, the editor
took special pains with the department of Religious
Intelligence, spending on it and grudging to it much
time and labor, — thanks to which it remains a chronicle
of worth for the exciting years that followed.

Lectures had lately become a very popular instrument of culture in Boston, four or five courses sometimes going on at once. In their limited field, Mr.
Gannett's corresponded to Dr. Walker's famous series
on Natural Religion, to Emerson's addresses, and Parker's five discourses. The church was filled to over-
flowing, aisles and pulpit-stairs, by listeners listening
two hours long. People suffered themselves to be
locked into the church at the close of the afternoon
service, to be sure of a good seat in the evening ; and
ministers, now gray-headed, then students in the Divinity School, remember their eager walks over Cambridge
bridge to hear the eloquent speaker of Federal Street.
He used to enter the pulpit with topics carefully laid
out and texts arranged, perhaps with his arms full of
books ; then, giving himself up to the themes, that were
at once those of his science and his faith, he would
speak on and on in a rapid flow of exegesis, criticism,
argument, and appeal. The people, musing, wondering,
groping for light as they were, welcomed the clear and
glowing statements. They were probably the last systematic expositions of " old-fashioned Unitarianism "
that won enthusiastic hearing in the city where its New
England disciples were first called by the name.

In spite of the crowded houses, the lectures by no
means satisfied the lecturer. The note in the Journal
was usually a word of disparagement: "Not fluent ; "

" Had not sufficiently laid up the topics, so was too dependent on my notes ; " " Used harsher language about other sects than I ought." Of the discourse on " Jesus Christ, the Mediator," he writes: —

"Lectured two hours and twenty minutes: on the whole was satisfied, excepting with the length and with some remarks at the close, which seemed like rhetorical flourish. The mistake of length arose from my attempt to give a thorough examination to the Orthodox texts, instead of making a selection from them. And yet I doubt if I did not adopt the better plan. I had finished this part of the lecture at the close of the first hour and half; but, had I stopped there, I should have left only a negative impression of what we did *not* believe : I preferred to go on, and leave as full a *positive* impression as I could. This obliged me, however, to be very rapid in the latter part. The audience were wonderfully attentive: very few went out. The house was entirely full."

But if the people did not go out, the lamps did : —

" May I, as the representative of many hundreds, beg of you to shorten your lectures? Their length has regularly increased on each successive evening from the beginning. The audience make no complaint on their own account, — nobody leaves the church, though hundreds were there upwards of four hours last Sunday evening, as I can personally attest; but we have the *most serious apprehensions for you.* Some inconvenience arises too from the failing of the lamps: they do not hold oil enough for so long a time, and four of them went out last Sunday evening."

Before the next winter gas had been introduced to meet the emergency that friends expected would recur.

The good parish voted him relief in the spring after these lectures ; but it could not be thought of then, and the sessions of the " Pierpont Council " ran far into the

summer (1841). Rev. John Pierpont, of the Hollis
Street Church, had been too uncompromising a reformer
to be good pastor, thought some of his flock; while
others stood by him as the bold champion of temperance and anti-slavery and the liberty of the pulpit. At
last by mutual consent the difficulty was referred to a
council, and the brother-ministers were summoned to
their thankless task. Because laborious and thankless,
Mr. Gannett believed they had no right to shrink while
a possibility existed of healing the torn parish. The
council exonerated Pierpont in the main, — not wholly,
for his tone and spirit had been sharp. Therefore the
decision satisfied neither party. Theodore Parker,
reviewing it in the "Dial," called it "a piece of diplo-
macy worthy of a college of Jesuits," — a piece of injustice to one at least that was keenly felt. Once engaged,
no one had been more anxious than Mr. Gannett to
effect successful mediation ; and the thick manuscript of
notes and details attests the conscientious painstaking
of his verdict. A slur thrown on his honesty of motive
always wounded him more deeply than any possible
condemnation of his deed.

At last in the autumn he escaped, tired enough, to the
White Mountains, and on to Trenton Falls, where some
dear friends lived who had brought their quaint names
and liberal faith from Holland. Trenton was a favorite spot. Again and again his journeying feet turned
thither for the welcome. At the Notch he writes : —

"I should not send an atheist or an irreligious person here
for religious impression. The scene is not majestic and
wild so much as desolate. Desolation and ruin are the
images these mountains leave upon the mind. They would
not humanize. They spoke to me of a cruel or gloomy

rather than a paternal God. The silence, however, of the
Notch this evening was impressive. The stillness and release from bustle, excitement, and constant *something-to-do,*
which I have enjoyed the last three days, have been exquisite.
They have given me a peculiar feeling of happiness, complete in itself, and yet composed of this one sense of freedom
from noise and toil."

After describing the ascent of Mount Washington, he
adds : —

"I was almost in despair before I reached the stage-road.
I doubt if I had mounted a horse before for four years, since,
indeed, I rode through the mountains of Westmoreland.
But a night's sleep, — oh, what virtues there are in rest
and sleep! Tell me that there is no indication of a Providence in life! There are more proofs of an infinite wisdom
and a paternal care exercised towards man in a single night's
rest than in all the grandeur of this mountain range. . . .
Crawford talks seriously of making a carriage-road from his
house to the foot of Mount Washington. It can doubtless
be done."

" A very pleasant journey," he says of it, on reaching
home, — " such a one as I wished, exercise of body and
rest of mind ; been gone just three weeks, and had fresh
proof of the goodness which crowns every day of my life."

But the work had, after all, gone with him. When
the wagon broke down in Franconia, out came the ink-
bottle to write " copy for the magazine." And, once at
home again, the engagements began to click into each
other like wheel-work from morning to late night. The
sermon-habit held full sway. Now and then two sermons came between the Saturday and Sunday supper-
times. This was the kind of toil which, with his two
canes, made him look already old. In one of the
mountain-taverns he had been greeted, " A smart, active

man for your age, sir!"— "How old do you suppose?"
— "I should say, fifty."— "Just forty." And the
kind of toil which was *making* him old. The next
winter's course of lectures was not over when the wife's
hand comes among the Journal-pages to record: "April
6. Sick. Dr. Bigelow six times and Dr. Jackson once."
A second quick, sharp warning, probably of the same
nature as before; and another two months went by
before he preached again.

In October of this year (1842) word came to Boston
from the country, — Dr. Channing is dead!

For eighteen years they had been joined in labor and
love for the one parish. Unlike as they were, few
friends could claim a closer nearness to his great associate than Mr. Gannett. It was his privilege now to be
the first to offer those tributes to the mind, the character, the spiritual insight, the life-giving influence, which
were uttered in so many sorrowing churches of both
the Englands, as the tidings reached them. As the
after-years went by, it was his delight to bring fresh
reverence to Channing's memory. Time and again, in
sermon and lecture, and once by special service of
remembrance, he caught anew the young man's attitude,
to speak his gratitude and keep the name a living inspiration in the church. The last sermon in the old
meeting-house and the "Fortieth Year's Sermon" but re-
echo what he said on the first Sunday of loneliness: —

1842. "After my connection with this society, he encouraged me in every plan I undertook, welcomed every sign of
increasing sympathy and energy among us, and cheered me
under every occasion of despondency. How often would my
spirit have wholly sunk within me, if he had not animated
me to new struggle with the discouragement of my own
heart!"

1864. " During Dr. Channing's life I knew that no mistake of mine could seriously affect the interests of the congregation.   On his forbearance I now look back with amazement."

In his magazine he also gathered up in three long articles the choicest words of others' reverence.   And, when the autumn came again, he made a pilgrimage to the spots in which Dr. Channing spent his last days.

October, 1843. " I have all summer, indeed for a year, wished to visit Lenox and Bennington this season, that I might place my mind more immediately in the midst of associations connected with Dr. Channing. . . . I am in Lenox, writing in the chamber occupied by him, delightfully situated, looking towards the south and west over hills and vales, with a little lake in the midst of the scene.   It is now rich in beauty from the autumn foliage; and I can understand how in summer he must have enjoyed the deep verdure, the graceful forms of the mountains and cultivated fields blended in one landscape, which he looked upon from the bosom of this quiet village. . . . Miss Sedgwick showed me a letter which Dr. Channing wrote to her from here that summer, full of playful sentiment, unlike any thing of his I ever saw before.   They told me of his great spirits while here, his high enjoyment of nature and a singular freedom of manners, and even extreme mirth, of his unusual health, too, up to the very time of his leaving.   He does not seem to have made much impression upon the people here, out of the Sedgwick family.   The landlord showed only that he knew an eminent man had been in his house."

At Bennington. " I am now writing in the room in which Dr. Channing died.   What scenes of life and death have hallowed it, — of true spiritual life, and of physical death. I *must* become a better man from my enjoyment of the privileges of his acquaintance and character.   Let it not be my condemnation that I have had such great blessings."

The ministers of the early day of Unitarianism were now fast passing, one by one, from sight. Dr. Tuckerman and Dr. Follen had gone two years before their friend; Greenwood and the younger Henry Ware followed him closely after. Mr. Gannett said the last prayer over Dr. Tuckerman, and from Ware's bedside bore to the brethren the good-by: —

"How glad I am that I went up to see him, and what a privilege has his friendship been to me! How richly have I been favored in the acquaintance of such men as Mr. Ware, Dr. Channing, Dr. Follen, Dr. Tuckerman, — such as I never expect to see again!"

He himself, now forty-two years old, was beginning to be counted among the elders and established leaders of the denomination. His parish-work was hardly greater than before the vanishing, but more demand for outside service came. He preached the "Election Sermon" of 1842, noting, "I had taken pains in preparing and in writing it, and am satisfied from the result that I cannot preach more than pretty well." The next year he gave the Dudleian Lecture at the College,— a clear statement of the relations of Natural to Revealed Religion, as he conceived them: —

"Let me attempt to enclose the result to which we have come within a single sentence. It shall be this. Natural Religion, by teaching the being and perfection of God, lays an indispensable and sufficient foundation for Revealed Religion; by its inability to teach more it renders Revelation both acceptable and probable; and by hints that it affords, which become available to any purpose of instruction only after the entrance of Revelation into the world, it confirms and expands the teachings which come through this latter source."

Harvard now conferred the title which will henceforth make his name sound more familiar in our story : —

Aug. 23, 1843. "To-day I received the degree of D.D. from Harvard University. In all honesty it makes me feel ashamed, when I think how little I deserve it. How do circumstances determine a man's visible position in the community, rather than his merits! Here are hundreds of men who are far more worthy than I to receive such a diploma; while I, who am altogether destitute of the learning or the character which might entitle me to it, receive it because I happen to be settled in Boston and to have been once the minister of President Quincy."

With such feelings, no doubt he hesitated before giving up the humbler magazine to assume joint charge with Dr. Lamson of the "Christian Examiner." For a while, indeed, he had a hand in both, till Frederic Huntington took the former wholly to himself, christening it anew "Monthly Religious Magazine." Through five years (January, 1844 — May, 1849) the regular Thursday formula in the Journal reads, "On the Examiner with Dr. Lamson;" and the study on that day became proof against the children's noise. Of his own contributions, which rarely exceeded three or four a year, several were upon the denomination in its various aspects. The most noticeable of all was an article on Theodore Parker and Transcendentalism.

These were the years in which that mysterious *ism* excited such curiosity and alarm in Unitarian circles. Few were sturdier in opposing it than Dr. Gannett, and few among the opponents more ready with justice to its friends. He was wary of "intuitions." What *was* this peering "consciousness," this "higher reason," that

seemed like feeling trying to play the rôle of intellect
while decrying intellectual processes and outcomes?
His own reason led him through plain processes of the
understanding to profound convictions clearly outlined:
at the same time he had the enthusiastic temper seldom
found with thought so logically fashioned, and absolute
sincerity of speech. No wonder, then, that his voice
was as strenuous against the "new views" as it had
been strenuous for the previous heresy. Rather wonder
if it had not been so. He had done his best to establish Unitarianism against the Orthodox attack; and now,
valuing that faith not merely as a result of free inquiry
in religion, but as the true result, the very truth itself,
he faced about with the same loyalty to *keep* the faith
against this fresh denial.

Signs in the Journal indicate what is going on. He
demurs a little at Dr. Channing's apparent leaning: —

Dec. 22, 1839. "Dr. Channing preached in the morning on
'religion a moral exercise of the mind,' — illustrated principally by remarks on the views we should entertain of God;
on the proper ground of worship and obedience, as not
being the sovereignty, but the moral character, 'of the
Divinity.' Dr. C. maintained that conscience is the foundation of piety, and 'the voluntary subjection of God to a
law of rectitude' its justification. I did not like the sermon.
It seemed to me to be based on the unsound philosophy that
morality is, in theory at least, independent of the divine will,
instead of being, as it is, nothing but an expression of this
will; and to be suited to do harm rather than good at the
present time, when *among us* loose notions concerning the
divine personality and government are so prevalent. As
an exposure of Calvinistic *superstition*, it was valuable; but
Dr. C.'s statements needed qualification. The close of the
sermon, in which he spoke, on the other hand, of attributing
to God an indulgent fondness, was excellent."

Jan. 5, 1840. "Dr. Channing preached a sermon of uncommon power, but of doubtful utility, in defence and illustration of the doctrine that the glory of Christianity consists not in any thing peculiar to itself, but in what it has in common with the teachings 'of reason and nature;' its most important truths, — *e.g.*, the being and unity of God, human immortality, and the presence and aid of the Divine Spirit, — being only clearer declarations of what had been whispered by these other teachers. Even the character of Christ and the character of God, Dr. C. thought, were excellent and glorious rather for what they had in common with other good beings than for any attribute which they alone possessed. The discourse was powerful and bold; but, without more qualification than Dr. C. introduced, I doubt if it was not suited to do more harm than good."

Here is another glimpse of the Boston Association in council : —

Dec. 9, 1839. "Walked to Association at Ripley's, and home in evening. One of the best meetings I ever attended. Present: Dr. Peirce, Frothingham, Parkman, Young, Capen, Ripley, Bartol, C. Robbins, Sargent, Hall of Dorchester, Hall of Providence, Everett of Northfield, Dwight, Lothrop, and I, — 15. Discussion began at $6\frac{1}{2}$, and continued without any pause till $9\frac{1}{4}$; Ripley, Frothingham, Bartol, and I taking the greater part, with occasional remarks from Parkman, Dwight, Capen, Lothrop, Young, and Hall of Providence. Subject, the comparative value of external authority, *i. e.* an outward revelation, and the inward judgment, whether founded on 'instinct,' reason, or experience. The discussion was singularly free and candid, calm but earnest, with variety of opinion, but with great harmony of feeling. Ripley expressed himself with more caution than I had expected. With such explanations and qualifications as he made, his views would do no harm; for he attaches great value to an outward revelation, speaks with the greatest gratitude of

Christ, and says we can never do without him, and, as I understand him, he does not believe in any suggestions of religious truth by our own nature which can afford ground of reliance. The revelation, — Christ, — he says, comes and awakens a consciousness, produces a faith, which becomes more and more experience; and the Christian, as he goes on, relies more on this experience than on any external authority for the justification of his faith. Dwight went farther in his statements than Ripley, and seemed to me to enter the region of indistinctness and error. It was throughout a pleasant and profitable evening."

And here the whole body of **Unitarian ministers** in the great Anniversary Week : —

May 27, 1840. "Berry Street Conference: did not get there till Mr. Damon had nearly finished, on miracles as an evidence of the truth of Christianity. Room full. Discussion on 'new views,' and the treatment which they, by whom they were professed, received; the speaking principally by the New-School men, — Ripley, who was very earnest and spoke very well, Stetson, Osgood, &c. I replied to Ripley and he to me upon the point of injustice, that it was mutual. Throughout it was a fair and kind, though warm discussion."

The meeting adjourned to the next day "for farther conversation on New and Old School; good attendance and good discussion. It has done good I am sure, made us understand one another better, and produced more instead of less harmony of feeling."

That evening "I had a very interesting conversation with George Ripley on his views, feelings, and situation. Talked there nearly an hour, and then walked home and talked here a little while. He expressed himself with entire frankness, and our conversation was to me most pleasant. He is uncomfortable in his present situation, is dissatisfied with the present religious and social institutions, and contemplates a change in his own mode of action; would like to preach freely, as did Brownson, or rather as Fox in London. He seems to me to be fond of a class of terms which he thinks denote important and neglected truths, but which are either symbols of error, or only peculiar forms of expressing familiar ideas. He considers himself in relation to his present views 'the child of Dr. Channing,' and says his faith is now, after ten years' study of theology, as firm as a rock."

April 21, 1841. "Parker of Roxbury here for an hour, talking about religious state of the community, and differences of theological opinion; liked him very much."

A month later Parker gave the famous ordination sermon at South Boston, on "The Transient and the Permanent in Christianity." Mr. Gannett was present, taking notes for the account in the magazine. The account won protest from the preacher, to the amazement of the reporter, who thought he had done little but quote Parkerisms: —

"MY GOOD BROTHER GANNETT, — . . . Your report of my poor sermon bears to my mind but few of the marks of truth which I have always so much admired in you. Don't fancy, however, I dream that you *thought of* misrepresenting me. I would not believe it, though an angel told me. I do not wonder at the treatment the sermon has met, though certainly I expected it would make no noise or stir. If I ever wrote any thing with a Christian zeal, it was that very discourse.   I remain very affectionately

       "Your Christian brother,

           "THEODORE PARKER."

Of the autumn lectures, therefore, which followed, interpreting the sermon, the reporter showed his notice, and altered it, according to the lecturer's suggestion, before sending it to press. Mr. Parker's vigor, heartiness, sincerity, and bold rebukes of selfishness were

praised, but not " the boldness, rather than the patience " and fairness, of his criticism : " he is certainly
not the representative of Unitarian opinions, and should
not be so considered, he would probably say, in justice
to himself, — we as decidedly say, in justice to them."

The previous chapter told how the excitement spread,
how the Boston Association of Ministers discussed the
plan of dissolution, in order to avoid exclusion, and how
they held a special conference with Parker, — a conference of which this was the close, in Parker's words :
" At last, a little before nine, Bartol spoke in praise of
my sincerity, which some had called in question, spoke
many words of moral approbation ; so likewise did
Gannett at length, and with his usual earnestness.
Then Chandler Robbins opened his mouth to the same
purpose. I burst into tears, and left the room." Two
years later, when Parker had been to Europe and
returned more zealous than ever for a reformation, and
in the Thursday Lecture had given omen of his zeal, the
question of fellowship again arose in the Association.
The younger members generally felt obliged to accept
the odium he brought on them, as one of the inconveniences of liberality, and would pass no vote of censure. Of the older members, Dr. Gannett, it is said,
was the only one, save Mr. Pierpont, who did not think
it necessary to exclude him from their communion by
some kind of action. To publish a simple disclaimer of
Parker's opinions, he thought would be right and would
be enough : the wisdom of even this course he apparently had doubted until now. He was one of the
committee of three delegated to hold a second interview
with the great embarrasser. " From ten A.M. to
four P.M." of a winter's day it lasted, in the house in
Bumstead Place. " Dined here," the Journal adds ;

and no doubt the talk kept right on across the table in the little dining-room. But no good was done. Parker soon wrote him : —

"I am sorry for the Association, but I cannot help it : I cannot take the *onus damnandi* on my shoulders. It would be to avow that there is good cause for my withdrawal. By their course towards Mr. Sargent, they have forced me to come to Boston to preach every Sunday morning. They have in a measure identified me with freedom in religious matters."

It was the moment of final break between the Radical and the Unitarians. There was much excitement. Several pamphlets passed to and fro, and among them Dr. Gannett's article on " Mr. Parker and his Views " appeared in the "Examiner" for March, 1845. It shows the character as much as it shows the thought of the writer. In part from this article, in part from two or three other sources, earlier and later, we extract his criticism of the intuition-theory set over against the evidence on which his own mind relied, and his opinion of the true " Unitarian " course to be pursued towards the disturber of the faith. Whether the intellectual position be accepted or rejected, here are the clear conceptions, the frank intent, the conscientious justice, both to his own belief and its opponent, for which all who ever knew him were wont to give him credit : —

Is Mr. Parker a Christian ? — " The real question we conceive to be a question concerning the foundations of faith. Why shall we believe religious truths? on this turns the controversy; not, what are religious truths? The historical facts of religion are, in strictness of speech, its proofs rather than its truths. . . . The distinction is important in view of the present controversy.

" For, adopting this distinction, we do not understand that

Mr. Parker denies the Christian truths. On the contrary, he both recognizes and insists on them, makes them prominent and authoritative, and calls for faith in them as just and essential to the true life. The doctrines not only of the divine government and providence, but of immortality and retribution; the paternal character of God, the fraternal relations of mankind, the great principles of love to God and love to man; the absolute importance of righteousness, and this not a righteousness of external propriety, but of the whole character, — universal and thorough rectitude, such as is seen only where there is fidelity to all our obligations and destinies; in a word, the authority of the law of duty as expounded by Christ, — all these points we understand to be as heartily believed by the one party as the other in this controversy. So far as they are concerned, he whose course has given so much pain to his brethren is a Christian believer; and, so far as the inculcation of these truths is concerned, he is most certainly a Christian teacher.

"But he denies the correctness of the grounds on which these truths are generally received as authoritative; and he presents other grounds of faith which we believe to be altogether insufficient for the purpose. He denies the miraculous character of Christianity. He denies that Jesus was sent upon a special mission in any other sense than that in which any other great or good man has a mission to perform, growing out of the exigencies of the time in which he lives and the .capacities with which he is endowed. He denies the inspiration of Jesus in any other sense than that in which it may be shared by any one of our race, — the same in kind with what we all have, and differing in degree only according to the larger natural endowment and moral or spiritual development of the individual. He denies the miraculous narratives of the New Testament, and holds them to be the exaggerations of an admiring but poorly enlightened faith. The resurrection even of our Lord he rejects from among the facts which he can believe, and

represents the Gospels as the most singular compound of
the true and the false that the literature or the religion of
any period of the world has ever known. It is plain, then,
that so far as faith in the supernatural mission of Christ, or
in the historical record of his life, is concerned, Mr. Parker
is not a Christian believer.

"And yet he may be a Christian man; that is to say, he
may have received from Christianity influences which he is
too slow to acknowledge, that have made him a pious and
upright follower of the Master from whom he withholds this
title. It may be a speculative, rather than a practical, denial
of Christ's authority which we observe in him ; and, notwith-
standing the instability of the foundations on which his faith
rests, he may cherish as strong a conviction as we of the
reality of the Christian truths, and draw from them the
strength and beauty of character which mark a true disciple." . . .

He rebukes the frequent lightness and sarcasm of
Parker's language where the religious sensibilities of
others are concerned, but does "not doubt that in the
jealous state of feeling which has been awakened a
great deal has been imputed to him which was never in
his heart or mind ; " and then calmly states at some
length the chief objections to his views. Those views
directly impugn the fact of the special revelation, they
undervalue its contents and its influence, they deprive
us of the only sufficient means of authenticating it, they
even make worthless all historic testimony whatever,
costing us the words as well as the deeds of Jesus ;
while "the theory of the intuitive perception, by mankind, of the nature and authority of absolute truth or
absolute religion, we hold to be purely a theory ; and,
for the support of our opinion, we appeal where he
makes his appeal, to consciousness and fact." . . .

Miracle and Intuition. — " In the modern scepticism as to the truth of the miracles, we have not so much to meet the shafts of the infidel as the doubts of those who sincerely adhere to our own religion. And it seems to me that this same controversy as to the real nature of miracles must of necessity be prosecuted for ages to come, as it has been for ages back. The very constitution of some minds inclines them to receive with ready faith what another class would reject as entirely inconclusive. . . .

" A divine revelation is a special interposition, essentially and intrinsically a miracle. It was requisite to save the world from utter ruin. And it was given. But, again, individual miracles were necessary in order to prove the authenticity of the revelation, — that it did indeed come from heaven. A miracle is the only sufficient seal of the divine character of a mission. No other evidence which may be adduced bears that peculiar stamp which can be impressed only by the hand of God. On what else can you rely for the proof of the divine attribute? Do you say on the *internal character* of such mission or revelation or doctrine. Why, then, were not the truths promulgated by the heathen sages, their excellent lessons of morality, their conjectures of a future state, — why were they not regarded and received as truths? They all commended themselves to the minds of men: why did not men embrace them, and lean upon them as on a staff which could not be broken? Because something more than all this was necessary to render them authentic, — to give to them authority.

" In more enlightened ages it has been said that our spiritual or *religious instincts* are sufficient to impress on us the truths of Christianity. ' The mind instinctively perceives truth; cannot mistake and cannot reject it; but confesses its authority and rejoices in its divinity.' To talk of spiritual or religious *instincts* in this sense is an abuse of the term. If there be any one peculiarity which, more than all others, attaches to the idea of instinct, it is that this quality is

15

always certain, definite, precise in its operation. It causes
just one thing to be done, and no other. Again, it is incapable of progress. It induces the immediate performance
of a particular act at the moment, it cannot extend to the
future. But the idea of religious instinct must necessarily
be different from this. It must include the law of progress,
which we suppose to apply to all spiritual things." . . .

"What are our *intuitions?* The persuasions of truth
which we entertain, that are not derived from a foreign
source, nor through a process of reflection. . . . I am doubtful of the merit of these intuitive perceptions. They may be
beautiful angels hovering over us and guiding us upward to
heavenly truth, but they float around us in so heavy a cloud
of mist that their forms can hardly be discerned. . . . With
each of us, of course, these persuasions, as they may be entertained, have authority. But how do we know that they are
not erroneous? That they often are erroneous is shown by
the fact that different persons entertain opposite persuasions,
each of them alleging intuitive perception of the truth; and
by the farther fact that the same person in the course of his
life will change the persuasions which for a long time he may
have held on this kind of evidence. Intuitions, whatever
they ought to be according to the theory, are not in experience invariable. . . . Besides this, it is next to impossible,
in the human mind, to separate what are called intuitions
from the ideas and habits of thought produced by education,
early association, and the influences of society. . . . In fact,
the language with which many persons are captivated is de-
ceptive. The three fundamental ideas of which it is said the
soul is conscious are God, the moral law, and immortality.
Yet the soul can only be conscious of its own exercises
and of its present state. Its faith in God, or in immortality,
or even in duty, can be nothing more than an inference
from certain facts of which it is cognizant, and which it
brings together in such a manner as to deduce from them a
result with which it is satisfied; so that its knowledge or

persuasion of the highest truths is secured through a process of reasoning, not through the affirmation of an intuitive faculty. . . .

"If we trust to intuitive evidence for our religious convictions, we shall find that it is too much like building our anticipations of the weather upon the signs of the sky. A few signs God has put there for the help of our judgment, and to a certain extent they are useful; yet how differently will they be read by different observers! . . . History lends but little support to the intuitive philosophy. Collectively, the human race has shown an inaptitude to discover or retain the great religious truths. Still less encouragement, if possible, does a study of individual experience furnish; for but few men perceive the handwriting of God on the walls of their own spiritual being, or evolve eternal truth from their own mental conceptions. . . .

"Our age has gone too far on this path of a transcendental philosophy. That certain fundamental or elementary truths of religion find their sanction either in ultimate facts of our being, or in processes of the most rigid reasoning, or in both, we do not deny. The existence and perfection of God, for instance, must be proved before we can begin to think of a revelation from Him. But all religious truth which it is important that we should know cannot be discovered by means of the reasoning or the intuitive faculty. There are great truths which must be *revealed*, before we can receive them with an entire confidence. They present themselves to the mind as conjectures, probabilities, hopes, till they are incorporated into our positive belief by the force of external testimony. Mr. Parker makes religious faith to rest upon three classes of facts, — facts of necessity, of consciousness or intuition, and of demonstration. Now the facts of necessity do not embrace all the wants of the soul; for that God should be merciful to the extent which our situation demands, cannot be regarded as a fact or 'truth of necessity.' Neither is the doctrine of Divine forgiveness included among the facts of consciousness or intuition. Nor yet among the facts of demonstration, 'for these are such as follow by way of inference from the two other classes; and where there are no premises, there can be no inferences. Upon this momentous doctrine of the Gospel therefore, if the Gospel had not spoken, we should have had no sufficient ground of faith. . . . In regard, again, to the purpose and results of the present life, it is Christianity which expounds these in such a manner as satisfies the anxious inquiries of the soul. Men indeed believed in immortality before Christ appeared to give them instructions, but their faith was either unsteady in its character or material in respect to the objects of its contemplation. Men may now collect arguments for belief in a future life from the domains of philosophy, but they forget how much the force of such arguments upon their minds depends on the influence which Christianity has insensibly exerted over their judgments and associations ever since their birth. Those persons who speak of Christian truths as necessary parts of human belief, when the spiritual nature of man has reached a certain stage of progress, overlook the part which Christianity has borne in bringing *them* to this stage."

" The inference, then, which we must draw, is that religion is an altogether distinct thing from an intuitive perception of certain religious truths. What we want in religion is *certainty,* — moral, not reasoning or mathematical certainty, but the highest degree of certainty which can apply to moral doctrines. Therefore what we want to believe in regard to the teachings of Jesus is that they were of absolute authority, and not matters of reasoning or inference. The assurance of this we have in his own language. He does not say, ' Thus it is said,' but ' I say unto you,' — a positive distinct enunciation of what he wishes to declare. We must rest upon miracles, because there is nothing else, no other authority in the nature of things, on which we can base our reliance in Christianity as an institution from Heaven. To every sensible Christian man, as we conceive, they must be the strong, im-

movable, imperishable prop of his belief, the foundation rock
on which his faith in Christ, as a teacher sent from God,
must be built. Without them the religious truths which we
embrace lose their character of certainty, their value as the
stand on which we plant our faith and from which our minds
derive hope and the assurances of peace."

How should Mr. Parker be treated by Unitarians? —
"Let him be treated as any other propagator of what are
deemed erroneous and injurious opinions should be treated.
Shall he be persecuted? No. Calumniated? No. Put
down? No; if by this phrase be signified the use of any
other than fair and gentle means of curtailing his influence.
Shall he be silenced, or be tolerated? Not tolerated: for
the exercise of toleration implies the right to restrain the
expression of opinion by force; but the validity of such a
right cannot be admitted in this country, and should not
be allowed in the Christian Church. Nor silenced, unless
open argument and paternal persuasion may reduce him to
silence. But, on the other hand, he should not be encouraged
nor assisted in diffusing his opinions by those who differ
from him in regard to their correctness. No principle of
liberality or charity can require any one to aid in the diffusion of what he accounts error, especially if he think it
pernicious error. Neither directly nor indirectly may he,
in justice to his own persuasions, promote the purposes of
another who wishes to divert public confidence from those
persuasions. We cannot understand that impartiality of
mind which is as desirous that one opinion as another should
be brought before the community. . . . If Mr. Parker had
confined himself to the inculcation of his positive opinions,
silence might then have been the only needed intimation of
dissent. . . . But so long as he considers it his duty to under-
mine the foundations on which the faith of the multitude
rests, and justly rests, so long do we conceive it is both
proper and incumbent upon those who differ from him to
express their difference in frank and strong terms.

"In similar terms, we say, let him speak who espouses opinions which we consider untrue and dangerous. He holds *our* views to be untrue and harmful. Let him say so. But let not silence be imposed on us, whilst the freest speech is claimed for him. . . . Christian liberality let no one neg· lect to cherish in himself, and Christian liberty let no on* attempt to wrest from another.

"Cases may possibly arise in the application of these prin ciples which will present some difficulty. Is not the liberty of him who is placed under any kind of exclusion violated, it is asked, and are not the principles of Christian liberality disregarded, when the pulpits of other ministers are closed against him? We think not. . . . By withholding from our neighbor the opportunity of using our pulpit for the propaga- tion of what we regard as error, we merely say that we con- sider it error, and do not wish to help in its diffusion; and this we may say, and ought to say, not only indirectly by such an act, but in the most direct and unequivocal terms. Our neighbor doubtless expresses elsewhere the same opinion respecting our discourses; and, if he is an honest man, he will be very likely to express his opinion in our pulpit. There are those who think it is as well that people should some- times listen to what is unsound in doctrine. We are not of this way of thinking, for we believe that truth is always better than error; and, to repeat the familiar but pertinent remark, what each man accounts the truth stands to him as the absolute truth, and demands from him the same loyal ser- vice, and therefore we esteem it a minister's duty to present to his people, not only in his own preaching, but also through him he may introduce into his pulpit, what he himself believes, and not what he disbelieves. If we are wrong in this decision, all that can be charged upon us is timidity, not exclusiveness.

"But it is contended that this is receding from the ground taken by the denomination to which we belong nearly thirty years ago, when the division arose between the Orthodox

and the Unitarian portions of the Congregational Church
in this Commonwealth. Possibly it is. We think, however,
that the ground of complaint against the Orthodox at that
time for refusing to exchange with Unitarians was that they
considered us as denying what was essential to salvation,
and therefore regarded our teaching as not only unsound,
but fatal. We remonstrated against this as a judgment altogether too harsh, and therefore maintained that the separation which it induced was unrighteous. . . . But we do not
remember that we have ourselves ever felt any disposition to
complain of Trinitarian ministers for excluding us from their
pulpits. We certainly should not seek an exchange with a
Unitarian, if we believed in the Trinity. We do not desire
an exchange now with one who accepts that doctrine, for we
have no wish to convert the Christian pulpit into the arena of
a gladiatorial theology. . . . Our present system is best suited
both to promote the improvement of the congregations and
to preserve kindly feelings among the clergy.

"Some persons, verging to the other extreme, demand
much more than the exclusion from their pulpits, by his
brethren, of him who makes it his object to spread what they
deem false and hurtful opinions. They require that he be
cast out from the professional sympathies of those with whom
he has been associated, and that a rebuke be administered
to him by some formal act of the denomination to which he
has been considered as belonging. . . . Is it said, as a reason
for such action, that the denomination are responsible for the
opinions advanced by one of their number, unless they subject him to rebuke or separate him from their society? Yes,
it is said; and by whom? By those who know that from
the first we have disclaimed responsibleness for each other's
opinions, and denied, in the most emphatic terms, the justice of holding us under such a responsibleness. . . . It is
not our way to pass ecclesiastical censure. We are willing
— at least, we have said we were willing — to take the principle of free inquiry with all its consequences. There never

was a principle yet, intrusted to men's use, which has not been carried to extravagant results. The principle of phil-anthropy, — of what follies and mischiefs has it been made the occasion! The very fact that for months the Unitarians have been urged from without and from within to denounce or renounce Mr. Parker, and yet have not found out how to do it, shows that it is strange work for them."

"That in our own number should be found those who com-plain because Mr. Parker has not been publicly censured, does greatly surprise us. . . . We have neither hierarchy nor synod to arrange the difficulties of such a case ; and, serious as we felt them to be, we have never for a moment regretted our independence of such means of abating a heresy. Much has been said because the Boston Association of ministers did not expel Mr. Parker, or, at least, publish some disavowal of his opinions. But expulsion of a member for not thinking with his brethren, however wrong his way of thinking, and however pernicious the influence of his teaching may be in their eyes, is not an act which that Association contemplate among their privileges or their duties ; nor do they come together to draw up statements of belief, either for their own benefit or for the satisfaction of others. All that they could consistently do was to express to Mr. Parker their indi-vidual views, and set before him, in free and friendly con-versation, the inconsistency of his course in continuing to exercise the functions of a Christian minister while he rejected the main facts of the Christian Scriptures. And this they did. They had no authority to depose him from his place, or cast him out from their company. They neither felt nor showed indifference in the case. They acted with firmness, and with justice alike to him and to themselves, to the cause of Christian truth and the cause of religious freedom. Others may see in this a proof of the wretched effects of Unitarianism ; but we are willing that Unitarianism should stand or fall by the judgment which an unbiassed observer, who understood the merits of the case, should pass upon the course pursued towards Mr. Parker by his brethren." . . .

" That it is a painful and anxious time through which we are passing, we do not attempt to conceal from ourselves or from others. The question at issue, as we conceive, is not what shall be the character of the popular faith, but shall our people have any faith whatever? This is a more important question than whether they shall believe in the doctrine of the Trinity or the Apostolic succession. Mr. Parker thinks his views will establish the faith of his hearers upon a more solid foundation than that on which it has rested, and that, if they should prevail, they would correct much latent scepticism. We believe that in most cases their effect, where accepted, will be seen in a vague confidence in religious truth, that after a time will end in the most painful sense of uncertainty or in open unbelief. They will, doubtless, secure many listeners, and some disciples. Still we are not alarmed. So far as our own denomination is concerned, we have little fear for the result; so far as Christ and his religion are concerned, none. Truth is stronger than error. Christianity is too divine to be overthrown by the mistakes or the denials of men. All that is required of us in the present exigencies — either as its defenders or its disciples — is to speak the truth in love: 'the truth,' for that is what we owe to our Master; 'in love,' for that is what we owe to our brethren; 'speak,' for that is what we owe to ourselves."

The two men, Parker and Gannett, differed very widely in other matters besides theology, — matters in which there was as little muffling of opinion as in that. Mr. Parker had incomparably the wider range of knowledge, and a much more slashing and effective stroke in all his championship. In mental justice towards opponents, in careful fairness of stroke, in reverence for others' reverence, Dr. Gannett was the superior. As to earnestness of conviction, sincerity of speech, and self-denying zeal, Parker used the right word in his letters, — they were brothers. At bottom they could not help

respecting each other. Two letters from the end of
1846 show the frankness of their intercourse. Parker
had written to ask if **Dr.** Gannett were the author of
a certain criticism on one of his sermons. The latter
told him No, but added: —

"But now as you have addressed me, and with great
kindness, on the subject, let me say that I was sorry you
penned and uttered some of the sentences in that discourse.
They are not worthy of you. They give the impression, so
far as I have had any opportunity of hearing what persons
think, that you have lost some part of the amiability which
all once ascribed to you. They are taken as indications of a
soured and irritated mind. I confess they have affected me
in this way. You have condescended to use taunt and insinuation, and to go out of your way (as it seems to me) to
give utterance to personal feeling. I wish you would drop
this style of remark, and go straightforward in the prosecution of the purposes you have at heart. You can do great
good in bringing many to take an active interest in Christian benevolence. And if you should do harm (as I, of
course, must think you will) by the inculcation of your
peculiar theological opinions, yet I would rather you should
do it in a manner that will leave your character free from
the imputation of any other than the highest and purest
motives.

"Pardon me if I have written with too much freedom. I
believe you will not misunderstand me.

"Yours very truly,
"Ezra S. Gannett."

Mr. Parker's answer came marked "*Private*" at the
beginning, and "I beg you not to show this letter, — no,
not to your wife," — at the end. He knew that the
rebuker to whom he opened thus his inmost heart could
be trusted. But the letter set in its frame of privacy

reads so nobly, that, with all these years between, it seems right to decide anew the question of showing it. At least, so think they who would be most careful of the writer's wish.

"WEST ROXBURY, Dec. 19, 1846.

"DEAR SIR, — I am glad to find that you did not write the article in the 'Christian Register;' and, if you did not, my end is answered, and I care little who did. I thank you for the remarks you make about myself in the letter. I like the frankness and plainness with which you speak, and both honor and thank you for it. You are the only one of the ministers who ever came and told me of a wrong-doing in my course. Had others done so, I should have been glad; as it is, I am almost wholly without counsel from the clerical body. *Fas est et ab hoste doceri,* how much more *ab amico?* . . .

"I don't suppose you will believe what I say, but *I* know it is true, *that I have never printed or preached one line which any feeling of ill-will or sourness has sullied in the faintest degree.* I know many would misunderstand it: but I know that God would not; that I did not; that the few noblest Hearts, which with me are far more weighty than a world's applause or a world's scorn, would also understand it. When I was a boy, I used to think that Christ was angry with persons when he said those dreadful things in the Gospels; that he felt a little soured at their malignant opposition. As I lived more, I saw it was not so. Yet the men who heard them said he had a devil. Now don't say I am comparing myself with Christ. I only mean to say that it was unavoidable he should be mistaken; and if he, why not so little a man as I am?

"Now I have sometimes suspected you of saying things in ill-temper, — yes, of saying them against *me.* . . . If you tell me you had no such motive, I think I shall believe you. Yet I don't ask you to do so, — certainly I would not for my own sake. The things which sound so hard when I say them or print them are said *wholly in sorrow, not at all in anger.* I weep when I write them. I wrestle with myself afterwards, say I *can't* say them, I *won't;* but an awful voice of conscience says, Who art thou that darest to disobey thy Duty! So I say them, though it rends my heart. Trust me, I feel no sourness, no disappointed ambition. I saw long ago what my course was to be, and submitted cheerfully, joyfully. I hope to do my duty; though I know that the more faithfully I do it, the more shall I be blamed. Yet I foresee great future good to come to men through what I am called on to do and to pass through. When my tears flow no longer, when the grass grows over my level grave, when my name has perished from amongst men, the hearts of men shall flame with the truths that I have tried to teach. Others shall reap where I have only mown down the thorns, and that with lacerated arms, men calling me *destroyer, ill-tempered*, and all that. These things I count nothing. I do not ask even you to do me justice: I know God will. If I have hard things to say, I *must* say them, — not that I would.

"I beg you not to show this letter to any one, — no, not to your wife.　　　　Truly your friend,

"Theo. Parker."

This account of their — friendship, shall we say ? hardly that — shall close with the good-by which Mr. Parker sent from his sick-bed, a hurried pencilling, mailed February 3, the very day on which he left the house in Exeter Place for Santa Cruz and Italy and death : —

"Boston, Feb. 1859.

"Rev. Dr. Gannett.

"Dear Sir, — I don't know when I shall see you again, — with the mortal bodily eyes perhaps never. Hence this poor scrawl with a pencil. In your sermons which I used to hear

in earlier life, either at Watertown or at Boston or elsewhere, you spoke words which sank deep into my heart,
helping to quicken the life of pious feeling which I think had
never slumbered there. I write now to thank you for the
good words spoken then. Let me also say that ever since
I have admired the self-denying zeal with which you have
worked in your profession, while so many slept, and felt
therein an encouragement. Believe me, with earnest gratitude,   Yours truly,

"THEODORE PARKER."

We return to the home-life. For the summer a sea-
side home had been discovered, a little fishing-village
whose houses straggled along the rocky shore of Cape
Ann's farthest point. Only two or three of the city-
folk had found it out besides himself, and for half a
dozen years they had it almost to themselves. All was
quiet and queer and old. One house still had its upper
story jutting over the lower, as it had been built, the
legend said, for protection against the Indians; and on a
seaward hill-top, amid a desert of big boulders, gaped the
half-filled cellars of the early Cape settlers, dating back
to the same primeval days. Thick woods lay between
the fringe of habitation on the shore and Gloucester
further inland. The people, like ocean-islanders, had a
certain sea-flavor of their own. One summer-day Mr.
and Mrs. Gannett, while riding round the Cape, espied,
behind a red-barred gate, a roomy farm-yard green to
the door of the sun-browned house which lay so well back
from the road. Hard by a great barn stretched, the
patriarch of a group of small out-buildings, round which
there drowsed and stirred the lazy barn-yard families.
Beyond in the sunshine were two or three green fields,
beyond them the blue ocean. All had a look as of

wide space, slow time, and simple, ancient ways. Here
was an ideal found real! They ventured in, begging
leave to stay. "Pa Babson" demurred, but "Ma'am
Babson" said Yes, and that decided. Once in, they
came back, sure of a welcome, for a few weeks of every
summer. "The Babsons are the same hospitable people as ever, and the neighbors I like very much." To
the children the "Old Farm" was the summer's paradise, the winter's dream.

Broken weeks only were the father's share of Paradise. Long after the city custom turned, his sense of
duty had effect to keep the church-doors open all the
hot Sundays. For the few who wanted meeting, he
must be there to meet them. For the very few who
wanted the second service in the afternoon, he again
was faithful at his post. Sometimes a parishioner lay
very low in sickness: that was a claim that took precedence of all else to keep or call him back. But how
he enjoyed the short stays at the farm, as he ran down
for the two or three days at a time! He was the same
active *doer* here as at home. "Doing" was essential to
the fun. He revelled in putting things to rights, and had
a gift for clearing up litters, slowly, — but so perfectly!
In the city the recreation could be indulged in only in
the garret or the cellar and the wood-shed. As no one
else would keep those places in proper order, he must,
— he used to say; and his tone of satisfaction in calling
the family to behold his triumphs of cleanliness and
beauty in ungainly spots, and the architectural finish of
his wood-pile, was very droll. Those days were rather
dreaded in the household. He always wanted companionship in this, as in all other interests; and large
were the. moral, besides the pecuniary, benefits resulting to the stray boys and men of whom he made allies.

One of them thought that, "if he could always work under a boss like the old gentleman, he should not care particular about drinking." In the country his genius had wider scope. Now a stile was to be made in the pasture-wall, now the kitchen-steps needed smoother flag-stones, and each summer the whole chip-strewn corner by the wood-pile must be cleared from the accumulations of a year. The farm-people laughed as they helped their limping reformer. Every one knew him, liked him. In such little betterments, in arranging picnics, — at which the more the merrier, — in talks with the country-folk, and notably with one "Farmer Knowlton," the Tom Paine of the village, who loved to pose the city-parsons with searching Bible-questions, he spent the days between the stage-rides homewards.

Aug. 15, 1844. "After dinner (it was a genuine country-picnic) we had singing and dancing by the help of a fiddle well played. I have not for a long time been so *conscious* of enjoyment. What a contrast to the affectation, display, and conventionalism of life in the city! All good-tempered, free, and simple."

October 2. "Another delightful day. Worked in the yard spreading sand on the new path, and fixing steps to the back-door. In the barn with the children to husk corn. Then I walked alone to the Cove and home through the fields, lay under the oak-trees, and enjoyed the day, the scene, and the associations excessively. I am almost unwilling to enjoy so much."

October 4. "We have most abundant reason for gratitude. Why am I so much blessed? It seems as if the Divine Providence was laboring to win me from my insensibility by its incessant bounty."

Each year the place grew dearer. No previous visit had been so pleasant as that in the summer of 1846.

"Anna has gained strength, and the children have not had a sick day. We have returned home well, and find all well. Let us be grateful, tranquil, and dutiful." After that season Rockport became memorial ground.

1846, December 22. "Brought home New Year's presents for the children for Anna to see. Sat up preparing 'Intelligence' for the 'Examiner.' Between 1 and 2 o'clock I fell asleep in my chair, and was waked by Anna coming into the study at 3 o'clock to ask me if I was not going to bed. I told her I must finish what I was doing, and sat up an hour longer."

December 23. "Came home from Cambridge printing-office in 8 o'clock omnibus, found Anna sitting in the parlor, writing at her work-table, bright and cheerful. She read proofs of 'Examiner' with me, and went to bed at eleven o'clock."

There the Journal stops for a week; and, when it begins again, it is crippled into one line records. The wife, the mother, had died on Christmas evening.

"It was a still and solemn moment, so tranquil, beautiful, holy, that we could not give utterance to grief. The chamber was as still as though no life were in it. I laid myself, almost involuntarily, by her side, and felt the calmness, whether of stoicism or of submission, I know not. I felt the influence of the scene. We all felt it. It subdued and tranquillized us all. She had gone, the patient and suffering one, the loving and faithful one; she had gone from pain and trial, and it seemed as if we knew she was more than at rest, — she had entered into a higher and freer life."

The words are taken from a book written by him for her children, — written slowly with pages added on the Christmases of many years. It was begun at —

Rockport, Sept. 9, 1848. " I am sitting in the chamber where she spent so many quiet and happy hours, near the window from which she looked upon her favorite view, the western window of the 'old farm' house. . . . And, while every thing reminds me of her, I am more than ever impressed with the features of this scene as suited to please her, — tranquil and beautiful, with the noise of the world behind us, and the quiet bay, with here and there a little sail, stretching off towards the setting sun. . . . Here let me execute the purpose I have so long cherished of recording my recollections of her last hours. Then will I add the memorials which attest the sympathy of those who loved her; and the whole shall constitute a precious book for her children and for me."

Thenceforward Christmas was a still and shadowed day in the household life, one which he spent in the seclusion of her room or in the study, except when he went forth to visit some friend in affliction. Towards nightfall the children used to gather round him and talk of their mother and say the hymns which she had taught them, till by and by all knelt in prayer and kissed good-night. A shadowed day, — for death to him was a mystery that brought awe, resignation, trust in the All-Goodness, but not the feeling of an unseen presence or bright sure visions of reunion. The mind was truthful with itself. Among the words of Christ — and save from them there shone no light at all for him upon the mystery — were none that promised glad greetings from old friends ; and he questioned much whether in their hastened progress and their ripened powers they again could be what they had been to those who, for long years perhaps, might have to tarry here. No wonder, then, that the dear name was ever after uttered in a hush, and that, if lightly called, we saw him shrink to silence. Into his love for her there entered that omnipresent element of loyalty. Eleven years married : the rest of the seventy years wore by, and still the Christmas memory was kept, and the Journals all through the years spring open at many a place where a flower, fastened on the page, chronicles a pilgrimage to the Mount Auburn grave.

When next he met his people, who had loved her well, it was natural to speak of her : —

" The strength of her character lay in its moral integrity. Her devotion to the right was almost marked with the certainty of an instinct. It had the force of a law which might never be broken. What was right must be done, cost what it would. This was the deepest and steadiest conviction of her soul. To this she clung through sickness and health, through hope and fear, in every season and under all experience. She dreaded nothing in herself so much as a departure from rectitude. She shrank from nothing in others with such an instant disapprobation as from a similar departure. Falsehood of every kind was so much her aversion, that she would rather disappoint or offend by honesty than conciliate by the slightest compromise of truth. In every exigency I knew she could be trusted, even as we trust the unchangeable laws of the Creation amidst the strains which overwhelm the earth.

" To this firmness of moral purpose was united an extreme gentleness of mind. The masculine in expression belonged not to her. She was a *woman* in her whole constitution and being. The delicacy of her sensibilities was such as could be seen, I think I may say, only in one of her sex. Her affections were deep and true. Where she bestowed her love, she gave all her heart. Yet even her most partial or intense affections could not make her swerve from the path of duty. I know she would have died for them who were dear to her; but I do not believe she would have done what her soul told her was wrong, even to gain their fondest gratitude. She saw their faults, for the purity of her moral sentiment reflected the images which fell upon it in their real character; and they affected her with the most painful emotions which she ever experienced.

" In her religious character there was much to interest as well as to satisfy those who enjoyed her confidence. With a natural inclination to the side of doubt rather than of faith, she had looked at the great truths of religion with the eye of an anxious curiosity. Years ago her mind took hold of the questions which lie at the foundations of all belief, the mighty questions of God and revelation. She had toiled through those questions, till her faith stood in the conclusions of the understanding, and not in the simple assent of the feelings. From these questions she advanced to others of less magnitude, but of deep importance. Providence presented to her view a scene which at once perplexed and exercised her mind ; but the progress which she was making through all its difficulties was most beautiful to observe. By sure steps she was reaching that solution of the great problem of life which so many never think of attempting, and so few approach, which harmonizes all apparent discordance, and leaves the soul free for other inquiries, — a solution which can be reached only by patient thought.

" Of her domestic life I dare not trust myself to speak."

From the memorial-book on different Christmas days : —

" She had calmly prepared for the event of her illness. A box was found containing all her New Year's presents for the different members of the family, carefully arranged, and with the address of each in her own handwriting; a characteristic example of the forethought and method and faithful attendance to every duty which distinguished her."

Dec. 25, 1848. " I think I never felt a disposition to complain of the Providence that had afflicted me, or to doubt

the goodness of God; and I know that it was from trust in
His perfect will, rather than from any hope concerning a
future life, that I drew what comfort I obtained. Immortality was a fact which I recognized in all my meditations,
but it was from the presence and rectitude of the Heavenly
Father that I derived whatever support my faith gave me.
One phase of this experience I distinctly remember. Perhaps a week, perhaps longer, after the separation, a sense
of mystery began to swallow up my other feelings. Every
thing seemed to be enveloped in impenetrable mystery, and
the burthen grew upon my heart till it was almost insupport-
able, and I was obliged to force my thoughts into some other
channel lest it should entirely overpower me. The first,
inevitable feeling of desolation was scarcely more dreadful
than this oppression of the *mysterious*, which seemed to en-
viron and pervade life. I also remember that, when I first
walked through the street after the event, it seemed to me
strange that people should be going on in their employments
as usual. A feeling of surprise was awakened, and I seemed
to myself to have expected that every one would look on life
with as different a judgment as I was passing upon it. The
Bible I found to be the only book that I cared to read:
other books interested me very little. Even hymns did not
meet my want. They were either too cold or too poetical:
simplicity and sentiment were lost in studying expression.
But the Bible, particularly the Psalms, appeared to have
been written for me. Wonderful was the adaptation of their
language to my case. I never before knew how much the
Bible meant, nor how near it came to the heart, how true
and exact a transcript it gave of human experience."

Dec. 25, 1851. " The *completeness* of the separation
seems to me strange. As I do not believe that we have any
instruction which justifies us in supposing we can hold the
least intercourse with the departed, this entire cessation of a
reciprocal dependence, which was once so intimate, does not
explain itself to my mind. ' It must be so,' am I told? I

answer, 'It is so, but why need it have been so? Why could not God have permitted us to have some knowledge of those who have left us, and to enjoy to some extent still their society?' It has pleased Him wholly to withdraw them from our communion, and I doubt not that He has done what is right and best; but I do not *see* that it is best, and I confess that at times there seems to me to be something violent and unnatural in the sudden and total extinction of inter-course. The reasons that suggest themselves to the mind for such a disruption of dear habits are not strong enough to overpower the *feeling* that some degree of intercourse might still be permitted. We must walk through the perplexities of this subject by faith, not by sight.

" I am again reminded of the influence which the memory of her character and her affection ought to have on me. Why am I not more as she would wish me to be, if she were here? Let me act more under the persuasion of her love and her life. She loathed all insincerity: let not me deal dishonestly with others or with myself. She was faithful in the discharge of every duty: let me not be dilatory or neg-lectful. God help me to do better the next year, if I should live, than I have done these last months! God help me to be faithful to my children and to my own soul!"

Dec. 25, 1854. " Eight years have passed, and this anni-versary renews the question, — Am I better for the discipline God laid on me? Alas! no. Yet I long for the faith, the peace, the humility, and the self-control, into which it was His purpose to lead me. I do not, however, believe that we can explain a bereavement, or any form of human suffering (but, least of all, death), by tracing the moral or spiritual benefit it may yield. During the last year the truth has presented itself to my mind with special force, that the providence of an Infinite Being must embrace details and connections which we cannot understand. A providence which our faculties could measure would not be divine. God, arranging the plan of human experience for all of us through the whole existence of each one of us, must have taken into this plan numberless events which we should have had neither the foresight nor the breadth of view to include. While we know that 'the very hairs of our head are all numbered,' and, therefore, nothing can be outside of the Divine Providence, in countless instances His providence must take effect in a way to confound our judgment. In the events that surprise and disappoint us, in the afflictions particularly that seem to us so strange, I find a proof that our lives are cared for, over-ruled, and guided by a wisdom and a love higher than ours, and discover the justification of faith as well as the need of it in the most distressful occurrences. It would be difficult to believe that all which happens to us is under God's tender oversight, if it were all within the solution of human faculties." . . .

There were three children when the mother died, eight, six, and four years old. Most conscientiously the father accepted the new responsibility, striving to be father and mother both; and all through the shaping years the mother's sister so filled the empty place with loving care that they hardly knew their loss.

Just before the Christmas day he had begun another course of Sunday evening lectures, this time upon the "Contents of the Scripture." Again the church was more than crowded; and again the fluent talk ran on long past the hour, filling nearly a broadside in two of the city papers. He maintained a theory of Inspiration that bore as hard against the Intuitionalists on the one hand, as against the Literalists on the other: —

. . . "I read and reread these affirmations with amazement. The Holy Spirit of God is said to have superintended the common geographical and statistical statements, so that

there might be no error! Why, error there *is ; undeniable*
error, in some of these more unimportant statements. . . .

"I do not, therefore, deny the inspiration of the apostles.
I assert it, and would maintain it to the last drop of my
heart's blood ; for, if I give it up, I give up my faith in Christ,
my hope in heaven. But I maintain that it was given in the
early part of their ministry . . . through a twofold illumination, — through the personal intercourse enjoyed with our
Lord, and through the fulfilment of his promise upon the
day of Pentecost. . . . Thus thoroughly qualified to go forth
and spread the faith of Jesus of Nazareth, they were then
left, in executing their work, whether as preachers or afterwards as writers, to the unembarrassed, uncontrolled exercise
of their intellectual and moral faculties. Their minds were
not superintended by a force which in any degree interfered
with the freedom of their mind's action. Their hearts and
consciences kept their memories faithful to the service which
they undertook." . . .

Whereupon the critics fell upon him, not always
kindly. Some one in the " Boston Recorder " smote
him thus : —

"You tread the path trodden by Celsus, Voltaire, Paine,
and Theodore Parker. . . I see in you an advocate of public
virtue, starting morality and truth from their deep foundation ; an ambassador to guilty men, rending your commission
before the eyes of the disobedient. . . You have filled up
the measure of Unitarian unbelief. . . That system was begotten in the pulpit you occupy. The old form of your faith
has for a long time been ready to vanish : what place so fitting for its exit as the place of its birth? How appropriate
that its author and its finisher should both stand in the same
pulpit ! . . I have been struck with the emblem of your
faith which is fixed in the rear of that pulpit. It has the
form of an anchor. But it resembles not that hope which
is an anchor to the soul. The transverse beam in the real

anchor is so constructed that the flukes *must hold :* in yours, the emblem is so arranged that they *cannot hold,* — the transverse beam is directly over the flukes, making the anchor worthless.   An apt emblem of that hope which you offer to guilty men, without the cross of Christ."

The crowds might come to hear the lectures, still the condition of the church was troubling him.   One after another the old parishioners were dying.   At times the Journal reads like a chronicle of death, the funerals follow each other so closely through the pages. And now and then a friend deserted the old pews for the sake of a fresh voice.   New listeners came, but the empty places were not all made good ; for the population had greatly ebbed away from that side of the city. Forty years before, when the church was built, — even twenty years before, when the preacher was ordained, — the neighboring streets held Boston's finest mansions, and the flock lived all around its Sunday fold.   But the warehouses had steadily pushed nearer and nearer, skirted with a front of Irish settlers, until, for a large part of the parish, the Sunday morning now brought long journeys ; and many persons had moved altogether out of town.   All the old churches in that part of the city suffered in the same way.   But in this preacher's eyes the fault was his : he could not preach as he ought, he did not work hard enough, with tact enough, with ability enough, at the various duties ; and he felt the diminution sorely.

Oct. 7, 1846. "—— came to tell me she was going to worship at ——, the reason being that ——'s preaching met her wants more than mine, as his was 'strengthening,' while mine, being addressed so much to men as sinners, discouraged her.   We had a long, free, and pleasant conversation."

But, on account of that conversation, probably, —

"In evening, very much depressed and disheartened."
Oct. 5, 1847. "Altogether distressed and perplexed about
my ministry. I dread the winter, as its duties present them-.
selves before me. The society must decline, and, unless the
present tendency be arrested, must perish. I ought, therefore, clearly to leave my people. Yet I have not the courage
to face the mortification, or to meet the inconveniences which
would follow such a step. I know I can never have peace
of mind or self-approbation so long as I stay here; but, if I
go, what will become of me or my children?"

Distressed and disheartened on that account, but the
trouble was more real to feelings than to facts. The
true secret was that the effect of the European trip
had by this time almost vanished. Even before the
sorrow in the home, the glow of health began to die
out of the days, and the old feelings of tired self-
reproach were lurking near to take their wonted place.
He felt that he was growing old. When he sought to
insure his life, the doctor's honest warning that old age
for him would depend on very cautious management
frightened off the Companies. He tried to "manage."
Especially he tried to begin the sermon on Monday;
and, if he succeeded, it was sure to falter, consume the
week, and linger into the late Saturday midnight, after
all. From time to time the sadness broke in, in a way
that augured ill for years not now far off. The mood
would pass, but would return again and yet again.
Friends understood him: "It was the weakness of
the flesh." No one knew him better than Calvin Lincoln, who wrote him, after some earnest talk with
yearning and self-accusation in it: "Your self-distrust
arises from an ideal of the true life too exalted for the

weakness of humanity.   There must be a deep principle
of piety, a deep well of Christian love, to sustain such
uniform activity in duty (as yours), and I cannot think
that you need that entire prostration of soul before God
of which we were speaking when together."

As a fact, his harvest of influence both in the city
and the denomination had but begun.   Trust, and the
new serviceableness that comes through trust and makes
the sweetest reward for faithfulness, were his in ampler
measure now than ever before.   The officers of the
parish hushed him at once when he spoke to them of
the decline of the congregation, the people passed resolutions warm with affection and gratitude as they strove
— and strove not seldom, but usually in vain — to make
him accept an increased salary.   Friends in New York
were again asking him to entertain the thought of
going thither, — to whom he made reply that the only
change he could contemplate was to a smaller, not a
larger field.   And in 1847 he was chosen President of
the American Unitarian Association.

The early misgivings about organization had died
away with the Fathers.   To build up a denomination
was the accepted policy of the second generation of
Unitarians, and it was strengthened by the excitement
over Parker's radicalism.   The Transcendental leaven
was working good, however.   Unitarianism, having
passed its controversial, and being well advanced in its
philanthropic era, was now thought to be on the eve of
a spiritual era.   The missionary spirit grew yet more
earnest, and resolve deepened to spread abroad the
gospel of pure Christianity.   The Association, just
come of age, obtained an act of incorporation in 1847,
and made ready for effective action.   Early in 1849 a
series of crowded meetings was held in Boston, of which

reports went far and wide among the churches. Not long before a new school for ministers had been opened, through the zeal of a few friends, in the backwoods of Pennsylvania. It was hoped that the West would get its Liberal prophets thence. Let us double the funds of the Association that we may aid the students, that we may print our books, that we may succor our weak churches, that we may send out teachers through the land to bless the thousands who are yearning for our nobler faith, — such was the appeal and such the stout endeavor.

Dr. Gannett was the right man to become President of the Association at this time of quickening zeal, when the higher officers were expected to be no longer honorary associates, but working helpers. The memorial reverence connected with Channing's church had made it in a sense the mother meeting-house of the denomination, the homestead where the faithful naturally resorted for their councils; and the heartiness with which its living minister seconded every effort kept up for many years the habit of resort, in spite of the increasing inconvenience of the place. He was fertile in practical suggestions, untiring at watch and labor. A few years before, his hand had written the report which led to the experiment of a Collation in Anniversary Week. " The only doubt has arisen from the uncertainty whether a sufficient number of persons, particularly of ladies, can be obtained at this late day to promise their attendance." A few years later, when it had become the favorite Unitarian festival of all the week and led to large expense, he wrote the plan which brought relief. Among his papers of about this date we find " Minutes of the Committee on Missions," and drafts of " Propositions for Increasing the Efficiency of the Association," and of a long appeal to the public in behalf of the general

movement. Of course, he took active part in the meetings referred to above. When he resigned his office in
1851, after four years' service, the "Examiner" declared:
"Our cause owes more to him than to any one among
the living. Though beyond all others of our brethren
he insists most emphatically upon Unitarian distinctions,
we do not think that he has ever made himself an
enemy, or lost the esteem of a single individual among
the sects around us."

The praise shows that he no longer edited the magazine. He had given it up two years before. The appeals for special service were coming often now, and
seldom were declined on any score of business or convenience. Doubtless then, as later, humility would
urge its veto strongly; but, if refusal was to throw real
labor on another's shoulders, consent was tolerably sure.
In 1848 he preached the "Convention Sermon" before
the Congregational ministers of Massachusetts, taking
for his subject the "Relation of the Pulpit to Future
Time." Nehemiah Adams assured him, speaking for
his Orthodox brethren, that there was no word in it to
which they could not all agree. A discourse before the
Benevolent Fraternity of Churches, on the "Object,
Subjects, and Methods of the Ministry at Large," bears
the same date; and in that year he also took a leading
part with other ministers in a movement against Licentiousness. The next year he preached the sermon
before the Ministerial Conference on the "Nature and
Importance of our Theology," — "Poor, poor," says
his Journal, — and one before the Fatherless and
Widows' Society. All of these were printed. In 1850
he gave the address to the Alumni of the Cambridge
Divinity School, on "The Minister's Devotedness to
his Work;" that at the Normal School Reunion in

West Newton, on " Education as a Means of Establishing
Woman in her True Position in Society ; " another lecture on Education before the American Institute of Instruction ; and a sermon before the Young Men's Total
Abstinence Society. It was known that he could do
well in emergencies, and sometimes the summons was
very short. Whether short or not by summons, by his
own delay and the press of other work the time grew
always scant before the task was fairly under way. The
funeral-sermon would be finished in the cars, the dedi-
cation-sermon on the boat, — where once he called for
lights, and sat up nearly the whole night writing in the
cabin.

About this time the " Lyceum Lecture " was added to
American institutions. Every large village must have
its course of lectures. They stirred the quiet winters
with a touch of literary life, and gave the country-
people a chance to face the famous city-men ; and the
authors and ministers, on their part, were glad enough
to eke out narrow incomes by playing the apostle of
culture. To this end, Dr. Gannett joined the ranks, and
for five or six winters took many a cold ride by car and
stage about New England. " Conversation," " Manners," " New England Ideas and Institutions," and
similar subjects, gave him themes. The venture was
successful, but his audiences did not laugh so often as
perhaps they wished to, nor so often as perhaps he
wished they would ; for he could never far unbend from
the preacher's earnest attitude : on platform and in
pulpit, his nature was the same.

In the matter of income, just now alluded to, a constant competition went on between the generosity of his
parish and his own sense of ill-desert and proper ministerial simplicity. The record of the race is comically

honorable to both. In 1840, although in debt, he refused an increase of salary: the people had been too good to him in Europe. The advent of the other children made a difference, so that in 1842 he consented to accept $500 more, which made the salary $2500. In 1846 another $500 was twice offered, twice declined. Two years later he concluded he ought to yield to wishes repeatedly expressed, lest he should seem insensible to the kind intent; but repentance came, — his conscience gave no rest till the sum was back in the treasurer's hands. The parish, however, provided with a conscience and a preference, too, as positively refused to receive it back, and kept on investing it yearly for his benefit. In 1851 they begged him to go to Europe, and in this way use the accumulating fund. No, he would not. The next year he finally accepted the increase for the future, forcing the reluctant friends to say no more about the four times $500 now untouched. To say no more to him; but twenty years later, when all was over, it remained in the parish treasury, and was offered anew to his children as the " Gannett Fund." There perhaps it still remains. In 1853 the European journey was again suggested: in vain. In 1858 a journey in the States with money for it: in vain. The next year, might they not pay his house-rent? No. And so on in later years, as we shall see.

This conscientiousness had no solitary reference to the parish. It was but one expression of his general feeling about trusts. In all transactions involving money, there was the same scruple to be just against himself. Taxes would be low, if all weighed their spoons and counted their dividends so carefully, and made such returns of property as he felt bound to make. Here, for instance, is a letter to the treasurer of Harvard College · —

" Boston, Jan. 15, 1849.

"Dear Sir, — I have long desired to do what now for the first time it is in my power to do. While a member of the Divinity School at Cambridge, in the years 1821–24, I received at different times, from Mr. Higginson, Steward of the College, various sums, which were given me as one of the Divinity students, I understood to defray or reduce the expenses of my theological education. I have no recollection, nor do I think, that the money which I received, or any part of it, was asked for, either by myself or by any one of my relatives; nor do I know on what ground it could have been bestowed, other than the mere fact that I was a member of the School. I was not then in need of assistance, having inherited from my father's estate more than what was sufficient to carry me through my professional studies. For many years, having unwisely brought myself into debt, I forgot this among more pressing obligations. Of late years, however, it has been a source of anxiety; and now, having just paid the last debt which could be demanded of me, I wish to return this money also, which it seems to me that I ought never to have taken. . . . Two hundred and ten dollars, therefore, constitute the amount which I seem to have received, and now desire to return to the source whence it was derived; and I beg leave to enclose this amount, subject to your disposal as Treasurer of the College. I do not add the interest, not only because I have not the means, but because it does not appear to me that I am bound to pay interest on sums advanced under the circumstances which I have described.

" Respectfully and truly yours,

" Ezra S. Gannett."

The classmates of 1820 were now turning the corner of their fifties together; and one of the band, Governor Paine of Vermont, invited them to meet at his country-home and celebrate old college memories. Fifteen

assembled at the welcome. " Gannett," as he again
became, took his two boys with him ; and thence the
three went on far into Canada, down the majestic
river, to the gorge where the Saguenay comes through
the northern wilderness. It was the little fellow with
him, not the classmates' greeting, nor the impression of
the river-solitude, that made that summer so dear for
him to recollect. When the next winter came, five
winters from the mother's death, a single line under-
scored in the Journal tells how suddenly the home again
was darkened : —

" Monday, Jan. 26, 1852, *ten minutes past twelve.*"

" Henry's illness was very brief. I went to my lecture
Sunday evening with a troubled heart, yet without defined
fears. The next morning he suddenly failed, and at twelve
o'clock passed away without any suffering. Three times I
kissed back his breath, and then he breathed no more. . . .
We miss him continually. When I came into the house, my
first salutation was from him, and his arms were round my
neck. Our home is changed. But I thank God for his life
and the joy we had in him ; and I ought to be willing, I
believe I am, that God should arrange the circumstances of
his future education. Now his life seems to me to have been
a dream of mine, so vivid in its passage and so distinct from
all present experience. He was a dear child, the most affectionate and joyous in his nature. He clung to me with all
the love of a child's heart, and I leaned on him, I knew not
how much, till he had gone."

Already he had written to a friend : —

" I am growing old with a fearful rapidity, or rather have
already become an old man. What shall you think if I tell
you that, few as our days are on earth, my life seems to me
to have been a long one. As we look back and see through
what changes we have passed and how many have left us,

do we all feel that we have lived centuries instead of years? I suspect so. And with this sense of age comes a partial weariness of life, a dread of yet more change and excitement, a desire rather for the security of another world than for the uncertain future of this. I am all the time longing for repose. Rest and progress, — how shall we unite those two opposite states of being? Yet they must be harmonized in our experience."

That was written the year before. It was more true now. From the time that Henry went, he was an old man.

17

ARLINGTON STREET CHURCH.

IX.

AFTERNOON: ANTI-SLAVERY AND WAR TIMES.

1852–1865.

THE home was in a country-nook no longer. On the garden at the foot of "the Court" the Music Hall was built; and the long bank where the cherry-tree and lilacs, the smoke-bush and the savin-tree, had grown, and the woodbines hung the bronzed and crimson veil in autumn, was now a sidewalk, where the throngs passed up and down to evening concerts and to hear Theodore Parker preach on Sunday mornings. On the other side, just through the parlor-wall, the hack-horses of a neighbor stamped, — towards whom the pastor's family and his parish felt the charity which sometimes faileth.

It was a minister's house. You would have known that not more by the books in the study than by the pictures in the parlor. The latter, gifts of friends, were carefully ecclesiastical or scriptural in subject, — Madonnas of Raphael, Christs of Ary Scheffer. The owner liked it so. He would have his house denote his work, as the pulpit-gown or the black coat denoted it. In all things the furnishing was plain. No minister should be over-comfortable, was his theory. Exceeding peace would seem to disfellowship the little ones of the flock. In the study, the couch and the great table, the little desk where the sermons came, — it had been his wife's school-desk, — and the book-lined wall, left small place for more. Few new books were bought, even in the favorite department of Bible-work. Those on the shelves, in the rusty leather covers, were the standard commentaries and metaphysics of his youth. Friends' faces made the pictures here, — Channing and Tuckerman, Henry Ware and William Furness. Judge Davis's bust looked down from a corner. The Judge had been one of the old parishioners.

Nor less a minister's household than his house. The morning-greetings were given, Bible in hand ; the children reading their verses round in turn, and kneeling with the father in his prayer. The burden of that prayer was the day's prophecy. If it were humble and penitent, he would be sad and weary ; if full of thanks for life and its opportunities, he was to go from door to door on errands of a pastor's love ; if full of fervor and sanctity, the Bible class or sermon was the day's work. Sickness, late rising, company, seldom interfered with this service, even if it were held with his children alone in the study. The family-week moved on to parish-time : Tuesday and Wednesday were " Bible-class days ; " Thursday was " Channing Circle day." A pile of Bibles waited in the china-closet, and the chairs were wont to flit about the house to be marshalled in the parlor.   The children were brought up to hand about sponge-cake and tea, and work quick miracles of transformation in the furniture.   Half an hour after the last of the sixty or seventy friends had said good-night, order reigned on shelf and in the chambers: all was back again in place.   Of the meetings in this later time, one who was a part of them writes: " The heavy step on the stairs as he came down with his arms laden with books was always the signal for a welcoming smile ; and then, as the talk grew earnest or the exposition knotty, his face lighted and the smiles quivered into one another. It was like a father among his children.   At the sewing-circle, — ' Channing Circle,' as it now was always called, — he was sometimes full of fun and humor ; while the confidences in the more serious Bible-class hours brought him very near to those who were searching for truth. It was in these meetings — and they were generally in his own house — that the remarkable love between the people and the minister was born and fostered."   They never were a weariness to him.   The hours given both to preparation and to lecture were among his pleasantest, and he was very happy when he succeeded in drawing the members into free conversation.   Nor were these hours allowed to put restriction on his calls, which were oftener made in the evening, especially at the tea-time.   As a rule, the well-known canes bore him from house to house from five in the afternoon until long after the nine o'clock bells rung good callers home.

And all days looked towards Sunday, the father's work-day.   It began on Saturday evening.   For the children, no party-going then, no noisy game, no novel after nine o'clock : even sewing after nine was mild sacrilege, against which the feeling brought from childhood

made a protest. He usually took tea that evening with
one dear friend close by. On returning, the week's accounts were puzzled out and squared. And then, the
world's work over, the children, as they came in to kiss
good-night, would see perhaps the first sheet of the sermon started, theme and text at top. The thinking for
it had been done before upon the streets. On and on
through the small hours the lamp kept bright. Down-
stairs the tea-pot simmered on the range, and a little
waiter held the slice of Graham bread and crackers for
the midnight freshening. The study-couch was usually
bed, and the morning found the sermon on page four-
teenth or fifteenth. Seven or eight pages yet to be despatched; but they were sure to come, the last as the
bells rang church-time.

Twice always the children went to church, besides
the Sunday school. No household task that could be
spared was done, that all the family might share the
Sabbath rest. Year in, year out, the cold corned beef
and Indian pudding, prepared the day before, appeared at dinner, — until at last a revolution happened, and a plum-pudding dynasty succeeded. Grave
books were read, — Paradise Lost, Butler's Analogy,
or smaller reading to match. In the twilight, as the
father rested on the couch or in the great arm-chair,
the children had their best hour with him: in younger
days, reciting Dr. Channing's little catechism; when
older, giving memories of the sermons, or telling what
they had read, and saying favorite hymns, among
which the mother's never were forgotten. Sunday
evening the table must be more plentiful, to honor
the likely guest; and after tea, if no engagement called
him forth, the circle was apt to be enlarged by parish-
callers. One lonely waif there was, of Boston fame for

friendlessness, who knew that, if Dr. Gannett were
only in, there would be a pleasant Sunday evening in
his dreary week, and some one who would listen to
him patiently while the words fell slów and large in
separate drops.   No wonder that he came for years
so regularly.

It was a home of principles rather than of rules and
strict exactitudes.   Life seemed to shape itself as a
matter of course to the father's standard and his necessary work.   Not his convenience, but his work, — that
was the centre round which all revolved.   There might
have been more careless grace in household ways ; for
the mother-aunt and the elder children felt the pressure
of his tired mood, and learned to watch and wait upon
his sensitiveness.   Henry, the youngest, with his impetuous loving ways burst in upon the shadows without
knowing their existence ; which made his going the more
bitter loss.   But, shadowed or unshadowed, there was
always in the house a presence that stood for perfect
truthfulness, for hourly self-denials and active thoughtfulness for others, for frank humility in confessing
wrong or ignorance or failure.   The children saw a
grown-up man, their father, trying like a child with
them to be and do just right.   To live with him, and
doubt that there were such things in the world as
supreme sincerity and unselfishness, would have been to
doubt that the sun shone in at the windows.

Great was the respect for anniversaries, and great the
children's corresponding expectation.   Fourth of July
brought the annual walk through the Common, the
glasses of colored lemonade, the weights of the family
registered in the memorandum-book, water-lilies, whips,
and canes.   To do less would have been unpatriotic.
Blessed was the child who fell to his generous care

that day. If the home provided none, the mall did. Thanksgiving was a grand family festival. To the young eyes the silent group of black puddings waiting in the dimness of the cellar had something awful about them. They brought to mind the Pyramids, and seemed almost as everlasting. The little pies and big rejoiced on every side. The entire quartette, mince and apple, squash and pumpkin, must glorify the table : not one should fail the yearning of the New England heart on that day. But the happy festival of all was New Year's Day, never forgotten even when the mother died, or the father was most ill. How good "the parish" used to be, — to father and to children too ! How promptly the door-bell was tended till certain packages sure to come in well-known handwriting had arrived ! And how he wearied in the shops till the right gift was found for each one in the wide circle, inside and outside the house, that he remembered ! The gifts would sometimes oddly mingle deference to another's rights of taste with honest disapproval of the taste. He would purchase no German books for a certain girl, — not he ! — preferring she should read devotional English ones, yet duly put into her hands the money to buy her choice, knowing well what it would be. The birthdays, too, were very sacred, and no growing up wore out their sanctity. Bundles, carefully wrapped, were sure to set out for the absent son, wherever he might be.

The constant giving, and the personal economies which made it possible, were in curious contrast to each other. The black clothes reached a shiny old age before they were set free, and he fairly revelled in the cheapness of his Oak Hall summer suit. If friends had not been generous, he would hardly have known what ease meant; yet, to vanquish his sure impulse, one had to *argue*

with him that refusal of the carriage or the Sunday
grapes would be disloyal to a kind intent. He seemed
to dislike taking almost as much as he rejoiced in
giving and sharing. The very children had to become
anonymous sometimes, to carry·a point of comfort for
him. Throughout the household life there was the
healthy pinch that keeps one braced with the sense of
having just enough, and mindful, therefore, of the many
who have less. A slight eater himself, almost a vege-
tarian by constitution, and trained to the sober solidities
of Puritanic diet, he eschewed most dainties. Tea was
the one great indulgence; for restoratives, peppermint
if he felt badly, molasses and water with ginger in it if
life were gladsome, until quite late in years. At times,
when chatting with a brother-minister, he used to
smoke a mild and cheap cigar. But a day came when
the rest of the bunch went into the fire, and he never
touched one afterwards: his boy was coming to an age
when the example might be dangerous. Yet the outfit
of ash-pans, cigar-cases, and the amber-tubes, was presently made over to the innocent! Perhaps from cosey
associations with the kitchen in the prim child-life, he
always loved a luncheon by the kitchen-fire. Various
were the devices employed to induce him to partake of
any slight luxury provided in the home. Habitual
butter, and not too much, was the line at which simplicity ended and luxury began. Jelly was tasted with
an apology, for its function claimed it for the sick.
More than once he succeeded in sending the roast beef,
whole and hot, from the table to some poor friend.
Once, probably when conscience had been chiding the
selfish extravagance of two courses at table while the
poor were with him always, he requested that hasty
pudding might be provided for an indefinite future.

Three or four days passed, when, forgetful of their fate, he brought home with him to dinner some hungry ministers. They shared his pudding, — and saved his family: thenceforward he restricted his restrictions.

And yet his hospitality was unbounded. The weeks were few in which the guest-room held no visitors; and the guests made most at home, and for the longest periods, were those who but for him were homeless, — some poor foreigner, it might be Irish, German, French, but oftenest English, perhaps an English minister and his wife. One brought his family of little children straight from the steerage to the shelter: it was summer, and the host kept house for them in the empty rooms. Of course the " Civil Rights' Bill " was in force at table. The girls in the family were made real friends, trusted and trusting: they shared in the good times and sorrows, and those who lived long there became and seemed to feel like relatives. " Anniversary Week " was the jubilee week of the year. Dr. Gannett was a city minister, and to the utmost corner of the rooms or table the house belonged that week to the " brethren." He dearly loved that name, especially in the plural. The week began with the " Association " to tea, — on this Monday trebled in number by the advent of the country-parsons. On the three great days of the Feast, there were dinner-parties; and the table sometimes stretched diagonally across the parlor to hold the two or three more guests, whom at the last moment he could not deny himself. They were curious dinners, such as were not often found elsewhere, — simple and neat in form, but side by side sat scholar and the farmer-minister, the eloquent speaker of the morning and the timid young beginner, all unknown, yet kindled into speech before the hour was over by the tact that bade him welcome.

At the evening teas, the brethren, two, three, four score,
dropped in by clusters, as they would.

His charities, too, were very large for his income, but
larger yet his patience and sympathy. The word " Engaged " was seldom allowed to be said at the door. The
story must be listened to ; and he would question and
cross-question the petitioners, chide, and give, all at the
same time. The entry-dialogues and his experimental
confidences became home-jokes. The funeral or marriage, be it of a stranger and poor, was rarely solemnized
without the fresh cravat. Those poor whom he had
adopted — his pensioners — came to him as to a father.
Was " Patrick's " boy in trouble, Dr. Gannett was
Chief Comforter in the case. Did his apple-woman on
the Common plan some wholesale purchase of a box
of oranges or a doughnut speculation for the Fourth of
July, Dr. Gannett was summoned to the council and
made banker. Unpaid rents, pawnbrokers' charges,
family disputes, " black Sarah's " funeral, all were
brought to him for settlement, often adding to the
complexity of Saturday night accounts, and sending
him to borrow money in advance of the quarter's salary.
On Thanksgiving eve, the eight or ten turkeys were
carefully weighed, tied, labelled, and despatched, mated
with the proper pies, to make the next day merrier for
certain friends. Not till he was sure that the woman
with four children had a ten-pound turkey and the
childless widow a six-pounder, was the sermon touched :
no one could arrange it but himself. In the same way
the grapes were distributed from the great vine that
clambered over the nursery windows : the neighbors
had their plateful of the little harvest.

And usually he was his own messenger of help. The
homes of the poor knew him well. A friend tells of

seeing him on a very slippery day, down by North Street,
feeling his way carefully along, the two canes grasped
in one hand, the other carrying a bowl. Espying M.,
he stepped into a door. As *his* spy turned the corner
and looked back, he saw the Doctor cautiously peep out,
and then begin again the perilous journey, —to some
attic, probably, in the neighborhood. The habits of
another friend, whom he had recommended to the pulpits, came to his knowledge, and he felt obliged to speak
of them at the Association. S. found himself cut off
from preaching, and was intensely angry with him.
The scholar, sick and moneyless, used to get young
Wendte to do his errands and ask assistance here and
there. One day, in a rain-storm, bound on some such
mission, the boy met Dr. Gannett. " Why, where are
you going in this rain ? " — " For the doctor." — " Is your
mother sick ? " — "No, it's S——." His face fell. " What
is the matter ? " Wendte described the poor man in his
wretchedness. " Where does he live ? " They parted.
The boy went on about his errand, and came back
an hour afterwards to find Dr. Gannett already there.
S. was out of bed, sitting in the chair, looking at him
with tears in his eyes. The Doctor, lame as he was,
had taken him up, made the bed, swept up the room,
and from somewhere got a bowl of soup.

> " That best portion of a good man's life,
> His little, nameless, unremembered acts
> Of kindness and of love,"

made a very large portion of this man's life. Sometimes their connection with an especial " cause " gives
such little deeds dramatic setting, and lifts them up to
name and fame. Not so with him and his. They were
scattered broadcast over the common ways of life, into

the lot of poor people, of tired, friendless people, of sad
parishioners, of " brethren " stricken with his own despondency who made his study their confessional.   To
these last he could speak words of wisest cheer, knowing — no one better — the secret in their heart, and how
to offer healing which he could not use himself.   Such
words and acts were seldom to be found out except by
accident, as in the cases cited just above.   By the doer
they were likely to be forgotten with the day.

Yet the detail, the thoroughness, of his help, was most
notable.   The service would last until the want ceased.
No one who found shelter under his roof left it until the
home or the occupation was obtained.   The widow fighting the wolf from the door was borne in mind this year,
next year, and year after, till the boys grew tall and
earned enough.   The North End missionary knew where
he could turn for an evening's preaching every season ;
and the solitary sailors'-preacher, who once or twice
a year came up from his Land's End to the Boston Mecca,
knew that one face would light up to greet him, and a
hand would find money for his cause, if need be.   Had
the old and penniless parishioner no relative, he would
render the last services himself as tenderly as if she were
a sister.   Were a tired friend starting for the White Hills
or for Europe, he delighted to write down the routes,
name the hotels, plan the excursions, provide the letters.
A young man entering the city-life brings him a letter
from the minister at home : " To my boarding-place he
came and to my place of business, always with the same
warm and earnest words, as of a father who had known
me from childhood.   How happily have I heard common
and unscrupulous men inquire, ' Is that Dr. Gannett ?
Mr. C., does he call to see *you?*   We rarely see such

men about here.' Indeed, the entire scene of a sales-
room would seem to change to quiet and respect at his
presence."

He was but fifty years old when his boy died, yet
one meeting him in the street would have said "the
old man." The black hair had early turned gray, the
grand, high head was bald, the slight form was bent as
the shoulders rounded with years of leaning on the
canes, and the face showed lines of wear. The eyes
alone looked young. They told the story of the strong
days and the public efforts; but the Journal shows the
other days coming oftener and staying longer. The
sensitive constitution must have been finely tempered
to have risen so bravely from the first break-down and
the quick after-stroke. Now, as it weakened, it ex-
acted slow penalty for all neglect and strain. He lived
in a broken body. To all duty, to all pleasure, he
dragged the useless, withered limb. Dyspepsia in some
form was almost chronic. Pain was frequent: he sometimes preached when he could not stand erect in its
grasp. The nerves had become most delicate metres of
wind and damp and heat: "An east wind depresses or
irritates me, a dry fine air exhilarates, or rather excites,
me. I need more self-control, more calmness, more
wisdom." The clothing to protect them ranged through
three or four grades of summer thinness, and as many
more of winter thickness. The wealth of well-darned
flannels made "which is which?" a standing problem,
solved over and over with the daughter's help amid
much tribulation. This delicacy was reckoned as another of his faults, of course, yet a mystery as well.
He never thoroughly accepted the fact that flesh could

so control the spirit. Now and then, as in the Rockport walks, the sensitiveness ministered to exquisite
enjoyment; far oftener it put an edge on pain. One
day an ordination called him back to Bedford: —

"Mr. Cushing took me to the old school-house, where,
thirty-seven years ago, I was frightened by the children, and
tried (and acquitted) by the school-committee. I remembered it as of yesterday, even to the place for wood in the
entry, and to the spot very near where Mr. Lane's house
stood in which I boarded. No other week of my early life
seems to have left such a distinct impression on my memory.
The air was delicious, wind from the south-west, sky clear,
and country verdant still. The atmospheric influence and
the mental association produced an almost painful consciousness of pleasure. A rare day!"

Or again: —

"A singular change to-day. This morning I came home
almost broken in spirit. After dinner slept two hours, and
woke up strong and almost presumptuous in feeling."

Such sentences were symptomatic. He analyzed his
pleasure, his courage, his sorrow, his failure, the sermon's worth, his bearing in the call or the discussion,
his ability for ministerial work. It was very strange.
He was absolutely simple, sincere, often too impetuous
in word and act: *after* the word or action, self-consciousness beset him, not prompting to selfishness or content,
but to the uttermost opposite of these. He was aware
of the tendency, lamented it, struggled against it; but
what so hard to conquer by struggle as the habit whose
one master is simple, self-forgetting Health? Sometimes, as has been said before, he seemed a very boy
in glee and banter. The amused smile which faintly
lingers in our frontispiece was quite common on his

lips. Many a guest must remember him in hours of
merriment, and, if he reads this book, will wonder at the
shade that overspreads it. It was hard to recognize in
the leader of a mountain party, standing and shouting
in the wagon, improvising the doggerel in his turn, buying cake for the sake of fairness at the hotel where
the party lingered for a moment, recruiting for picnics,
making the fire, cutting the branches, — hard to recognize in him the troubled, tired minister of the winter.

What he needed to make him always glad was the
power to be successfully busy according to his ideal:
but that is equivalent to saying that he might have the
good time, but never the spirit of good cheer; that he
could not win peace, but only an escape. He lacked
the elements which help to balance moral earnestness;
lacked belief in the body's rights and the duty of diversion; lacked the sense of humor, — that safety-valve of
conscience; lacked the sense of beauty in any rich development. Music, save as hymns where he could hear
the words, was an unknown language. Pictures had
more meaning. The theatre, often visited in college-
days, was afterwards wholly given up in deference to
common expectation; for he thought it duty to observe
that etiquette of dress and bearing and amusement
which buttresses a minister's good influence with a community. The American circus, however, remained legal
fun, and the children always had the treat. Flowers
had strangely little charm. At funerals, in church, at
the communion-service, he could not bear their presence: the brightness, the laugh in them, seemed irreverent. Clouds were to him what flowers are to most, a
dreamy wonder and delight. Nature as landscape was
loved dearly, and in nature the mountains best. He
would sleep in the country of a spring-night on purpose

to hear the birds sing once in the morning. As to
books, he read little, and made hardly any thing his
study, save the Bible : duties among men and women,
and the press of necessary writing, used the time all up.
A novel could not be read with easy conscience, even
on a sick-bed : " It always seems as if I were wasting
time," — a pang that somehow was not roused by newspapers. He seldom went to poetry for rest, nor to
science for fresh fields of curiosity. A solid argument
with some moral or religious bearing suited best. He
was very humble, too humble, about this ignorance of
books ; for, when he read, it was as men do who think
much outside of books : he was not at the author's
mercy, but caught the strong and weak points at a
glance, and judged a ready, reasonable judgment of
his own.

This was poor provision by way of balance to that
conscience. Only system, and something like a resolute, wise selfishness, would have helped in such a strait.
Had he deliberately done more for himself, he would
have been able to do still more for others. In spite of
the hopeful plans with which, after the Sundays, he so
often faced anew the weeks, there was no system in
the labor, no economy of time and strength. Always
delaying, he felt always pressed. Between those little
deeds done for others, moments slipped away which
should have been compressed into reserves for rest, for
books, for quiet thinking. Other moments vanished in
disproportioned painstaking about trifles. All must be
punctiliously nice, from the linen and the hands to the
wording of the slightest note and the package tied with
twine. So the months passed in a constant sense of
things undone and waiting, things poorly done and condemning. Rarely was a quiet singing moment his, a

half-hour of simple peacefulness. Now and then, if on a Sunday he had preached his twice and the new sermon had been a little better than usual, and he knew no tired friend to whom he ought to offer help in an evening service, — now and then, at such a time, the sound of hymns would come from his lips as he rested, and he really *enjoyed* the pause. But such was not the usual reward of even Sunday.

In the Journal of the later years the struggle left its signs in many a single word or sentence that hints a whole sad day : " Discouraged," — " greatly depressed," — " talked with —— about resigning," — " wasted years " (this on his birthday), — " would go, save for the children," — " impossible to write, duty to give up," — " tired, sad, conscience-stricken," — " sunk in gloom, sleeping to forget myself," — " slept fifteen hours " (a Sunday night), " yet rose so aching with fatigue that I was obliged to lie on the couch again before dinner. Well as I look, I am fast growing old ; and conscience, busy with its terrible reproofs and prophecies, makes life miserable."

These are the secrets of the private diary, but they escaped sometimes into his look, his gait, his talk, his letters. He was fifty-five years old when the last lines were written. Not only very tired,—by this time he was lonely, too. So many had gone whom he loved that he sometimes felt that he belonged more *there* than here.

Dec. 25, 1857. " Eleven years since she was taken. It seems to me longer, much longer. I have grown old since that time. My children have grown up, and my work in life seems not to have been done, but to be past being done."

One sister had gone long before, both his brothers recently, leaving to see each other here only the elder sis-

ter and himself, the oldest and the youngest of those
who knew the Cambridge homestead.   Few of his work-
mates in close sympathy with his thought and his en-
thusiasms lingered in the field.   Two or three times in
the course of the ten years between 1850 and 1860
he wrote to the parish letters of resignation, — which
friends persuaded him to withhold, — and returned
to the Ministers' Association the office of Moderator,
only to resume it at their earnest, affectionate request.
Very touching already was his sense of humility before
the bright young brothers abler for work than he, the
work in which he once had been as strong as any, and
which he still loved more than most.   A friend who
detected the sad tone tried to tell him how tenderly
he was regarded amid the changes in their religious
fellowship : —

April, 1856. "There is a tone of sadness in your last note
to me, which I wish I could in any way cheer. . . . When I
call back the occasions when as a Divinity student I walked
in from Cambridge to attend your Lectures in your church,
the Athenæum Hall, and the Tremont Temple, remembering
what throngs waited eagerly on your longest discourses,
and how earnestly they listened to your most eloquent and
cogent expositions of the strictest form of Unitarianism; and
when I compare these memories with the changed state of
things now, as regards both doctrines and men that engage
enthusiasm among us, it would be insincere for me to deny
that you do not fill your old place *in the old way.* . . We must
all reconcile ourselves to the very peculiar character of our
community.   I do not think it is relatively so well balanced
and well regulated as it was at the time that our denomination first took its stand.   The class of men and women who
were then earnestly religious are not so now. . . Parents
generally will not exercise that kind and amount of religious
control and care over their own families which they did but

a score of years ago. There is a different way of doing most things in our profession. . . I think I have noticed during the last fifteen years a growing tendency to a perfect isolation among our brethren, and yet I believe it has nothing at all to do with personal likes or dislikes between themselves. . . . The more energetic and influential men then were, the more emphatically they were identified as leaders with the movements of the past, the more will they seem to be thrown into the shade by a new set of men and measures. . . You have held in our denomination a place of honor and influence which only your own modesty has led you to underestimate, and which only a tendency to desponding feelings — if you will allow me candidly to say so — leads you now to suppose that you have lost. You will stand for ever identified with the most earnest and vital championship of the most distinct form of Unitarianism. . . It is, after all, *your* speech at a convention which combines all the best and effective appeals that can be looked for on such occasions. If your favorite views are not made as prominent in the minds of others, your spirit and devotion and entire single-heartedness of zeal are the admiration of all of us. You may be sure that words of yours, which you may have been the least inclined to follow with the expectation of great results from them, have mingled with the best religious elements in the hearts of many hearers." . . .

After a minister has been at one post for thirty years, little new experience breaks in on old ideals and old routines of parish-work. Days add themselves together into seasons, and each one brings fresh interest and fresh performance, yet fresh in instance rather than in kind. But in the record of more public service a few new items must be placed, belonging to these years of " afternoon."

From 1857 to 1862 Dr. Gannett was President of the Benevolent Fraternity of Churches, which he had helped

to found so long before, and done all he could to foster
ever since. It had become the strong Unitarian mission
of Boston, supporting several ministers and chapels.
Under his appeals, his church was always one of the
largest yearly donors to its treasury, as well as to that
of the Unitarian Association.

For a long period (1835-1858) he was one of the
Overseers of Harvard College. The elaborate notes for
the speech in which he urged a kind of pastoral professorship for the college-boys, and his long report as chairman of the committee appointed to investigate the
subject, would seem to indicate that the measure owed
its success in no small part to his earnestness.

Over the Divinity School he watched as a grateful
son with very special love. Once before, when it was
in danger from the lack of funds, he had worked among
its saviors. In 1857 there was long talk about its reor-
ganization, and the directors of the "Society for Promoting Theological Education" held many conferences
to promote the scheme. He was among the most zealous of the schemers, and his hope embodied large change.
The School should be adapted, he thought, to the two
classes of men that offered themselves to the ministry,
and were needed by the churches, — those with, and
those without, a thorough education : a two, a three,
and a four years' course would best meet the want, of
which time a fourth part, more or less, should be spent
with a settled minister in getting practical acquaintance
with the life ; the students should live in private families, not camped together in a monastery ; an inspiring
principal, a professor of Biblical study, and an outside
corps of lecturers, — settled ministers, — should furnish
the instruction. These were the leading features of the
" Plan of a Theological School" according to his ideal,

or according to his vision of what might be made real.
It proved but a dream, however, then : the only result
attained by all the schemes and talk was the appointment of two non-resident professors.

Antioch College in Ohio was winning reputation at
this time under that rarest of inspirers, Horace Mann,
but had been so sadly crippled by early errors in its
management that some great effort was needed to save
it from financial bankruptcy. It was the unsectarian
college of the West; it was a college where the experiment of coeducation of young men and women was
on trial with rich promise of success; and the moral
standard aimed at was so high as to make it in still a
third way an experiment. Emulation had been entirely
discarded as a motive to study ; and the President, act
ing on the belief that his college was to form character
as well as mind, had publicly promised that no one of
vicious habits, whatever else he might be, should ever
receive the diploma of graduation from his hands.
Antioch must have rescue at the hands of Unitarians.
Half well-disposed, half-doubtful, Dr. Gannett went
Westward and attended its Commencement in 1857.
He returned to be its eager advocate before the denomination ; and his word carried weight. Among other
modes of urging it, he published in the " Quarterly " of
the Unitarian Association a plea, which President Mann
wrote him was " of inestimable price." " No man," said
another of its champions, — " no man could do as much
as you *have* done to propitiate the good-will and confidence of the Unitarian body towards the Institution."

A great event in the quiet life was now at hand.
The home so much endeared by its associations, so

much profaned by change, was at last abandoned for a
snug house in a crevice running in from Boylston Street.
But — event greater far ! — the people had at last decided
to leave Federal Street Church ! To the minister's feeling
life held few incidents that meant so much. The old
shi ir e was very dear, and the spot itself historic. Its first
ha l wing dated back to Boston's lane-and-pasture era.
The primitive meeting-house appears to have been a
barn on " Long Lane " made over in 1729 by a party of
Scotch-Irish settlers who brought their Presbyteriai,
discipline into this heart of Congregationalism. The
building before long erected in its place became memorable in 1788 ; for there the Massachusetts Convention
adopted the Federal Constitution, — an occasion that
gave the street its more honorable name. Just before
this happened, the society had voted to give up their
old fellowship and join the Congregational neighbors.
A few years later young Channing was preaching in the
pulpit of what had by that time become a little " Liberal " parish ; and the third meeting-house was that
which his attractiveness speedily made necessary to
hold the growing congregation, and then made famous
as the cradle of Unitarianism. For a long time now it
had lingered among the warehouses and the swarming
population of the by-street tenements, a relic of the past.
Three attempts to procure a new site that all would like
had failed, because some of the old worshippers clung
so fondly to the wonted place. " I am sorely disappointed," the pastor wrote after one such veto, " and at
first felt that my only course is to resign my ministry ;
for I consider it a suicidal decision, as the society must
crumble away where they are, and I cannot consent to
see it perish in my hands. The indifference, of course,
is a consequence of my ill success as a minister." A

fourth effort resulted in a vote to move to the " new land " which Boston was creating for itself out of its hugging waters. And, so far as the choice of location was concerned, the departure proved, after all, well-timed; for the congregation, being the first to move in that direction, secured the beautiful site just ready on Arlington Street fronting the Public Garden. Within the dozen years since they settled there, a goodly company of towers and steeples, most of them the homes of exiles fleeing like themselves before the push of business, has risen in still newer streets beyond.

One day in March of 1859 the high-backed pews were crowded by friends to hear and look the last good-bye. The pastor's morning sermon sketched the history of the meeting-house; and in the afternoon nine other ministers, all children of the church, though not all bearing still its denominational name, gathered around him in the large old-fashioned pulpit to take part in the closing service. The pilgrims were very reverent. A carefully made model preserves for future generations both the outside and the inside aspect of the church, while parts of Dr. Channing's pulpit were wrought into furniture for the new vestry and into tokens for the relic-lovers.

Nearly three years of tabernacle-life passed by before the new temple stood ready for its dedication. The graceful building was significant of the changes which half a century had wrought in Boston culture. With proud rejoicings, — to judge by an ode written at the time, — the fathers in 1809 had turned their wood to brick. Their children transfigured the plain brick to freestone and the architecture of the Italian Renaissance. The pulpit descended nearer to the people, and the pews a little lowered their backs; but their but-

toned doors, and the gallery with its separate row of
windows, and the high-perched organ-loft and white
walls untouched by fresco, keep up, amid the arches
and the stately columns and the richly moulded panels,
a pleasant feeling as of elder ways.   An aged deacon,
one of Dr. Channing's generation, outlived his friend
just long enough to add as his gift the chime of bells.

   The dedication sermon no less significantly hinted,
in its way, the change in Boston faith.   The previous
church had been erected in a time of theologic stir by
Liberals standing consciously on the verge of a great
heresy.   Now the whole Unitarian controversy lay dim
in the years behind.   A cycle of thought had been completed, and men were growing conscious of another wide
suspense of faith.   The minister in Federal Street read
the omens well.   He dedicated the new church to a
positive Christian Faith.   The necessity and glory of
strong conviction in religion was his theme : " I am not
come to destroy, but to fulfil."   To fortify faith rather
than encourage doubt, to urge truth possessed rather
than seek to find new truth or to abolish error by attack,
was the function of the Christian Church, as in old
time, so in new, he said; for Faith — Faith as a mighty
assurance of truth believed — was the secret of the
highest character, the loftiest purpose, the most glorious achievement, was the cement of society no less
than the bond which unites earth to heaven.   Neither
doubt nor unbelief was sinful.   Scepticism had its
rights, and had done good : Christendom at this day
held a surer faith because of its jealous inspections.
But denial, as a habit and delight, impoverished the
mind, starved the heart, beggared the conscience.
Freedom was neither the end of life nor a means to
that end : it was nothing but an opportunity.   Free

Inquiry was a method, not a result. The New Testament merely pronounced an axiom of the spiritual life, in declaring with such stress that they who live without Faith must perish.

" Criticism has its place and its value. Religion neither abhors nor dreads it. Christianity neither despises it, nor trembles before it. Let the Bible, the gospel, the teachings of the Church, the beliefs of the past, the assertions of the present, be subjected to the most severe and impartial examination. Detect every blemish, expose every weakness; cross-examine the witnesses, canvass the miracles; tear the diadem of glory, or the crown of thorns, if you can, from the head of the Anointed One; analyze, dissect, curtail, decry revelation; lay bare or overturn the foundations of faith: so long as all this, or any part of it, is done, as all honest work should be done, with a good purpose, and by fair means, let it be done. But it does not belong to the Church to carry on this process. It may permit certain parts of the work to be conducted within its borders; but it is not the business of the Church, through its officers or its servants, to make men doubt. Who ever thought it was one of the functions of government to foster rebellion, or of a tribunal to destroy confidence in its own decisions?" ...

" Faith, as it stands in the Bible, is a grand and glorious word. It sweeps over the universe in its significance; mounts up to the throne of God, and lays a reverential hand on the attributes of the Most High; runs through the past to the beginning, when the heavens and the earth were made; reaches forward, till it grasps the results of the Divine government and human agency through the periods of an endless duration; and brings within the mighty burthen of its meaning the spiritual realities which science cannot measure, and philosophy cannot reach. Let not the dogmatist nor the bigot degrade it to the uses for which alone they think it fit. Shall the sword with which Michael drove the arch-fiend from heaven be seized by every puny arm that would lay an adversary low? I ask neither one school nor another, the philologist nor the theologian, to give me the definition of faith: I find a better than they can furnish in the text, which, in the only terms commensurate with the height and breadth of its true import, declares that 'faith is the substance of things hoped for, the evidence of things not seen.' . . .

" If, under the restrictions of the gospel history or the requisitions of the Christian argument, the word obtain an immediate connection with him who is pronounced the 'Author and Finisher of our faith,' it does not lose the broad and lofty character which we have ascribed to it. It is still belief in facts of which the senses do not take cognizance, and in truths disclosed to a higher faculty than reason. Man's chief endowment being that through which he acquaints himself with God, reason is not his highest endowment. The reason points to God, but does not lead us to him, simply because it cannot. Reason may legitimate the processes of the spiritual understanding, but it cannot create them. Neither can the spiritual understanding, by which I mean the religious faculty in our nature, educe them from itself. They must be awakened by an external influence, as the life of the plant must be stimulated by the air. That influence obtains access to the soul through the consent of faith. Revelation is an indispensable necessity of man, if he would realize the fact or obey the law of his own perfection. . . . What reason cannot do, faith will do, — connect the soul with God by availing itself of the soul's receptivity of Divine influence. Christ awakens this receptivity, and then supplies the soul with the knowledge and the aid, of its want of which it may have been but faintly conscious before his approach. . . . The gospel seeks man as made for God, yet as having through sin lost sight of God; and, by its disclosures of the character, mercy, and will of the Heavenly Father, enables him to lay hold on that knowledge which is 'eternal life.'

" Now, what relation has reason to this history of the re-

generated and perfected soul ? The relations, first, of herald,
and next of interpreter; in the first instance authenticating
by proper tests the credentials of the messenger from God,
and then determining by just methods what meaning should
be put upon his instruction, even as Daniel, in the presence of
the Babylonian monarch, pronounced the hand which traced
the mysterious characters on the wall to have been sent by
God, and then gave the interpretation of the writing. Reason is neither ignored nor undervalued by the believer; but
it is neither exalted above revelation, nor lifted into equal
dignity with it. Its place is not on the top of the mountain,
by the side of Him who taught the multitude, but with
them, listening with reverent admiration. It should stand
at the foot of Calvary, not with the scornful exclamation,
'Let him now come down from the cross and we will believe
him;' but with the awe-struck confession, 'Truly, this was
the Son of God.'"

By planting, strengthening, extending Faith positively, not negatively, he repeated, had the Church
prospered in the past: only by increasing Faith in the
same way could it in the future prosper. It was its
function, for example, to stand for the reverence due to
the Bible as the store-house of divine influence, for that
stupendous fact of Mediation which constitutes the
thread of its history, for the solemn doctrine of Retribution and the indestructible relations which exist between
righteousness and happiness, sin and suffering, in this
life and the life to come, — to stand positively for these
faiths rather than to lend its strength to nurturing the
temper which distrusts them.

"Who can conceive of the change that would come over
the prospects of truth, if, instead of cavil, doubt, or denial,
we set ourselves to the task of exposition, defence, and entreaty. Entreaty! why, the truth itself persuades men,

when they can see and hear it, as if an angel spake to them. What results has not the preaching of a single truth often wrought in character and in society! When I observe how much may be done in recommending error by an earnest advocacy, I long to see those who hold the simple gospel go forth in God's name, and call their fellow-men to salvation with the irresistible voice of strong belief. Oh! were we ourselves moved as we should be by that one short line, 'Our Father, who art in Heaven,' would it not be the very sword of the Spirit in our hands, with which to strike down the rebellion and self-will of men? Rather would it not be as music which arrests the busy, and cheers the weary, and fills the heart with a strange delight? If any one of us could go out into the world, believing what those six words convey with his whole, whole heart, and preach it as he then could not help preaching it, it would sink into other hearts as the rain into thirsty ground, to soften and enrich and clothe it with a perpetual verdure. Ay, give to the weakest of us such a faith as we all may have, and Napoleon's victories would be nursery-tales in comparison with the conquests he might achieve." . . .

" We dedicate our house of prayer in troubled times, when the sight of armed men is familiar in our streets." The words are not needed to remind us that we must now turn far back in our story. One thread firmly twisted into this life, as into the life of every American during the years of which this chapter and the last one treat, has been purposely omitted hitherto, that it might be drawn out by itself.

Dr. Gannett was poorly fitted to take part with other men in any work to which he could not give the whole of himself. His conscience, once engaged, made him the closest, truest of allies. It also hindered much alliance. " No man had more the courage of his opinions than he," says one who knew him well, and differed widely from him. To belong to a party was to labor for it, give his name and time and strength to it, accept its foremost duties, bear its reproaches, and be its champion everywhere. But, where he was to co-operate, he needed to see not only a right end in view, but what, in his own eyes, were right motives and right methods. He could not go hand-in-hand with men who used what he deemed outrage, even to overthrow what he might at the same time deem much greater wrong. A cause might have his deepest sympathy, while its specific party, if unjust in urging it, in vain would claim his presence : he had to be absent or be untruthful to himself. And the same courage of opinions that marked his adherence was apt to make him outspoken in opposition.

For several reasons, therefore, in the long Anti-Slavery crusade he could never join the band of brave crusaders ; and they regarded him as more hostile to them than almost any other Unitarian minister. The time may not yet have come for doing such men as he full justice for the stand they took. Those who at the time condemned them bitterly would still condemn, no doubt ; yet some, perhaps, would moderate their past words, if they could. " Anti-slavery " he always was, but slavery was the thing abhorred : it did not follow that the slave-holders necessarily deserved abhorrence, nor that their institution was a wrong to be righted by fiercely lashing tongue more than by fierce attack of hand. The Abolitionists seemed to him to systematically denounce all at South or North who did not accept their watch-words. — They also seemed to ignore responsibility for the likely consequences of the watchwords. To him likely consequence was part of a word

or a deed, and one could not lightly discharge himself
from liability for it. He saw that a Northern demand for
" immediate emancipation " meant " disunion," and did
not see that disunion would bring relief to the enslaved :
he thought it certain to bring worse enslavement. He
saw that complex issues of civilization were involved in
any deep cure of the evil, and that the most valuable
results of civilization would be imperilled by its rash
treatment. The stopping of the outrage where it existed, not a mere Northern avoidance — more nominal
than real — of participation in it, was the end in view, —
and an end that could be reached only by influence,
not compulsion, he believed. His own standard of
right was ideal; but where hostile minds were to be
brought to the ideal, he was a man of methods rather
than of " watch-words." He was under bonds of his
nature to work towards the absolute right by helping to
make actual the best right possible. By constitution he
belonged to the class who calculate practical effects and
have to act accordingly in the " causes."—Moreover,—it
is but saying the same thing in a more specific way,—he
was too good a Peace-man to be an Abolitionist ; for he
saw what some Abolitionists could not, and others would
not, see, that disunion almost certainly meant war.
And that meant, besides all other horror, failure of the
Republic and shock to the great cause of popular government throughout the world. — And finally, apart from
that reason for his devotion to the Union, the whole
strength of his nature, conscious and unconscious, was
reverent to organic order and visible law. The same
predispositions that in religious thought kept him so
firmly planted on the authority of an outward revelation, that in *all* loyalties made him so strenuously true,
also made him one who only in the very last extreme

could have ventured on immediate anarchy to compass a higher future peace.

As year by year the nation neared its woe, feeling on both sides deepened. Many at the North, who stood quiet through the Texan annexation, burst out in protest when the Fugitive Slave Bill, in 1850, by legalizing better modes of capture, turned their Free States at last into good slave-hunting grounds, and when they saw black neighbors actually caught back from their consenting streets to doom. Others, who gnashed their teeth, but kept lips shut at that, remembering the old compact on which the Republic had been built, felt patience suddenly desert them when the Missouri Compromise was broken by the planters and their friends in 1854, and new territory was thrown open to the encroaching curse. There had been a day of mobs against Emancipation lecturers in the North : now came a day of mobs to rescue fugitives for freedom. Among others who changed ground were the Unitarian ministers. A few of them had long been leading Abolitionists : many now enlisted in the ranks. In their meetings, anti-slavery resolutions had at first been put aside as irrelevant, then mild votes were passed, and finally majorities grew earnest.

But Dr. Gannett held fast his first belief that the subject was irrelevant to the purpose of those meetings, and he uniformly opposed the introduction of such resolutions. Certain expressions that probably fell from his lips on these occasions in some excited moment of debate are still held in stern remembrance by the old champions, then fighting against such heavy social odds. It is said — he only believed it himself because men like the Mays were willing to take oath the words were truly reported — that he called the Abolitionist temper " the

hellish spirit alive and active here in our very midst,
even in New England, which left little comparative
need for us to go South to rebuke an evil;" and he is
charged with having said, after the Fugitive Slave Bill
had been passed, that "the perpetuity of the Union
depended on the support of that law," and that "he
should feel it to be his duty to turn away from his door
a fugitive slave, unfed, unaided in any way, rather than
set at naught the law of the land." If he ever said that
last, he had unsaid it before as he unsaid it afterwards,
by intimating in published sermons what he really
would do in the case. At one of these Unitarian meetings, — it was in 1851, just after Mr. Sims had been
restored to slavery, — he rose, after a denunciation of
the commissioner who had ordered the return, to urge
that the officer had acted "from convictions of his con-
stitutional obligations as an upholder of law and as a
good citizen, and that a wrong was done by the resolutions in stigmatizing him as a ' cruel ' man because of
that return." The word was cancelled.

The other saddest week that Boston ever knew came
three years later. Rev. John Parkman writes : —

"I stayed at your father's house during Anniversary
Week, in the spring of 1854. During that week Burns was
arrested, tried, and sent back to the South. While the trial
was going on, Dr. Gannett never lost an opportunity of
having a fling at the Abolitionists. I was accustomed to
hear him denounce their violence and fanaticism, with a due
degree of patience; but sharing in the excitement of this
particular juncture, being in fact a member of the Vigilance
Committee, I did not listen to him as patiently as I was
accustomed to do. I was especially annoyed by the — as it
seemed to me — indifferent and unfeeling way in which he
spoke of the poor fugitive slave. 'What an ado about a

mere single incident of slavery?' 'What good is going to
come of all this excitement?' 'What is one man set against
the continuance and safety of the Union?' he said, among
other things. I finally proposed to him that we should not
discuss the matter further. This state of things lasted two
or three days. On the day when Burns was given up, the
first person whom I met on entering his house was Dr. Gannett. 'Is it true that he has been surrendered?' he asked,
in those plaintive tones which all who knew him well remember. On my replying 'Yes,' he threw himself into a
chair, buried his face in his hands, and then, in a voice broken
by sobbing, burst out, 'O God, forgive this guilty nation!
What will become of us? what dreadful judgments are in
store for us?' He said more, that I do not remember exactly,
but these particular words I am sure he used. He recovered
himself in a few minutes, but was miserably depressed
through the whole day. I met no one during that week
who seemed to take so much to heart the event which made
it so sad and memorable.

"I am quite aware that what I have just written adds
emphasis to the question, How, then, do you explain the
silence in the pulpit of this strong hater of slavery, and his
counsel to others to follow his example? I will only say that
whoever discusses that question is in duty bound to keep
this truth in mind, — that specific acts or omissions ought
obviously to be interpreted in the light of character viewed
as a whole. Those who think that Dr. Gannett's course in
reference to slavery was determined by unworthy considerations, by shameful timidities, by lack of conscientiousness,
hint at anomalies of character in which no candid, no wise
man believes.

"I have witnessed other similar struggles between opposing tendencies in your father's intellect and temperament.
I used to tell him when he talked about his having a sinful
nature, and how he felt wicked when he rode on Sunday, that
he had his ancestors' Calvinism in his bones. On the other

19

hand, he had a *horror* of the doctrine of the Trinity that I never witnessed in any one else. He looked on Trinitarianism as a kind of idolatry, an impiety!

"Then, again, I remember his saying with the utmost warmth he never would recognize Parker as a Christian minister, by exchanges with him. Yet there was no minister for whom Parker had a greater esteem, or against whom he made so little complaint. If I remember rightly, he somewhere expresses this feeling in print."

Here is the daughter's memory of the same week : –

"I do think Father's love for Order should be emphasized : it was more than that, it was loyalty to the powers that be,— to God, to the government, to elderly people, all representing authority; and this leaning on his part sprang from his Puritanical child-life and his humility. I don't know whether Father ever said he would turn from his door, &c., I don't *believe* he ever did, and I KNOW he did say on the Burns day that he would shelter the slave, and then offer himself to the law on his own confession. I know that he expressed disapprobation at our school-girls having stood at the window to watch the rendition. I know that he then said to me it was right, but a terrible day to witness, and that it almost persuaded him that it would be better not to obey, and then (this a strong impression), 'No, obey now! but the revolution must come, and such a general revolution is not disobedience.' I *know* that I said to him, 'What if the slave came to your door?' and I know that he answered solemnly, 'I have thought of that; and if he comes to-night, or any time, I should shelter him and aid him to go further on to Canada, and then I should go and give myself up to prison, and insist on being made a prisoner, would accept of no release; (for' — this in brackets a strong impression — 'I have decided what to do as an individual against the government, and therefore I should abide the result.') I know that I have heard him say the same to others, for his manner when speaking of it could never be forgotten. It was intensely quiet and determined, his hands clenched, and he set his teeth each time. *I know it.* And it shows the struggle and the man and the conscience and the thought, Loyalty to the Law. It has a very glorious side."

To Mrs. S. W. Bush we owe this vivid recollection of another scene in the anti-slavery times : —

" Years and years ago I saw advertised a meeting to be held in Boylston Hall, by the Unitarian ministers, for the discussion of somê point relating to the actual work of the body. Though not then in the habit of attending such meetings, I went to this one. The audience was small, but most of the well-known preachers of the day were present. The subject (which I have forgotten) was announced, and some one rose to open the discussion. As soon as he took his seat, Mr. S. J. May rose. I need not tell you what was his subject, or how he brought it to bear. Brows clouded, the gentlemen on the platform became uneasy, faint cries at first, then louder, of 'order,' 'order,' appeals to the chairman to stop the speaker, as he was introducing a subject entirely irrelevant to the one under discussion. Mr. May stood firm, erect, waiting for the storm to subside, endeavoring to put in his word, yet without clamor. Once he took his seat, and it seemed as if the meeting would come to order, and the proposed subject be again brought up; but some one rose who wished to prove that the anti-slavery work was entirely outside of the ministerial work, that it belonged to politics, not religion. Again Mr. May was on his feet, entering his earnest protest against such atheism as that. A dozen ministers started up to refute him; they threatened to put a stop to the meeting if Mr. May was not silenced. At that moment a sound was heard from the midst of the audience, a hand fell with more than the weight of the speaker's gavel, and the uproar was quieted, as your father rose, pale, emaciated, from recent illness, but with such a light in his

eye, such power in that voice, as he said : ' Brethren, I suppose
there is no one here less able to be present than myself; but
I will sit till morning, before I see Brother May put down.
I do not sympathize with him in many of his views or his
ways of carrying them out, but I claim for him as for all
others liberty of speech.' He sank exhausted into his seat,
but those few words had thrilled every heart. Mr. May was
accorded the floor, and, himself deeply touched by this plea
for him, made only a short statement of his ideas and with-
drew, leaving the subject for which the meeting had been
called to be quietly discussed. I do not believe any one
present could ever forget the majesty which seemed to fill and
surround your father, as he stood up in his bodily weakness,
the vindicator of perfect liberty of speech. It was a glorious
moment, one full of inspiration; and I doubt not went forth
into many lives, as I am sure it did into mine, to leave its
impress indelibly upon the character."

Nor is this the only story of the kind remembered of
him. At a Unitarian Convention in Salem where the
Fugitive Slave Law was under discussion, and James
Freeman Clarke was about to be put down by parliamentary ruling after one of Dr. Gannett's earnest
speeches, the speaker was again upon his feet, pleading
that the Convention be guided by the higher Christian
rule, even if it sacrificed the parliamentary one : the
members had listened to him, it was but justice for
them to hear the other side. And it was done.

Had he lived at the South, with the outrage within
sight and hearing, the same demand for justice would
have been very apt to place him high in the calendar of
anti-slavery martyrs. It was this same instinct which
made him so careful to own that Southerners might,
in good faith and without wilful sin, believe their
institution right, and so indignant with denouncing

Abolitionists. In a letter written very early in the troublous times, he tells a friend: —

"I must insist that genuine, primitive colonization, and sound, thorough anti-slavery doctrine, are not incompatible. I hope, therefore, to maintain both. But there is one characteristic of the anti-slavery movement which I cannot approve or excuse, or for a moment cease to deprecate. I refer to the injustice which is, as it seems to me, continually and systematically heaped upon all those who do not adopt the principles or advocate measures of the Abolitionists. There are exceptions, I know, to the universal manifestations of such a spirit, and I am glad to say that I have never thought that you betrayed or felt this spirit. But the general strain of language of Abolitionists towards, — not only slaveholders, of whom I mean not now to say any thing, — but towards Northern men who do not agree with them, is, I think, unchristian, bitterly and fiercely unchristian. With a party which glories in such a course, I cannot strike hands. I may sympathize in their objects, while I dread and abhor their spirit. Here is my objection, my sole objection to the Anti-slavery movement. Discuss the subject, the Abolitionists may and should; but when they denounce other men, who, believing such discussion pernicious, would discourage it, and hold them up as confederate with the agents of wickedness; when, for example, a Colonizationist is *therefore* set down and set forth at once as an apologist for slavery, or when a Christian minister, because he in his soul believes that the Abolitionists are doing harm by the manner in which they conduct their discussions, and hence refuses to throw upon their side whatever influence he may have, is therefore publicly branded with the seal of condemnation, and the confidence of his fellow Christians is taken from him, — injustice is done, cruelty is practised, and they who are loudest in their inculcation of brotherly love are its most flagrant transgressors. The Abolitionists have a right to act on their convictions, and to require that they should be respected for obeying their convictions; but the same right belongs to other men. In principle, I am with you. In spirit, I rejoice to believe that you and I would be one. But there are those with whom you are connected, persons who seem to me so to distrust the goodness of all who differ from them, and to look down upon all such with so great a consciousness of moral superiority, that I feel myself when in their presence to be in a situation not unlike that of a criminal before his accuser and judge."

The judges were not wont to mince their words in passing sentence. Of course he suffered personally much reproach from them. To his regret the church-committee at Federal Street refused to lend the Anti-Slavery Society their house, when that Society wished to pronounce a eulogy on Dr. Follen, the noble German, lover of liberty, who perished on the "Lexington." Pastor as well as people had to bear the lash for that refusal. To cite another instance : —

April 7, 1840. "Unexpectedly met —— at Hillard's office, and had a few minutes' conversation with him, plain and earnest but not uncourteous on either side, about his speech at Lynn, in which he said 'no words could describe the baseness and meanness of my conduct' in refusing to read from my pulpit a notice of the annual meeting of the Massachusetts Anti-Slavery Society."

Yet by some of the strongest Abolitionists at home he was known well enough to have credit for principle as sincere as their own. Not so with English acquaintances, who in their newspapers spared no rebuke. One friend, however, though not himself agreeing with Dr. Gannett, took generous risk to show that he was misrepresented. To this friend, Rev. Russell Lant Carpenter, he writes at one time and another thus : —

"Your letters on Slavery in the 'Inquirer' impressed me with their evident candor of spirit and fairness of statement. You can do good in England by representing the truth; and, in this age of partisanship, a man who is blamed by each wing of the social state may congratulate himself that he has reason to believe himself 'about right.' It is the vice of philanthropy in our day that it condemns and traduces every one who will not use its own terms or adopt its most extreme measures. The time must come when reasonable men, at least, will see that a subject so encumbered with difficulties needs to be managed with judgment, and may be regarded under different lights by equally honest minds. . . .

"The course taken by some of the English Unitarian ministers, I confess, gives me pain, because their votes seem to forbid any intercourse, and exclude the continuance of sympathy between me and some whom I have loved. . . . I have two or three times been moved by misrepresentations connected with my name in English Unitarian Anti-slavery papers, which were sent me to reply by a simple statement of the truth; but I have found that they who are so careless in their censures are generally slow in retraction, and I have preferred silence to controversy. . . . You may be assured that I entertain no other than kind feelings towards ——, but I wish you would say to him, that, if my conduct in regard to other points of duty had been as well sustained by my judgment and my conscience as my course in regard to slavery, I should feel little self-reproach or little anxiety for the future.

His closest view of actual slavery was gained in 1853, when he spent a week or two in Charleston and Savannah. Among hospitable friends, he saw it in its very best aspects of city and plantation life; saw kindness on the part of masters, seeming affection and content on the part of slaves. But it made his heart sick, — "the fact of irresponsible ownership of fellow-men, as if they were beasts of burden, or part of the household stuff;" and in a sermon after his return he gave solemn testimony against it. Nor then for the first or for the last time was such testimony urged against —

"The grievous wrong, utterly indefensible and unjustifiable, to be held in universal and immitigable condemnation. . . . It is the attempt to degrade a human being into something less than a man, — not the confinement, unjust as this is, nor the blows, cruel as these are, — but the denial of his equal share in the rights, prerogatives, and responsibilities of a human being, which brands the institution of slavery with its peculiar and ineffaceable odiousness."

But with this utter condemnation of slavery he joined that conscientious devotion to established Law, to Peace, to Union, which in the issues of the hour placed him practically on the side opposed to Freedom. The struggle in his mind; his revulsion from the inevitable clash; his slow yielding, only inch by inch; the looking to God in perfect ignorance what the country ought to do; and, among other things, his clear intention what to do himself in case a fugitive should ever reach his door, — are displayed in many a passage of his printed sermons.

While the Fugitive Slave Bill was impending, February, 1850, he spoke thus: —

"*Freedom, Peace, and Order,* — these three constitute the gift of Heaven to this Union; and woe to him who lightly puts either of them in jeopardy! . . . These three, be it remembered, belong together. Try not to separate them. Concede something of opinion, something of preference, something even of your judgment of abstract right, for the sake of their conjoint preservation. When you come to deal with actual relations and positive evils, consider how society is knit together; and bear it ever in mind that patience and hope are more effectual means of introducing the triumph of right under a perfect constitution of society, far more effectual than discord and violence. Freedom, peace, order! — he who sacrifices one of these, in his anxiety to secure the largest measure of either or both of the other two, is at best a blind enthusiast, if he be not a mad fanatic. They must stand together like the States of this Union, inseparable, and cherished with a common love by every one who cares for the welfare of his country or the progress of mankind."

November, 1850, soon after the Bill had passed : —

Calamity of Disunion. — " I cannot contemplate the possible overthrow of the American Union but as a calamity too great for the common speech of men to describe. I cling to the Union, and pray that it may be preserved from dissolution, because such an event would involve the disappointment of the dearest hopes of the philanthropist, and put back the world, that now seems to be coming to a comprehension of the blessings which the Creator intended it should enjoy, for I know not how many ages. I cannot foresee the extent of evil that would follow on the failure of this attempt to demonstrate the worth and durability of free institutions, — an attempt made on the grandest scale and under the most favorable circumstances. I can only hear the sorrowful regrets of those whose hope would be extinguished, and the exultant sneer of those who begrudge the people every right which they now have the power to exercise or the courage to demand. Not freedom only, but civilization, would suffer incalculable detriment. The progress of opinion would be arrested, the sanguine would be disheartened, the energetic intimidated, and another period of apathetic gloom — to last, no one can tell for how many generations — might come over the nations. If this sound to any one like the language of extravagance, let him consider the position which America now holds in the regards of the civilized world, and he will be slow to pronounce such anticipations visionary.

"But, whatever should be the result abroad, there can be no doubt respecting the consequences which would ensue here upon the overthrow of our present government. I, finally, cleave to the Union, both theoretically and practically, because these consequences are too dreadful to be anticipated without the keenest sense of misfortune. I esteem it a fit occasion for praise to the God of our fathers that they constructed a Union, the preservation of which will prevent such terrible disasters. Should the Union be dissolved, it would be on sectional grounds. . . . Rival states would take its place, mutually jealous and mutually hostile, with causes of irritation springing out of their past history, and occasions of strife continually arising out of the new relations in which they would stand to one another; — rival states, between which, even if an amicable rupture of the bonds that now hold them together were possible, war would be enkindled before a year had expired, — war that would be marked by the atrocities which hatred, stimulated by opportunity, always begets. Border incursions would ripen into prolonged warfare. It has become a proverb that they who were once nearest, when estranged, make the most bitter enemies. One cause of ill-will, especially, would gather force with every day. The institution which is the principal mark and ground of difference between the North and South would breed perpetual mischief, as those held in bondage on one side of a national boundary would escape to the other side, and what is now a source of vexation would then induce an immediate resort to arms. There is no need of calling in an exuberant imagination to describe the horrors that must flow from the erection of two or more independent governments, whatever internal form they might take, out of the present United States. The dullest foresight may descry evils of such magnitude that the heart grows sick at their contemplation.

"And what would be gained as an equivalent of all that would be lost? Would the North be freer or happier, more prosperous or more religious, than she now is? Let the history of every period signalized by the prevalence of evil passions and the effusion of blood furnish the answer. Would the South grow richer, stronger, or more worthy of respect? With every disadvantage under which it now suffers aggravated, and the benefits for which it is indebted to the Union withdrawn, certainly not. Would philanthropy behold the accomplishment of its wishes, or oppression relax its grasp on those whom it dooms to perpetual servitude? On the contrary, when both the right and the opportunity of exerting some influence for the amelioration of the evils of slavery, which the citizens of the free States now have, should cease, and the colored race should be left to the interests and habits of masters who would then carefully exclude alike interference and observation, their condition would be more hopeless even than at present. Would slavery become extinct through the speedy or gradual ruin of the Southern country, which, deprived of the alliance that now sends some currents of life through its languid veins, would sink into poverty and imbecility? Even if this should be the spectacle which the future would unroll, I do not envy him whose prophetic eye can look on such a result with satisfaction. Nothing would be gained by dissolving the Union, — nothing, — nothing. And much would be sacrificed, which, if it were possible that a time should come, when the members of the republic thus rent in pieces would wish to restore its unity, could never be recovered. God save us from disunion! I know that slavery is a political and a moral evil, a sin and a curse; but disunion seems to me to be treason, not so much against the country as against humanity. The curse would not be removed, the evil would not be abated, no one would be benefited by it. And only the historian who should record the long series of misfortunes and crimes to which it would give rise could tell how much all would have lost.

"Would I then maintain the integrity of the Union

always and for ever? Are there no possible circumstances that would compel us to renounce our allegiance to the constitution under which these states have arisen to greatness? I do not say this. Would I submit to every law which might find a place in the legislature of my country? My answer would be in the negative. But there is a wide difference between refusal to comply with a law which we hold to be immoral, incurring, of course, the legal penalty of such refusal, and an assault upon the institutions under which unwise legislators have had an opportunity of doing a wrong thing. No one denies the existence of a higher law than any which can proceed from human legislation. The real question at issue concerns the interpretation of that higher law. Does it abrogate loyalty to an earthly government, or does it add to the sentiment of loyalty the force of religious obligation? This is not a point on which conscience gives one decision, while worldly interest or personal cowardice gives another. There is conscience on both sides. My neighbor's conscience and mine may not pronounce the same sentence. Each of us may act from a sense of the highest obligation, and yet we may act very differently."

In June, 1854, after the rendition of Mr. Burns to slavery: —

Union may cost too much. — "Until that solemn crisis arrives, which in the providence of God is the ultimate fact of political history, when a people are driven upon the right of revolution, and society returning to its first principles is dissolved into its original elements, — a crisis which no thoughtful man will contemplate but with dismay, — we must avoid all conflict with the laws or the legal authorities of the land. We may present a passive resistance to an enactment or a mandate which it would violate our consciences to obey. Else our obedience to human law may supplant our respect for what we believe to be the requisition of God, which would be fatal to integrity and purity of character.

But in this collision between the claims of an earthly and a divine government, each of which we recognize as legitimate, we must accept the penalty of disobedience to the former, — suffering, not fighting, for conscience' sake. . . .

" I repeat that, while a law stands in force we must either consent to its execution or bear the penalty of disobedience. But when the execution of that law not only inflicts a pang on our moral nature, but is made doubly painful by the frequency and zeal with which it is carried into effect, we cannot, or, if we can, we ought not to fold our arms and close our lips in patient acquiescence. The principle of the present Fugitive Slave Law was embodied in the similar act of Congress passed more than half a century ago, but for more than fifty years the South was content that the act should remain comparatively inoperative: let it take the same course now, and the North would acquiesce in the legal validity of a claim seldom enforced. But if the South evince a determination to put Northern feeling to a trial on this question whenever it shall have an opportunity, Northern men will not consent to witness often such scenes as we were made to endure a few days since. The question will not be simply whether a law shall be executed or be resisted: a deeper question will arise, when the Southern master shall use the free States as the ground on which to assert the immaculate character of slavery. The alternative will then present itself, whether we will become ready participants in upholding a system which we abhor, or will seek a dissolution of the bond which holds us and the South together.

" This is sad language and fearful. I have loved the Union as dearly perhaps as any one. I have clung to it as the guide and hope of the oppressed nations of the world. I have lost friends and been traduced, — that is no matter, save as it shows how I have spoken, — because I maintained that the Union must be preserved at almost any cost. I say so now. But it may cost us too much. If every manly and honest Christian sentiment must be subjected to continual indignity, then

will sober men, who have loved the Union and clung to it,
ask whether a peaceable separation, with all its prospective
issues, would not be preferable. . . . Our national adminis-
tration and our free soil must not be used to promote the
interests of slavery; and if, in maintaining this position, a
result which five years ago, or a year ago, we should have
regarded as among the most extravagant suggestions of a
gloomy foresight, should become inevitable, and even be followed by disasters, at the thought of whose possibility we
tremble, we may deplore the situation into which we shall
be brought; but how can we, with self-respect or in consistency with our holiest persuasions, avoid it? We must
do our duty, and leave the issue with Him who ruleth over
the affairs of men. Precious as our national history and
national hope are, righteousness and liberty are still dearer
possessions.

Then came the day, in June of 1856, when Brooks of
South Carolina assaulted Charles Sumner in the Senate
Chamber. Massachusetts shook as if the blows fell
on each head in the State! " War ? " Not yet, is his
word: be earnestly, religiously calm before we act!

" I read with sadness the language of Christian men and
Christian ministers, whose brave words, if they be well considered, are bloody words. To me the musket and the Bible
do not seem twin implements of civilization. . . . Let the
alternative involved in the relation of slavery to the Union
be brought before me under circumstances which compel me,
if I cling to the one, to encourage the other, and I shall
know that God has called me to the sad duty of helping to
destroy the citadel of the world's hope. But, till I see that
duty too plain to be mistaken, I will pray that it may not be
made the test of my submission to a solemn and dark providence. I think that, if the hour of final decision had come,
we should see it more clearly than we now do. This is
the time for lowly and importunate prayer. There need

not be less of bravery because there is more of piety, less of righteous indignation because there is more of humble confession, nor less love of freedom because there is more reliance on God. Be watchful to detect the first sign of duty, and ready to obey the first call to action that shall come from a higher wisdom than that of man. Be patient till the hour comes; be prompt when it comes; be firm while it lasts. God give us all the discernment and the determination which the exigency demands!"

And then John Brown's attempt: —

"This sad affair at Harper's Ferry I cannot write about, the maddest attempt ever made by one of the noblest of men."

To the very last he recoiled. On that Thanksgiving Day of 1860, when the whole country was rocking with excitement, he still could say: —

"Truth and right constitute the tribunal of final appeal to whose decision the soul and the community and the land should bow. Never will a faithful interpreter of the Gospel of Christ say that the Union may be preserved at any cost, however great. But truth and right have not yet decreed that these United States must cease to be one people. . . . The hour does not plead with us in behalf of concession, but of sobriety and candor. Delay in action is often as clear a duty as sincerity of purpose."

The war began. Among the Abolitionists were some whose conscientious attack on slavery had hastened the crisis, and whose conscience, when the crisis came, bade them, as followers of peace, stand quiet and wait to see the glory of the Lord. What could this man do who had been too consistent a lover of peace ever to join the Abolitionists, and believed that they were in part responsible for the war? He could simply stand and wait with them.

"To me war, if inevitable, is an evil, and hence arises before my mind a conflict like that of which you speak between 'right and apparent necessity;' for no evil can, under God's government, be unavoidable. We, poor mortals, — for I do not think as highly of human nature as you do, or as I once did, — cannot reconcile these elements of contradiction; and therefore must either adopt that part of the alternative which seems to us preferable, or remain perplexed and distressed."

He could do nothing for the war. After it was over, regret came that his cherished peace-principle had yielded to the very slight extent to which it did **yield** by acquiescence. Such men as he are sorely racked at such a time. Even when age or circumstance saves them from suffering publicly, they are among the real sufferers, — "martyrs of moderation," earnest men bound by sense of duty to keep still while all around them are uprising in enthusiasm. No " war-sermons " rang from his pulpit, no young men of the parish were urged to enlist. — " May, 1861. Declined to subscribe to the Massachusetts Volunteers' Fund this evening." Only in the Freedmen's Aid Society, " the great charity of the age," as he called it, did he actively engage. It seemed a delight to find one work of the time in which he could heartily incite the parish to co-operate.

But, after the war was a settled fact, neither could he preach against it; believing that on the victory of the North depended then the very things in whose behalf he had so earnestly deprecated war before, — the national existence, the success of republican institutions, the suppression of slavery. Now and then, as the sad four years wore by, he even spoke of their terrible necessity, and took much pains to make English friends better understand the issues that were involved. Once, when the mob-spirit broke loose in New York, came a preached Amen to the use of force, and then he spoke from that same reverence for government as " organized society," which underlay his whole course in regard to anti-slavery. " A mob's single purpose in the beginning is resistance, its final work destruction. Tampering with it is like giving a wild beast food enough to whet its appetite ; retreating before it is like inviting a pack of wolves to follow you to your home."

But this was a unique exception. In general, he could only watch with intense interest the influence of the war on personal and national character, and lift up his voice from time to time amid the excitement to recall his people's minds to the thought of God. This, to him, was the minister's sphere ; here lay his duty of speech. Faithful and frequent was his warning against the faults engendered by our prosperity, — the worldliness, the extravagance, the dishonesty, the arrogance, the recklessness of human life, the wish for future vengeance on the Southern white, the impatience with the black. Remember God! remember God! was his one great thought, his constant message, through the dark hours and the bright. God's purpose, he felt, was in some strange way carried out by all the bloodshed and the evil: in His providence, it was sure to turn to final good, even if disaster should first overwhelm the country. And, when at last the blessed peace came, it was not the generals and armies, but He whose instruments they were, that had given us the victory. " God's Overruling Care of War;" " Repentance amidst Deliverance;" " In Time of War prepare for Peace;" " Our Coming Work and Duties," — the sermon-titles suggest what his people listened to when he spoke of the nation in its trial.

July, 1863, after the battle of Gettysburg. — "On the recent anniversary, which seemed to be doubly consecrated by the recollections of the past and by the congratulations we were exchanging over the intelligence just received, my strongest feeling, after the long breath of relief had been drawn, was the desire that some one could lift up his voice at the corners of the streets, amidst the congregated crowds of the city, and through the dwellings of the land, crying, ' To your altars and your closets, ye American people! There fall on your knees before Almighty God; and, while you bless Him for the deliverance He has granted, confess your sins before Him, and with penitent hearts resolve on better lives. To prayer, to humiliation, ye people whom the Lord has blessed, and let praise be the vestibule of repentance!' "

To a friend, in 1863 : —

"My faith in a Divine Providence overruling the movements of this civil strife has grown much within the last six months. If the North will only be true to freedom and order, the result is sure and near. The war will not last a year longer. The Federal forces may suffer defeat once and again; but, unless we are disloyal to our own opportunities and duties, we, *i.e.* the Government and the free States, must succeed. I am not reconciled to war as a means which man should choose for the vindication of the Right; but during this war we have been led as by a visible hand of Divine Power, from one conclusion to another, till we almost seem to be the blind instruments of the Eternal Purpose by which we are controlled. A shorter war would not have left the interests of the country in as safe a position as they would hold, were a peace concluded to-morrow; and probably a struggle of six months more will place them in a still safer position.

"On the whole, we are wiser, stronger, better, than we were two years ago. Our virtues have grown rather than our vices. Sympathy, self-forgetfulness, practical benevolence, force of character, patient submission to suffering, intelligent loyalty, are oftener seen than formerly, and the rights of our fellow-beings are more justly and more generally apprehended."

To an English friend, in March, 1864 : —

" I have thought once and again that I would write, but the one subject which seems now to stand between England and America, dividing instead of uniting us, — the war, — has kept my hand still. Why write only to complain or to recriminate? I have said. He and I cannot take the same view, and our difference is but made more plain by an attempt to reconcile opposite opinions; yet I am not willing that our friendship should be buried in silence, and at least I may thank you for sending me the articles which you have inserted in the ' Inquirer.' The one error which marks them all — pardon me for saying it — is insensibility to the vital question which the war presents. Deeper even than slavery lies the national life. Ours is a struggle for existence. The principle on which the assumed right of secession rests is fatal to any nationality. The success of an experiment in which all lovers of popular freedom should be interested is brought into question. I cannot understand, without imputing to England most unworthy feelings towards the United States, how she who holds her own national life with such a conscious pride can treat with cold contempt our desire to preserve the Republic from dissolution. I am a peace-man; as truly, I think, as you. It was, long before I could be in any degree reconciled to the course which the Government was forced to take; but as I came to see more distinctly that the alternative was resistance or death, a defeat of the Southern enterprise or a disintegration of the Union into independent and mutually hostile States, I submitted to the dreadful necessity, and, though I have not given a dollar to support the war, I have looked on with the most intense interest. In the

Divine Providence, a result is close at hand, which few could foresee even in the remote distance. Slavery is perishing, the death-blow given by its own hand. The problem which neither politician nor philanthropist could solve is disappearing from the anxious inquiry of both. With the triumph of the Federal arms, not only will slavery cease, but the negro will have vindicated his right to stand side by side with the white man in upholding the social interests of the land. The war has been prolonged as if, without our knowing it, for this end. Grievous mistakes have been made, enormous expenses have been created, a terrible loss of life has been demanded, flagrant crimes have been perpetrated, and whether the moral tone of the country has been raised or lowered is doubtful; but we confidently believe that in a year's time we shall be able to say that free institutions have been saved from overthrow and their blessings been extended to every man through the broad extent of the Union. . . .

"You may be assured that this conviction of the impossibility of yielding to the Rebellion without the utter loss of national life, and not a love of war nor hatred of the South, has reconciled a large number of our people to the prosecution of this bloody strife. Conservative men unite with radical Republicans on this ground. All feel that the government must be sustained, and the war be brought to an end by a practical refutation of the Secession doctrine. Till this is accomplished, we shall not only have no peace in the country; without this, we shall have no country."

Fast Day Sermon, April, 1865. — "*What is the result?* These free democratic institutions of ours have in the last four years been put upon such a trial, been cast into such peril, been so searched by events and so exposed at every weak point, as they never had been before, as they never can be again. No possibilities of political history could have made the trial more terrific or more conclusive. And they have come out of it unscathed; bearing, perhaps, some marks of the ordeal through which they have passed, but firmer, more trustworthy, more admirable than ever, entitled to our fondest reliance, and sure to extort from the eastern hemisphere an acknowledgment of their integrity."

"This I account the great result of the war. In so regarding it, I do not overlook the importance of that other effect, which has necessarily occupied a larger place in our field of vision, — the overthrow, the total and permanent overthrow, of slavery. Rejoicing in this effect as heartily as any one, I still must ascribe greater importance to the vindication of a popular system of government from the suspicions which had been cast upon it, and the anxieties which even its friends entertained. For if this system had been found unequal to the exigency, if the country had failed in maintaining itself against intestine discord and foreign envy, what would have been the consequence? Not only would slavery have perpetuated its dire injustice, but civil freedom as the hope of man in every land, would have received a wound that might not be healed in many generations; the flag, of which our Governor speaks in the Proclamation under which we are met, as 'the symbol of equal rights to all men under its folds,' — and to all men everywhere, let us add, the symbol of what they may claim, and must at some time realize, — would have been in their eyes a badge of disaster and token of discouragement; the progress of civilization would have been arrested, and the name even of Washington have shone less resplendent in the firmament of political history. Thank God! this has not been the result. Our institutions have not been prostrated by the hand of violence, nor have they fallen through their own inherent weakness. The Union is saved, and the Republic is safe. Popular government has shown itself to be as strong as regal government. The people are as capable of guarding the functions of sovereignty as the most despotic monarch on earth."

July, 1865. *Thanksgiving for Peace.* — "I am prepared for the contempt with which an enthusiastic love of peace will be met, and for the sarcastic inquiry about Peace Societies and their idle hopes, ' Where are they now? ' Just where they were five years ago, — in the hearts of those who believe in the religion of Christ as a religion of love, and in the sure promise of our faith that the love of the right shall prevail, not by means antagonistic to that which is true and good, but by the diffusion of Christian influence over the land and over the world.

" Shall we be less confident in our interpretation of the mind of Christ and the will of God, because disappointment has again fallen upon our too sanguine expectations? Why, delay is the invigoration, as well as the test, of faith. Ashamed of peace principles! No. Never was there more reason for trusting in them, and never a more proper time for insisting on them. Let the soldier call us fanatics, and the politician deride us as fools. The foolishness of God is wiser than men, and the weakness of God is stronger than men, and that is Divine wisdom and strength which we draw from the New Testament. Tell us not to wait till the world is better before we talk about an end to wars. Let us make the world better by preventing war. Let us make it so good that it will not think war is inevitable. Instruct men in the *principles* as well as in the arts of peace, and they will find some other way for maintaining their rights. Only when the gospel of the beatitudes shall be taken as the law of every life and the inspiration of every purpose, will the interests of humanity be safe from the assault of violence? What an absurdity — is it not, clear-headed reasoner? — to pronounce suffering and destruction the necessary — I do not deny that they may be the indirect, but not a necessary — means of advancing civilization! What a contradiction, thou warm-hearted disciple of the Lord Jesus, to believe that he came to make men brethren, and in the same breath to hold that they must be brought to that moral elevation at which they can comprehend this truth by forming them into hostile armies, whose business shall be mutual injury! "

Meantime, through the four anxious years the various parish-work went on more vigorously than ever. The society grew larger, freed itself from every debt for the church, and gladly used the opportunities of the new location for more active helpfulness. A permanent missionary was employed to visit in the by-streets of the district and gather the poorer children into sewing-school and Sunday school. The ladies formed a " Union " which offered occupation and cheap clothing to needy mothers. A branch of the Freedmen's Aid Society furnished support and supplies for two or three teachers at the South. Subscriptions for one purpose and another followed each other closely through the busier months, and often the week-days held three parish gatherings in Bible class or vestry-meeting or in a " Channing Circle."

The beautiful church was the pastor's pride and delight. Many were the hours he spent in adding privately to its beauty and convenience. For one thing his money could be spent without counting, and his time without regret. No corner from cellar to loft escaped his watchful reverence. For instance : —

" In belfry of the church from 10 to 4.30 with Messrs. Munroe, putting in the tongues of the bells which had been annealed; then with Patrick, cleaning the clock-tower, bell-deck, and Jewell's room.

" Bought for $125 the portrait of Dr. Channing for our vestry, where it hangs under the clock. Friends gave me $90.

" At vestry, hanging portrait of Dr. Belknap and changing other portraits. Have now done all I wish to do for the vestry."

For a year or two, under the first excitement of the change, his spirits had brightened ; but, as the church approached completion, he questioned himself more and more severely whether he ought not to withdraw betimes in favor of some younger man. He was not conscious of the failing strength, he said, but knew that age was creeping on him. A place upon the school-committee of six schools proved no sinecure. In the Ministers' Association, the brethren refused to let him leave the Moderator's chair, for which he felt himself continually unworthy. He was the remembrancer among them, having already been called on for that memorial of the Fathers of the denomination that was quoted in an early chapter. And tributes to the old ministers, as they disappeared, came naturally from his lips at the yearly " Alumni Meetings," or in the commemorative discourse for which some sorrowing parish asked him. He was in request at ordinations, especially for the ordaining prayer : " No one else so filled up our idea of the reverend father in God." The sister died : he was the patriarch in the family circle. His daughter married ; but he gladly felt that the marriage only wound more love and shelter round him. All three, father, daughter, and the new son, dwelt together ; and the other son came back from time to time. The old anniversary still kept its spell : —

Dec. 25, 1863. — " I have spent the greater part of to-day, as I would always spend this anniversary, at home and alone. I seem to gain strength by quiet, and the remembrance of the past throws a serious and subduing influence over the present. If I could only be taught a filial piety by God's goodness to me, and could acquire simplicity of character, I should need no change of outward circumstances to give me peace. I do not wish for happiness, but for a wise and calm thoughtfulness."

The summer of 1864 finished forty years of service

with the single congregation. Older men stood in
certain pulpits, but not one had been so long in charge
of any other parish in the city. The anniversary
sermon was painfully grateful and humble. He had
lately expressed by letter his readiness to go, and now
again entreated his people to be frank. " Frankness is
kindness, silence may be cruelty. . . . Even if I remain
with you, my stay cannot be long."

" I have acted on the belief that both preacher and people
may derive from the cordiality of personal relations a com-
pensation for the poverty of his discourses. This truth alone
could have saved me from despair in the earlier years of my
connection with the Federal Street Society; and, when the
duties of the pulpit fell almost wholly into my hands, my
hope of usefulness rested on the associations which my hearers
might have with me as with one who had shared their sorrows or gained their confidence. . . . It has been to me a
constant source of embarrassment and regret that I could not
attract the young; nor can I hope that that which was difficult when I was myself a young man will be found easy or
practicable at this later period of my life."

Looking back over the years, he recognized four lines
of thought with which he had tried to make himself
and them familiar: self-consecration, as the basis of a
religious character; faith, a positive definite belief respecting God, Christ, a miraculous revelation and its
authentic record; righteousness, as essential to an experience or a hope of the life eternal; and, " grandest,
holiest, dearest theme of all," the possibility and joy of
close communion between the human soul and God: —

" Rising from the base of consecration, and converging,
faith becomes more demonstrative and righteousness more
internal, till the two meet in that point from which the soul
ascends to a still more intimate acquaintance with Him who

is boundless Truth and everlasting Rest. Under such a definition of the religious life, death has appeared but as a change of circumstances, and immortality as an unlimited expansion of being."

He spoke of the change in Unitarianism since he entered on his ministry: —

"Then we who rejoiced in giving the name of 'Unitarian' to our form of the Christian faith foretold its rapid diffusion over the land: now we are glad if we may believe it holds the influence which it had at that time acquired. Then the great theological controversies hinged on the proper interpretation of the Bible: now they involve the authority of the Bible, and the value of a supernatural revelation. . . . By some persons it would be thought doubtful commendation, to speak of but little change in the convictions by which an honest mind had been governed through a period of more than a quarter of a century. They who regard progress as not only a beneficent requisition, but the supreme law of human life, cannot feel sympathy with one who holds nearly the same views of truth, both practical and speculative, which he embraced forty years ago, . . . with which he was familiar when he sat in youthful reverence at the feet of such teachers as Ware, Norton, Channing, — teachers, now as then, with whom I am willing to lag behind the age." . . .

"In regard to two articles of faith, my preaching may have indicated a slight divergence of opinion from statements I once accepted and repeated. My study of the New Testament, together with the pain I have felt in reading books and papers of comparatively recent publication, has led me to a more reverential appreciation of the offices by which the Lord Jesus Christ continues to fulfil the work which the Father gave him to do on earth, and to a less peremptory statement of his relations to God. Those relations transcend human ability to define. While my faith in the supreme and sole deity of the Father has grown stronger rather than weaker, the place which Christ holds in the scale of being is a subject on which I wonder that others speak with so little hesitation. I leave it among the things which are hidden beyond our sight.

"My views of human nature have also undergone some change. I cannot use the language of which I once was fond; still less, the language which marks a school of thought in which I have never been able to take the first lesson. Neither consciousness nor observation permits me to interpret man as the philosophy of intuitions reads the constitution of the human being. The erroneous views of Christ and the Bible which prevail so widely, if they have not their origin, find their support, in this philosophy. I rely on an authority external to myself: for in man I see capacity indeed, but present weakness rather than strength; crude judgment, want, sin. Human nature needs to be guided, upheld, and protected. The radical error of our times, I soberly believe, is a false estimate of the powers and prerogatives of human nature. . . .

" Of late, perhaps more than in earlier years, I have laid stress on the word 'trust,' and on its vast and gracious contents. As experience has disclosed to me more of the infirmities and wants of which time makes us all conscious, I have repeated that word with more emphasis; and, if I have been thought to say that, in its last analysis, religion is but the exercise and expression of trust in God, I have not been greatly misunderstood. . . .

" In a word, I have learned more of my own ignorance than of any thing else. I am more ready to allow mystery as a vast region which neither knowledge nor faith can penetrate; and more ready to walk by faith as a light which shines on passages redeemed from mystery, but not open to knowledge. Once I attempted to explain that which I now resolve into the wisdom of a perfect and eternal Will. As I stand at this moment of time, and look back upon the past; as I stand on this spot, and look out over society; as I stand by an open grave, and look into the future, — I think less of man and more of God, I understand less and believe more. I have little confidence in human speculation, and more gratitude than I can express for Divine revelation."

That same summer he printed four discourses in quick succession, — the one just quoted, sermons memorial of his old associate on the " Examiner," Dr. Lamson, and of the venerable Josiah Quincy, and a ringing installation sermon on " Loyalty to Christ." An elder brother-in-work wrote him : " Three such discourses in so hot a summer show that your vigor is unabated. Long may it be so ! What with progress and what with reaction, I do not see but that it will soon rest almost entirely on your shoulders to uphold Unitarianism as it *was* and the gospel as it *is*." The words apply still more fitly to the Brooklyn installation sermon, an eloquent, compact argument for the old as against the new Unitarianism. The ministers were again discussing theological differences, and Unitarians in general were conscious enough of a drift in thought and uncertain enough of its tendency for Dr. Gannett's clear-toned warning to make a deep impression. It was much liked and much disliked.

But the vigor of a sermon tells little of the man who writes it. " Depressed, frightened, asleep, — O shame ! " are a type of the words which mark the autumn-days in the record, — asleep to shut out the dark moods and quiet the unstrung nerves. It was not time, however, to stop trying to improve and to do : —

Nov. 8, 1864. " Began course of Lessons in Elocution from Mr. Taverner, with Rev. Messrs. Chaney and Foote, in my parlor."

November 14. " Saw Dr. Clarke, who calls the trouble physical, a want of nervous force."

November 20. "A.M. preached new sermon on Genuine Charity. P.M. preached new sermon on Religion Natural."

And so on. All through the next spring, as the war was closing and men's hearts were growing lighter, he grew visibly more tired and weak. The watchful friend last named prescribed a journey to Fayal. "What would be the use? Temporary respite and relief, — nothing more." Then in the strange revivals the old hopes seemed possibilities, and plans were renewed and he could not believe himself a sick man.

Feb. 28, 1865. "Called on Dr. Clarke to tell him I am better, and, instead of going away as he proposed, will do three things: 1. go to bed at 11 o'clock; 2. not sit up Saturday nights; 3. spend one day in every week out of town in recreation."

On May 30, in very trembling hand, is written : "Went to Festival in Music Hall between six and seven o'clock. Mr. Eliot unexpectedly called me up, as I sat upon the platform. Spoke ten minutes, and was kindly received." The "call" is worth telling by another. He went late to avoid notice, but could not decline the invitation to the platform, so took his seat in a corner behind one of the tables, too far off to hear distinctly: his head was down, and resting on his hand. The chairman spied him there, and presently began to speak of one whose name was in all the churches for his zeal and helpful life: as he turned to aim the summons, he saw the old man sitting unconscious of any reference to himself. "Yes," continued Mr. Eliot, "I told you of his modesty, — he doesn't dream I am speaking of him," — and so proceeded laughingly till all eyes in the Hall were fastened on the white head in the corner. Some one touched him, saying, "Mr. Eliot is calling on

you." Turning with a start, he caught sight of the looking faces and half sprang to his feet, not knowing what
had happened, whether he was waited for or not. It
was such a picture of surprised unconsciousness, amid all
the praising words, that the whole audience broke out in
a tumult of applause and welcome. Then, leaning on
the table where he was, he spoke a few moments in
his earnest way about the Unitarianism which he loved,
and sat down again amid the hearty loud response of
those who fondly listened.

He is still a " watchman on the walls: " —

May 31. " Ministerial Conference in our Vestry. . . . Our
duty in reference to National Congregational Convention
brought up by me from Boston Association: the protest I
had prepared and read to our Association was read and
approved; and E. S. Gannett, C. A. Bartol, and George E.
Ellis were appointed to take such action as they should think
proper."

For the Orthodox Congregationalists, who were about
to hold a Council in Boston, had styled themselves in
their official documents the " National Council of Congregationalists," " the entire body of Congregationalists
in our country." The discourtesy to Unitarians was of
little consequence, but, if borne in silence, might possibly at some time be made the ground of practical injustice. The benefit of certain funds, for instance, still
belonged to members of both sects in common. Hence
the protest, — a few quiet words published in the papers.
An Orthodox friend urged that it be brought more directly to the notice of the Council: he answered : —

" It seems to me that, on the whole, we took the course
which self-respect and courtesy would concur in recommending, when we made a brief and unimpassioned statement to

the public, by which we hoped to guard our own rights, instead of suing for a favor before the Council, or attempting to embarrass their proceedings by our remonstrance. Our sole object was to maintain our position as Congregation-alists, which we have tried to do in the simplest way. If the Council, with the facts before them, of which they cannot now be ignorant, choose of their own will to repair the injustice which has been done by their committee, however inadvertently, we shall be pleased; but we prefer that they should act from their own sense of right, and not on any solicitation of ours, as if we came either seeking a favor or demanding an apology."

Still a watchman, — but getting ready now to yield his post : —

June 6. "Mr. Sweetser here to persuade me to go to Europe. Told him I could not."

June 22. "Mr. Sweetser, Mr. McGregor, and Mr. James Read here with a paper signed by gentlemen and ladies of our congregation asking me to go abroad, and enclosing a check for $3,000!! Told them, after a moment's thought, that I would go; not because I needed it, but because I did not see how I could refuse such kindness, pressed upon me in such a way, and after previous refusals. They wish me to be gone through the winter and spring, but I said I would only take four months. They wish me to go soon, but I cannot leave home till the close of July, without neglecting things that I wish to do."

And they wished him to take the $3,000, but he would only take $1,000.

When he crossed the sea before, although more broken down than now, he had youth in him to help recovery. Now he had old age; and the work was mainly over at the best, and he felt that he must hurry home to do a

little more while the day lasted. Then his companion
was the wife just married: now a grown-up son went
with him, who but dimly remembered the mother's face
that so long since had vanished from the home. Between the two journeys and companionships lay nearly
thirty years of an earnest trier's life.

His plan had been to spend the time in England,
renewing old acquaintance there with friends and pleasant places. But the first fatigues and excitements were
more than he could bear. He would ignore the weakness till utter weariness held him fast. " Was very
tired by the foolish feat," he writes, of climbing the
worn stone stairway that winds to the top of St.
Botolph's church-tower at Boston. There were other
" feats " and many such fatigues. Besides, he was disappointed and offended by the English sympathy still so
loudly manifested for the South. On the former journey, the continent had proved more restful: perhaps it
might again. So they crossed the channel. The two
days on the Rhine were full of dear, sad memories.
" At St. Goar I think I recognized the very house and
chamber, and old associations crowded hard upon me."
A leisurely month in Switzerland, in which he jaunted
from place to place, every three or four days rejoined
by the young men travelling on foot, brought the first
health and joy. " The first record I have been able to
make in my journal since I landed. Am writing in a
nice little chamber in Hôtel Suisse in Interlaken, feeling
better in body and mind than at any time since I left
Liverpool." While here, he notes: —

" Went to the English Church under the same roof with
the 'Catholic Chapel.' Heard a good and true sermon from
'Work out your own salvation; for,' &c. 1. The duty.

2. The motive. Stayed for the Communion service. As the minister went down the aisle to change his dress, I took his hand and whispered, 'I am a Unitarian minister, may I commune with you?' He answered instantly, 'Yes;' then added in a kind manner, 'Looking unto Jesus.' I went to the altar with the rest, knelt, and received the elements. He said nothing unpleasant, and I enjoyed the service, and hope it was sincerely used and gave me strength."

After loitering at Berne, Geneva, and the Leukerbad with its wonderful mountain-ride and the odd scene in the tanks, traversing the Simplon, and pausing two or three days among the Italian Lakes, he recrossed the mountains, and by long rides down the beautiful, wild Engadine reached Innsbruck. Sight-seeing on two canes, with a conscience behind them, was no play. The quick run through the German capitals and Paris sadly tired him; for he *must* seize the opportunities — his last, he kept saying — of learning what he might. But then followed three pleasant weeks in England among kind greetings from the London ministers, and cherished friends in Bridport and Bristol. Three months from the time he left the steamer, he again entered it at Liverpool, brightened, but not greatly strengthened. The seasickness that began in the Irish Sea lasted to the wharf in Boston harbor. He grew so weak that the doctor feared he might not reach the land; but Charles Humphreys was with him, and the son-like care was given constantly. When they arrived, one Thursday afternoon, there was careful anxiety that his schedule of foreign trifles should be duly reported to the custom-house officials; and then he was helped off the vessel, and borne to the home and the welcome. Mr. Little, one of his parishioners, had bidden the peo-

21

ple to his house to greet their minister. Although he was too weak to stand, as he sat there in the arm-chair feeling that they loved him, it was a happier evening far than any he had spent away.

The next Sunday he stood in his pulpit and preached!

ARLINGTON STREET PULPIT.

X.

A FATHER IN THE CHURCH.

1865–1871.

THE sermons defending the faith at the dedication, the "fortieth anniversary," and the Brooklyn installation, have revealed the fact that change in the faith was going on. The later, like the earlier, trip to Europe happened to fall at an important moment in the Unitarian history.

Since the days when Emerson first lectured and Parker preached, the mental outlook had widened, — widened on many sides, from many causes. Eyes were no longer rare that saw in the "new views" truth fitted to make men glad. Unitarian laymen, not a few, and many of the younger preachers, no longer thought the Fathers' thought. Two "wings" had slowly been developed in the body. The term "old-fashioned Unitarianism" had come in vogue, while, denoting some-

thing divergent from it, the term " Liberal Theology "
was winning a new meaning from the age. Besides the
change in actual ideas, minds had grown more liberal
in temper. The Unitarian principle that exalted good
life above creed, good or bad, had steadily won its way.
Those who occupied the ground on which the West
Roxbury heretic had stood were no longer sharply
challenged ; and the space on the other side which separated " old-fashioned Unitarianism " from Orthodoxy
had also many settlers, — deep-hearted Unitarians and
fresh-minded Evangelicals fraternizing there quite near
each other. More and more stress was laid on " unity
of the spirit." One natural consequence, however, was
resulting from this stress, — a certain blur around ideas,
a loss in clear thinking and expression. The standard,
too, of ministerial scholarship had fallen, as such scholarship became less specialized. And this happened at
the very time that the other sects, who shared quite as
largely in the impulse of the age, were adding scholarship and culture to their means of influence. Compared
with them, the Unitarians as a sect had been losing social
and intellectual rank. In the general advance, the rear
had pressed forward towards the van; while those who
were now the foremost no longer represented any one ecclesiastical connection. Of course, the Unitarians claimed
and, although with exaggeration, rightly claimed, that
this gain in religious culture and liberality throughout
the land was itself in part their spiritual harvest, the
effect of their brave stand for freedom.

As early as 1860 Dr. Gannett thus suggests the situation in a letter to Rev. Mr. Carpenter, his English friend :

" I cannot tell you — for I do not think any one can tell
— how theological or ecclesiastical matters stand with us.
Every thing is at loose ends. We are good-natured enough ;

but all sorts of opinions shelter themselves under the protection of 'Liberality,' — this is the favorite word just now, 'Unitarian' having gone out of fashion. Our young men are bold, careless, crude, one is often tempted to say: our old men are driven too far by reaction. Mr. Parker's death has called out several sermons, which deal more in eulogy than in exposure of the serious error which belonged to his theology. Where we shall end, I know not."

And again, in November, 1862 : —

" The palmy days of Unitarianism have gone by, union and co-operation have yielded to individualism, and the 'Liberal Theology' of the present time embraces opinions of every sort, from semi-Trinitarianism to ultra-Parkerism. However, God will take care of His own truth; and, if we are not worthy to uphold it, the charge must pass into other hands."

No break as yet. But certain signs betokened that a break might be near at hand. The ministers began to ponder their relation to each other, and the possible limits of pulpit-exchange.

"Feb. 13, 1865. A. M. Ministerial Union; address by Rev. J. F. Clarke on Union, against a Separation, in the Unitarian body. Earnest discussion.

" P.M. Ministers' Association meeting at Rev. Dr. Nath. Frothingham's. Large meeting, — thirty there, — several not of the Association. Subject of discussion, Our Differences. Dr. Frothingham said we were all Rationalists, all Naturalists, all Supernaturalists; defining these terms in his own way, and having acknowledged and spoken of a centre and two wings in our body."

" Feb. 20. Ministerial Union, to hear address from Rev. Dr. Bellows on the New York Convention, or rather on the opportunity thrown before the Unitarian denomination. Discussion turned very much on the differences between us, which most of the speakers considered unimportant, their idea being that the Christian spirit and Christian work made a man a Christian. The liberal, or progressive, or left wing, evidently meant to control the future action of the denomination, and to silence the more conservative part of the body."

" March 13. Ministerial Union. Rev. O. B. Frothingham read an elaborate, able, and brilliant address on the Ground of Unity among us, in reference to the New York Convention; not unity of spirit, nor unity of work, neither of which, as he showed, is a basis in itself, but unity of thought, which he described us as having in respect to God, Christ, the Bible, liberty, &c.; imputing to us views which some of us would reject."

At the same time, these very signs and others showed that the practical tendencies of the denomination were about to flower into a new enthusiasm. Never since the early days had the opportunity seemed so good for promoting a liberal form of Christianity. It was just at the close of the war. The sympathies wakened by the four years of struggle had crossed sect-lines as well as State-lines. Dogmas had paled before stern tests of life and death, and differencing creeds grew small by the side of the helpfulness in which all joined heart and hand. To earnest Unitarians, the opportunity spoke like God's command to strip off the traditions of culture and aristocracy that had so long stifled influence, and to press among the people with their gospel. In April, 1865, they met in National Conference at New York, to carry out their purpose. The whole body seemed to be vitalized. The churches were soon organized into Local Conferences, reporting to a General Conference every year or two. New missionary effort, both in East and

West, was resolved on, and far larger contributions than were ever asked before were easily obtained. City-theatres were engaged for free Sunday services, and the great audiences seemed to show that the people had been reached. Here and there " Unions " sprang up for benevolent work and social fellowship. A popular monthly — a magazine less of ideas than of stories embodying ideals, and of records to stimulate practical progress — took the place of the scholarly " Examiner," that had crept the round of the ministers' studies for so many years. Before long a new Theological School, with a lowered standard of education, was established, in the hope of inducing more young men to enter the Liberal ministry. And the doctrinal basis of the denomination was widened as far as the National Conference could widen it while remaining distinctly " Christian: " " Other Christian Churches " had been invited to join the Conference; and presently, to meet the objections of certain friends disturbed by a creed-like phrase in the Constitution referring to the " Lordship " of Jesus Christ, an article was expressly added to declare that all such expressions represented only the belief of the majority, and bound none who did not freely give assent. — Possibly this uprising and girding of the loins for a mission among the people may by and by be recognized as the beginning of a new era in Unitarian history.

Had Dr. Gannett been a younger man, no one would have leaped more instantly to the front to engage in such a mission; and he had gifts of enthusiastic conviction and eloquence that would have fitted him for special service in it. But now by age he was disabled, and the years that had weakened the body had tempered — not destroyed — enthusiasm. He was revered on all sides as a noble example of the "elder type of Unitarianism." Such reverence implies a growing loneliness for the one revered. He was not so sure as many were that the age was yearning for "Liberal Christianity," and that the West was a field white already to its harvest; he did not see all prospects in the sunrise light that gladdened other eyes. Yet, so far as he was able, he joined heartily — and heartily with him meant actively — in all the new plans.

In February, 1867, he again writes his friend in England about the situation : —

"The Unitarian denomination here is in a strange state. On the one side a strenuous effort is made, and not without success, to produce more organization, compactness, unity; and, on the other side, individualism and radicalism were never so outspoken before. It is no longer unkind or invidious to call certain gentlemen Radicals. They adopt the title, and seem to delight in it. They have a periodical under that name, ably conducted. They are found in the ministry and among the laity. They value the Bible and the teachings of Christ, but allow an intrinsic authority to neither. Most of them, if not all, are earnest men, thoroughly sincere and religious. Many of the younger ministers are found among them. It becomes a serious and a difficult question how far co-operation may be, or can be, secured between 'the old-fashioned Unitarians,' as they are called, and the 'new school.' We meet this question at every turn. It is continually bringing into view inconsistency in this man and in that man. Some few are in favor of separate organization, which others discourage. Here and there one like . . . stands aloof from all participation in Unitarian movements. —— has been led by his exclusive devotion to the doctrine of 'the Spirit' into statements that seem almost to discredit external revelation. The 'Christian Register' and the 'Liberal Christian' try to prevent discord and separation, and are therefore amusing, if not painful, examples of a literal self-*denial*. Their columns represent Unitarianism as prospering and spreading beyond all former times. I doubt the accuracy both of the statistics and the conclusions which they are made to support. Our churches in Boston are stronger, probably, than they were five or ten years ago; but so are the churches of every other denomination. There is more activity in the religious world. The war taught people to do and to give, and now they turn their awakened energies into channels nearer home."

The address which he delivered in July, 1867, at the semi-centennial celebration of the Cambridge Divinity School, reveals in part his own answer to what he calls the "serious and difficult question." It was a somewhat notable occasion. The Alumni gathered from far and near, — old pastors, resting from labors that began in sheltering the infant Unitarianism from Orthodox exposition; the well-known preachers, strong leaders of the day; and fresh-faced graduates just entering the work. Of all the listeners, not more than five or six were older than the bending, white-haired man who spoke to them, and probably no one still in active service was so old as he. That "question," hardly to be avoided in any case, happened to be specially pertinent; for the School had just been made the object of sharp criticism for fostering so many young Radicals. On this same day, the venerable Professor Noyes, sitting in his chair before his old pupils, made his last address to them to vindicate the right of his young men to think away from their teachers without incurring disrepute as irreligious. The grateful tributes which Dr. Gannett rendered to Norton and Ware, his own professors, have been already cited in another chapter. After reviewing the history of the School, he went on to speak of the methods of management which the changing times demanded : —

"When gravitation ceases to hold the world together, the Bible may cease to be the all-pervasive influence of a Divinity School; or, if the latter change should precede the other, the institution will fall to pieces as surely as would the material world, were the mighty power of gravitation withdrawn. You may have something else without the Bible, and it may be something in which men shall take a senseless or a just pride; but it will not be a Divinity School, and, least of all, a Christian Divinity School. . . .

"The modern style of thought — which makes human nature the starting-point of religious inquiry and religious faith — has come into our Theological School through open doors. Have closed doors, with ingenious fastenings, kept it out of Andover or New Haven? Shall we turn it out and shut the door against it? . . . An institution that did not feel the movement going on around it would be more venerable than useful. On the banks of the Rhine stands a castle, which, while others at no great distance have fallen into ruins and modern civilization has reared its dwellings in the neighborhood, has been fondly kept from decay, with its furniture renewed after the old pattern; and there it stands looking down on the busy river along which the steamboat rushes back and forth, and the wire of the telegraph transmits intelligence with electric rapidity, as it looked down upon the long silence or the sudden fierce conflict of the mediæval times, — a memorial of the past, which holds a half-dozen sleepy guardsmen within its walls, and receives an annual visit from its royal owner. We want no such literary or ecclesiastical structure, perched where the spirit of the age cannot have access to its apartments. . . .

"If Radicalism means only uprooting, and they who accept the name expend their strength in denial, there is no ground of sympathy left between them and believers; but if they, too, have real faith, though it do not answer to our idea of Christian faith, and join with it religious sensibility and a conscientious attitude of the soul towards a spiritual life, there is room for mutual respect and confidence. . . . For the sake alike of peace and of prosperity, for the sake of the School, and for the gospel's sake, the *control* must remain in the hands of those who represent the original design, which was, as we have seen, to make Christian ministers; and this control must be exercised in the interest of a reverential and grateful faith towards him who is the Head, even Christ. To admit to an enjoyment of privileges is one thing; to invite into a share in the government is another thing. The former may be nothing more than justice; the latter, nothing less than folly."

" Address better received than I expected; but I omitted all mention of Dr. Follen, having forgotten his connection with the School." — But the secret wish was disappointed : he had hoped to inspire an effort to *do* something for the School. " A grand opportunity was lost," the Journal adds, for there was no time to consider his suggestion : —

" Is there no rich man who will give the forty thousand dollars that would found a Professorship in our School? There must be more than one such man, if we could only bring the facts just as they are before them. Then *we* will raise, — we poor ministers, with the grace of God to help us in our address to our people, will raise ten thousand more. . . . And then," with the other funds at command, " our School would have its proper organization, under a sufficient body of teachers; which it has never had from its beginning to this day."

In two or three sermons written not long after this address, to kindle his people to zeal in the new work, the same " question " had again to be met and answered : —

"What is our duty towards those whom we have been accustomed to style our brethren in the faith, although now the household be sadly divided?   It is a twofold duty, — to respect the rights and to expose the errors (as we consider them) of those from whom we differ.   Every one has the right to think for himself, and the right to avow his belief in such terms as shall not be scornful towards others ; the right to be esteemed sincere, unless his dishonesty be palpable, and to be accredited as acting from pure motives ; the right to be understood and represented as he intends, and the right to pronounce opinions which he rejects false or hurtful.   Without the mutual concession of these rights, there can be no profitable controversy nor pleasant intercourse.

"With such concession, it may be unwise to maintain a union which is rather nominal than real, and which is made the occasion of much friction and frequent misunderstanding. I frankly say that, if it were possible to draw the line of separation, it seems to me it would be better — better for the truth and better for ourselves — that they who hold opposite opinions respecting the supernatural work and Divine mission of Jesus Christ should stand apart, relieved from their present embarrassment and left free to follow their own convictions.   But, while the broad space between the extremes is filled by gradations and complications of belief and unbelief, any such sharp division is impracticable ; and we can only be careful that we neither trench on the rights of others nor compromise our own.   Let it be remembered that we cannot exercise our right of free speech without virtually admitting that they from whom we differ have the same right, which they may exercise in condemning our opinions There is too often a disregard of this fact, that can be explained only by taking into view an infirmity of human nature, which makes it difficult for most men to do justice to an opponent.   If conservatives have been reluctant to acknowledge the sincerity or conscientiousness of Radicals,

—these terms are no longer invidious, but simply descriptive, — the latter have been as slow to grant to the former the privilege of saying what *they* think. Both parties are guilty of violating the first principles of Christian morality. The anti-supernaturalist has a right to inculcate both his belief and his disbelief; and I have a right to say, in as public a manner as he, that I think the one is as pernicious as the other is unsound. Without impugning motives, we may, each and all of us, stand up for the truth."

"There never has been an attempt" among Unitarians "to impose silence on honest and decent speech. They who have been pained by what others have said, who were connected with them in ecclesiastical relations, have disavowed responsibleness or participation, and have strenuously resisted the imputation to a religious body, without their consent, of the belief or disbelief of any member of that body : was this wrong? The Unitarian ministers of this or that Association never excluded or persecuted Mr. Parker. They refused to be made responsible for his opinions by any conventional position in which they were placed, and they claimed the right—the same which they accorded to him—of declaring and defending their own convictions. This was the height of their offence against Christian liberty, — an offence which proved them to be its consistent vindicators. The unhappy feelings of that period—for such feelings there were—have passed away ; but the history of that period has been unfairly told, and I wish here and now, for the sake of the younger members of this congregation, to bear my testimony, founded on a close acquaintance with the facts of that time, to the open, honorable, and Christian treatment which Mr. Parker received from his brethren. If they disliked his theology, if they thought it inadequate and unscriptural, might not they copy his example of frankness? Had they practised deception, I should not have a word to say on their behalf. They but exercised the right, of which on his side they had neither the power nor the desire to deprive him, of announcing their

dissent from what they on theirs held to be unsound doctrine. That right has never been relinquished or betrayed.
It is as sacred to-day as it was twenty or fifty years ago."

When the National Unitarian Conference inserted in
its Constitution the explanatory article to conciliate the
Radical brethren, most of the ministers on reaching
home probably told their people what they thought of
the attempt. What Dr. Gannett said is again characteristic of his tenacious faith, his outright speech, and
his spirit of justice : —

"I have been sorry to hear a victory claimed for either
side, Conservative or Radical, or to hear the word ' compromise ' used as pertinent, for I do not understand that there
has been concession or defeat. We have merely put into
the Constitution of the National Conference a statement of
these two facts, on which we have always insisted, that the
Unitarian body through their common belief accept Christ
in his official relations to mankind, but that they neither
exercise nor arrogate the right to compel any person to hold
this belief under the penalty of exclusion if he renounce it.
They may form and publish and prize a creed, longer or
shorter, as the inheritance, possession, or distinction of the
denomination, but may not force the humblest or the weakest
member of the denomination to wear that creed as a badge.
"It appears to me that we are still loyal to Christ and
true to the traditions of our history. That history began in
elevating righteousness above dogma, character above creed,
and in subverting the pretensions of ecclesiastical despotism.
Our fathers were at once disciples of the Lord and the
Lord's freemen. They would accept no formulary of belief
with the menace of Divine displeasure for doubting its truth
held over them, and they extended no formulary with a similar
menace to others. It was their office to unite earnest faith
with practical freedom. I conceive, therefore, that we are

following their example when we cleave to Christ, yet leave others to obey their convictions. It does not devolve on us to be the arbiters of any fate but our own.

"You know, my friends, how tenacious I am of faith in the miraculous mission and superhuman authority of Christ. To me his gospel is the very word and grace of God. Without him as a divinely inspired, a special and a sufficient Teacher, I should' have no mercy to lean on, no hope to cherish; for I cannot discover in natural religion instruction adequate to my need as a sinner and as one over whom death will assert its power. . . . The decay of faith in him, I am persuaded, would turn back the current of civilization and deprive man of his dearest spiritual resources. It is through Christ alone, as I think, that men are authorized to call upon God as the Father, or that a sinful world can ever realize the salvation after which it is groping. . . .

"But I have never dared to say that men must think on this subject as I think or be lost, I dare not pronounce scepticism invariably the fruit of an evil heart, nor do I wish to call a man an infidel because his appreciation of Christ is different from mine. I cannot ask the Trinitarian nor the Radical to respect my rights, unless I respect theirs. The Christianity of neither the one nor the other is my Christianity, and I do not believe it is *Christ*ianity; but it does not fall within the obligations or the privileges of my life to divest them of a name which they account theirs as rightfully as I account it mine. If they are good men, humble, devout, benevolent, true, I will try to convince them that they still lack one thing, I will do all that I honorably may to prevent the diffusion of their opinions through the community, and I will pray to God to open their eyes that they may see the whole truth; but I will not, I may not, I cannot, heap on them terms of reproach, and pronounce them sciolists, heretics, or knaves. Of the Radicalism of the day I will speak as pernicious, and happily short-lived; but, among those by whom it is professed, I see too much goodness to permit me to become

their accuser. . . . From the inmost places of my being, I
cry out for the one Mediator between God and man.   But
I do not the less abhor the temper which imputes evil motives to those who will not sit at his feet, and ascribes all
unbelief to a bad heart.   Such loyalty to the name of Christ
is disloyalty to his spirit and example."

The theses of the college-graduate in 1820, and the
last published exposition of Unitarianism which he gave
in 1871, are essentially the same.   He had not been
ashamed of the faith when it needed champions to win
first standing-ground ; nor was he ashamed of it now,
when the force of thought in his own denomination was
going more and more against it.   But it should be
added that his belief, while centring firmly where it
did and keeping its old outlines, seemed to grow less
rigid at the outlines as he grew older.   Friends of former days noticed in his preaching a different, a brighter
tone, — less appeal to conscience through the head and
more through sympathy, less of law and more of grace.
" Of late, perhaps, more than in earlier years, I have
laid stress on that word, ' trust,' and on its vast and gracious contents," he said of himself.   And yet " life,"
the spiritual life, " the Life of God in the Soul of Man,"
had been the one prevailing theme of all the years, the
thread running through the sermons and coming to open
sight in hundreds probably ; the prayers had always
been most earnest worship ; the old hymns, " Greenwood's " hymns, had always thrilled with the feeling
which his heart read into them ; — perhaps it was chiefly
the old man's face and tones that seemed to make the
service now more tender and impressive, and the benediction sound as if it gave for the moment the gift that
it invoked.   Even towards the young men, though their
tendencies hurt him sorely, he lost somewhat of the

faithful challenger's feeling. As men, he had never done them injustice; but, living on, he saw more surely that reverence and piety could coexist with the views to him so strangely irreverent. After reading the Life of Parker by John Weiss, he notes: " It has raised my estimation of Parker immensely. He was a *very* learned man, and a tender, true-hearted man, honest and thorough." A letter, written to Mr. Carpenter in 1860, contains a sentence which shows him half-conscious of the change: —

" I have never acknowledged your kindness in sending me your lectures on the Atonement. I was the more pleased with them, because you have sometimes seemed to me less zealous for Unitarian doctrine than I am moved to be. Mere pugnacious Unitarianism, however, I value less than I once did. Is it an inconsistency — I hope not — that, as I grow older, my faith in Unitarian tenets strengthens, but my anxiety for their diffusion abates? I have seen so much of sectarian interest which yielded no spiritual improvement, and feel so much the need we all have of a religious life, that I wish it were possible to take for granted that men hold the right belief and we might expend all our effort in trying to make them Christians in heart and life."

His reverence for the masters always remained that of a young man. It is pleasant to see one whose age had elected him for the Memorial Address at Cambridge laying his work before his own elder for approval: —

July 12. "Called on Rev. Dr. Frothingham, and read him my Divinity School Address, nearly finished. He seemed to like it, and suggested no change."

A few months later, the same feeling led him to suggest and carry out another commemorative service of

22

rather an unusual kind. On the first Sunday in October, 1867, the church was filled with old parishioners and friends. A quarter of a century had passed since Channing's living voice had ceased.

"It seemed but right, at the close of such a period, that we should join in some expression of gratitude to him from whom we had received the best instruction of our lives, as well as of admiration for one who had secured a place among the world's benefactors." . . .

"I was obliged to take some part, relying on other gentlemen to make the occasion what it should be. Mr. Edward Wigglesworth presided. We had four admirable addresses. Dr. Walker spoke of Dr. Channing as a reformer, Dr. Hedge commented on his writings, Mr. Hillard described him as preacher and pastor, and Dr. Clarke spoke of his general relations to society."

The pastor's own contribution referred chiefly to the sources of Channing's wondrous influence as a preacher, — his intense faith in the truth he uttered, the depth of personal experience from which the utterance came, the absolute integrity of purpose and mental fairness which lifted his vision above sectarian bounds and kept him always a learner, always the fearless advocate of freedom, yet never of that freedom which disowns reverence and humility.

This was his attitude towards the elders. Of his way among young men, Mr. Fred. F. Lovell, one of his pupils in the new Theological School alluded to a few pages back, sends the following pleasant picture. It was during this same autumn (1867) that Rev. Mr. Hepworth's zeal founded the new School. Several Unitarian ministers gave their services as instructors, and Dr. Gannett was pressed to teach "Systematic Divinity," or, as he preferred to call it, "the truths of religion." It was famil-

iar work.   Again and again had he gone over the themes
at church and vestry-meeting.   And yet he was reluctant to take the place, doubting much his " fitness " for
it.   He finally consented, but made his relations with
the students far less professorial than friendly.

"He came to us old in Christian life, yet humble as a child ;
perplexed sometimes by what seemed to him flippant cavil-
ling, and his brow would knit in pain, yet he was always
forbearing.   I think he united in himself the faculty of being
severe, just, and kind, in a greater degree than I ever knew
in another.   He always felt it to be proper that a student
should freely express his opinion, however much opposed to
the ideas which were deeply cherished by himself.   This expression sometimes took a form that seemed to him irreverent.   He instantly apprehended the departure from logical
argument to ridicule or scoffing, and would so kindly yet
firmly and pertinently point out the error, that the very
mildness of tone made it only the clearer, and left the objec-
tor confused and silent.   Never in the most heated debates
did he lose that regard for the opinions and feelings of others
which was so marked a trait of his character.   I fear we sometimes hurt him more than we should have hurt a less sensitive man.   Some of us would choose oft-times to assume the
rôle of Gamaliel himself rather than sit at his feet and learn ;
and in this ignorance we would smile at his mannerisms, and
the systematic arrangement of his books preparatory to the
exercises.   But somehow he drove a wedge into all our
hearts, and, taking out much that was crude, rough, and
mean in them, set a love for natures like his own there in its
stead.   He bound himself to us by a stronger tie than we
knew, until an event occurred that told us how much we
loved him.

"You may perhaps catch my idea better, if I illustrate by
an incident.   Among the gentlemen of the School was one
of middle age, strong in physical life and equally strong in

all his opinions. He had been used to the exhortations of the Baptist school, was rough, outspoken, but royal-hearted, good and honest, more conservative than the Doctor himself. I think the Doctor loved the man for the very honesty of purpose that caused him to combat some of his favorite points so sturdily. But their mental contests over the vexed questions of Divine Sovereignty and Human Free Agency were frequent and vehement. Upon one hot July day, near the close of the month, the Doctor came to us a little more worn than usual. His face bore upon it a look of weariness as he placed his canes upon a chair and took his accustomed glass of water. It was our Baptist friend that passed the water, and he could not refrain from at the same time driving a peg of his pet theory of 'man's subordination to circumstances.' No one thought the Doctor's reply severe at the time; it excited no comment from any of us. But he, upon reflection, feared that the answer had sprung from the uncomfortableness and irritability of the moment, and that it was not a judicious refutation of the idea put forward. To feel himself to have been in error, with Dr. Gannett, was to make immediate reparation. So on the following morning, as we were gathered for our Elocutionary Exercises at the Church of the Unity, the Doctor came in, and, during a pause in the recitations, motioned our friend to him, took his hand, and said loud enough to be heard by all: 'Mr. K., I don't know but that I spoke somewhat hastily in answer to your query yesterday. If I did, you must forgive me. I was a little irritated from the heat and walk, and hardly took proper time to consider my reply.' Nobody else could have said that as Dr. Gannett said it, — it was so dignified yet so gentle, so beautiful in its simplicity, so grand and Christlike in its humility. They are both in the Eternal Fields now. The soul of the honest Maine missionary went first, and I am sure came joyously to welcome the dear old master to the home where the problem was solved.

"The winter of 1869 commenced with dreadfully cold

weather, streets filled with snow and walks covered with ice. It was apparent to all of us that it was only by a great exertion of will that the Doctor was able to dominate the physical suffering, which the going to and from the college, together with the mental labor, occasioned. The exhaustion consequent upon great anxiety lest he should fall and break his limbs in the fearful state of the streets, encumbered as he was with canes and books, left him so weak that, upon reaching the chapel, he would often seem unable to speak for several moments. Then he was always afraid he should not do enough. He made a more rigorous standard for himself than for us; and one day, as I was assisting him over the sidewalk, he phrased it in this fashion : 'I am afraid I am not doing the young men as much good as I ought. I suffer greatly, and sometimes it is quite difficult for me to keep my thoughts upon the lecture.' I said we all felt it to be asking too much of him that he should come so far. 'I don't mind that; but I may have to give it up from inability to present the subjects as I think I ought.' This feeling seemed to grow upon him, until one morning I received from him a note asking me to read his resignation as 'Professor of Systematic Theology' to the School. The reason given was substantially the same as stated in his conversation; viz., 'that he feared he was not doing the good he ought, and that perhaps some one else could better fill his chair.' *So* great was the humility of this saint among men!

"I was made heartsick by it. It occurred to me that Mr. Hepworth (then our President, and who appreciated better than any other the work the Doctor was doing for us) could suggest the best thing to do. So I at once submitted the letter to him. He was much moved by it, for he knew the Doctor so well that the suffering and labor were all brought to his mind by this uncomplaining relinquishment of his duties. 'Poor old man,' he said, 'the strongest yet the weakest, the most exalted and yet the humblest of us all.' He walked over to the School with me, and talking with us all in the chapel said, 'This must not be: if we can prevail upon him, we must, for no one can take *his* place here now.' So we all got together and wrote out about as heartfelt a petition to our dear old father as ever came from human bosoms; asking him, if possible, to come back to us, telling him how he had grown into our hearts, and that no one else could be to us what he was. And I doubt not to him, as well as to many others, the most satisfactory part of this petition was the eagerness with which those most obstinately opposed to his conservative ideas signed it. It was one unanimous outgoing of all hearts towards this old man, made doubly dear by the thought that we were to lose him. I took the request to his house, and found him, as usual, busy with his books; but he spared me a few moments, took the letter in his hands, read it through very carefully, laid his head back upon the chair, and said, in his own simple and sincere language that went straight to the point, 'Well, I am glad that they think I have done them good: I will consider this, and, if I *can*, will grant their request.' I went back hopeful and happy. A few days afterward a favorable answer was sent me in a short note, asking that it be given to the School. It was joyfully received. So long as he remained with us, the pleasure was greater and greater to us; and I believe it gave him augmented satisfaction to feel that we did try more studiously than before to satisfy his requirements.

"The time allotted for the lecture was one hour, but it oftener consumed three. He always came thoroughly prepared; his subjects briefed out on half-sheets of note-paper, the books he wished before him. We often were negligent and inattentive: he never was. No matter how cold or warm or how much exhausted he was, with rigorous exactitude he commenced and pursued the points marked out for the lecture. He would generally take up the subject that was to form our next essay to him, and talk upon it for an hour, the students taking notes and occasionally asking questions. The themes were, — 'Inspiration,' 'Revelation,' 'Divinity of

Christ,' 'Origin of Sin,' and other subjects suggested by
Scriptural study and our talks upon the lectures. In com-
mencing his 'talks,' as he loved best to call them, his tone,
though distinct, would often be but little above a whisper;
but, as he continued, his voice would grow louder, and he
appeared to speak more easily to himself. At times, when
treating of subjects of more vital importance, it always
seemed, to him than to most men, — such subjects as 'Human Accountability,' 'Forgiveness of Sin,' and others relating to the kinship between this world and the next, — a sort
of inspiration would appear to take possession of him, his
voice would become resonant, his eye brighten, and his deep
faith in the truths he spoke, coming from a man who lived
them out, gave to them almost an imperative force, and
lifted the speaker into a sublimity borrowed from the
grandeur of the precepts that were eternal. The conversation would at other times become general, each one defining
his position upon the mooted question. It was always his
custom to shake hands with each one upon coming and
going. The essays written on the subject of the lecture of
the week previous were taken home by him, and, after careful correction both as to manner and matter, were returned
on the next lecture-day. The annotations and corrections
were often copious, and in so great a number of essays
required much time and labor: often he used a sheet or two
of note-paper in reviewing the subject.

"As I write, so much that he said and did presents itself
to my mind that I find myself running on to an indefinite
length. His kind, gentle, loving ways, always making us
welcome at his own home, and greeting us cheerfully whenever and wherever he met us, made on some lives, I know,
an impression that can never die out. Guileless as a child,
no man could know him and his nature and not grow purer
and become ennobled by the intercourse. Whenever I have
looked for a life that combined in one man my ideal of purity,
simplicity, and Christlike self-forgetfulness in duty to others,

the name that has come to my lips almost unbidden is that
of dear, blessed old Dr. Gannett."

From the Journal : —

May 20, 1868. "Twenty-eighth and last lecture at the
School. On the whole I have enjoyed these exercises. The
young men have given more attention and shown more interest than I expected. Reading and correcting their essays
have taken up a good deal of time, but I believe writing has
been very good for them."

With all young ministers he was a most generous
talker. The Sunday tea brought many a friendly controversy with them. Never did he take advantage of
age, experience, or study, to overawe the crudest boy
he spoke with on religious subjects. On the contrary,
such a boy would be taken at his best, would perhaps
hear his argument stated for him better than he himself
could state it, before it was opposed. The old man was
the one to feel the loneliness of the dissent, and often
he did feel it bitterly. To hold discussion with him
was a constant lesson in humility and noble fairness, as
well as in frank enthusiasm for one's own belief. Now
and then a word like this occurs in the later Journals : —

"Ministers' Association met. Discussion on the state of
our Theology. Dr. —— opening, and answered by Drs. ——
and —— on Radicalism. I explained, and claimed justice
for the young men."

May 3, 1871. "Annual meeting of the Society for Promoting Theological Education. Discussion about requiring
beneficiaries" (at the Cambridge Divinity School) "to sign a
declaration that they 'intend to enter the ministry of the gospel of our Lord Jesus Christ, contained in the New Testament;' . . . and I insisting on requiring nothing but the
terms used in Mr. Williams's bequest, 'intending to enter the

Protestant ministry.'" (The vote went against his opinion
of right.) "I declined a re-election as one of the directors,
because it would put me in a false position. In my speaking,
I was egotistical and vehement as usual. When shall I learn
self-control?"

The impatience that occasionally broke out thus in
discussion was seldom directed against any one but himself and his own inability to demonstrate to another
what to him was sun-clear. But the memory of the
ruffled words many a time sent him hurrying back to
amaze some friend with a petition for forgiveness! The
stories of his apologies are touching and amusing. Late
one night, a friend heard the limp and the well-known
canes coming along the sidewalk, and wondered what
necessity brought Dr. Gannett at that hour to his street.
A neighbor's door-bell rang. He heard an upstairs window open, and then the Doctor, standing below, pour
out contrition for some hastiness that he feared had
given hurt: after which, the canes clicked lightly off
into the silence, — the conscience was at rest. And
this, save as to the midnight, was instance, not exception. To believe himself to have wronged another,
was to tell that other so. Mortification, so constant in
him in some forms, seemed unknown as a deterrent from
confession. Not to confess would be increasing the injustice, would be simple dishonesty: at once he set
out for the house, or sat down to write the note. He
often humbled people to the ground by his own humility,
— never in any other way. Indignation he knew:
contempt or triumph was a feeling that had absolutely
no place in him. At least, the nearest approach to contempt he ever showed was a feeling, half-indignation,
half-amusement, towards certain supercilious attitudes
of American Episcopalianism.

A few passages from letters to his son written during these latter years will show how conscientiously, at the same time how fairly, tenderly, humbly, he would, as a father, urge his faith. The last two or three extracts contain other words of counsel for young ministers: —

"Feb. 5, 1861.

"I do not quite agree with you about the *progress* of Unitarianism, or the constant 'march' of thought. There must be truth somewhere, and I do not know where to look for it, if not in the Bible. Now, if I think the right interpretation was put on the Bible twenty-five years ago, departure from that interpretation, whether in one direction or another, must be a loss of truth. Of course the Trinitarian or the Calvinist would say the same of any deviation from his understanding of Scripture; and he ought to say so. By every man what seems to him the truth should be held in fond regard, and he must be sorry that others reject it. Still no one should question another's right to his own interpretation. Each must value his own opinion (or faith), and accord to others the same privilege. The point on which I insist is that stability, and not movement, is essential. Growth must proceed from a root. The mind which has no fixed conclusions is not in a healthy state. It must have not only principles, but conclusions. Inquiry should not be all the mind covets or defends. Inquiry is good for nothing, except as it leads to faith. Some of our young men and some of our preachers seem to think that the great business of life is seeking for truth. It seems to me our chief duty consists in using truth; that is, in turning settled convictions into elements of character."

Spring of 1866.

"You ask me to give you my opinion about your entering the ministry. I have wished not to influence you, for the decision on so serious a question should and will rest with you. But, as you desire me to write you, I will answer your inquiry so far as I can. Upon reading your letter, I was pained by the necessity which you felt for using such strong language in regard to your distaste for 'a life of praying and preaching.' I was relieved in a measure by turning back to your remark concerning the 'real motive of the minister,' that it 'should be a wish to do *God* service,' as 'quite a different thing and implying quite different purposes from a wish to do *people* service.' I think you have mistaken this service towards God. Do you consider '*living* to the glory of God' something very different from living for the good of others? What truer consecration of ourselves to God is there than that which consists in devoting ourselves to the benefit of His creatures, in leading them to a knowledge of His character and a spiritual apprehension of His presence? I am inclined to think that you have in your own thought dwelt too much on the professional or ritual offices of the ministry, and too little on its general design and work. . . . As I believe you lie under a misapprehension, I certainly cannot on this ground dissuade you from it.

"There is another point of view, however, from which to examine the subject. Have you faith enough, or the right faith, to make you a *Christian* minister? Whether you have faith enough for your own salvation, or for the usefulness you covet, is another question. Have you such faith as is needful for a preacher in a Christian church, is the question you (or I thinking about you) wish to settle. . . . The Bible will *grow* on you. Giving up its authority on grounds which seem to you untenable (on some of which I concur, on others differ from you), you will see in it an adaptation to human want, a *sufficiency*, and a power, which belong to no other book. The speciality of Christ's position is what I most insist on. . . . It seems to me that if your preaching should proceed on the basis which you have indicated, trying to build up faith on what you regard as its strong support, and not endeavoring to destroy confidence in other grounds of belief in the same truth, it would be essentially Christian preaching, and you might be a useful as well as sincere Christian minister. If you accept Christ as the Light of the world, kindled by the Divine Hand for the sake of illuminating the path along which the generations of men should seek God and find at once their duty and their satisfaction, you can preach in his name and in his spirit. . . . We puzzle ourselves over definitions, when we dwell upon the miraculous and the supernatural; but, if we believe that Christ's mission and work were *special* through a Divine purpose and gift, we have the essential truth, I believe, which clothes him with authority. . . . I agree with you in holding indefinite, rather than precise, views of Christ's nature and rank. I probably differ from you in supposing his peculiar spiritual consciousness to have been in part the result of an inspiration or influence specially communicated, and for a special purpose, by God, and not purely a consequence of his own intellectual integrity and moral aspiration. . . .

"I am more inclined than I was to recognize the essential authority of Christ where his special authority is not allowed; although to me, and I think to most men, that is needful, and I read in the New Testament a continual assertion in its behalf. I am more and more persuaded that there are different forms of truth and different kinds of evidence for different minds. The great question is, not what does a man reject, but what does he hold, and is it to him authoritative Divine truth. If he heartily believe it, let him preach it, not antagonistically, but positively, practically, and spiritually. Some of the men from whom I widely disagree, on the Rationalistic as well as on the Orthodox side, claim my admiration for personal worth and professional industry. A great deal of error may not prevent one from being both good and useful. I dislike the tendencies of thought around me, yet they awaken mental activity, and will probably lead to some firmer results than have yet been reached. Cavil and scoff, arrogance and bigotry, are insufferable, but honest and humble inquiry has its function to discharge in the religious world. I have no doubt of man's need of the Bible, and its just authority over human convictions and human lives will be established by the discussions through which the age is passing.

"One word more: do not take your idea of the ministry from what you have seen in me. My temperament and character make me a most unfortunate example of the clerical life. Other ministers, if you knew them, would show you how much they loved it, and how much their own experience recommends it.

"May God guide you to a right decision. Ask his counsel and keep your heart open to receive it, and He will lead you.   Yours affectionately,

"Ezra S. Gannett."

"Boston, March 16, 1870.

"My dear Will, — Did I not once tell you that Mr. J. M. Barnard told me that Stuart Mill said that Jeremy Bentham's 'Theory of Legislation,' Austin on 'Jurisprudence,' and Maine on 'Ancient Law' were the three books to be read on the subject? Maine you have, Bentham is said to be out of print (here at least), but I have been successful in finding one copy of Austin. Will you accept it as my birthday gift? I have not forgotten that the day is past and gone, — for I thought of you much last week; but it was a week of utter weariness and wastefulness with me, during which I scarcely went out of the house. Forgive me. . . . I do wish you held different religious opinions; for my conviction of the Divine origin and special efficacy of Christianity grows stronger, as my consciousness of moral defect and spiritual need increases. I need Christ as both a Teacher and a Saviour. I need the supernatural in the Gospel to give me an arm of help or a ground of hope. Human nature is not sufficient for itself, and God's interposition is man's salvation. I long for you to see this.

"Yours affectionately,

"E. S. Gannett."

"Jan. 24, 1869.

"That delay in the sermon-writing, Will, is very bad. Pray do not follow my bad example. Do not put off writing till the choice is between Saturday night and nothing. I have been half ruined by it. Don't, don't you begin in that way. Resolve that your sermons shall be written on Wednesday and Thursday. Two days will give you time enough, and those two days set apart and keep for this purpose. Now is the time to save yourself from a lifelong bondage to a miserable habit."

"July 23, 1869.

" It seems to me you make two mistakes about preaching: one in thinking too much of the immediate effect, the other in not believing that people come to church to worship, and therefore may be benefited by a sermon intellectually poor, which yet falls in with their devotional predisposition. . . . The immediate effect of a sermon is seldom its best effect. The influence of preaching may be like the influence of character, cumulative, and imperceptible; that is, the hearer's convictions, purposes, feelings are gradually determined by the trains of thought to which he listens, even though the separate discourses may make little impression. Does not a minister's usefulness lie very much in the slowly increasing influence of which he may be ignorant, and of which his people may at any one moment be scarcely conscious? The pulpit should *educate* the people in right thought and good living."

"Nov. 1869.

" I believe stronger ties of interest will be woven between you and the people. They will all feel these bereavements. . . . I have found that they whom I have approached in their sorrow have been the persons with whom I have afterwards held the closest relations; and this I suppose every minister would repeat. Your preaching and your conversation will acquire a tone that only actual suffering could give them. The earlier trials in a minister's life are full of instruction, his later ones may be less profitable — through his fault. The secret of a minister's usefulness in a bereaved house seems to me to lie in the naturalness of his sympathy. If he can go as a friend, and let the ministerial element come in (or come *out*) as it may, he will do more good than by professional counsel. But there are two difficulties in the way, his own consciousness of an official relation, and the unwillingness of the people to forget that he is a minister. He must pay some regard to their expectation that he will give them comfort, and must *begin* the conversation. I feel that I have done the best in the case, or all but the best, when I have led the mourner to open her heart. If the afflicted will talk to you, you will see how to talk to them."

The years now were filling with the thought that he must lay down work. On one of his bright days he writes : —

May 4, 1867. "Sixty-six years old to-day. Looking back on my experience, I feel that I am old; physically, too, I am not as strong as I was; and my memory holds nothing. But in desire to be busy and useful (without excitement) I am more conscious of a right purpose than perhaps ever before. I wish to remain in the ministry, in spite of the example of those who, because they have passed sixty, have resigned their pulpits. Shall age be a disqualification for the ministry? At the annual meeting, this week, of the proprietors of the church, no discontent, as I learn, was expressed; but a wish that I would take the salary of $5,000."

The highest yearly salary that he ever would receive — and that for hardly more than a single year — was $3,500.

"Shall age be a disqualification for the ministry?"
The question constantly beset him. He recognized the
changed views of the pastoral relation from those held
when he was young, but yet maintained that a character
ripened with time, that a man ought to be wiser at sixty
than at forty, and therefore that the connection between
a minister and his people, like a family-tie, should not
be broken by increase of years, if they brought not increase of weakness. In the hottest days, when the
blood circulated freely through his chilled system, he
wrote and preached and visited, and felt that he had
time and strength for all future duties. As the cold
weather came, the physical prostration would return,
with the gloom consequent upon it, — a gloom that he
endured in silence as long as nature would permit. Nor
did he indulge in lengthy delineation of his feelings in
the Journal. The entry of day's doings oftener ends
with "Tired, very tired," — that perhaps was all.
Rarely was the line as long as this: "What does it
mean? These alternations of feeling from despair to
hope, from utter weakness to natural ability, are destroying my life." He grudged the necessary hours spent
in self-forgetfulness and sleep obtained by sedatives;
still more he dreaded the reaction bringing "horrid
self-consciousness." After great pain endured, the
record simply runs, "I have been very tired and sad
this week, feeling that I must and that I *ought* to send
in my resignation."

Again "the letter" was prepared. But, as long as
the seasons of relief and strength were at all frequent,
he could not make his mind up either to withdraw,
or to ask for a colleague, or to "accept a pension," as
he called it. To one friend before all others outside of
his own home he used to turn for comfort and counsel.

It was the wife's sister, the children's mother-aunt through all these many years. Another dear helper was the old college friend: " You really think, then, that I can stay a little longer? I will then." And when the door closed, he would draw his chair up to the table, — " Lincoln thinks I can do something still." And in the parish there were still other loved and loving listeners. His physician said, " Do not decide until you are calm." He still waited therefore, teaching the young men in the School, taking his turn at the Theatre-preaching, now and then giving one of the Local Conference sermons, besides attending to all the regular parish-duties. The grandchild that had come into the house helped to play away the sadness. As soon as the tea-cup was pushed aside, the little head would bounce into his lap and the white hair was covered with thumping fingers, — the merriest moments of the day. Christmas (1867) was —

" A quiet day, as I wish it may always be. Alone; the past seeming to me less real, — or less sad? — as the present seems to me so near its close. My hold on earthly things appears to me very slight. The past is a far way back, and the other life but a little way off. Oh that I was prepared for it!"

He often now of summers visited the White Mountains. Jefferson, a little village lying full in face of Mount Washington, was the favorite spot. In the course of a long ride with a party of friends in 1868, he found himself at Dixville Notch. The boy was in him still on the strong days: —

" Came back to the foot of Table Rock, one of the loftiest pinnacles. The young people, John the guide, and I, went up. The worst ascent and descent I ever made, — constantly precipitous, and the slight path composed of loose stones and earth. I could not use my canes; could only give one hand to Will, and scramble up and down with the other; was made dizzy, if I looked back; fifty minutes going up, forty coming down. The view from the summit hardly rewarded the effort."

During the next autumn, many were the hours passed on his beloved couch. " Tired and sleeping, but calm; at home on couch," — " miserable; at home, on couch, sleeping and thinking," — " sleeping and reading, weary and troubled." There was a touching pathos in his love for this sofa. It came, among other household gifts, from his people some twenty years before. From it his youngest child had entered the other world; in his own life, it was the home within the home, the spot of surest rest and peace; round it his children had gathered on Sunday and Christmas evenings; and thereon he hoped to pass away.

At this very time the Committee on Theatre-Preaching wanted him to go forth among the cities as their missionary. He told them that he did not know how to preach, and each year was less able to get hold even of the true theory of pulpit or public address. Yet he consented to meet the young men at the School once more.

He *must*, he *must* resign: the conviction was slowly wrung out of his heart after days and weeks of suffering. It would appear an easy thing to do: to him it was a terrible, ghastly effort to send that " letter." It was written and rewritten. At last, one Sunday in December, there came a sermon on " Farewell." On Monday the letter went. When it had actually been given into the hands of the messenger for delivery, there was the stillness of death in his room. The deed dreaded for years was done. It seemed to him necessary, right, the only right course, — but like the suicide of all his past endeavor, all his hope. He had loved and served his people with his strength through almost four and forty years, he yearned to love them to the end and die in service. " Receive us . . . to *die* and live with you," had been the text of the first sermon. " Be thou faithful unto death " had been the motto on his favorite seal. Now it was all over, — and life remained. Here is the letter : —

"Boston, Dec. 21, 1868.

" My Friends, — It becomes my painful duty to ask to be released from the ministry of the Arlington Street Church. I have slowly and reluctantly come to this conclusion; but I can no longer doubt what I ought to do, for your sake, even more than my own. I feel my inability to meet the demands of the present time too sensibly to bring the little power I have to bear upon the work. You need an abler and younger man in your pulpit, and a more genial friend in your homes; such a one as I trust you will soon find. For the many acts of generosity I have received from the proprietors in their corporate capacity, and from the Prudential Committee as their representatives, as well as for the numberless proofs of kind and patient regard which members of the congregation have bestowed, I can only express in these poor terms of acknowledgment my heartfelt thanks. I have but one prayer to offer in your behalf: may the Divine blessing increase and perpetuate your congregational prosperity, and the Divine grace fill all your hearts.

" Shall I trouble you to call a meeting of the proprietors, as soon as may be convenient, to accept my resignation, which I should like to have take effect at the close of the present month ?

" With ever faithful regards, yours,

" Ezra S. Gannett.

" To the Prudential Committee of the Proprietors
    of Arlington Street Church."

That Christmas was " a wretched day. Broken down in heart and hope. On my couch."

But the patient, loyal friends again urged him not to leave them, to take another absence, — for a year, if need be, to rest and travel at their expense. Letters, gifts, kindnesses, poured in, amazing the sad, humble heart.

" The past month has been to me very strange. It seems like a dream. The expressions of esteem which I have received, so many and various, have confounded me. I cannot write nor think with a clear mind. Only one thing seems to me plain, — that I may remain the minister (or *a* minister) of our church." — " Dr. Clarke says I must go away: if I will take four months' rest, I may be sole minister two or three years more; if I do not, I shall certainly break down again."

So he accepted a part of the generosity offered him, — of course the church-treasurer had his usual struggle, — and went away. And with him went Calvin Lincoln. The two gray-haired pilgrims had been close work-fellows for fifty years. They travelled towards the South, visited the other classmate who from those college-days had ministered at Philadelphia, went on through scenes where the signs of war still lingered, visited the Freedmen's Schools in Richmond, stopped at the Sea Islands for a glimpse of the emancipated farmers there, and at last sought what little soothing Florida might give. Then, turning Westward, they climbed Lookout Mountain, groped in Mammoth Cave, rested in St. Louis with friends, and by boat came up the river, pausing at the large towns, until they reached St. Paul. By that time, the rest and change, the friendly greetings everywhere received, and the brother's presence with him, had begun to do the sick man good. In

Milwaukee a large circle of pleasant welcomers awaited him. The Unitarian society opened its church-parlors, and seven of the city-ministers of other denominations accepted invitations to the kind reception.

"I find here a very pretty Unitarian Church, with organ, Sunday-school room, *parlor, kitchen,* &c., after the latest pattern of ecclesiastical arrangements; and, what is better, a degree, or at least a manifestation, of cordiality among the ministers that amazes me. The Trinitarian Congregational, the Presbyterian, the Baptist, and the Methodist ministers have a Monday morning meeting in one of their vestries, in which they give a little account of their preaching on the previous Sunday, and spend an hour or more in pleasant talk. To my surprise, my son had been invited, and had attended the meeting; and had been asked to bring Mr. Lincoln and me. We went this morning, were received with the utmost friendliness. I was asked to open the meeting with prayer; and we, in our turn, were called upon for the subjects of our yesterday's sermons. Could such hospitality to different beliefs have been shown in Boston?"

Thence home by Niagara and Trenton, after a ten weeks' journey of five thousand miles.

Hardly a third of that time passed in work again before the Journal says: "At home, very tired;" and soon, "Tired and troubled." The year dragged painfully by, a conflict with many discouragements. He longed — how he longed to *do!*

"How fast the months slip away! October three-quarters gone! And life, with so much to do, and so little ability to do it, and, what is worse, so little resolution to summon that little ability into exercise. Ought we not to be glad that God takes care of the world?"

When he wrote the words, he was toiling in a new way for his friends, the students. Arrangements had

been made in the theological course at Harvard to ac-
commodate the special class of young men for whom the
Boston School had been begun, and the latter had therefore ceased.   Dr. Gannett favored the new plan.   As
his sketch in 1857 shows, he thought the work of the
two Schools could be carried on in one, where all advantages should be concentrated.   But the change sent to
Cambridge a large number of students with little means
of self-support.   To and fro among the Local Conferences he therefore went this autumn, asking for aid to
establish a cheap club-table at their Hall.   Generous
response was made to the appeal, and the table still
exists.   After dining one day with the young men, he
notes with evident satisfaction the bill of fare : " Excellent dinner of·roast beef, potatoes, squash, bread and
butter, and baked Indian pudding, nicely served."   A
well-timed "Visitation ; " for Indian pudding always
transfigured dinner in his eyes.   It was his last service
for the School he had loved so long and well, — his last
prolonged effort of any kind in public.   The success
repaid him, but its cost was speedier prostration for the
volunteer.

Still a few weeks longer the Bible classes and the two
Sunday services were cared for ; still on Saturday night
the lamp burned on till far towards dawn, while week
by week the sadness in the little study grew heavier.
Again it became a question of life or death ; and
again he wrote out his sentence, and sent it to the
church-committee.

His people received the message very tenderly.
There could be no more delay.   They accepted the
resignation so far as regarded his active duties and
responsibilities, but voted, — " That Dr. Gannett be
requested to remain as senior pastor of the Arlington

Street Church, in order that the Church may continue to enjoy the benediction of his presence, and the members of the society, whose steps he has so long and faithfully guided in the Christian way, may have him among them during the remainder of his earthly life, to encourage, comfort, and inspire them." They voted, further, that his full salary be still continued; and in an affectionate letter told him what he had been to their fathers, themselves, and their children, in that long service which had made him the oldest minister of Boston, according to the period of pastorate; and how his work was twined with that of Channing in their hearts, and how warmly they remembered the public loyalty with which he had upheld the interests of a pure Christian faith. They also asked him to prepare for publication a volume of the sermons he had preached to them to be a permanent memorial of his faithfulness.

Dr. Gannett received the committee conveying the foregoing votes with a quiet that told the depths of his sorrow. A month later he answered them as follows:—

"Boston, Jan. 24, 1870.

"My dear Friends,—It has not been from insensibility to your kindness, nor from ingratitude to those whom you as a committee represented, that I have so long deferred a reply to the communications which you brought me. The votes and the letter of the proprietors of our church not only expressed a warmth of regard for which I was not prepared, but proposed an arrangement so different from any which I had contemplated, that I could not without much thought frame an answer to my own satisfaction. And now I know not by what fit expression to convey my sense of the tenderness and generosity which have been shown me. I can only sincerely thank those who have relieved one of the most painful acts of my life of much of its peculiar character, by converting it into an occasion of gratitude and trust.

They invite me to remain in Boston, and propose to furnish me with ample means to defray the expenses of residence in the city. A provision so liberal as they would make, I cannot accept. Even as a testimony of their esteem, in which light alone I can regard it, it exceeds the utmost limit of a just consent on my part. For the present I most gratefully accept one-half of the amount they proffer; yet let me add, that I take so large a sum only because I believe it is the wish of those by whom it is bestowed that my enjoyment of a home in Boston should involve no pecuniary embarrassment or anxiety.

"The proprietors of the church have also expressed a desire that I should prepare a volume of sermons for the press. It is a request for which I cannot but be grateful, but with which I could not comply without a change in my estimation of the discourses, on which they pass too favorable a judgment. I have seldom left the pulpit without a feeling of disappointment that I had made so little of so great an opportunity; and the feeling would, I think, not only be revived in me, but be shared by the generous friends who ask for them, on a perusal of the sermons which must compose such a volume.

"And now will you oblige me by bearing to those to whom I am so much indebted the assurance of my profound gratitude and sincere love? To a more kind or faithful congregation never did a minister hold the pastoral relation, through many or few years; and for him that shall succeed me, I need only ask that he may enjoy the same intimacy of affection and the same candor of judgment. So long as it shall be my privilege to remain a resident among you, the sympathies of my heart, if not the labor of my hands, will be at your command; that, whether rejoicing together or sorrowing together, we may abide in the love and truth that shall make us one in Christ Jesus.

"Affectionately yours, Ezra S. Gannett.

"To the Committee of the Proprietors of the Arlington Street Church."

Already on the first Sunday of the year in a sermon about " The Old and the New," he had acknowledged the love of his people, speaking to them face to face. As he gave out the text, " Old things are passed away: behold all things are become new," those who listened knew the meaning that underlay the words to him, and many echoed them with feeling only less deep than his own.   He told them how, amid the ceaseless mutation, within, without, ruled ever by ceaseless law, we could trust absolutely the goodness of the infinite Will, of which " immutable law is the shadow falling everywhere, the revelation of an unseen intelligence."

" Faith must reconcile me, and you, and all men, to that progress of events which is the constant, and often the unwelcome, evolution of the Divine will; faith in God as absolute goodness as well as supreme power; faith in a love too tender to be tyrannical, and too wise to be indulgent; faith in God as a father, and as my Father, the Father of every one and therefore my Father, — not mine more than others', but theirs and mine, beyond denial, doubt, or a whisper of unbelief.   Give me this faith, establish it in my understanding, plant it in my heart, and I shall neither tremble nor complain ; but will open my arms to embrace and take to my bosom all life's experience, changeful and strange and sad and irreconcilable with my notions of wisdom and goodness though it seem to be.   Let such a faith come, whence it may, — from the depths of my own nature demanding and therefore finding it, or from the high heavens disclosing it in compassion for my want, — let such a faith come into my weary soul, and I will sink into a rest sweeter, a thousand times sweeter, than the repose of a tired child in its mother's arms.   Open upon my spiritual sense, O thou vision of an infinite love, and inspire this faith in him whom I call God, but who has a dearer name for them to use who know Him as He may be known ! "

At the sermon's close the thought at his heart came forth, and he spoke of the change about to take place between himself and his people. This was his word of entreaty and benediction : —

"If I may condense into one line all the counsel that I am anxious to press upon you, dear friends, it shall be taken from the lips of the Master, to whom we unite in ascribing an authority that belongs to no other. 'Have salt in yourselves,' said Jesus to his disciples, 'and have peace one with another.' Keep within yourselves, each of you, that sanctity of character which at once gives it flavor and preserves it from decay. Let religion be the vital element in your life. Let Christianity be in each of you light, force, and satisfaction. Depend not on institutions, however highly you may value them; lean not on one another, in disregard of your own strength. Trust not even to your minister, as if he could bear your burdens. But 'have salt in yourselves,' and 'have peace one with another.' Obedience to the first precept will secure obedience to the second. The personal life, if it be what it ought to be, will make the congregational life what it should be ; while, on the other hand, congregational union will promote personal excellence. It has been a characteristic of this society ever since I have known it, as I believe it was long before, that it has been free from discord or the indulgence among its members of any unfriendly feeling. We have had our differences, but have never had quarrels or heart-burnings. We differed about the removal of our house of worship, but we all rejoiced in the completion of this edifice. We differed about the use of a Service-Book, but we both made the trial and relinquished it without strife. We always have been, and are to-day, a harmonious congregation. Our charities are well sustained through a common interest. Our hearts cherish the same desires in regard to the welfare of this society. May God bestow the wisdom needful to make its future history yet more memorable than its past. . . .

"Dear friends of this religious society! May God be with you through all coming years, — in this your sanctuary, in your homes, in your hearts. Christ be with you, in his influences that enlighten and strengthen and solace the believer. The holy Spirit, the Teacher and the Comforter, that cometh from the Father through the Son, be with you in all the vicissitudes of experience. May this church remain for generations strong and happy in its ecclesiastical existence. May its members live as both heirs and partakers of the life everlasting."

Letters could not be kinder than came to the old minister from his brethren, when they heard that his hands had dropped the life-long task. They knew, best of all, the pain it cost him. Letters from the Fathers even older than himself, who welcomed him into the waiting-season; letters from the men in active middle life, telling him how well they remembered his comings to the pulpit to which they used to look up from their boyish cricket in the pew; letters from young men. We must give one or two.

"CAMBRIDGE, May 18, 1870.

"MY DEAR DR. GANNETT, — I was very glad to receive and to read your farewell discourse, — a farewell not to your people, but to the active duties of your long pastorate. How many years have passed away since you preached your first sermon for me! And how many are the undertakings which come up to my mind, wherein you and I have acted cordially together! Do not you remember what we did towards founding and building up the Unitarian Association, while many of our elders shook their heads and held themselves aloof? Don't you remember our frequent attempts to reform the Boston Association of Ministers, in all which good Dr. Porter snubbed us and put us down so beautifully? Well, the company is pretty much all gone, and they are beginning to blow out the candles; and I, for one, am content to follow.

"I have now been laid on the shelf for ten years, and you may like to know how it seems to an old stager. A thousand times better than I expected it would. Indeed, until the death of my wife, which left me quite alone in the world, and except for that event, I can certainly say, with Mr. Quincy, that the happiest period of my life has been since I laid down the burden of all public cares. I welcome you, therefore, to what seems to me to be a most natural, appropriate, and happy close of an anxious and busy life, — a few years of comparative leisure and rest in which to settle up our accounts with this world, and prepare for the next. What we want is to be rid of the chafe and fret of responsibilities, to which we feel ourselves becoming more and more unequal. There is no one in the whole circle of my acquaintances who better deserves this boon than yourself, and I hope you will enjoy it as much as I do.

"My locomotive powers, I am sorry to say, continue to fail me little by little; otherwise I should have called upon you before this, in order to testify in person the regard and affection with which I am very

"Sincerely yours,   JAMES WALKER."

"BOSTON, Dec. 28, 1869.

"MY DEAR FRIEND, — We had a pleasant meeting in your parlor yesterday, although we were all very sorry that you were not able to be with us. I think this afternoon conference meeting will give us, after a few trials, the social and sympathetic intercourse you have so long desired to have among the brother ministers. But I should not write you to-day, merely to give an account of the meeting. I have something else to say. I tried to say it to your daughter, and she promised to speak for me. But that does not altogether satisfy me. I must speak for myself.

"What do you enjoy most in this world? If you could have fulness of health and property, and an influential position, what would you do with them? You know what you would do. We know what you *have* done.

"You would use them all to help other people. You enjoy helping people who need you. That is your life. That gives you happiness.

"Well, did you ever think that for you to have that happiness, there must have been somebody willing to receive your help? You have helped people by giving, and you have enjoyed it. Can you also help people by receiving, and enjoy that? That is the question. I have a friend who is always doing something for me, and will not let me do any thing for him, except by violence. I cannot call him selfish. He is not. But what is he?

"I was hasty in saying that the question was : 'Can you be generous in receiving as well as in giving?' That is not all. Can you have faith that, in spending the last years of your life in giving your people your benediction, you are truly helping and blessing them? Is the benediction in your service the least of all? It seems to me the best of all. I delight in that tradition of the apostle John, that, when he was old, he used to speak to the people with trembling lips ; and his sole sermon was, 'Little children, love one another.' You have preached us a grand sermon in your life (I use great boldness), now give us your benediction, best of all. — Pardon whatever is amiss in this note. I have not written a word I meant to when I began. It must be some other that has written to you. I should never dare to write in this way, though I am truly and affectionately yours,

"G. L. Chaney."

The answer was not sent till long after its date. "I have been thinking earnestly about my duty," reads a line of explanation on the back of the rough draught from which we copy : —

"Boylston Place, Sunday evening, Jan. 9, 1870.

"My dear Chaney, — I have not answered your most kind note, because I wished to do it both deliberately and quietly. Yet it is not with an unmoved heart that I can reply to the terms of personal regard which will make that note one of my treasures. I believe I long for the good opinion of my fellow-men more than I ought, and to know that one whom I hold in fond esteem is my friend fills me with delight. That a young man should have any love for me seems just incredible; and yet the faith in your sincerity which I can never lose impels me to trust in your affection, and thankfully to accept it.

"You allude to the arrangement which my people, if I may still call them mine, have made for my future wants. The convictions of years forbid me to accede to an arrangement which has no limit in its generosity. So much of what they offer as will enable me to live among them without an anxious economy, I shall gratefully take; but I must not lay on their good-will, sincere as I believe it to be, any heavier burthen. I do not mean to prescribe a rule for other ministers. With larger expenses and with active duties, they are not only justified, but bound to take a salary which I neither am bound nor, as I think, should be justified in receiving.

"And now, let me hope, that, though we may not often see each other, our friendship will never be less cordial than in the past days when it has been to me so pleasant. You have made yourself very dear to us all, as we have looked with admiration on your ministry, and have been admitted to closer acquaintance with a character every year growing richer in its acquisitions and freer in its sympathies; but no one can rejoice more truly than I in subscribing myself both

"Gratefully and affectionately yours,

"E. S. GANNETT.

"Rev. G. L. CHANEY."

In the Ministers' Association, he resigned his Moderator's place with thanksgiving words: "It is delightful to think that for forty-five years I have enjoyed a confidence irrespective of age, on whichever side of the line between the old and young I have stood." This time the request came back signed separately by each brother that he would stay and keep his wonted seat among them. But now he held the purpose strong, confessing to them that in the past he had often occupied that seat " when so oppressed with a sense of unworthiness to preside among men who knew so much more, and *were* so much more, that the duty, simple as it was, became painful." — " How many would thank God, could they have your life to look back on ! " was the thought, phrased in one form and another, that kept reaching him. On that sense of ill-desert, so simple and sincere, it fell as constant surprise that hardly even carried cheer. To all such notes the most grateful, humblest answers were returned.

At first he was very sick, — too sick at times to see any one ; and through the whole next year he needed all the comfort that friends and daughter and home could give him. What they could give was very little in proportion to what they offered ; for no rest, no kindness, could possibly uplift at once the feeling of disgrace that overcame him. He yearned to work, to preach, to help his church in some way, to do any thing to get the sense of use and self-respect. He could hardly bear to touch any portion of the salary he had not earned. He begged permission to hold the Fast Day service which the people were now going to omit for the first time. Might he give the benediction ? Might he administer the Communion, or call as pastor in the homes ? were questions that sorely troubled him. The forebodings were all fulfilled. It hurt him to see little things left undone, or changes quickly instituted which did not quite approve themselves to his reverence so careful of old ways. The sentences along the Journal-pages are very touching to one who remembers how they were stereotyped in the sad look on his face as the spring-months went by : —

March 13, 1870. "Evening, doing nothing but grieving."

April 11. "My strength has left me surprisingly; am less excitable, but much more weak than I was."

April 27. "Called on Mr. Hunnewell to say I was ready to tender any assistance he might desire about the pulpit next Sunday or at any time, if Dr. Ellis needed it."

May 4. "My sixty-ninth birthday. I cannot write about it. The last six months have changed my relation to all the world."

May 14. *To Rev. Henry W. Foote.* — . . . "It has been a dark and weary season with me this last winter, but I hope for calmer and brighter days. That I needed this discipline which I have been undergoing is plain to me, and I am trying to thank God for it. Better habits of life would have saved me from this disappointment; but now repentance for my errors, and submission to the perfect Will that overrules all things, are the privileges on which I may seize. Of your friendship I can never be forgetful.

"Sincerely and faithfully yours,   EZRA S. GANNETT."

May 20. *To another Friend.* — "The change from regular professional employment to a release from all engagement is not pleasant, and Sunday is a strange day. Our pulpit has been admirably supplied by Dr. Ellis."

By the end of June he ventured to invite to his house his old classmates. It was the fiftieth anniversary of their graduation. Of twenty-two still living, twelve were present at the gathering.

The summer, in a measure, brought revival. He again found his way to his old haunts at the Mountains, and to a new place, a hill-top farm at Whitefield, where the sadness perceptibly yielded to the quiet and beauty. One Sunday he preached for the Methodist minister: —

"He having asked me to, though I told him I was a Unitarian, I unwisely consented. . . . I certainly am losing what-

ever power I once had of clear and consecutive thought or
of appropriate language. I will extemporize, if I may, once
more; and, if I fail, let it close my preaching. . . After dinner
sat behind a rock in the pasture, and read. Such perfect
stillness it seemed to me I never knew. A holy Sunday
afternoon to be remembered."

In the autumn any little fatigue or excitement brought
back the dreaded hours. But he had at last half-learned
the two lessons, — to deliberately rest, and to trace dark
hours of the spirit to causes physical; so that all went
more easily. It had been very pitiful before to see how
the self-reproachings of his weakness drew lurid color-
ing from the Calvinism he had learned in childhood.
As in delirious sickness the mind sometimes wanders
back to a language caught in infancy and long-forgotten,
so with him the pictures of wrath and judgment then
impressed rose up to torture the morbid conscience.
With the return of calm and strength they gradually
sunk back to their buried hiding-place.

Parish-visits to the sick and grieving could now be
attended to. How thankfully they were made — he
could do that much! And a weekly Bible class came
to his house. Now and then, with the doctor's leave,
he even preached, and after the old way made the most
of his opportunity: the sermon on Thanksgiving Day
was "fifty-five minutes" long. And again a little later
occur these entries: —

"I preached in our church, a new sermon, fifty minutes
long, occasioned by Mr. Storer's death. . . . He was, in my
eyes, a faultless man, and the most true of friends. . . . I found
no difficulty in writing or in preaching. Wrote on sermon till
6.30 in the morning, but with little weariness. Still I see
that, had I continued to preach, I should have obeyed my
old habit of night writing, and am glad I have retired."

" Glad." It is the first word of the kind with such a reference in the Journal. One " Happy New Year " more of the old kind in the home : —

Jan. 1, 1871. " New Year's celebration by distribution of gifts. . . . The presents were put on the piano and little tables, each with its address (of to, and from, whom) and given out successively; so many that an hour and a half were consumed. Then we had tea in the parlor, and closed a pleasant evening. How different from last New Year's! And how thankful ought I to be ! "

It was a very happy day throughout, made so by the thoughtfulness of friends; and when the good-night hour came, he laid down his pen with a glad smile and peaceful, loving words. The clouds were surely break-ing. The smile and peace gave promise of serene months to come. " At evening time there shall be light."

As he grew stronger and friends noticed the quiet coming on the face, invitations to preach oftener found their way to him. Sometimes he spoke at home, some-times for a brother elsewhere. The discouraged com-ment was apt to be, " It is time for me to retire ; " but the next call was very sure to be accepted. His own church began to hear candidates with reference to the choice of a new pastor, and the old pastor offered to preach by exchange with them in order to save the par-ish money. He took part in forming " a new State Temperance Society on exclusively moral and religious grounds. I suggested two difficulties which we must remove or avoid. 1. Not even to seem to oppose or wish to hinder prohibition ; 2. Not to ignore or dis-credit the old Massachusetts Temperance Society." He also delivered the introductory lecture of a course on Christian doctrine as understood by Unitarians. It was a popular summary of their religious beliefs, of which some friends thought so highly that, several months later, they had it reprinted from the stenographer's report. The last time on his old theme! No wonder he "found it easy to speak" over the hour, "without using my memoranda and without excitement." And he came home almost triumphant, for the church was too crowded in every part, and the words of welcoming and thanks too hearty, not to have a special meaning. Of course he preached the Fast Day sermon again, and it made him "sit up all night without sleep, writing."

In April the "Christian Register" celebrated its semi-centennial anniversary by a dinner. "I went reluctantly and distrustfully, but found a welcome from several in the drawing-room," and he describes the pleasant time. When it came his turn, he spoke as one who could remember the birth of the paper and the Unitarian zeal of the early decade from 1820 to 1830. Laughter broke in once and again as he recounted the tribulations that beset the infant sheet when it represented the religious radicalism of the day. Something which he did not say Mr. Bush told after him : —

"I want to say a word in relation to our friend Dr. Gannett's relation to the paper, and I shall tell something which I dare say he has forgotten, and which perhaps he will get up here and deny. He does so much good that he forgets it. Perhaps he does not remember how much he has done for the establishment of the 'Register' on its present footing. The paper which led to the present organization, the 'Christian Register Association,' was drawn up in his study, by his hand. Then it was no easy matter, at the outset, to get men to subscribe for the stock. At one of our meetings, when it became necessary to complete the subscription, if the plan was to be carried out, it was what he said and did — for his words were enforced by deeds — that secured the enterprise. Then, in the third place, when it was found that we had not organized quite according to law, we met in his own parlor (if he denies it, I will show him the record on our books), and perfected the organization. You see, therefore, that we are indebted to him, not only for the 'Register' of the past, but for the 'Register' of the present. He must take some of the glory, and he must take some of the shame."

And still the face grew brighter : —

May 4, 1871. "My seventieth birthday! I feel and would acknowledge the great goodness of God to me in the circumstances of my life, and in His wonderful patience; while I look back and look in upon my own wickedness with bitter regret."

In Anniversary Week the previous year he had hardly shown himself outside his house. This year he attended a few meetings, and at the Communion Service broke the bread. Once, twice, more the Sunday sermon brought back the old night-work, and the Journal adds again : —

"I am convinced that I could not be writing sermons every week, and not in a month be broken down. I did right to resign my ministry, and God in His great goodness is reconciling all things."

On June 25th he preached all day at home : —

"In the afternoon a sermon written yesterday and last night on 'Constant Growth in the Religious Life,' from 2 Peter iii. 18, 'Grow in Grace.'"

They were the last words spoken to his people.

With but two or three clouds upon the days, the summer passed most happily. He had not been so happy

for years. Again he was at Mr. Dodge's on the Whitefield hill-top, and most of those whom he loved best
were with him there. He spent the time reading and
riding and working out of doors, — holding service
every Sunday, either for the Baptist minister in the
little village, or in the Unitarian chapel at Lancaster, or
with the friends gathered in the parlor of an evening.
He had promised to "supply" at Lancaster during the
minister's vacation, whenever no one else was at hand
to fill the pulpit. Nothing was more real enjoyment to
him than a chance with a country audience, to whom
he could talk with voice and face and hands for a long
hour, freshening the sermon with yesterday's memories
of their streams or hills. That was to do the chosen
work in a chosen place. As at Rockport in younger
days, so here "clearing up" was the other labor of love.
The words read very naturally : —

"At work round the house and barn, removing stones
and lumber. And in the house reading 'McDonald on
Miracles.'" "On the chips." "Removing and piling
boards." "His very recreations took the form of useful
activities," wrote one who spent part of that season
with him : —

"He was continually occupied in manual labors for the
improvement of the place, and worked so constantly at this
humble and self-imposed task that the door-yard gradually
looked as renovated as a meadow when the fresh grass of
spring takes the place of the waste that winter leaves. At
favorable points for the best views of the mountains, he had
benches built for the accommodation of his fellow-boarders.
I cannot say how many times he gave up his own room to
some new-comer against the strong remonstrances of all his
friends. His ruling desire was to make everybody in the
house happy and comfortable."

And another, till then a stranger, adds : —

"The entire household at Dodge's loved and reverenced him as a father. His cheerfulness was the life of the company, and we know that they will always feel a special sanctification blended with their recollections of those few summer weeks which were to be the last of the good Dr. Gannett upon this earth."

Twice he was summoned home to Boston by funerals at which his voice was longed for. As always, to this call he went, against all entreaty of those who knew how much the double journey, down and back, would tire him. On one of these occasions, having to pass the Sunday alone in the city, he went to a Methodist Church near by. It was the Communion Service. "I went to the rail and partook," having first asked a young man, who told him he was free to do so. . . . When he went back to Whitefield, it was with a croquet-set to add to the good time of the guests upon the hill.

Once more he stood on Mount Washington, this time ascending by the railroad : —

"We spent the night at the foot of the mountain. He was the last up at night and the first in the morning, looking at the machinery of the car. I shall never forget the rapt expression of his face and his eager bending forward as we went up the mountain, nor his leaping from stone to stone up there, nor his wanting us all to dine at the Tip-Top, as fairer to the hotel-keeper than to bring our lunch."

Here are reminiscences, from one and another, of the Sunday evenings in the parlor : —

"We had had the parlor evening service, — a service I can never forget. Unitarians from Cambridge, Providence, and New Orleans; Methodists from Vermont; an Orthodox lady from Rhode Island; and the Baptist family under whose roof we were met, — formed the congregation. After the prayer and singing and the reading of a part of the Sermon on the Mount, Dr. Gannett read us one of his most thoughtful and spiritual discourses. The subject was the old, old theme, — man's knowledge of God. The central thought of the sermon was the impossibility of finding God by the searching of the understanding; the possibility of knowing Him by the reverent approaches of faith." . . .

"I could not help thinking, as I looked at his saint-like face and listened to his earnest words, how appropriately the remark would apply to him, that his 'very presence was a benediction.'" . . .

"The last Sunday I was there, he read one of Collyer's sermons, and then bowing his head prayed. That same night, after most of the boarders had retired, he and Dr. Thompson fell into discussion on Nehemiah; and Dr. Gannett rapidly turned over the leaves of the book, finding the passages which confirmed his view that Nehemiah was a self-conceited man, — 'I, Nehemiah, did this or said that, and even spoke of his washing.' He laughed as he read, and we all were very merry over it; but the next morning he was depressed, because he thought he had done so wrong in laughing at the Bible." . . .

"He was keenly sensitive to any want of earnestness or spirituality on the part of religious teachers. He held others up to the same strict standard which he required of himself. I remember how much he was disturbed when a number of the 'Register' came, which seemed to him to have too much secular matter in its columns. His idea was that a religious paper should be exclusively devoted to the concerns of religion, that it could not contain too much spiritual food, or give too much matter which would tend directly to deepen and strengthen personal piety. Equally sensitive was his denunciation of whatever in religious controversies or reviews appeared to him to be unfair or unjust to any side. His last communication to the 'Register,' touching a review of Dr. McCosh on the 'Boston Theology,' shows how keenly he felt what he regarded as the unfairness of some references to 'old school' Unitarians." . . .

It was fitting that this last word in print — it appeared in the paper of August 26 — should be that of a Defender of the Faith.

July 31. "For the first time on this visit I have felt as I did last summer."

August 15. "Felt miserably, like last summer. I hope the old gloom is not returning upon me; yet the recollection of a wasted life and the consciousness of spiritual and intellectual inability overpower me."

August 20. "Preached in the Unitarian Church at Lancaster. Extemporized from Rev. iii. 21 ('To him that overcometh will I grant to sit with me in my throne, even as I overcame and am set down with my Father in His throne.') Fifty minutes, poorly. Stopped at Sunday school and talked with Mr. Clarke's class of adults."

And he expressed his willingness to preach a second time, if it were customary.

"Evening. Service in the parlor. I read Scriptures, offered prayer, and read sermon from 2 Peter iii. 18, 'Grow in grace.'"

So the last sermon written for his people was the last he preached; and the last Sunday on the earth was what he would have had it, had he known, — a working-day. With thoughts of promised triumph, never self-applied, and of earnest speeding forward, always self-applied, he closed the life-long services.

The next day he wrote to the old dear friend, Mrs. Torrey: —

"I shall not be sorry to go home, as I purpose to do this week. The freedom from social pressure which one enjoys here is the great attraction, even beyond the grandeur of the scenery. Nature, however, has a wonderfully *soothing* power. Rest, without torpor, seems to be the law of life in this region. The mountains are calm, and the whole scene is peaceful. Sunday is, above all other days, delightful. The people then — they are never in haste — drop their labor, and the stillness would be oppressive, if it did not seem at once cheerful and holy. . . Remember me affectionately to Mr. Torrey, and believe me

"Ever, in true friendship, yours,   EZRA S. GANNETT."

August 24. "Evening. In the house, reading and packing."

And the Journal ends.

The next day, Friday, he came home. We have this glimpse of him on the way : —

"As we entered the car, the first person we saw was our beloved friend, occupying the front seat, and busily engaged in reading 'Mount Washington in Winter.' Never shall we forget the happy smile that filled his face, and the hearty earnest shake as he took us by the hand, and expressed his pleasure in thus meeting friends away from home. Never have we known him to be more social, cheerful, and lively in conversation, than on this day, as we rode along together, chatting on various topics."

The home was nearly empty. Two little recollections remain of the next few hours, — of cheering words spoken by him to an old and lonely worker, and a vision by another of his own bowed face covered with both hands ; so there were probably sad hours in the day to the old man coming back from his summer-rest to meet again the fact that he was a servant with no work to do. But for the morrow, at least, he had work to do, — he was to preach at Lynn; and, when his son left him in the morning, he was planning to take the late 10 o'clock train. The day passed quietly in the house. Perhaps he was lonely, for he changed his purpose. As dusk came on, with the worn sermon-case and the canes that had so long travelled with him, he took the early evening train, — seating himself in the back part of the rear car, near the light that he might read his paper. — Six miles out from Boston an express-train from behind dashed into it.

No friend knew of it, — no one recognized the poor disfigured face till the afternoon of the next day. Then from the floor where they lay he was borne home by a kindly stranger; and into a thousand happy summer-places the name was flashed. He was but one of many victims. In many a home that day a name turned all the summer-light to darkness. — What mattered it to him? Oh, very little. He never would have been *ready* to go : on the eve of a journey, he always used to sit up late, perhaps all night, doing the last of the un-done work. He never would have been ready, — in his humility he always would have felt himself an unfaith-ful servant, and longed to give more service before he went. In that one possible moment of sharp agony, what thoughts mingled with his pain? As if we had seen his mind, we know: he thought of his children left with no good-by, of his parish and the thousand things not done for it, of the long and empty life : — and then he was with God in His hereafter, whither " their works do follow them."

Very tender were the last words said over him. First in the home, with only the home-circle, by the friend of fifty years. Then once more he rested in the church he loved ; where round him gathered, not his people only, but the citizens who knew him well, the humblest and the highest. Ministers by scores were there of all de-nominations. And many aged people : he had said the last words for their children and their children's chil-

dren. The hymn was sung that had kept a special
meaning in the home since he chose it, years before, for
the wife's funeral. The Bible lent its Beatitudes, of
which each one fell on the ear like a chosen word of
quiet welcome, and its shining Revelation-vision. And
one told how, " body, soul, and spirit, as much as in him
was," their friend had done the work of an evangelist
in their city for nearly half a century, in words and acts
of love ; how his fidelity was a proverb and an axiom, a
first principle from which men reasoned when they discussed the preacher's and pastor's mission ; and how
good it had been, after the season of suffering, to see
once more the old smile, and hear the strong voice persuading truth, before the death-touch so swiftly came.

" At the grave-side a gentle rain fell, while the sunshine glinting through it seemed to tell what a great
light and gladness were at the heart of all these tears
and sorrow. One offered a prayer ; and then another
told us how often Dr. Gannett had closed his services
with the grand hymn

' From all that dwell below the skies, '

and asked us to join in singing it. ' And after they had
sung a hymn, they went out.' " The seventy years
were over.

XI.

AFTER - GLOW.

THE life was over; but, when seventy years of unselfish, earnest life have gone, they leave a bright and pleasant light behind. On the next Sunday, in many a church, — and not in Unitarian churches only, — the sermon touched on the ideal of character just passed from sight. When his own parishioners had come together from their summer's scattering, Calvin Lincoln, the old friend, and Dr. Hedge, spoke for them the love in which all hearts were one. In Chicago, the four Unitarian churches joined in a memorial service. From St. Louis came the sermon of a father in the ministry, who himself looked up as a son to this older father. From little country-places, from the pulpit of city-missions, from church-conferences, from various Benevolent Societies, came grateful messages and resolutions alluding to seasons when he had given fellowship and help. For a few weeks, wherever in New England Unitarians greeted each other, anecdotes of Dr. Gannett were apt to mingle in their talk; and in their respective newspapers men of other faiths were glad to express their hearty reverence for his life.

Some of these memorials are here preserved, written chiefly by brother-ministers who knew the man they wrote of long and well. Their voices echo each other in confirmation of the story that has been told, and make our book the joint tribute of a band of friends. Tireless activity in duty is the great characteristic on which all dwell, and with this, as if it were a part of it, his deep humility; then, the quick sense of justice and the truthfulness, and his abounding hospitality and self-forgetting kindliness. The words are grouped below somewhat according to the quality or the service that they emphasize most strongly. Among them will be found impressions also of his intellectual power, his eloquence, his theology, and his service to the denomination that he so much loved.

HON. WALDO FLINT.

" FELLOW PARISHIONERS AND FRIENDS, — A great loss has fallen upon us, as a society and as individuals, since we last met in this place. Our beloved minister, — I use the term which, I am sure, he would have chosen, before all others, to designate his calling, — our dear familiar friend, ' with whom we took sweet counsel and walked to the house of God in company,' has been taken from us. His death, though sudden and in its manner most shocking to our feelings, came not too soon for him ; for who can doubt that, at any moment, for him ' to die was gain ' ? but we cannot help feeling that it was too soon for us. His health had so much improved, under the influence of rest from harassing cares and toil, that we indulged the hope that he might again be able to instruct us, at least occasionally, from the desk which he had so long and ably occupied and adorned, and that he would often gladden us by his presence in our families. But God, in His all-wise providence, ordered it otherwise; and we would bow in humble submission to His will.

" And now that he is gone, we cannot but recall, even more vividly than when he was with us, his constant and untiring labors for our benefit, the persuasive eloquence and earnestness with which he addressed us from the pulpit, and the ever ready and warm sympathy with which he entered into all our joys, as well as all our sorrows, in the more private sanctuaries of our homes. I was a member of this parish when Dr. Gannett was settled, and I have known him intimately for about forty years; and I can say, in the full assurance of its truth, that in the whole course of my long life I have never known a more unselfish man, — indeed, it sometimes seemed to me that he went beyond the requirement of the law, and loved his neighbor better than himself, — a more devoted Christian minister, or a truer friend than he ; and I call upon all who hear me, and especially on all who knew him as well as I did, to bear witness from their own personal knowledge that there is no exaggeration in what I have just said.

" We cannot fail to remember how humbly he thought of himself and of the work he had done among us; how depressed he was at times, because his apparent success in his ministry had not risen to the height of his aspirations ; how often he lamented — and this was not cant : our friend was guiltless of hypocrisy in any of its forms — that he was doing so little for us, while we thought all the time that he was doing more than he ought, more than he had strength to do, more than we had any right to expect of him. The fact was, I suppose, that his standard of duty was higher than ours, — higher, perhaps, than any one in the present state of society could reasonably hope to maintain. . . .

" And so our friend worked on and ever, and literally wore himself out in our service, — his indomitable will struggling all the while with incurable bodily disease, and sometimes, by its determined persistency, seeming almost to have gained the victory.

" Let us thank God that he was spared to us through so many years."

REV. CALVIN LINCOLN.

" To his mind there was habitually present a most exalted ideal of the sacredness of the pastoral office. He considered himself, in the full meaning of the term, the minister of his people, religiously bound to perform for their benefit every service to which his time and strength were equal. . . . In deciding what should be the extent of this service, he knew no limit inside of their wants and their wishes. . . . He would brave the fierceness of the storm, the freezing cold of winter and the oppressive heat of summer, and force himself over long distances from his home, if by so doing he could speak words of comfort and hope in the dwellings of the bereaved, or at the bedside of the sick and dying. . .

" You can never forget . . . how entirely he became one with you, forgetting for the time that he had any life or any cares of his own to engage his thoughts or to occupy his time. . . . He became at once the personal friend of every family in his society. His acute perceptions, his ever-flowing sympathy and the sensitiveness of his own nature, enabled him to understand and appreciate the trials, and to share in the joys and hopes of those to whom he ministered. Hence it was that there was such a peculiar delicacy and tenderness in his manner, such appropriateness in his thoughts and language and in the tones of his voice, as gave you the assurance of his perfect sincerity and deep personal interest in your welfare, — that he entered your homes with none of the formal utterances of one who believed himself authorized to instruct others, but that he came to you because he wished to encourage and to help you, by bringing before your minds those great truths of the gospel which awaken life and strength and hope in the soul of the believer. . . .

"But in his own home, in his care for those whom God had committed to his immediate protection, you beheld the full beauty of his character. His love for those around him was an exhaustless fountain. He lived in them, and for them. He was ever watchful for their virtue and their happiness. Faithful to his obligations as the head of a Christian household, he was continually devising methods to increase their comforts, to secure for them some new satisfaction. He shared in all their joys and hopes. The advance of age had no power to abate the strength or the tenderness of his affections. His heart was always young. He forgot himself in his efforts to make others happy. In their service no toils were too severe, no sacrifice of personal ease too great. These services of love were not confined within his own family circle. Connections and relatives, near and remote, shared most freely his kindest offices. All that he was able to do in advancing their welfare was as readily done as if they alone had a claim on his time and labors. . . .

"He esteemed himself a debtor to every human being to whom he had the power of doing good. Hence he became an active member of numerous associations es-

tablished in the interests of morality and religion. In
accepting the advantages arising from united action, he
never consented to surrender the right of private judgment. .. His opinions regarding the rectitude and wisdom
of any proposed measures were deliberately formed,
distinctly avowed, and firmly maintained. . . . However ardently he might desire the success of any favorite
measure, he would never allow it to be adopted through
a wrong impression of its real character. His whole
soul revolted from any thing like management and
craft. Whatever he accomplished must be done in the
full light of day. No failure could disappoint him so
severely as the failure to do ample justice to the reasoning of an opponent. This love of justice, this keen sense
of the requirements of honorable dealing, were, if possible, more conspicuous when, in speaking or writing, he
referred to the motives and characters of those maintaining views of religion which he believed to be false,
and of hurtful tendency. He would always state with
the utmost fairness any doctrine the truth of which
he wished to disprove ; and, while urging all fair arguments to show its unsoundness, he was always careful
to give full credit to the purposes and characters of its
defenders. In this connection, I am reminded of the
remark of one who differed very widely from Dr. Gannett, in his estimate of the authority of the New Testament. After listening to his discourse at the funeral
of a deceased brother, Theodore Parker remarked, " I
would as soon leave my character with Dr. Gannett as
with any man living."

REV. JAMES FREEMAN CLARKE, D.D.

" We all felt a little better and happier for knowing that
Dr. Gannett was living among us. He was one of the

men who gave character to the city. Wherever he was
seen passing with his rapid step, jumping along on his
two canes, men felt the presence of the sense of duty.
Conscience was incarnate before their eyes. The moral
sense was made flesh, and dwelt among them. Such a
man, by continuing to live, does more for a city than
half a dozen banks, and is more of a power than the
whole Common Council. . . .

"All of his life was a preparation for death. I think
he was the most conscientious man I ever knew, — he
was even *too* conscientious. His conscience was often a
morbid one, or rather a tyrannical one, and ruled him
too despotically. He never seemed to forgive in himself
what he willingly forgave in others. He went mourning all his days because he could not attain his own
lofty ideal of duty. He was only contented when he
could be making sacrifices, renouncing comfort, giving
up something to some one else, denying himself and
taking up his cross. That, to him, was the chief command of Christ, and he lived a life of perpetual, remorse-
less self-denial and labor. He ought to have been an
anchorite, — a hermit, living on herbs, in a cave, in order
to be satisfied. And certainly, when we think how our
life runs to luxury and self-indulgence, it was a great
thing to have among us one man who never indulged
himself, but always longed to bear hardship as a good
soldier of Christ.

"I do not think he ever quite saw that side of the
gospel which brings pardon and peace to the soul,
and makes us feel as safe in the love of God as the
little child feels safe sleeping in its small crib by the
side of its mother. I often longed that he should see
more of this part of Christianity, and thought what immense power he would have to shake society, and pour

into it a new revival of faith and love, if to all his other gifts he could have added the full faith in the pardoning love of God. I do not mean that he doubted or denied it, but he never seemed to me to realize it. He could believe that God would pardon the sins of others, but not his own. This deprived him of a portion of the power he otherwise would have had, and threw a certain gloom and severity into his services, which made them too severe for young and sensitive natures. His young people sometimes left him for churches where there was more of comfort and hope, and then he blamed himself for it, as he did for every trial that befell him. But it was no fault of his, he was made so: his conscience was too strong for him, and, as I said, too despotic.

" And yet how sweet he was ! What a lovely smile of affection played on his lips, as he met you! how warm and generous his greeting ! how glad he was to do full justice to the work of others! how tender his sympathies! and how his sense of justice flamed against evil and wrong everywhere ! . . .

" He was one to whom that often used, much-abused word, ' eloquence,' might justly be applied. When he kindled into flame, his words had a singular power, which pervaded and charmed an audience. I never have known a greater magnetism than they exercised at such moments. His power of language was so great, he was so fluent and affluent in his expression, and so inspired by his passion, that he swept away all our coldness, and was almost sure of carrying his cause, whatever it was, right or wrong. . . . His sincerity of passion was very apt to make even a poor argument triumphant. . . .

" In losing Dr. Gannett we have lost, I fear, the last man who had a sense of ministerial brotherhood. He believed with all his heart in the brotherhood of the clergy. No man ever stood by his order as heartily as he. How he loved the meeting of ministers! how he welcomed them to his hospitable table! what loyalty he manifested to all his brethren! He never could think ill of a brother minister. He always gave to thèm 'the benefit of clergy'! When a young man passed from the ranks of the divinity students into that of the ministers, he felt himself welcomed by that cordial hand to a new sphere. No matter who gave the formal 'right hand' at his ordination, the pressure of Dr. Gannett's was the real 'right hand of fellowship.' It almost seemed as if he regarded ordination in the Catholic sense, as a sacrament communicating some new spiritual quality to him who received it. To him all his ministerial brethren were sacred and sanctified. Brother A. might seem to others stupid, brother B. a bigot, brother C. a self-indulgent sluggard, brother D. a cold, dry man of the world. Not so to him. He refused to recognize any thing but good in them. He himself, the very opposite to them in all these things, never seemed to have the sense of their defects. Or, if his sharp eye could not help noticing them, he spoke of them with a smile, as one notices the trifling blemish on a great work of art. He was 'The Last of the Brethren.' "

REV. RUFUS ELLIS.

" The days which were strength and usefulness have been many. . . . I say 'days which were strength,' and yet almost so far as my remembrance of him runs back, it was strength of the spirit rather than of the flesh; it was outward weakness which seemed to provoke him to labor, when the strong with almost one consent would have made excuse. Which of you has not heard from the silent street the fall of the two staves upon the sidewalk in the evening hour, signalling, against his will, the way of our dear friend to some one who needed sympathy and counsel? I think it must have rested him to work, — at least, I have tried to think so, when dividing vacation-time with him: it was so hard to keep him away for a few much-needed weeks of relaxation from his pulpit and his people. Body, soul, and spirit ' as much as in him was,' and that was not a little, he has done the work of an evangelist in this city for nearly half a century, in word and in act; and, various as are the duties of the minister of the gospel, who ever said to him, ' This ought ye to have done, and not have left the other undone'? who ever said to him, ' The sermon last Sunday was earnest and able, but during the week a bereaved parishioner looked for you in vain'? who ever said, ' We were glad to see you in our home, but we missed in the discourse from the pulpit what we gained in the parlor'? His fidelity was a proverb and an axiom, a first principle from which we reasoned when we discussed the mission and the prospects of the preacher and the pastor in our day. And it was not the fidelity of an official person, but of the man in Christ, who is the same man in the pulpit, in the study, in the street, in the social gathering, in his household, speaking the truth, because he can no other. Sometimes he saw, or thought that he saw, interpretations and methods which would make the work of the ministry more telling. I wish that he could have seen them to be also scriptural and true; but, failing that, he accepted the overweight and the smaller result, and hoped and labored for what he saw not, always intellectually honest, true to the reason and understanding and revelation by the Christ which

God had given him, and to that abundance of the heart out of which his mouth spake words as fit and well ordered as they were burning.　And this life-long work of his was a work of love.　Conscientious service, the most eminent, could never have called forth such affectionate loyalty as waited upon this ministry, and made you willing — as myself I always was — that he should call you brother, because you knew that upon his lips it was no word of custom or of cant, that he loved the brotherhood, sympathized with the young clergyman, and was ever ready to befriend the less favored.　And though he laid upon himself burdens heavy and grievous to be borne, there was in his nature a great capacity for enjoyment, a keen delight in human fellowship, very often great joy in the common conditions and fellowships of life.　And so I say they have been years to thank God for. . . .

" We are here because for this world they are ended. . . . The angel of death was one of the swiftest, and the departure, though sudden, was not unprepared for ; and, for one who could not learn to be idle and be happy, the best lay on the other side. . . . In that last hour he was on his way to serve, — the burden of the Lord upon his heart for a waiting people."

REV. CYRUS A. BARTOL, D.D.

" I think of the words applied to another, — ' The zeal of the Lord's house hath eaten him up.'　He gave the last mite as though he had not poured gold into the treasury.　All we mean by character in him was almost incomparably displayed.　But one virtue, of Patience, . . . is for him struck from the list.　He no longer painfully endures, — he purely enjoys.　For his labor that

Sunday he had rest: what Sunday did he have it before? A prophet of such holy zeal, not unmeet like Elijah to go up in a chariot of fire, — a worker toiling to threescore and ten, — a servant wearing out the last thread at his task, spinning for the spiritual fabric when the fibre of his frame was gone, like one turning the wheel when the wool gives out on the spindle, — it was fit he should be dismissed from the field for some refreshment and that music of welcome for those who have well done."

REV. ANDREW P. PEABODY, D.D.

" I have never known a man who seemed to me to have more of his Divine Master's spirit and character. What most impressed me in him was, not the fervor of his spirit, though where have we seen a warmer glow of devotion? nor the versatility of his powers, though who has had a wider range of beneficent activity? nor his eloquent utterance, though from whom have we heard more kindling thoughts or more burning words? — but the entireness of his consecration to duty, Godward, manward, and most severely and self-denyingly selfward, — his tender, rigid, self-sacrificing conscientiousness, so that the words applied to the Saviour, ' Lo, I come to do Thy will, O God,' seem to have been the formula of his life ; and, as nearly as human infirmity will ever permit, he might, but for his lowliness of heart, have summed up the record of his threescore years and ten, ' Father, I have finished the work which Thou gavest me to do.' His conscience knew no rest, made no truce or compromise, admitted no exception or excuse ; and it was to him inspiration, genius, power. It made him master of his own soul ; it gave him a kingly presence among men, and the unction of a holy priesthood before his

God. A thorn, sometimes, in the flesh, it was ever a spur to the heaven-seeking spirit. A bondage, often, outward, it gave him the glorious liberty of the children of God."

REV. A. D. MAYO.

" As I write this, I keep glancing up from my paper to a beautiful picture that hangs upon the wall close by. You all know it, — the face of him whose life among you so many years was an illuminated commentary along the margin of your Bibles. We used to wonder how he could bear all his own burdens, — a frail, overworked, weary man ; bending under the weight of everybody's sorrow and sins, haunted by a sense of duty that drove his body like a leaf before the wind. But now we see that he kept himself alive for years by bearing every man's yoke. As long as he could feel the weight of some poor creature's poverty or scepticism or sin or folly on his shoulders, his spirit was 'renewed like the eagle,' and he went about your streets a messenger from Heaven. Such a man is an answer to a myriad false theories of human nature."

HON. GEORGE S. HILLARD.

" No servant of the Lord ever worked in his Master's vineyard with a more devoted and self-sacrificing spirit. Neither ill-health nor infirmity, nor the depressing influence of a desponding temperament, could abate his energy or chill his zeal. The work he did was enough to task the most robust health and the highest spirits. He had all the Christian virtues, and especially the peculiarly Christian virtue of humility. In no man of our community were the characteristics understood by the term 'apostolic' more marked than in him."

EDWIN P. WHIPPLE.

" Perhaps in this testimony to Dr. Gannett's worth sufficient emphasis is not laid on the peculiarity of his disinterestedness. Fanatics are usually impelled by enthusiasm : Dr. Gannett always appeared to us a fanatic of duty. After spending all his energies in Christian work, after doing all that God had given him strength to do, he was profoundly depressed by his shortcomings in his high calling. His virtues of commission seemed to him as nothing when compared with his sins of omission. Though a strong Unitarian, he had a good deal of that spirit of self-abasement we notice in Evangelical saints. His activity in good works amazed those who knew him, and his friends and parishioners were always more anxious to abate than to stimulate it ; for they saw he was always stretching his powers of endurance to their utmost capacity, and that he must at some time utterly break down. The colleague and successor of Channing, he was in disposition his opposite. Channing carefully nursed what health he had : Gannett squandered his prodigally. Channing was tranquil in the calm contemplation of his ideas : Gannett was disquieted by his incapacity to do what he conceived to be his work. Channing's mind was particularly occupied by his grand abstraction of the dignity of human nature : Gannett's heart was stirred by the spectacle of its concrete and most ignoble specimens, and by the thought of his duty to give them a lift upwards. Channing was serene, because he had faith in ideas. Gannett was despairing, because he could not do all he wished to save and elevate individuals. He was in truth one of Duty's fanatics, the noblest of all fanaticisms. He was so constituted that he could have no peace in retirement from active work; and he died in harness, a true soldier of the Lord."

REV. JOSEPH F. LOVERING.

"I shall never forget his manner and appearance the first time I was privileged to hear him. He was to deliver a discourse in the Federal Street Church. I was fortunate enough to secure a seat in the gallery on his left. I remember, with the clearest distinctness, how feeble he then seemed, nearly fifteen years ago. Then his form was bent; then he bore the look of one who held frail tenure on earth; then the white locks were a halo about his brow. I remember the calm self-restraint with which he began, the gradual kindling with his theme, the vigorous outstretching of his right arm, while his slight frame quivered with the passionate earnestness within; and I remember the sad, sweet face, glowing with the saintliness of his pure soul. If there was one designation, more than another, which he deserved, it was — the preacher of faith. What he himself wrote concerning Dr. Channing can be said of him: 'One quality was common to his earlier and his later discourses, — intense faith in what he was saying, as the needful impulse and rule of life. . . . He preached from himself, not from books; not even from the Bible as a statute-book, but as a source of inspiration that was received into his own being before he attempted to communicate it to others. The spiritual electricity was transmitted through himself.'"

REV. RUSSELL LANT CARPENTER.

"It was as a preacher that he was best known in England. His fame had scarcely reached this country when he first visited it in 1837, but he made an impression which could not be forgotten. We had never been carried away by such a flood of impassioned extemporaneous eloquence. On his second visit to this country, in shattered health, in 1865, his eye was not dimmed, nor was his fire quenched by the sorrows and trials of more than a quarter of a century; but, when he preached in Bridport, his powerful utterance in the evening moved us less than the gentle breathings of a filial and chastened spirit which pervaded his morning sermon on 'Blessed are the pure in heart: for they shall see God.' Never shall we forget his tones in the hymn, as he read the words '*My* Father and *my* God.'

" Those who only knew him as a preacher, however, had a very imperfect estimate of his value. His illustrious colleague has an influence in every continent as a thinker and a writer; but in New England, and especially in Boston, it was even more emphatically true of Dr. Gannett that he made full proof of his ministry. There were some who said of Dr. Channing 'he was a word, not a deed.' The saying was unjust, for his word, like his Master's, was with power; but no one could dream of bringing such a charge against his indefatigable colleague and successor! . . .

" More than twenty years ago, the writer went to America, intending to spend a year there in becoming acquainted with its people and enlarging his ministerial experience. He felt somewhat desolate when he landed there; but from the hour when he reached Dr. Gannett's house he found himself at home. He had not the slightest claim on his regard save as the son and biographer of one who was loved in all our churches; but no brother could have shown him more devoted kindness. For many weeks, at intervals, he opened to him the endearments and sanctities of his home and his heart, besides facilitating, as no one else could have done, an acquaintance with valued members of our body in every part of the United States. . . . We could not but be touched when we saw how desirous he was that we should make the acquaintance of men who had a claim on our regard, but whose public course he strongly condemned. All his attachments showed the intensity of his nature ; but he seemed to us remarkably free from bigotry or exclusiveness, for his affections united him to many from whom his opinions separated him. . . . We should not have referred to a personal experience, had we not clearly seen that this kindness of his was the outflow of a deep and bountiful nature. What he was doing for us we found him perpetually doing for others. Whilst almost too grateful for any benefit rendered him, he delighted to spend and be spent in the service of others."

REV. JOHN H. MORISON, D.D.

" Dr. Gannett was not a man of intuitions, but was gifted with a very large development of the reasoning faculties. He saw what he saw at all with perfect clearness. His faith in what he believed at all was without any shadow of doubt or misgiving. He was, therefore, impatient of religious musings which have no substantial intellectual basis to stand upon. He felt himself shut out from that whole region of spiritual speculations or imaginings, into which many devout persons are led by their affections, and where they dwell amid visions of ideal life and beauty which they learn to love and cling to as objects of Christian faith. There was no place for him beyond what is distinctly revealed by reason or the Gospel of Christ. This caused him to appear to some people to be hard and bare in his doctrines, especially in his views of what awaits us when we pass beyond this mortal life. This peculiarity may have lessened his power in dealing with some of the finer sensibilities and affections. But no man could be more tender in his ministrations to the afflicted. No one could enter into their feelings with a more delicate sympathy, or make their sorrows more entirely his own. Whatever consolations his reason allowed him to accept as true, and to receive into his own heart in his times of tribulation, he would pour into their hearts with a gentleness and pathos which only those who have known him at such times could understand. Wherever he could find his stricken and afflicted parishioners, whether near or far off, through cold or heat, through storm and darkness, this seemingly diseased and almost helpless man took his way to them, and with a voice and countenance full of the sweetest sympathy soothed and comforted them.

"But his strong forte lay in his logical ability united with religious fervor. This, with his sense of fairness to others, his almost superstitious reverence for what he regarded as the truth, and the perfect clearness of his intellectual conceptions and statements, gave him peculiar power as a controversial theologian. His rapidity and logical exactness of thought, his precision and felicity of expression, united as they were with a glow of religious enthusiasm increasing in freedom and fervor as he went on from one to another branch of his subject, peculiarly fitted him to be an extempore debater. In this department of professional duty, he had no equal in his own profession, and, as we once heard a distinguished lawyer say, no superior in the legal profession. His greatest success before the public was in the different courses of controversial lectures which he gave on the great doctrines of Christianity. They were given to crowded audiences, and listened to with absorbing interest. They were sometimes two or three hours long. But we have been told that there were persons who allowed themselves to be locked into his church at the close of the afternoon service that they might be sure of a seat in the evening lecture. Many of the truest gifts of eloquence showed themselves at those times. He needed the excitement of the occasion and the audience, with the pressure thus put upon him, to bring all his faculties into full and vigorous action.

" When he was speaking extempore, there was a peculiar aptness, and sometimes a remarkable poetic beauty, in his illustrations. One we remember, but not the words he used, ten or twelve years ago, when speaking at one of our anniversary meetings of the brethren who had been associated with him in the early period of his ministry. ' We no longer see them,' he said, ' but the very place is filled with the fragrant memories which they have left behind. As I think of them, I seem like one walking by night through gardens of flowers, where he sees nothing, but the air is filled with perfumes which tell him how sweet and beautiful they are.

" He loved his brethren in the ministry. There was no one who would go farther or submit to greater discomfort in order to do the humblest among them a favor. . . . He was strenuous in defending his own views, but equally strenuous in securing a hearing for those who differed from him. . . . If, in the heat of a discussion on some exciting topic, he should happen to use what might be considered a harsh expression, how quick he was to see and acknowledge the wrong ! One evening, in talking with a young minister, he said something which it seemed to him, after his friend was gone, might convey an unjust imputation against him. Late in the evening as it was, this dear good man went out across the city in quest of the young man whom he felt that he had wronged, and, reaching his house after eleven o'clock at night, begged to be forgiven for the injury that he had done."

REV. FREDERIC H. HEDGE, D.D.

" Measured intellectually, he was not one of those to whom we accord the name of genius, and place in the highest rank of minds; and yet intellectually, in his own way, a man of very extraordinary ability. If we class the minds of intellectual men in two categories, the intuitive and the executive, Dr. Gannett would rank, I think by general consent, in the second class. His was not an intuitive mind, not the sort of mind that discovers truth, that receives it at first hand; not the sort of mind we call original, not a leader in new paths, not an originator of new ideas or new methods; but rather one who rested in authority, who followed tradition without question, and leaned on the past; intellectually conservative, cautious, although by temperament impulsive, daring, who, if his vision and theological convictions had pointed in that direction, would have been among the boldest of the radicals. For never was man more faithful to his vision, never one with whom conviction and avowal, conviction and action, were more indissolubly joined. Not a man of commanding imagination or exuberant fancy, and without the charm and play of thought which those qualities engender, but one who possessed in a supereminent degree the faculties proper to his class, — the executive class of minds: a clearness of perception, a precision of understanding, a thoroughness and tenacity of mental grasp, a vigor and alacrity, withal, a facility of representation and a power of industry in which he had few superiors among us, and which in early youth secured for him the foremost place in school and college. . . .

" Predominant in his mental constitution was the logical faculty, — the faculty of consequential reasoning from given premises. . . . He was unsurpassed by any of his fellow-laborers in the power of saying precisely what he meant, of setting forth in clear and cogent speech what he saw and thought; for thought and feeling with him were one: he thought through his feelings, and he felt with his thought. And this mutual interpenetration of the sentimental and intellective in him constituted the charm and power of his discourse. Very eloquent he was, as all who heard him in the days of his strength will testify, when engaged upon a topic he had thoroughly mastered, or which, through the interest he felt in it, had mastered him. And the secret of his eloquence was his intensity. He surrendered his soul, his entire being, to the theme he handled: it bore him irresistibly on, as a strong, swift river bears a floating thing on its bosom; and it bore his hearers with him, if not by intellectual assent to all his positions, yet in uncontrollable sympathy with the torrent sweep of his impetuous soul. He was greatest, I think, in extempore speech. The exactitude of his perception, the perfect precision of his thought, and the marvellous command he had of his powers, their prompt obedience to his will at all times, in all places, gave him a mastery and success in that kind of performance, — a combination of fluency and force which I have rarely seen equalled, never surpassed. . . .

" As a theologian, he was fixed and defined by every demonstration we had of his faith. A thorough and zealous Unitarian, — a Unitarian not by lineage or home influence or early bias, but by election, by deliberate investigation, by independent conviction, — a Unitarian of the old type, with Arian proclivities in his doctrine of Christ, and with Puritan leanings in practical religion, but on the question of Divine Unity, in opposition to all Trinitarian dogma, fast grounded, immovable ; a zealous champion of Unitarian views, and through all his professional life an efficient co-worker in all institutions and instrumentalities aiming to establish or promote the Unitarian cause. . . .

" Friends of the Arlington Street Society, yours has been a privileged church ; enjoying the ministrations of two men, of whom, though differing with the widest difference, each has been a model in his kind. The intellect of Channing, the heart of Gannett, have been yours. It were difficult to say from whose sowing has sprung and is to spring the richest fruit. The name of Channing has gone out through all the earth, and his word to the ends of the Christian world. Translated into many languages, his wholesome and inspiring thoughts have been bread and wine to how many thousands who hunger and thirst for the unadulterated truths of the Spirit. The mission of Dr. Gannett will have, it may be, a narrower orbit, and shine with less conspicuous light ; but his work will strike as deep a root, and act, though unseen, with a power as great on the life of the world. His mission is his character as developed in his life : it is the influence that character has had and will continue to have on all who came within his sphere, and in and through them, by a law of moral solidarity, on others and countless others

who never saw his face and will never hear his name.
Who can compute the radiations of a righteous soul,
or guess how far its action may reach, or what latent
germs of goodness in distant spheres it may quicken
into life ?   The great Giver bestows no gift so precious
as when he sends such a soul to dwell and work among
us.   Then he plants his own seed, whose lineage never
dies, but abides in the world, a power for ever."

REV. EDWARD EVERETT HALE.

" So soon as he entered upon the duties of his profession
he was appointed to be the colleague of the celebrated
Dr. Channing, the first preacher of his time in America.
He filled the place to which he was thus assigned, at
once so delicate and so honorable, with such fidelity
and assiduity, he spoke with an eloquence so hearty,
from convictions so profound, that he at once earned for
himself a reputation all his own.   He did not need to
be spoken of as Dr. Channing's colleague.   He gave
support, energetic, wise, and hearty, to such measures
as the friends of Liberal religion concerted for using
most effectively their forces.   Indeed, of many of these
measures, he was himself the first deviser as he was the
ablest advocate.   He shrank from no hardship, and was
ready to undertake manfully any duty which might be
assigned to him in discussion or in organization, with his
pen or on the platform.

" Nor was the work which thus devolved upon him,
and the men around him, any trifle.   It is easy enough
for the men and women of to-day, in an atmosphere
wholly different from that of half a century ago, to say
that freedom of religious inquiry is a thing of course,
and to reckon it as one of the postulates in any calcula-

tion. But they ought not to forget that the organized ecclesiasticism of the country did not mean to have it a thing of course, and that, if it is universal now, we owe the breadth of our position to men who have fought for it and fought manfully. Of these men the Unitarian leaders of that day were among the most efficient; and of these leaders Dr. Gannett was among the most energetic, hearty, and laborious. The work he loved best, and therefore, probably, which he did best, was his work in the pulpit. But as president of the Unitarian Association, as founder or leader in a large number of charitable institutions, as editor at one or another time of different periodicals founded in the interests of religious literature, he rendered ready and manly service, which it is difficult fully to estimate, now that the success of such exertions has completely changed the field in which they were made necessary. . . .

"The time has fully come for some competent person to prepare a comprehensive history of the several charitable organizations founded in Boston on deliberate system, by the men of Dr. Gannett's generation, largely with his advice and assistance, under the immediate influence of that new theology which taught every man to 'honor all men.' . . . The set of men, ministers and laymen, who first gave themselves here to the establishment of the ecclesiastical methods of this 'new theology,' meant that its theories should be treated under their own eyes in practice; and, with diligent study of the best lights in social science, they set on foot a series of institutions, to the endowment of which they contributed liberally, and to the management of which they consecrated their lives. Thus they established a general Christian 'Ministry-at-Large,' . . . pledged to meet, by religious influences, any evil it should find at work in the

town ; . . . a central society ' to prevent Pauperism,' of
which the function has been . . . to nip in the bud, on
a comprehensive system, the evils from which pauperism
grows ; . . . and a ' Provident Association ' for the wise
and systematic relief of the physical wants of any person
in want in the town. These three agencies make a complete system of internal organization, by which they
meant, when Boston was a town of forty-five thousand
people, to see if, in her increase, they could meet the
problems which have overwhelmed the larger cities of
the world, in what is falsely called their prosperity.

. . . " If the Boston of to-day, a city of three hundred
thousand people, is in any sort free from the dangers
they considered, . . . the reason is that the men of
whom we speak, deliberately, and with their eyes open,
studied in time the social order of the world, and founded
those central institutions which from time to time,
through half a century, have been picking away at bits
of the great iceberg, and have melted those bits in the
atmosphere of Christian life and love. Of these men,
Dr. Gannett was one of the most eager and active. He
and his immediate friends consorted in the plans we have
described, and are to be credited with the issue."

REV. HENRY W. BELLOWS, D.D.

" His services to the Unitarian body were of the first
order. . . He had inaugurated countless plans of religious and philanthropic service. Largely endowed with
talents for the ministry, carefully improved by study and
experience, he added to them a temperament so fervid,
a will so vigorous, and a heart so warm, that his intellectual and moral powers were exalted to a pitch of
efficiency and force that made him the necessary leader

of his generation of our ministers, and of the denomination to which he was so ardently devoted. . . . In the days when strenuous controversy raged, he showed himself a polemic equipped with all necessary learning, acumen and zeal, and able to urge the views of his theological party with an astonishing power and eloquence, in which logic and fire were equally present. When skill in extempore utterance was rare, he had attained an excellence in it which has not been yet surpassed. Who can forget the eager and patient crowds that winter after winter listened to his vigorous and impassioned pleas for the theological opinions he had embraced? And with what resolution, constancy, and labor did he not advocate and maintain the practical measures called for by the wants and opportunities of our misunderstood, rejected, or persecuted faith! How zealous he was in regard to all our earlier missionary movements! how important his contribution to our theological tracts, his editorial labors and his ringing appeals in our public assemblies! And, while he advocated the truth as he saw it, how scrupulous he ever was not to assail the adversaries he opposed with unlawful weapons! How carefully he kept the spirit of Christ and of charity in his most earnest and enthusiastic partisanship!. . .

" And while, with a broken frame and distempered nerves, he worked with the force and effect of two able-bodied men, who ever knew him to indulge in any complacency in his labors or to claim any recognition for his services? Painfully humble and self-accusing, he never had the support of even a just estimate of himself and his self-denying and consecrated life. . . . He was ever contending with those appointed to pay him the laborer's hire, and balking by every device the re-

ceipt of the salary he had so many times over-earned.
Absolutely free from cupidity, a foe to ease, and sus-
picious ever of comfort, he only needed to have been
born in an earlier age and another communion to have
become a Francis of Assisi or a Peter the Hermit.
Nobody ever dared suspect the purity of his motives or
the sincerity of his humility, the absolute truthfulness of
his word or the genuineness of his piety. He was by
universal consent held among the saints, concerning
whose worth and essential goodness all doubts and fears
and questions ceased after he had once fairly shown himself forty years ago."

REV. WILLIAM G. ELIOT, D.D.

" He was one of the most saintly men — there is no
other word to express it — I ever knew. With a natural
temper of impulsive vehemence, with a nervous sensibility of almost morbid quickness, he had yet so learned
the lesson of self-control that only for a moment did
the flashing of the eye and the trembling voice reveal
it: he was quickly again self-governed and quiet, and
with a loving smile. He felt wrong and injustice keenly,
but bore no malice, and forgave with that perfect forgiveness which forgets the wrong and shields the wrong-
doer. . . . I have known him in private conversation
to be severe in invective against whatever he thought
wrong or base. His indignation would burst out in a
torrent which seemed like a prophet's wrath. But his
deliberate word was always calm and dignified, and the
remainder of his own wrath he knew how to restrain. . . .

" His life was so full of noble deeds, his eloquence was
so masterly, his wisdom was so reliable, his capacity of
working was so wonderfully great, his readiness to work

for every good cause was so inexhaustible, that he continually found himself at the head of every enterprise, and
men counted upon him as a host; and, whether he would
or no, he was for all these forty-five years of service a
leader and standard-bearer among men who were themselves qualified to be such, but who yielded to him, or
forced upon him the precedence. And yet his humility,
his self-depreciation, his lowly estimate of himself and
of all he did, were so unaffectedly sincere that, when
all men were praising and looking up to him, and crowds
hung upon the words of his lips, and there were none
to answer, he was oppressed with the feeling of his
insignificance, and prayed that God would forgive his
shortcomings and inefficiency. I doubt if he ever said,
' I *have done* this or that;' but only, ' I have tried, and
am sorry that it was no better.' He was not naturally
of a sanguine or hopeful temper, and in so far the motive
and encouragement to work were not so great to him
as to many. He often thought that things were going
very wrong. But in his own work and duties his conscientious earnestness took the place of every other
motive. To do his part well was the great necessity
imposed upon him, and he worked with a will. He
might discourage you, but he would work for you and
with you, and command the success he did not dare to
promise. . . .

"He was ten years or more my senior, but the intimacy of close friendship was always between us as
between a teacher and disciple; for he was my pastor
for many years, and I always regarded him as such and
called him so to the last. . . . It was in his pulpit that,
in the summer of 1834, I was ordained as an evangelist
to come as a missionary to this place [St. Louis]. . . .
The brave words of Dr. Gannett, and the hearty grasp

of his hand, gave me a God-speed upon the unknown errand. . . . Thirty-six years ago, when I was a beginner here, and we were about to make an appeal for help to our New England friends, he heard that I was going there for that purpose, and with his frank honesty he wrote me a long letter. I have it yet, and read it over only a few weeks since. He advised me not to undertake any such thing: 'You will only bring disappointment upon yourself and your cause. You may beg your tongue off, and little will come of it.' That was not encouraging, but it did me good, for it showed there was no easy task before me. I went on, certainly expecting no help from him. But he no sooner saw me than he entered into all my thoughts and plans ; and to him, more than to all others put together, we owed whatever success we gained." . . .

REV. THOMAS J. MUMFORD.

"It is not often that any man wins the universal respect and affection of his denomination to the extent that was manifested in the case of Dr. Gannett. All parties honored and trusted and loved him. Whenever he arose at our general assemblies, he was received with the heartiest applause. In vain did that meek face express its astonishment, and that upraised hand deprecate the honor of which he felt so unworthy. The more he abased himself, the more delighted and the more determined we all were to exalt him.

"Dr. Gannett's passion for hospitality must be remembered by all who knew him, for there was never a man more given to it. His brethren in the ministry have countless sweet and tender memories of one whose ears were always open to their trials and successes, and his doors never closed to their forms. Sometimes he had a poor minister, with his wife and children, at his house, for days, if not for weeks. Anniversary weeks, when other clergymen often left the city to avoid the crowd and the excitement, Dr. Gannett seldom had an empty bed under his roof or a vacant chair in his dining-room. Around that memorable board, as nowhere else, might be seen the young and old, the obscure and the noted, the radical and the conservative, all equal in their welcome and his impartial attentions. He is now mourned not only by his peers in station, but by plain pastors of humble flocks, and threadbare mission-aries far away, who remember, gratefully, that when they were in Boston there was at least one man of high rank who sought them out, and gave them a brother's greeting."

THE BOSTON ASSOCIATION OF CONGREGATIONAL MINISTERS.

"DEAR FRIENDS, — The Boston Association of Con-gregational Ministers direct us, as a Committee of their number, to express to you their sympathy with you, and their abiding sense of personal sorrow and loss in your dear and honored father's departure from earth. For forty-seven years a member of our Association, and for many years our Moderator, there was no one so inti-mately associated with our best fellowship; and the void which his absence leaves among us can only be filled by our affectionate remembrance of him and our gratitude for all that he has been to us for two generations.

"We are proud to bear in mind the great service which he has done in this community for truth and goodness, the brilliant gifts which he consecrated to holy things, the eloquent tongue and fervid pen, the power with which he has fulfilled the highest and severest duties of the Christian ministry which he supremely loved.

"But we are yet more glad and grateful for the encouragement of his example. His Christian life was known of all men, yet was wholly known only by the God with whom he was in such near communion. His fervid temperament labored on for more than thirty years, disregarding physical infirmities which would have crushed a less indomitable spirit, and made itself felt a quickening impulse and a rebuke to younger men; his energetic goodness sped on, outstripping their fresher strength; his fearless loyalty to what he saw to be the truth brought the spirit of apostles and martyrs into our own time as a reproof and an inspiration. The intensity of his religious nature wrought in him an enthusiasm too exciting for the frail body to bear without yielding to the strain. It wrought in him also a spirit of self-sacrifice, which never demanded of others as much as from himself, yet which held up before his hearers the loftiest ideal of duty; and a humility, which sometimes pained us who loved him by the resolute refusal to take the comfort in his noble life-work which was his right.

"Many differing voices have united to bring their tribute to his generous nature and Christian ministry, and have testified how, more than the witness of his eloquent, earnest speech for Christ, the silent power of that character so imbued with the spirit of Christ has told on this city, and has approved the Liberal Christianity which he has so long adorned. But only his brethren and sons in the ministry can fully tell how warm his heart was toward them, how he greeted the youngest as a brother and a peer, how the light of his smile was their benediction.

" We sorrow that we shall see his face no more : but we rejoice in all that he has been, and in all that he has done, and above all in the faith in God and the love for his Master which have now been changed for him into open vision.

" With affectionate and Christian sympathy, we remain your friends,

" Henry W. Foote.

" Edward E. Hale.

" Wm. Phillips Tilden.

"To Mrs. K. G. Wells,
   Rev. Wm. C. Gannett."

REV. JOHN W. CHADWICK.

" e. s. g."

"' At eve there shall be light,' the promise runs
   In the dear volume that he loved so well;
Ay, and for him the promise was fulfilled,
   When rang for him the solemn vesper-bell.

His was no day of sweet, unsullied blue,
   And bright warm sunshine on the grass and flowers;
But many a cloud of loss and grief and pain
   Dropped its deep shadow on the fleeting hours.

Clear were his morning hours, and calm and bright;
   His sun shot up with splendid fiery beam;
And men were glad and revelled in its light,
   And leaped to welcome it from sleep and dream.

Then came a cloud and overshadowed him,
   And chilled him with a presage as of death;
And never did it quite forsake his sky,
   But sought him often with its eager breath.

For still, though hours were his serene and still,
    And radiant hours of steady, glowing noon,
That cloud of pain was ever near to touch
    With quivering sadness every brightest boon.

And as his afternoon drew on to eve
    And still he lingered in the whitened field, —
The reapers were so few, till night should fall
    Fain would his hand the heavy sickle wield, —

Darker it grew and darker o'er the land,
    And he was forced to lay his sickle by;
But did it brighten, then his hand was quick
    To seize once more its opportunity.

So the day faded, and the evening came:
    And then the clouds rose up and went away,
And a great peace and beauty welcomed in
    The evening star with her benignant ray.

And all the air was hushed and whispering,
    And all the sky was purely, softly bright,
And so the blessed promise was fulfilled:
    'At eve,' it said, 'at eve there shall be light.'

But that fair evening did not end in night,
    With shadows deep and darkness all forlorn;
Just at its brightest he was snatched away
    Into the golden palaces of morn.

And surely since the Master went that way,
    To welcome there earth's holiest and best,
He has not welcomed one who loved him more
    Than he who leaned that eve upon his breast."

By and by his people raised within the church a
memorial of their love. On each side of the pulpit
they placed a beautifully sculptured tablet, one for

Dr. Channing, one for Dr. Gannett. The latter bears this record, prepared for it by his friend and parishioner, Mr. Charles C. Smith: —

IN MEMORY OF

EZRA STILES GANNETT,

FORTY-SEVEN YEARS
MINISTER OF THIS CHURCH.
BORN AT CAMBRIDGE, MAY 4, 1801.
ORDAINED JUNE 30, 1824.
DIED AUGUST 26, 1871.

AN ELOQUENT AND LOGICAL PREACHER,
A DEVOTED PASTOR,
A STEADFAST FRIEND,
HE ILLUSTRATED THE DOCTRINES
WHICH HE TAUGHT,
BY A LIFE OF SELF-SACRIFICE
AND OF CONSCIENTIOUS FIDELITY
IN THE DISCHARGE OF DUTY.

AN EARNEST AND INTREPID ADVOCATE
OF CHRISTIAN FAITH
AND CHRISTIAN LIBERTY,
A VIGOROUS AND POLISHED WRITER,
A WISE AND PRUDENT COUNSELLOR,
HE WAS AN HONORED LEADER
IN THE DENOMINATION
TO WHICH HE BELONGED.

A GENEROUS AND ENLIGHTENED CITIZEN,
HE LABORED WITH UNTIRING ACTIVITY
FOR THE MORAL AND SOCIAL ELEVATION
OF THE COMMUNITY,
AND RENDERED IMPORTANT SERVICE
IN THE FORMATION AND MANAGEMENT
OF MANY ASSOCIATIONS
DESIGNED TO LESSEN THE EVILS
OF POVERTY, IGNORANCE, AND SIN.

THIS TABLET IS ERECTED
BY THE SOCIETY TO WHOSE INTERESTS
HIS LIFE WAS DEVOTED,
IN GRATEFUL RECOGNITION OF HIS
TALENTS AND VIRTUES.

At Mount Auburn, a cross rises near his grave, in form like the cross which he asked should be placed on the church-wall above his pulpit. On the rock-work at its base rest the two well-known canes; and, behind, lies an open sermon-case, on whose leaves are inscribed part of the text of his first and the text of his last sermon as the pastor of his people: —

JULY 4, 1824.
" RECEIVE US . . . TO DIE
AND LIVE WITH YOU."

JUNE 25, 1871.
" GROW IN GRACE."

"THE STUDY," BUMSTEAD PLACE.

XII.

SERMONS.

The book will not be a true " Life " of Dr. Gannett, unless it include a few of his sermons, to show in his own words on what subjects he was wont to lay the stress. The " Journal" that has been so often referred to in the previous chapters merely keeps the thread of the days' doings; those self-revealing letters, too, which make so many memoirs autobiographical, with him were very rare; and the absence of this inner mind and deeper heart in the record of a ministry so expressly loyal to a special faith may have suggested that the minister valued " doctrine " more than all besides. Such an impression would be most unjust. Although he believed that firm intellectual conviction must underlie warm religious feeling and strong religious motive, although his own ideas were cast in Unitarian forms, and from beginning to end he stood before the public

as their ardent champion and expounder, yet it was that
faith as wrought into experience and embodied in
character, not as held by the mind, that was the transcendent thing with him. The "doctrines" that he
loved so much were little more than the fundamentals
of the spiritual life, the few all-embracing ideas under
which a man believing in the Christian revelation con-
ceives our relation to the Eternal Reality of Being.
Some sermons are therefore added, that friends may
find in them the missing side, — it is the inside of all,
the inmost spiritual man, — as he gave it Sunday utterance. It is a side which cannot well be pictured, save
by one's own utterance. Dr. Gannett spoke himself
out in sermons, and in no other way. Save sermons or
essays of a sermon-nature, he published nothing, and
wrote very little.

These that have been selected contain his main
emphases, those oftenest repeated from week to week
in the home-pulpit, and from place to place as he went
about upon exchanges. The themes that he loved most
were those of the Inward Life, with Faith as the belief
in unseen realities for its beginning, — Faith ripened
into fellowship with Christ and God as its consummation. The "Christian consciousness," the soul's experience in the process of "salvation," — experience of
sin, repentance, and consecration ; of "regeneration,"
temptation, struggle, failure, and victory, and growing
"sanctification ; " of serenity and peace, the realizing
even now of the heaven-promise ; and, on the other
hand, the perfect sureness of a just retribution in the
hereafter, — directly upon these experiences a very
large part of his preaching centred. Next in number
are the sermons that treat of the *aids* to this True
Life ; above all, the aid vouchsafed in Christ's revelation

of the Father's mercy and our immortality, in Christ's cross with its appeal to the heart, in Christ's character with its perfect example, in his religion as the inexhaustible source of the world's spiritual vitality. And next, or perhaps not less in number, are those that urge the expression of this inward Life in outward Righteousness and Holiness, — not "practical sermons," so called, but sermons of religion-in-practice, the bond with God never being lost from sight. " Integrity " was a favorite word with him, applied to man, to Christ, to God. Says one who was in the meeting-house on almost every Sunday of his preaching, " The impressions left upon the minds of those who heard him through many years were, I think, the necessity of Personal Responsibility, Personal Integrity, Personal Purity, Personal Spirituality, as credentials of fitness for Heavenly Inheritances."

For every sermon-length here printed, one hundred and twenty-five manuscripts lie in the drawers. They number about seventeen hundred and fifty, — to say nothing of the piles of lecture-abstracts and of little sheets containing the heads of extemporaneous discourses. He used to record on the back of the manuscripts the place and time of each delivery, so that the elect sermons are easily traced. The first three found below had several times been off with him, wrapped in the old case, on an exchange. Several of the others were the preparation made for an ordination-service, and represent more deliberate work, or perhaps the recasting of two or three of the quick Saturday night productions. They have been freely handled in the editing; that is to say, while nothing has been put in save, here and there, a connective word or two necessitated by compressions, parts have been left out, a sentence or paragraph has sometimes been set in new

27

position, and in three or four cases parts of kindred sermons have been knit together to fill out the thought.
Such knitting is indicated by a double date or in some
other way; but it has not seemed worth while to star
the print over to mark the minor changes.

" Out of the Depths " was a cry out of his own depths
not long before his resignation.   Those who heard him
give it can hardly help supplying the face and the tones
that went with it.   Then come two sermons on Mystery and Faith, the latter embracing an extract from the
discourse with which Rev. Dr. Peabody was ordained
at Portsmouth, in 1833.   And then a series on the Spiritual Life, beginning with what the young man said at
a still earlier, a " Christian," installation at Portsmouth,
in 1829.   The larger part of the sermon on Salvation
through Christ was given at Rev. John C. Kimball's
ordination in Beverly; and the next at Rev. James
De Normandie's, once more at the Portsmouth church,
in 1862.   The seventh is part of the sermon preached
at Rev. Dr. Morison's installation in Milton. This and the
one that follows it treat of the Largeness of Christianity
as shown in its truths, its Teacher, and its inspiration for
common life.   The ninth again strikes the key-note,
" Life," dwelling more now on its outward aspect, and
presenting it as the distinguishing emphasis of Unitarianism.   This leads to some extracts on the Importance of
Opinion in Religion and the True Sectarianism.   And
then, although so much has already been said about Dr.
Gannett's Unitarianism, it seems natural to repeat here
its beliefs as he used to preach them.   For that purpose,
a few paragraphs have been selected from a sermon
delivered in 1845, at the dedication of the church in
Montreal; others from an address before the Ministerial
Conference in 1849; and a longer and more popular

statement, — the extemporaneous lecture that was delivered so near the end.

Several pages follow, in which he has unconsciously drawn his own portrait in picturing his ideal of the Minister's Devotedness. The passages are mostly gathered from the counsel which he gave at different ordination or installation services, — a few out of the very many in which he took part, — those of Rev. Dr. G. E. Ellis (1840), Rev. J. I. T. Coolidge (1842), Rev. E. E. Hale (1856), Rev. G. Reynolds (1858), and Rev. J. F. Lovering (1860). The extract marked 1839 is from the sermon he delivered before the Graduating Class at the Harvard Divinity School, and that of 1850 is from the Address before the Alumni of the same School.

And the sermons close with some words spoken by him of two cherished friends, Rev. Dr. W. B. O. Peabody, of Springfield (1847), and Rev. Dr. E. B. Hall, of Providence (1866), — again, words that have a strangely perfect fitness for himself.

Last of all will be found a list of the sermons and articles which in various forms were published.

DEC. 8, 1867.

OUT OF THE DEPTHS.

PSALM CXXX. 1: *"Out of the depths have I cried unto Thee, O Lord."*

OUT of the depths he cried, and was heard. Man never cries in vain, out of his extremity. He is permitted to go down into the depths, that his prayer may acquire a vehemence which shall make it effectual.

Does man ever cry unto God in vain? It would be sad to

believe that the ear of Infinite Love is closed against any entreaty. It would be more than sad : our faith in God could not bear such a shock. But He may let us sink very low, that we may learn the mighty prevalence of prayer.

When we are in the depths, we are apt to think no one ever sank so low before. But we know only our own experience. How sorely another is tried we cannot know, unless we can look into his heart. In fact, " the thing that hath been is that which is," and which " shall be." Others have suffered as we suffer, and to-day there are aching hearts — God only knows how many ! — besides ours. He knows them all. And that is the precious truth. He sees each one of the weary and worn, the disappointed, the troubled, the disconsolate, the self-condemned. He looks down into all depths, and hears alike the groan and the sigh. The soul that feels itself alone in this great world of mankind is, in its most desolate hour, alone *with* God, not without Him. *That* cannot be. And therefore there is no condition of body, mind, or estate, out of which the soul may not address its supplication to Him.

Of estate, did we say, hastily repeating words with which we are familiar, and not considering how inappropriate they may be in this connection? Yet not hastily, but purposely, did we use them; for it is a mistake to separate our worldly condition from the presence and will and love of God. Out of the depths of trouble *in their affairs,* men should cry unto Him. They need His help : why shall they not seek it? Ask God to help them in their business ! Some persons may be offended at the suggestion, as if it savored of irreverence. Is it not they who narrow the ground of reverence? Does not God's eye rest upon us in our worldly business ? Does not Divine judgment wait upon the merchant, and cast up the columns of loss and gain in his books? If he be prosperous, does he not thank God for the success which has crowned his enterprise or his industry ? Why shall faith be an inmate of the counting-room on one day and not on another? No one needs to fill his heart with piety more than the man who, amidst the uncertainties of business, is now solicited by a great temptation, and now is overtaken by a great disaster. The most religious part of the community should be they who handle money. Instead of separating their business from their prayers, they should make their business the subject of their prayers. Let a man pray every morning that God will direct him in his transactions through the day, let him offer up a petition to be divinely guided in every transaction before he enters upon it, would there be any impropriety in such address? Would it not throw a protection around his character under the moral exposure it might encounter?

Now, if God may be a defence against trouble, may He not also be a refuge in the time of trouble? No one is more liable to severe disappointments and sudden reverses than he who embarks his fortunes with the mercantile community. No one perhaps suffers more than the merchant, whose word has been as good as his bond, and his bond as good as gold, when he finds himself on the eve of bankruptcy. — his sagacity, if not his honesty, called in question, his family deprived of means of enjoyment, if not of subsistence, the hard steps which lie at the commencement of a business career to be retaken, unless still heavier disasters prevent, and the whole aspect of daily life changed. Some men meet the crisis with brave hearts, but hearts that bleed ; and others succumb, their courage broken, their hope gone. Is not this the very time to cry unto God? Are not these the men who *ought* to cry out of the depths? Cry that He will restore their prosperity, or will avert the calamity they dread? Yes : let them ask for *that*, if they can join with the prayer perfect submission to the Will that may choose other discipline for them. Whether they ask for that or not, whether they escape mercantile ruin or not, they may implore aid to carry them through the period of suspense, which is worse than the final event; support that shall make them both strong and patient, giving them a calm mind and clear judgment, and bring their integrity out of the trial unharmed. He is safe who can say, " Out of the depths of my anxiety and misfortune I have cried unto Thee, O Lord."

There is other trouble besides that which comes in the way of business; trouble into which any one may be plunged by his own want of sound judgment, or by the folly of others, or by circumstances which seem to involve no one in blame, yet cause bitter distress. There are few households in the land that have not some spectre stalking through the apartments, and casting a shadow over daily enjoyments. Home is a word that covers many associations, not all of which are pleasant. There are seasons in young life when the heart is ready to sink under a burden which it knows not how to bear or to cast off. There are years of parental life, through which the child to whom affection clings is an occasion of continual disappointment and alarm. There is many a personal experience, unwritten and untold, that cannot be described even in the poor words which but *shadow* forth reality, without filling our eyes with tears. Thousands of hearts go down very far below the surface of life, to its deep places, where the hand of God must be reached out to hold them up, or they will be overwhelmed. These are the hearts that should cry out for Him, cry *to* Him. "In my distress," said David, "I called upon the Lord, and cried to my God; and He did hear my voice, and my cry did enter into His ears." "Thou hast enlarged me when I was in distress," he writes in another psalm; and, encouraged by the past, renews his supplication, "Have mercy upon me, and hear my prayer." One book of the Old Testament is a long wail of lamentation. "My sighs are many, and my heart is faint," says the prophet, speaking in the name of an humbled and crushed people; yet from those depths of national dishonor and personal grief he exclaims, " The Lord will not cast off for ever." "I called upon Thy name, O Lord, out of the low dungeon. Thou hast heard my voice. Thou drewest near in the day that I called upon Thee: thou saidst, Fear not." What sweeter encouragement can be drawn from the heart of the gospel? That old Hebrew piety was a wonderful anticipation of Christian faith.

Out of the depths of *affliction* we may cry unto God. To whom but to Him, who is the same for ever, shall we look in the great sorrows of life? The heart, bereft of its earthly delight, needs to draw comfort from Heaven. We *must have* sympathy. Absolute loneliness is a slow consumption of the soul: its very immortality is assailed. There are few real mourners, who have not found the inadequacy of human friendship. They who love us come at such a time and sit with us, and speak words that soothe and strengthen us, and then leave us to ourselves; and the loneliness that we felt before they came we feel when they go away, and we felt it while they were with us. They cannot go down into the depths where we are struggling. They pity us as far as they can, they sympathize with us; but they cannot walk with us through the billows. There is only One who can attend us, only One who is as really on the stormy deep as He is in the serene heavens. A strange truth, a sacred mystery! He who dwelleth in the light inaccessible walks with us in the darkness. And we need only to cry unto Him, and His arm will surround our failing strength. How plain a type of the Divine help was that act of Jesus, when Peter, as the wind grew boisterous, became afraid, and beginning to sink cried, " Lord, save me!" and immediately Jesus was at his side and bore him along in safety. God is always near, waiting, — no, not waiting for our cry; but because, in that confused state of faith and unbelief in which the heart finds itself after bereavement, it must utter the sharp, blind cry of its want, He is ready with an answer of love.

Suffering under any form is the call which the heavenly Father extends to us to put our trust in Him. We need many such calls, and therefore *many sorrows* enter into our experience. But the pain that we endure through the loss of those who are dear to us, though it be the keenest, is the kindest of all; for, if only by dying could they for whom we would gladly give up our lives be clothed upon with immortality as the imperishable garment of their souls, God fulfils our best desire on their behalf, when He takes them out of a mortal state, and so is kind to both them and us. But, because in our weakness we had leaned on their companionship as needful to us, we cannot at once take in the full comfort of this truth, that death is life; and then the same heavenly Father, because His love is as patient as our want is various, hears the cry of our anguish, and folds us in His arms as tenderly as a mother the babe of her own bosom. There is rest for the weary spirit in His arms, and large communion for the lonely one, — a higher communion and a better rest than the morbid grief, that will not forget itself even in Him, craves. The cry must not be that God will supply the place of our friend with the light of His own countenance, — for such a prayer may show as much of selfishness as of faith, — but a cry like that which broke the silence of midnight in Geth-semane, when he who was in an agony prayed that the Father's will might prevail over his will, and from that prayer rose calm and strong. It is such a cry that befits us as we accompany our dear ones through the valley of the shadow of death to that point where the road begins to ascend, and we must part for a little while. You will find these lines in a book just published: do they not report the truth concerning trouble ? —

> " It is
> The darksome labyrinth wherein a God
> Doth graciously lead men, that every one
> May prove his life: that the bad man may know
> His wickedness and learn to cease from it;
> And that the good may by experience
> Know his good spirit and enjoy it. For
> We see the bad come forth from sorrow's cloud
> A better, and the good a kindlier, man.
> And is there one whom God has never tried ?
> For what one of the children whom He made
> Loves He not ? "

Shall we go down into yet lower depths ? *Are* there depths lower than these of which we have spoken, and yet with which man must become familiar ? With which he may, — not must. The necessity is laid on him only by his own choice. If he *will sin*, then the suffering which he shall bring on himself may lie beyond any help which others can extend, too far down from the light and warmth of day for any human hand to offer deliverance. We have read of travellers among the Alps who have fallen into chasms where no eye could follow them, and whence their cry could not clamber up the sides of the icy sepulchre in which they have lain bruised and bleeding till they died. We shudder at the thought of such a fearful death. But worse, far worse is *his* condition, who, crossing the treacherous ground of sinful indulgence, finds it giving way as he sinks into the cold and dark misery, where his fellow-men, ignorant of his situation, or inattentive to it, leave him to perish. Let him then come to understand himself, who shall depict the anguish that will seize upon him? He may have never prayed, or he may have made prayer a cloak to hide his sinful life from his own sight. Can he now pray, out of the depths of remorse? You may remember, my friends, the account we had, not long ago, of men who were buried alive in one of the coal mines of England. In vain did their companions toil, day and night, to rescue them. The chamber in which they were confined was reached too late. But *there* was found proof that they had sustained one another by words of holy faith and submissive prayer, and had sung hymns that were strains of everlasting life. And so the terror was taken from their hearts, and the horrors of that fatal imprisonment down in the bowels of the earth seem to have been converted into the glories of martyrdom. A deeper burial from help and hope, his, whose sins have overwhelmed him ; shutting out light and closing every passage by which he might escape from himself. What shall he do? To whom can he cry? Society does but send back the echo of that mournful confession which with parched lips he incessantly repeats, "chief of sinners," "chief of sinners." Friends take compassion on him, and attempt to divert his thought from his own wretchedness. As well attempt to turn back the incoming tide. Some say he is of unsound mind, but *he* knows it is an unclean heart that torments him. He cannot sing hymns, nor commit his soul to God in patient faith, as did those miners when death came to give them deliverance. Death has no kind message for him. If to live here in the consciousness of abused powers and wasted opportunities and violated obligations and habitual ill-desert be torture, what must life hereafter be, with that consciousness exasperated as the naked soul encounters eternal realities? Oh, where shall he find relief? Even where one of old found it, where a believer in Christ cannot fail in finding it. " Out of the depths have I cried unto Thee, O Lord. If Thou, Lord, shouldst mark iniquities, O Lord, who shall stand? But there is forgiveness with Thee, O Lord." Forgiveness for the chief of sinners. He need not climb up to heaven to lay hold upon it. Let him from the depths of his shame and ruin send up the cry, " God be merciful to me a sinner! " and the gospel of Christ is a pledge, as sure as Divine truth itself, that his cry shall be heard. There is no degradation so great that mercy will not go down to meet it, no ruin so complete that it cannot be repaired by Divine grace. " God be merciful to me a sinner! " was never breathed from a contrite heart in vain.

" Out of the depths," — how fruitful in suggestion are these words! To how many of us do they recall passages in our lives when the waters went over us! Does our recollection enable us to repeat the whole verse, " Out of the depths have I cried unto Thee, O Lord " ? Have we occasion, while these words are on our lips, to doubt the goodness of God? Have we ever cried, and not been heard? It is possible; for the cry must be wrung from the heart, not go up from the lips alone. There *is* prayer that is no prayer; prayer that has no efficacy, because it has no importunity; prayer that lacks meaning, because it lacks faith. Two conditions should be observed to give our cry power to pierce the ear of Heaven.

First, it must be prompted by a consciousness of the want, peril, or misery in which we are placed. Only when we apprehend the reality of our condition, can we truly ask to be lifted out of it. Unless one believes that he is actually in danger, it will be a false cry which he raises for relief; and, though it may at first deceive men, as soon as they find that he is trifling with them they will cease to pay attention to his call. Only a child or a fool will play with the sympathies of his companions in this way. Yet how often do men treat God as they would not treat one another, repeating words of the weightiest import as carelessly as if they were void of meaning. It may be difficult to say which is the greater offence against society, — to put counterfeit money in circulation among those who will accept it as good, or to pour empty phrases into the ears of men who will take them as symbols of truth. The former offence is a crime of which the law and the courts take notice: the latter may pass without incurring the penalty which it deserves. Let it be transferred from the domain of human to that of Divine judgment, it will not escape detection. What an affront to Almighty God, to make daily confession of sin as a form that might as well be repeated in dreamy sleep where one knew not what he was saying! or to ask for Divine protection, when one trusts to his own ability to extricate himself from the trouble into which he may fall! Some men need to be cast into "the depths," that they may learn to pray sincerely, and we may presume that for this reason they are put in great perplexity or imminent peril or extreme distress; for, if the end can ever justify or explain the means, does it not in a case like this, where the end is the communion of the soul with God? Such is our definition of true prayer. Speaking is not praying. Neither is a life of active obedience prayer, though it has been so styled. Prayer is the intercourse of the soul with God through offices of faith and supplication.

Here we touch the second condition which must be fulfilled to obtain an answer to the cry that goes up from the depths. He who sends up the cry must have faith, perfect faith in God, — in God as one who is attentive to every want and every request of His creatures; not bound by His love for man to grant every request with which He may be approached, — for such an obligation would make Divine power the dependent minister of the human will, — but ready and sure to arrange the discipline, if it may not be taken off, in the way most suited to benefit the sufferer, and even to yield him a better experience than exemption from the discipline would be. This is faith in the answer to prayer, about which there is so much mistake among religious people. Man may not dictate the reply he shall receive, but he may rely on the Divine compassion to do just that which is best for the suppliant, whether it be to remove the trial or to send down strength to bear it. It is while *in* the depths, and through long continuance in them, that the children of God often realize the largest assurance of His love. The cup did not, according to the terms of his prayer, pass undrained from him who was the best-beloved of the Father, but a peace such as the Father only could give settled upon his spirit.

" Out of the depths have I cried unto Thee." Must we not be glad that the old psalm which begins with these words was written, and has come down to us, — as true to our experience as it was to the experience of a devout and suffering soul thousands of years ago? Mark how it soon passes into another strain, not less true then or now. " I wait for the Lord, my soul doth wait, and in His word do I hope. . . . Let Israel hope in the Lord : for with the Lord there is mercy, and with Him is plenteous redemption." Hope in the depths? Yes : *there* more than on the level ground or the mountain-top. *That* is the place for hope, because there it is most needed, and what we need we may have. Prayer and hope and trust and peace and strength in the depths. I think they are more sure to enter into our souls there than anywhere else. " I have chosen Thee in the furnace of affliction," — that was what the Hebrew theology enabled the prophet to say in the name of the Lord. Is the Christian theology less clear in its revelation of a love which uses affliction as the channel of blessing? " Out of the depths have I cried unto Thee." I love those words. They have the mingled flavors of earth and heaven in them. " Out of the depths " men- have cried unto God in all ages, and been heard. Not with groans only, but with praises also, have " the depths " been filled. The saints who have passed through much tribulation have made them the hiding-places of their piety, and the peaceful skies have shot rays of light into those dark places. The elect of God have been educated there for a higher life. Men have become angels by passing through the deep, when the waters went over their heads and God was their only salvation. Take courage then, O my soul! bear your lot without a murmur or a fear. There is firm and pleasant ground beyond the depths, — the heavenly ground, which you must reach through this your appointed way. " Brethren, count it all joy when ye fall into many trials ; knowing this, that the trying of your faith worketh patience. Only let patience have its perfect work, that ye may be perfect and entire, wanting nothing."

1857.

MYSTERIES.

1 Tim. iii. 9: *" Holding the mystery of the faith in a pure conscience."*

Our life is embosomed in mystery, the universe is wrapped in a garment of mystery. The unknown infinitely exceeds the known ; the incomprehensible outweighs beyond all comparison the intelligible. To some persons this is an unpleasant fact. Yet, properly regarded, it would give them great comfort. *Religion* conducts us to the borders of mystery. Whatever direction we pursue in our religious inquiries, we are soon brought to a pause by limits which we cannot pass. With some persons this is a special occasion of surprise, disappointment, and complaint, while it should, on the contrary, strengthen their faith and enliven their gratitude.

" The mystery of the faith " seems to be a contradiction in terms. Whatever is an object of faith is believed, and belief embraces only statements which the mind can use as materials of thought. We may repeat words that convey no meaning to the mind, but they are not believed unless they represent ideas. An idea is something which the mind grasps. And therefore faith cannot include mystery. Spiritual truths pass out of the region of mystery into that of faith through the teachings of revelation, just as physical truths pass out of the province of the unknown into that of the known through the discoveries of science. When the apostle spoke of " the mystery of the faith," he indicated those truths of religion which had been revealed by the gospel; such as the character and love of God, the impartial offer of His grace to all mankind, the mercy of which every sinner may avail himself, the immortal destiny of the human being. Before Christ arose as the light of the world, these great spiritual facts were hidden in an obscurity which the reason of man could not penetrate. Christ placed them before the distinct perception of the believer, enlarging the domain of faith by just so much taken from the realm of mystery. Paul reminds Timothy that these are facts of a practical kind, affecting life, and should be held with a pure conscience. In almost every instance where the word occurs in the New Testament, it has a similar force, denoting what had been hidden, but was made plain by the gospel for the instruction and comfort of men : as the Apostle expressly declares when he speaks of the "*revelation* of the mystery which was kept secret since the world began, but now is made *manifest*," even "made known to all nations, for the obedience of faith;" and as our Lord indicated, when, in reply to his disciples' question, " Why speakest thou unto them in parables ? " he answered, " Because it is given unto *you* to know the mysteries of the kingdom of heaven, but to them it is not given." Revelation and mystery stand opposed to one another just as light and darkness, the one displacing the other.

Still there are profound and solemn mysteries to which we are *guided* by faith ; and our persuasion of the existence of these hidden realities is one of the most comforting and strengthening elements in the soul's experience. Everywhere, as we have said, we encounter mystery. Why? Because everywhere we meet the thoughts of an Infinite Mind expressing themselves in the forms which He has seen fit to adopt. Now the thoughts of an Infinite Mind are not such thoughts as our minds can entertain. As no mirror which man could make would reflect an image of the sun that should correspond in its dimensions to the sun's magnitude, so no conception of ours can represent the Divine Intelligence. " As the heavens are higher than the earth, so are my ways higher than your ways, and my thoughts than your thoughts," was language which the Prophet of old ascribed to Jehovah, —

language as true to-day as it was in the time of Isaiah. God is the Infinite Reality. Religion is the connection between God and the soul. At one extremity, therefore, it touches on the Incomprehensible; and the more religious a man is, the more he feels the thrill of this connection between himself and the Unsearchable Greatness. Everywhere we find that which we cannot explain. The most common things, if we examine them, confound us: the smallest flower that grows suggests questions which no botanist can answer. A drop of water involves the action of laws which enclose and pervade the universe. Religion more immediately brings God before us, its purpose being a vital union between our consciousness and the Divine Will. Brings Him before us, yet only as One the trailing of whose garments we can see when He passes by us. It is the shadow of His glory, which rests on us. The Eternal Glory itself is more entirely beyond our apprehension than is the globe on which we live beyond the capacity of a child's hand. A fearful yet also a gracious truth was signified in that fine passage of the Hebrew narrative, where we read that to the rash request of Moses, that Jehovah would show him His glory, God replied: "I will make all my goodness pass before thee, and I will proclaim the name of the Lord before thee; but thou canst not see my face: for there shall no man see me, and live. And the Lord said, Behold, there is a place by me, and thou shalt stand upon a rock: and it shall come to pass, while my glory passeth by, that I will put thee in a clift of the rock, and will cover thee with my hand while I pass by: and I will take away mine hand, and thou shalt see my retiring form: but my face shall not be seen."

Religion, then, has its revealed truths and its hidden truths. In the former we are interested as rules of life; how, it may be asked, can the latter become sources of benefit? By the assurance they give us of God. *By the assurance they give us of God.* The unknown belongs to Him whom no eye hath seen. That which confounds our understanding reminds us of the Incomprehensible One, the mysterious proclaims the Infinite. Therefore we say that mystery helps our faith. If we could comprehend all we see and all we experience, we should have nothing within or around us that would force us to recognize Divine agency. Every thing would come within the possibilities of the finite; and life, instead of requiring, would, so far as its testimony went, disprove a God. Atheism would be the logical and the practical result of a life free from mystery.

Is it useless for us, then, to seek an acquaintance with the Divine Mind? Certainly not; for if we "cry after knowledge and lift up our voice for understanding, if we seek as for silver and search as for hid treasures, then shall we understand the fear of the Lord, and find the knowledge of God." Ought we to prefer mystery to faith? Certainly not; for God shows His goodness to us in converting one and another portion of mystery into an article of faith. But, on the other hand, let us neither wonder that there is so much which we cannot understand, nor complain of the limitations which our knowledge cannot surmount. Let us not through discontent lose the benefit which we may derive from the character of our present existence. Every barrier which we cannot pass reminds us of the Power, Wisdom, and Goodness which constructed the universe, — a goodness as well as a wisdom, and a wisdom as well as a power, which we cannot comprehend, because they are Divine and *we* are human. If they were within our comprehension, they would be human, not Divine; and we should lose our God out of the universe. Power, wisdom, and goodness are the attributes of the Creator, which we need as foundations of trust or hope. Which would you rather have to rely on, infinite or finite attributes, Divine or human? When I reach the inexplicable, I feel a presence that awes me: it is the presence of God. It awes, but it sustains me.

As we advance in religious knowledge, do we lessen the presence of the mysterious on our souls? To this inquiry we may return both an affirmative and a negative answer. Just so far as we succeed in bringing any truth within our comprehension, we remove it from among the secret things of God, with which it may have been hidden. But the effect of this increase of knowledge may be to enlarge our sense of the unmeasured extent of spiritual truth. As when one stands at the entrance of a cavern, and sees only a depth of space overhung with darkness, he can form little conception of the length or the height of the interior ; but as he traverses one portion after another, now proceeding straight on and now diverging to examine some side passage, the distance to which it probably runs is better appreciated by him, and the farther he penetrates the more he feels the oppression of mingled gloom and grandeur : so, as we gain a larger acquaintance with religious truth, the immense range which it covers spreads itself out to our view with a wider horizon at every step. Just as all learning discloses to us our ignorance, and the youth at twenty perceives that he knows less than he supposed he knew at fifteen, and those who are conversant with the highest results of science are most sensible of the vast field which invites farther investigation, so progress in religious knowledge opens successively wider and wider views of the unknown. Take, *e. g.*, the questions which a theist will raise in regard to the Divine character or government, and compare them with the loftiest conceptions or most adventurous curiosity of the heathen mind ; or contrast the far-reaching speculations of a Christian believer with the narrow judgments and incurious acquiescence of an ancient Hebrew. The single doctrine of immortality which Christianity has placed among the treasures of our faith, what a boundless region of inquiry and hope has it disclosed to us, — like the Polar Sea, if the comparison may be allowed, to those who for the first time since the world began looked on its open surface, and by what they saw were enabled to imagine what stretched beyond thei. vision ?

Every truth has a background of mystery. No statement that we can make presents all that is true of the subject to which it relates. How easily, then, may we distinguish between knowledge (or faith, which in regard to religious truth is equivalent to knowledge) and mystery, and how clearly discern their mutual relations ! Whatever falls within the compass of faith we can state in intelligible propositions. Such statements are believed. Behind them and beyond them lie the mysteries of

28

religion, or unknown truths, which we cannot define and therefore do not believe, but the existence of which we recognize as necessary. We believe in the existence of many things, of which, *i.e.* of the things themselves, we cannot be said to have any belief. For instance, we believe there are laws of the physical universe which science has not yet discovered. What they are we do not know, and therefore it would be false to say we believe them ; while yet believing in the existence and force of such laws, and in their probable discovery by future students of nature, we are relieved from anxiety at what perplexes us, by our confidence in these hidden yet determinate methods of Divine action.

Or let another illustration explain our meaning. A person wrecked on an apparently uninhabited island by and by perceives proof that human beings have been on that island before him. The fact, therefore, he believes, — just this fact, and no more. Whether they are still on the island or have left it, whether they are or were civilized men or savages, how they found their way thither, and whether he shall meet with farther evidence of their occupation of the ground, are all unknown to him. As yet all these subjects of inquiry are mysteries, and he *believes* nothing about them. So behind the truths of the gospel lie questions to which we can give no replies, or only such as are conjectural. The answers which we frame out of our own conceits we may believe, but they are not God's revealed truth. Leaning on them, we trust in our own thoughts, not in His communications. Where we dare not even propose a reply, we must leave the subject as God has seen fit to leave it, — unrevealed, unexplained.

This difference between known truths and truths unknown, or between faith and mystery, is one of great practical importance. If properly considered, it would prevent a large amount of presumption, bigotry, and unbelief, — the bigotry and presumption of some persons driving others into the opposite extreme of unbelief. Truths which God has brought to light through the gospel, we may press upon the reception of men, by all the arguments which reverence and gratitude towards God, or love and hope for man, can prompt us to use ; but our solution of the mysteries which He has kept within His own knowledge, or has disclosed only to beings in a higher condition than ours, should be proposed with a modest distrust, as possibly or, at most, probably true, and only, therefore, worthy of attention. Let this rule be observed, and three-fourths of the controversies which have tormented the Christian Church would disappear.

A single example may illustrate this remark. In modern times, particularly, the warmest disputes among theologians have gathered around the doctrine of the atonement. The most angry feelings, the fiercest denunciations, the most solemn importunities, have been connected with the different interpretations put on this doctrine. The various disputants must therefore have all believed in the atonement ; for, if they did not, it would not have constituted a ground of debate. They all have believed in it as a Christian doctrine ; for it is the atonement of Christ that they have endeavored to explain. Why might they not have been content with the fact ? or have calmly and diffidently proposed their several explanations ? The Unitarian who sees only a moral value in the death of Christ, and his brother Unitarian who thinks there was something more, though what he dare not and cannot say ; the Calvinist who regards the suffering of Christ as an equivalent accepted by the Father in place of the condemnation of the whole world, and his brother Calvinist who speaks of the cross as an exhibition of the Divine displeasure against sin ; the Christian who, at one end of the long line of theories respecting the atonement, maintains that God freely forgives the penitent without any extrinsic consideration ; and the Christian who, at the other end, affirms that, if Christ had not taken upon himself the sinner's guilt, not a soul could have been saved, and all those who plant themselves on the intermediate solution of the mystery of the cross, — might hold their several opinions with mutual good-will, if they would but distinguish between the doctrine and its explanation, between the fact and the reasons which induced the Divine mind to include that fact in the gospel. The fact is the essence of the gospel, and only they who, in the apostle's phrase, "have received the atonement," can have any personal knowledge of Christ as a Saviour; but the reasons which influenced the Divine mind, in introducing that fact, to wit, the atonement as the reconciliation of the sinner to God through the death of Christ (and not by some other means), into the objective history of God's love, we need not understand in order to be saved. I repeat it, — I would to Heaven it could be repeated, with the voice as of many waters, that should drown the confusion of foolish, scandalous strife! — the mystery that lies behind the cross is not a subject for faith to lay hold of. That is God's secret counsel, which we should be careful lest we ignorantly, and therefore profanely, discuss.

The presumption of many honest and earnest men is one of the most painful results of the weakness to which we are all liable. They who know the least often talk the most recklessly. What title could be given to a book that should betray more manifest disregard of the limitations of human knowledge than this, borne on a volume that not long ago found considerable favor with a certain class of readers, — "The Philosophy of the Plan of Salvation"? *Plan of salvation,* — this phrase is objectionable enough in itself. But when one of our fellow-men propounds a *philosophy* of the plan of salvation, we are tempted to ask, "Who is this that by searching has found out God?" The mysteries which lie back of our redemption, and which may be said to constitute the philosophy of the gospel, are known only to Him from whom the gospel came. Vain man, you cannot explain the processes on which your own bodily life depends, and yet you venture to walk where angels tread with caution, if they tread at all, — amidst the infinite thoughts with which God has strewed the pathways that His mercy follows in its dealings with His sinful creatures! Learn reverence and humility, thou who wouldst be a teacher on earth!

Paying constant respect to the distinction which I have now endeavored to make clear, we are prepared to see the relations of mutual aid which exist between faith and mystery. That we believe compels us to admit that there is much more which would be an object of faith, if our minds were capable of receiving it, or if God had been pleased to reveal it; while, on the other hand, the unknown forms a support as indestructible as the Divine perfections, against which our faith may lean. If we reluct at mystery, we must hesitate about faith. If we will not admit that there is more than we can embrace within our belief, we shall find that there is nothing for belief to accept. Faith necessitates mystery, and mystery is the supplement of faith. Again let us take a single illustration. We live under a providence, *God's* providence. We believe this truth, though we never see an outstretched arm of power nor an overhanging canopy of love. We never *see* them : yet we believe that the Divine Goodness overarches our lives and the Divine Will leads our steps. So far our faith carries us to this conclusion, which is enough for us to know. But, if the providence under which we live be *God's* providence, it must include a great many surprises and disappointments of our hearts, must often frustrate our labors, defeat our expectation, and inflict pain on our bodies and on our minds. It *must*, I say, — because, being a providence which infinite wisdom has devised and infinite goodness conducts. it must include facts and methods which we cannot understand. There are not only perturbations of the planetary world which the astronomer has not yet calculated, but numberless and serious disturbances of our experience which we can neither foresee nor explain. If there were not, we should not be living under the care of an intelligence higher than our own.

Doubtless, to some extent we can interpret the Divine Providence. That God chastens those whom He loves is not a mystery ; for they are made wiser, better, and in the end happier.

> " As the harp-strings only render
>   All their treasures of sweet sound,
> All their music, glad or tender,
>   Firmly struck and tightly bound :
>
> So the hearts of Christians owe
>   Each its deepest, sweetest strain
> To the pressure firm of woe,
>   And the tension tight of pain."

Still, in each case of painful discipline, questions arise that weary and baffle us. We can only be still, and know that it is God whose hand holds us in its grasp ; and where the least can be seen, the evidence is strongest that the hand from which we cannot escape belongs to Him whose love is unsearchable. The inexplicable in experience compels us to believe in providence as superhuman, self-consistent, perfect, Divine. Take away the mystery, and you unsettle faith. Nay, disallow mystery, and you deprive the soul of its sweetest satisfactions ; for how can we "know the love of Christ, which passeth knowledge," or how taste of that " peace of God which passeth all understanding," if we be confined to the intelligible, the explicable, and the familiar ? I must recognize a faculty in my nature higher than reason, call it faith, insight, or what you will. I long for sympathies and delights of too spiritual a character to be clad in the coarse garments of a vocabulary borrowed from the senses.

There are mysteries in religion, and I am glad that there are ; for by them is my heart opened in its confidence towards God. In him is mystery that no created mind can comprehend ; and therefore may the universe of created minds trust while they adore. There are mysteries of which the gospel is an intimation, and for them I am thankful ; for by them I am established in my conviction that it came from the Being whose ways are past my finding out. There is that in Christ which I cannot understand. I dare not attempt to explain all I read in the New Testament, as if it were a child's elementary reading-book. Contradiction I would disallow, for Divine truth cannot destroy itself. What may be contrary to reason, I will not look for in Scripture, since the two revelations which the Father of spirits has given to man must be harmonious ; but what is above and beyond my reason, I expect to find there, and I will gratefully receive it. There are mysteries in my life, — God be thanked that they are many ; for so does He multiply the proofs of my dependence on Him, and the testimonies of His interest in me. There are mysteries in my spiritual experience. If there were not, how poor would that experience be, — poorer than my social or my bodily condition! He who is impatient whenever he encounters the unintelligible must be continually offended with himself. He who would live without mystery must live without faith, without religion, without God.

1865.

THE MYSTERY OF GOD.

Job xi. 7: *" Canst thou by searching find out God! canst thou find out the Almighty unto perfection ?"*

Of all the words which come into use in speaking on religious subjects, none includes more in its true signification, or should suggest more to the human mind, than the name which we most frequently give to the Supreme Being. Yet no other word in our language is probably so little understood — or, perhaps I should rather say, presents to our thought so little in comparison with its real meaning — as the word God. The term is too vast for human faculties to measure. It contains more than can be weighed in the scales of human thought, it embraces mysteries of being which transcend our utmost endeavor to grasp them. Yet this fact, that no effort which we can make will enable us to comprehend the Divine Being, offers us matter for profitable consideration. *The mystery of God* is a subject which will be usefully treated, if it shall lead us to inquire, first, why we can know so little; and, secondly, how we may be saved from the grosser ignorance in which so many persons are sunk.

First, God is incomprehensible in His nature. We know that He is a Spirit; but how much of *positive* knowledge is conveyed by that expression? Of His mode of being we know nothing. Uncreated, — not even self-originated, because origin implies beginning, — but from eternity self-existent and unchangeable, how can we comprehend Him to whose eternal consciousness our own inward experience presents no analogy.

Again, the infinity of God will not allow us to bring Him

within the province of ideas with which we are familiar. Who can give more than a negative definition of infinity? Illimitable, *i. e.* without limits, not finite, — this is all we mean by infinite. If we take up the Divine attributes, each of which has this quality, the introduction of the quality prevents our entertaining an adequate notion of the attribute. *Omnipresence*, — can we conceive of this, except as we break it into fragments, as it were, and gather up a few of them to represent the whole? *Omniscience*, or the knowledge of every thing, — how can they who know scarce any thing understand this perfection of the Divine Mind? The *Holiness* of God, — did the most spiritual man on earth ever rise to more than a contemplation of some of its external aspects? The Divine character in *manifestation* may be a subject of study, because manifestation is so far a removal of the veil behind which it is hid. But that character itself — in its essence, I mean, in its integrity, its absolute reality — can never be revealed to a created intelligence. God alone can read the mystery of inevitable and spotless holiness.

The Divine Providence also is inscrutable. We ascertain some of the laws which it observes, and use them as grounds of reliance in the arrangements which we make for our outward life. Scientific men have traced the action of these laws through the convulsions which in past ages have rent or rebuilt our globe, and in the relations which prevail among the heavenly bodies. The historian of the present day takes the idea of a Divine plan as his clew in traversing the passages of national and social experience. But how often is the keenest penetration at fault, and the most carefully constructed hope turned into disappointment by the event! We can see but a little way around us, a little way before us, even but a little way behind us. Yet the providence of God reaches from the beginning of the creation onward through all its stages, at once including all facts and included by them, the most comprehensive and the most delicate of forces, the guardian and guarantee of order, and at the same time a labyrinth of wonders. How can we explain such a providence? The history of a single human life is more than we can decipher, the growth of a blade of grass more than we can understand.

Again, we speak of God as the Moral Governor of the universe, indicating the most important relation which He holds to us or to any of His creatures. Indicating, but not describing it. For what are our best attempts to translate the will of the Supreme Mind into intelligible forms of expression but, as it were, the rudiments of a language which a higher intelligence than ours must frame into sentences? The essential principles of the Divine government we may be said to know, because we ascribe to God both unimpeachable rectitude and inexhaustible goodness, and from His moral perfection draw the assurance that His omnipotence must always act in the interest of holiness. But, when we have assumed or decided so much, we only open a door for faith to enter and bow in adoration before an incomprehensible wisdom. The progress of human affairs confounds our moral judgment, and tempts us again and again to ask how what we see can be reconciled with that regard for the right and the good which must be a constant element in the Divine care of our world. It is not reason only that is baffled, but faith itself is sorely tried.

Still more difficult is it to apprehend that intimacy of God with the human soul, which nevertheless is the foundation of our best acquaintance with Him. To apprehend, I mean, by any act or force of the understanding. It is here that we realize in its highest sense the meaning of the Apostle's remark that spiritual things are "spiritually discerned." This spiritual discernment of the Father of spirits belongs to a region of the consciousness more interior than the intellectual faculty can penetrate or the terms of human speech describe. The all-surrounding, indwelling Presence that upholds me, searches me, inspires just thought, quickens every good purpose, informs and aids conscience in the discharge of its office, meets the aspiration of an humble heart and rewards it with the joy of a communion as sacred as it is real, — what is this Presence but a condescension, we might almost say, a limitation, of Himself, on the part of the Infinite One, — an experience, an exaltation almost above himself, on the part of the creature, which any attempt of ours to put into words reduces at once to a contradiction and an impossibility? Yet the intercourse of the soul with God is the most precious and vital fact of our being, involving all that is dearest in our present history, and justifying the purest and loftiest hope which we can cherish. It is a fact, however, enveloped in mystery. The soul is abashed and overwhelmed at the thought of God's nearness to its most private exercises. I am never in such multitudinous companionship as when I am alone with God; never so *little* alone as when conscious that *He* is with me whom "no eye hath seen nor can see." Let me extend my thought beyond myself and try to seize upon the truth, that He is as near to every other human being, — at the same moment cognizant of all wants and all occurrences throughout the universe of which our largest discoveries have taken in but a little part, — and I find myself like one who in a frail skiff has put off on an ocean of unknown magnitude, without sail or instrument. In my closet, I am taught by my own meditation that it is not *my* prayer alone which is heard. The praises and the supplications of myriads of hearts reach their common object, without being lost in confusion by the way, or failing of distinct notice by Him to whom they are all addressed. I *believe* it is so; I know it *must* be so: yet it is as impossible for me to conceive of such a personal relation of one Being to all other beings as it would be to grasp the sceptre of Almighty power and assert my right of sovereignty.

The mystery of God deepens upon us the nearer we approach it. As all knowledge shows us our ignorance, so the mo e we know of God, the more clearly do we perceive how little we know. What, then, shall we do? what shall we say? Shall we pronounce faith a delusion, and speak of the Unseen One as if He were but the ideal which a religious imagination has framed for its own purposes? Shall we follow the Pantheist into his irrational conclusions, or the Atheist into his dreary unbelief? Has the mystery no edges of light, no crevices through which shines an illumination from the Infinite Reality? Are we like men who have entered a cavern, only to be terrified by the distance which they *feel*, rather than see, stretching before them into darkness? Are we in worse, ten thousand times worse, condition than the beasts, which have no idea of a Supreme Intelligence to torment them with its own inadequacy? Such impious thoughts we cannot indulge. Such questions as these we would rather trample into the dust. There *is* a God, unsearchable in greatness, yet revealed by His own will and act to the believing soul.

Nay, if He were not incomprehensible, He would not be the great God, the only Living and True. The mystery, which like a halo of glory conceals, yet makes us sure of the Infinite One, imposes a healthful and needful discipline upon us, rebukes our arrogance, chastens our self-esteem, and teaches us to walk in humility along the borders of this ineffable glory. We may find in it a motive for pursuing our inquiries in this humble spirit. That which is level with the understanding excites comparatively little interest. It is the unknown which we wish to know. The difficult rouses energy, the inaccessible enkindles desire. In obedience to this law, an honest heart will be drawn towards God by the boundless perfection which is His alone. Hereafter, what provocation will be given to the soul, through the successive periods of immortality, to bring itself into better acquaintance with the Author and Ruler of all things! May we not confidently say that the great employment of eternity will be the study of the Divine perfection, now in its various forms of exhibition, and now in its personal integrity? To know God is the pursuit of angels, and still higher beings, if higher there be. It is a pursuit that can never reach its termination, since the Infinite is always removed from the experience of the finite by a distance which the latter can never overcome.

How may this distance be lessened, is a question that naturally follows the remarks to which your attention has been drawn. It is a question in which every one ought to take an interest; since a knowledge of God, though it be difficult and partial, is more important than any other acquisition that we can make. Difficult, do we say, and have we been saying all along? Difficult only as an exercise of the intellect. Theology, as a science, consists, on the one hand, of propositions which transcend the understanding ; and, on the other hand, of proofs which the understanding must accept. Here lies the embarrassment of which we have been speaking. We are compelled by the laws of human thought to ascribe to God the infinite attributes which cause us so much trouble in the attempt to apprehend them. Pure theism is at once the most rational and the most unsatisfactory of beliefs. Nature, life, tradition, the highest wisdom, the meanest experience, all concur in teaching us the Divine perfection. Yet what is it that we are taught? Or, rather, what is it that we learn? Not the whole of what is included in the Divine perfection ; nor much of it ; nor, as we have said, more than a very little. Like a child learning his alphabet, we get certain necessary sounds. To exchange those sounds for adequate ideas is a task to which our minds are unequal.

Are we, then, left to an ignorance the more painful because we are continually reminded of it by facts that bring the Divine action under our notice ? No : let us with the utmost emphasis deny that we are placed in so cruel a condition. Knowledge is of two kinds, speculative and experimental, — in the head and in the heart : knowledge about which we may argue and dispute, and have our doubts, and involve ourselves in hopeless perplexity ; and knowledge which is not a subject of discussion, but an element of the spiritual consciousness. If we try to enlarge the former kind of knowledge in respect to Divine things, we are liable to disappointment, we cannot indeed escape disappointment. We *cannot* " by SEARCHING find out God." Searching is not the way to arrive at an acquaintance with Him. *That* is mental effort in a direction in which such effort will be wasted. We must *receive* the truth, not hunt after it ; look up to the heavens and wait, instead of digging into the earth with vain toil ; open our hearts, instead of racking our brains. The best knowledge always comes in this way.

I sit down before a picture of some great master of art. I cannot explain it, except in the most superficial and unmeaning manner. I cannot tell you where its excellence lies. If I have learned the technical words which the painters use, I only expose my ignorance by attempting to apply them. I cannot *describe* the picture when I leave it. Yet as I sit silently gazing, studying, absorbed, moved perhaps to tears, the canvas becomes a living spectacle. I see more than the eye sees. I take in, — a homely phrase, indeed, but how true! — I take in and carry away that picture, and it is mine to enjoy as long as I live. So it is with our penetration of the Everlasting Reality which we call God. In the silence of thought I look and study and feel, and begin to apprehend, and at last *com*prehend, — take in, not as an idea, but as a fact, the Divine greatness, goodness, holiness, every attribute in that infinite and incomprehensible Nature, and carry it away in my soul, and keep it there, — God in me, of whom I may be able to say but little, because there may have been but little mental activity. That is a very instructive line, " Be *still*, and know that I am God." And this is faith, — this experience of the soul, this answer of the spiritual consciousness to the inquisitive reason. Better, oh! incomparably better than any answer which the reason could construct for itself; for the best answer which the intellectual faculty could frame would be but paper bearing an accredited yet not a real value, while the interior experience is pure gold, the product of an inexhaustible mine.

I need only add that, in entering upon or maintaining such an acquaintance with God, we derive the greatest assistance from the revelation which He has made of Himself by Christ. This revelation is twofold.

First, verbal. Christ has taught us to call God, the Supreme Being, " our Father."

[1] Father! the word implies affection, solicitude, care, delight, whatever enters into the conception of personal interest of the closest kind. Always. everywhere, our Father, — then never absent from our need or our approach. Infinite? Yes; but

---

[1] This paragraph and the next are inserted from a sermon of **1861** on " A Near God."

what an amount of meaning is added to the name of "Father"
by this quality in His being! Because infinite, only the more
intimately present with all His creatures and at all times. Illimitable and inexhaustible love must we ascribe to an infinite
Father; and therefore we have an argument of the utmost
strength to assure us that He is very near us, nearer than any
other being, nearer than any other influence, so near that His
presence makes a part of our life.

The difficulty, too, which our sins erect as a barrier to our intercourse with the Father of spirits, is overcome through our
faith in the testimony which Christ has borne concerning the
Divine forgiveness. A *merciful* God is our Father in heaven.
It was man's sinfulness that brought the Son of God from the
bosom of infinite love to our world. Because man was self-
betrayed and on the brink of ruin, God sent His Son to extend
the help he needed. To our sin we are indebted for the confidence which we have towards Him who would not that we should
perish. Yes: even so, even so. The man who is most painfully conscious of his ill-desert, whose transgressions have been
more than tongue can tell, he it is who has the most satisfactory
proof that God cares for him with a pity as unutterable. Have
you ever seen parental love yearning towards an ungrateful
child the more tenderly, the more perverse he has shown himself?
a mother, whose heart would have broken if it had not been
strong through love, making every sacrifice for one who has re-
quited her with fresh occasion for sorrow every year and every
day, yet who thinks more of the wanderer from her arms than of
all the rest of her household? The patient mother watching for the
opportunity which shall enable her to regain her influence, the
mother whose most earnest desire is expressed in the thought,
"Oh, if he would but let me forgive him!" — that human parent
shows us faintly — faintly, I say — the interest which God feels
in one of His sinful children, according to the revelation which
He has made through and in Christ.

But this revelation is not instruction for the mind to analyze
or measure. If I wish to know the meaning of the word "father,"

I do not go to the dictionary, nor to the statutes of the Commonwealth, nor to legal decisions, but to my own childhood and my own home. I recall the days of parental guidance and affectionate care : the image of one passed into the heavens rises before me ; and, becoming again a child, I am able to put a true interpretation on that dear domestic title which was so familiar in my early years. Or I ask my heart to-day what the word means, and the love of which I am conscious informs me. It is through the affections that we receive the import of words which owe their place in our language to an exercise of the affections.

Secondly, the revelation through Christ is personal. He is himself a manifestation of the Divine, of the Perfect. To know Christ is to know God.

[1] The *character of Christ*, — on this infinite theme I wish it were possible for me to utter my own feelings. I call it an infinite theme, for such it appears to me. It comprises, I believe, a revelation of all that can be known of God or of human duty. Unlike every other being that has appeared on earth, he was sinless and perfect. We behold in him an unparalleled combination of virtues. He united the most dissimiliar traits, — dignity with humility, consciousness of power with meekness and tenderness, the most delicate sensibility with an adamantine fortitude, devotion to the will of God with boundless philanthropy, abhorrence of sin with compassion for the sinner, excellence on the broadest scale with fidelity to duty in the minutest details. There was no defect and no excess. We cannot imagine his character despoiled of a single attribute and not perceive that it would be injured by the loss. We cannot add a single grace that would not mar its symmetry. It was his prerogative, and his alone, to reply to one who desired to see God, " He who hath seen me hath seen the Father." In him were hidden all the treasures of knowledge and love. In him was truth em-

---

[1] This paragraph and the next are borrowed, in compressed form, from a sermon of 1833, on " The Christian Ministry," preached at Dr. Andrew P. Peabody's ordination at Portsmouth, N.H.

bodied. In his character the everlasting principles of the Divine government, the essential doctrines of religion, were manifested. " I am," said he, " the truth."

Here Jesus Christ stood alone. " Greater works than these shall ye do," said he to his disciples ; but not a greater miracle than I *am* shall you offer to men's admiration, — he made no such promise. Peter, John, Paul, was not a second Christ. No : he was alone in the grandeur and beauty and perfection of his character. We must assign to this prodigy an adequate purpose ; and while I can discover nothing short of that which considers it a revelation — not an evidence nor a sanction, not the credential nor the seal, but a revelation — of truth, while I find nothing short of this that will satisfy me, I rest here in the conviction that I have found its meaning, its purpose, its justification, its worth and its glory.

But how is Christ known ? By an intellectual examination, or by a moral appreciation ? Neither through metaphysical nor through psychological study shall we find the avenue to an acquaintance with him on whom his enemies endeavored to fasten the charge of blasphemy because he called himself " the Son of God." We do not put ourselves in relations of intimacy with Christ in this way. Is it, then, by making ourselves familiar with every incident that the Evangelists offer for our study, till we can describe the whole outward life of Jesus as if it had passed under our eyes ? If our knowledge of him be confined to the external history, we might almost as well have studied Worcester or Robinson as Matthew and John. They know Christ who approach him through sympathy, welcome him through faith, receive him into believing *hearts*. There his character discloses its beauty, its power, and its value as a revelation of the One Character, which, like the Divine Appearance, can only be made known by sign or by reflection, never in its awful radiance. He that hath realized the spiritual influence of Christ is alone able to understand that personal superiority which made him the image of the Majesty on high, the milder type of the inaccessible Glory.

The sum of our remarks is this : God cannot be known as His material works are known, by scientific investigation ; nor as abstract truth becomes the property of the mind, by hard thought : but as we discover what is beautiful or good, through a use of the moral faculty which distinguishes us, and through that exercise of faith which is the prerogative of the soul. The mystery that has confounded and distressed us begins then to clear away. We discover enough of that which it hides for our daily use, our present comfort, and our final hope. It is not to the curious or the bold, to those who think that " by searching they can find out God," or can by any process " find out the Almighty unto perfection," that the revelation of the Unseen One is given, but to the humble and the " pure in heart." We have been told of a traveller who could make no use of the organ of sight ; but who, as he passed from place to place, so appropriated to himself the features of the spot which he visited, understanding and enjoying the outward beauty by a sympathy which interpreted verbal description, that he knew more of the scene than many who had lived there all their lives. By a kindred power of moral apprehension, the invisible glories of the Divine Being may be felt, and in a measure be understood, by him who has but a faint intellectual discernment even of lower things ; while others who are wise or learned in matters that lie within the province of what we usually call knowledge may be ignorant of the God in whom they live and move and have their being. *The mystery of God* gives to the universe a foundation for its security, and to the believer a justification of his faith.

1829.

RELIGION THE CONSCIOUSNESS AND CULTURE OF A SPIRITUAL LIFE AND OF SPIRITUAL RELATIONS.

Rom. viii. 6 : " *To be spiritually minded is life.*"

MAN is connected with two states of existence, is an inhabitant of two worlds, one material and visible, the other spiritual and eternal. By his senses he communicates with that which is seen

29

and present, with the objects and circumstances of earth, is affected by them, lives in them. By his mind he holds intercourse with that which is unseen yet present, with the beings and hopes of heaven, is influenced by them, lives among them. Man, therefore, is a partaker of a double life, — the one the life of sense, the other the life of faith, — the one outward, the other interior. For this twofold existence he was designed by his Creator. It is his natural being. The foundation of religion, I repeat because it is often denied, the foundation of religion is laid in man's nature by the hand of his Creator in his religious capacities and affections, which as truly belong to his nature as do his intellectual faculties and social affections; and, if the consciousness of these latter indicates that man is designed for an intellectual or social life, the consciousness of the former indicates that he is designed for a religious or spiritual life. The poverty of language, however, obliges us when speaking of the soul to employ terms originally appropriated to the body. Thus we discourse on the spiritual vision, the inward ear, the moral taste.

It is the office of Religion to excite and cultivate these interior senses. Religion opens and purges the eye of the soul, enables it to hear spiritual truths, and causes them to be felt. Its chosen province is the soul. Its kingdom is within us, its rule is spiritual, its subject is what the apostle Peter styles the hidden man of the heart. Wonder not that man often seems to be, and is, unconscious of the elements that lie in his soul as the life of the plant in the seed, which, apparently destitute of a vital principle, needs only heat and moisture to stimulate it into action. The vital principle of religion must be excited by causes that are without it, that yet combine themselves with it. The spiritual nature must be unfolded and exercised upon suitable objects of thought, affection, desire, hope. These it does not find in human society, nor among sensible things. They are revealed and embraced through faith. By this, man is introduced to a new society, and to the knowledge of higher relations than those of time. As he becomes more conversant with the beings and hopes of a spiritual world, their relative importance grows in his estimation. His affections fasten themselves with strength on worthy objects. He perceives that he stands in the midst of infinite relations. There is a light within him brighter than the rays of the sun, and in this light he beholds spiritual and everlasting things.

Faith, I say, introduces him to this new world. Now faith rests on various kinds of evidence, and extends its vision over circles of various dimensions. In its nature it is simple, a single act of the mind, belief. There is no mystery in faith: nothing is more intelligible. It is a persuasion of the truth of certain facts, past, present, or prospective, with which our senses do not make us acquainted. It is through faith, historical faith, that I know that Jesus Christ lived and died and rose again. It is through faith, religious faith, that I know that I shall live hereafter and experience a righteous retribution. Christian faith is a belief of Christian truths. The end of Christianity, to which all its truths and precepts are subservient, is the preparation of the human soul for a future life; and this end it effects by calling the soul, during its residence in the body, at once to an anticipation and a participation of this life. Christianity is thus a religion of faith and of experience. Faith brings the human being to the knowledge of certain relations, to which he is now, and will hereafter be, subject; and, as this knowledge becomes the motive and rule of character, faith is converted into experience. As the student of art, first believing on the testimony of others that there are sources of beauty and delight which he may unseal, gives himself with confidence to his profession, till his mind, kindled into sympathy with the genius which has expressed its conceptions in such glorious forms, is taught by its own emotions the truth that it before received through faith. Assent becomes knowledge, experience, enthusiasm.

Having thus glanced at the origin and support of the spiritual life, let me enlarge on its nature and excellence. The man who is conscious of it dwells in the midst of thoughts and feelings which are not born of flesh, nor earth, nor the will of man. He regards this inward life as far more important than that which connects him with an ever-changing world. The things of religion are to him realities, not distant and visionary, but present and substantial. His soul is familiar with spiritual images and associations, and they impress him as the circumstances of external condition impress other men. He lives with God, nigh to Him, in communion and an humble sympathy with Him. To him God, though an infinite, is an individual being; though incomprehensible by his understanding, yet embraced by his affections. His piety is nourished by every moment's experience of the Divine goodness; for he is so habituated to the contemplation of God that he sees His image, as it were, reflected from all His works and all the aspects of His Providence. His own soul is the temple in which he perceives the glory of the Most High; and it is to him far more sacred, consecrated by a deeper as well as a more rational reverence, than was the Holy of Holies to the ancient Jew. Devotion is in him at once a sentiment, a taste, and a habit. God dwells in him, and he in God.

He feels also a personal relation between himself and the Lord Christ Jesus. This friend, benefactor, Saviour, sustains these offices not only to the body of his disciples, but to this one disciple Jesus is regarded as his Master and Redeemer, to whom he is united, in the language of Christ himself, as the branch to the vine, drawing thence the nutriment which diffuses strength throughout his character and clothes it with beauty. He considers himself likewise allied to orders of intelligence, that rise above him in successive gradations towards the Infinite Father. The universe is full of spiritual life. He sympathizes with the universe. His imagination, trained to its early flights by faith, soars beyond the limits of time and ethereal space. The creation is his home. The influence of God is felt everywhere, and wherever this is he finds something to which he is attracted. Saints and angels and all ministering spirits constitute one brotherhood, in which he is embraced. With the conviction of this alliance, he is armed with a power over evil, he scorns low associates and impure pleasures; for he belongs to a society into which are gathered the good of all worlds and ages. Tell him of heaven? He carries within himself a better picture of heaven than words can ever delineate. A picture of heaven, did I say? He is in heaven even now. He is with God and Christ and holy spirits, and what other heaven can eternity unveil?

There are other objects of interest in the spiritual world than the beings who inhabit and constitute its glory. Truth and virtue, perfection and felicity, are treasured there; and for these the Christian seeks. He hungers and thirsts after righteousness with spiritual appetites that he can never indulge to excess. And he shall be filled; but his desire and capacity grow with the supply. He is continually aspiring to something better than he has yet reached. It is a holy ambition. He is ever craving more riches, the riches of a sanctified intellect and a devout heart. Infinity is before him, and he would penetrate its depths as far as a finite nature may pursue its course. His soul is therefore animated with celestial hopes, which he knows cannot disappoint nor mislead him. His mind is ever active among holy thoughts. The perfections of the Deity, the excellences of our Lord's character, the capacities of the human soul, the influences and promises of religion, open to him unnumbered paths of meditation. He can never be idle and never weary; for his heart is in his employment. He loves religion, and it rewards him with a happiness which earth can neither give nor take away.

Another peculiar property of this life remains to be described. The Christian is conscious of immortality. I beg you to receive this declaration literally. He not only expects to enter on a conscious existence after death, but he so intimately blends the two states that they seem to him to constitute but one. Hence I say that he is conscious of immortality. He more than anticipates it, he already enjoys it. In the apprehensions of most persons, the life that now is, and the life that is to come, are two distinct and vastly dissimilar modes of existence. Not so with him who lives through faith. He regards the future as the continuation of the present, and death the line, the gate which separates them. This line must be crossed, this gate be passed ; but the domain which lies beyond will, in its essential character- istics, correspond with that in which the child of God preferred to dwell while on earth. This idea of the coincidence of the spiritual life here and hereafter cannot be too strongly pressed. Eternal life is a present possession, not an expected good. He that entertains this persuasion is delivered from the bondage in which men are held through fear of death, —

> " What cause for fear
> Of death, when this same death we die
> Is life continuous, and to die
> Is but to live immortally ? "

The man who cherishes this conviction is always inquiring what effect his conduct will have upon his interior life. There is no one so watchful as he to preserve himself unspotted from the evil that is in the world, since his spiritual senses would be darkened and blunted by sin. His conscience is a moral micro- scope by which the presence of folly is discerned where it assumes its most minute shapes. His tastes and sympathies choose whatever is noble and pure and is assimilated to the divine. He is always accumulating stores of heavenly wisdom and felicity. He is perpetually advancing in the way of salva- tion ; forgetting the things that are behind, and reaching forth unto those which are before, he presses towards the prize of his high calling of God in Christ Jesus. This goal is perfection, never to be reached, yet a progressive approach to which is the noblest employment and the only true happiness of the soul. What a glorious capacity is this, of everlasting improvement ! What an energy is possessed by the soul that is conscious of its impulses ! How lightly does it esteem labor and obstacle ! Its course is ever upward. Press on, press on, is its unceasing com- mand to itself. It turns difficulty into an occasion of triumph, gathers strength from combat, fixes its view ever on the most distant point, and obeying the will of God revealed in its capacity of indefinite progress, it rejoices amidst adversities and conflicts and temptations, seeing that by suffering it is purified as the precious metal in the furnace, and is prepared for other degrees of spiritual life in the mansions of the blest.

The doctrine of this discourse is a key to much of the lan guage of the Christian Scriptures, and unlocks the meaning of many passages that are often thought difficult. Such are those which represent the union that exists between the believer and his Saviour and his God. "If any man love me," said Jesus, "he will keep my words, and my Father will love him, and we will come unto him, and make our abode with him." "As thou Father art in me, and I in thee, that they also may be one in us." "Your life," wrote the apostle Paul to the Colossian brethren, — "your life is hid with Christ in God." "The life which I now live in the flesh," says the same apostle, "I live by the faith of the Son of God." Of a similar import are those clauses which suggest, if they do not convey, the doctrine of the Christian's entrance on eternal life, while he is yet in the body. "He that heareth my word," exclaimed the Author and Finisher of our faith, "is passed from death unto life." "These things," says the apostle John, "have I written unto you that believe on the name of the Son of God, that ye may know that ye have eternal life."

In a like manner, Christians are said to be crucified and to rise with Christ. No term could more happily express the effect of Christian faith upon a mind which had been buried in spiritual darkness than the resurrection. It was an awaking to the consciousness of a new life. Thus Paul reasons, "If we have been planted together in the likeness of his death, we shall be also in the likeness of his resurrection." That much vexed phrase "being born again" may in our age be adopted in a more literal sense than that in which our Lord employed it, in conformity with the popular diction of the Jews. May it not be said, almost without a figure, that a man enters on a second life when he begins to feel the relations which bind him to God and eternity? What a new character has his own existence assumed! How differently do all things appear to him! The change which would be wrought by converting a barbarian into an inmate of refined society is not so great as that of which he is conscious, who has led a vicious or worldly life, and is made to contemplate himself in the light in which he is regarded by the Omniscient Judge, as an immortal and accountable creature. I doubt whether, in the extent of God's government, there be any change that approaches so nearly to a new creation, a new life, as that which occurs in one who, having for years been insensible to God and duty, is awakened to the perception of them. Such a rush of strange ideas and feelings into his soul, such a crowd of fears and hopes hitherto unknown, such a burst of light to which his moral vision is not accommodated! God have mercy on him, and help him in that hour when conviction of spiritual truths comes like a torrent, to sweep away old associations and to turn the thoughts into new channels! God guide him to life and peace!

Indeed, I detect this doctrine in every part of the New Testament, running through it as a vein, to guide our researches in this mine of divine instruction. I perceive it veiled under the terms in which the office of Christ is described by the evangelist before he begins his narrative. "To as many as received him, he gave power to become the sons of God, to them that believe on his name, who were born of God." I hear it proclaimed among the first words which our Lord uttered after he commenced his ministry, "Blessed are the pure in heart, for they shall see God." I welcome it again in his discourses with the people, and in his conversations with his disciples in language which I need not repeat. It greets me again, as I examine the pages indited by apostles of the Lord. I am constantly taught that the Christian is partaker and guardian of an inward life, that heaven begins on earth, that the essence of religion is an obedience of the soul to those convictions which originate in faith. The doctrine is a reasonable one, my own nature responds to its truth, I gladly receive and would habitually recognize it.

It is often said that such views as have now been offered are mystical and useless: Religion should be intelligible and practical. Certainly it should. But this charge of mysticism, as it is the most easily made, is in general urged with less pertinency than almost any other. When men dislike what they understand of a doctrine, or from indolence or prejudice are indisposed to its examination, it is very convenient to retire behind the cry of mysticism and the adage that religion is a practical matter. Now let this subject be studied candidly, and it will appear to be clothed in no peculiar mystery either of ideas or of words. It is as simple and as rational as the command to love the Lord our God. The truth that religion consists in a consciousness of spiritual relations, and an habitual regard to them, is singularly practical, since it touches and sanctifies every circumstance of the exterior life. It links the future to the present by such intimate dependences that it might almost be said to spiritualize humanity and immortalize time. It brings the whole of our social condition under the cognizance of a law, which, proceeding from God, embraces the present and the future in one band, on which is inscribed, in letters that glow before the spiritual eye, the awful word Retribution. The sense of the relations which we hold to the Creator gives a just and solemn interest to every event, however brief or trivial in its nature. Its consequences are combined with infinite results.

Under another aspect may the practical character of this doctrine be seen. It explains the purpose of moral discipline, and solves that enigma which so long perplexed Pagan philosophy, the existence of evil in the world. It convinces us that God does not afflict nor grieve us but for our good, that we may be prepared for the joys of a future being. It reconciles us to trouble, by showing its salutary influence on character and its power of expanding the purity and strength of the soul. Of disappointment, it tells us that it is sent —

> " To minister to those who are designed
> Salvation's heirs ; commissioned from on high
> To chase the vagrant Hope, that, like the dove,
> Flies o'er the troubled waters of this world
> And finds no rest ; to plant its cloudy form
> On every smiling spot that lures her on,
> Till, taught by this she has no home on earth,

> Hope to the eternal Rock of Ages looks,
> And settles there."

Ought a doctrine from which such wisdom and consolation flow to be stigmatized as destitute of practical utility?

Brethren, bear with me, while I add a word of personal exhortation. Is the spiritual life developed in us? Are its functions performed sluggishly, or freely and effectively? This inquiry it would be wise in us to answer before our consciences. It embraces our highest, our everlasting welfare. The responsibleness under which we lie cannot be described in words nor measured by thought. Its limits are hidden in the depths of the unfathomable future. God is inviting us to His love. Christ died that he might show us the way, our own souls are crying to us for the satisfaction of their natural wants. All, as if with one voice, enjoin on us that we be spiritually minded. If we are faithless, we betray ourselves, we forfeit heaven, we fall from eternal life. Misery and folly too great for language to depict! If we believe and obey, we secure a happiness that makes us the rivals of angels. He who abides in God is secure against loss and harm. The principle of spiritual life evades the touch of disease. Sin alone can prostrate or impair its energies. It incorporates itself with the soul, and passes with it unharmed through the gates of death. Ah, ineffable is the bliss of that intercourse which the soul enjoys with its Author, when God is known not through reason nor through faith, but through love! This is the pledge and foretaste of the joy which awaits glorified saints hereafter.

1859–1860.

THE SOUL'S SALVATION THROUGH FAITH IN CHRIST.

JOHN iv. 14 : *"The water that I shall give him shall be in him a well of water springing up into everlasting life."*

1 PETER i. 9 : *"Receiving the end of your faith, even the salvation of your souls."*

To a poor, ignorant, half-heathen woman whom he met now for the first time, and whom, after leaving that part of the country, he probably would never see again, we find Jesus speaking of the innermost experience of the soul, its deepest need and its holiest satisfaction. Is not this a significant fact? Does it not show us that Christ saw in every one a nature capable of recognizing its own spiritual wants and of appreciating the supply of those wants which he would furnish? And does not his language remind us of that property of his truth by which it penetrates and sanctifies the private consciousness? " The water that I shall give him shall be *in* him." *In* him; or a personal experience, a secret action, a consciousness attesting the adaptation of this new agent to the soul's wants.

The *religious* wants of our nature are as real as its mental or moral wants, although moral men are often inclined to discredit them. We may, however, bring the question to the test of experience. Men, women, the old, the young, do feel a want, a dissatisfaction, a discord in themselves, which they but partly comprehend. There is a sense now of unsatisfied desire, now of unrelieved pain, with which we are familiar. In some bosoms it is an uneasy discontent with themselves and with circumstances. In some a vague apprehension and an equally indistinct hope. While in other hearts it amounts to positive self-reproach, a sense of guilt, a dread of the future, the recognition of an ill-spent past and a judgment unprepared for. The secret history of many persons includes yet more, — struggles, conflicts, misgivings, rallyings, discouragement, infirmity of purpose, vacillation, debatings with one's self, half-prayers, half-victories, nothing complete, nothing satisfactory. All these forms of experience belong to a consciousness lower down in our nature than that which is reached by social intercourse, — a consciousness altogether personal, private, secret, known only to the Searcher of hearts, and intended doubtless to produce very intimate relations between our hearts and Him. This experience — this lowest stratum of consciousness, if I may so describe it, this innermost realization of self — Christ addresses now, as he did almost two thousand years ago, when he said: " The water that I shall give shall be a fountain in the soul springing up into everlasting life."

It is in this consciousness that we must lay the foundations
of a religious character. What is religion? Uprightness, conscientiousness, usefulness? Partly, but not chiefly nor primarily.
Men may lead useful and irreproachable lives, and not be religious. Religion connects us with the Unseen. Theoretically, it
is the bond by which the soul is held to an Invisible and Infinite
Presence: practically, it is the recognition of that bond by the
soul. Piety, therefore, is the essential part of religion. Faith in
God as an active principle, a ruling sentiment, an immediate
satisfaction, and a prophetic assurance, constitutes personal religion. *Such* a faith, — *i.e.* a faith in God that habitually influences
one, guiding, controlling, satisfying, and sustaining the human
being; making him devout, and conscientious because he is devout; making him pious, and happy because he is pious; making
him religious, and, because he is religious, useful, — such a faith,
the basis and the strength of character, the inspiration and the
law of life, is not cherished, we have reason to fear, by the
greater number of decent, orderly, estimable people. People of
this class are good — *i.e.* they do right and try to keep themselves
right — from various motives, some honorable, some equivocal;
from a regard to opinion, reputation, success in life; from what
is called a sense of character, which means a preference of that
which is just and pure over that which is vulgar or base; from a
conviction that personal injury must always be a consequence of
wrong-doing. To give to motives higher than these the influence to which they are entitled; to awaken in the soul a consciousness of delightful relations with the Eternal Spirit; to
reveal to man the unexplored depths of his own nature; and to
make him independent of all external circumstances by developing
an internal life of which God should be not only the primal
cause, but the final end, — were the great purposes of the Saviour's
mission. . . .

No one can read the New Testament and mistake the purpose which Christ had primarily in view. The truths which he
unfolded, the precepts which he delivered, his counsels, warnings,
promises, were addressed to the private consciousness. Faith in

God he makes to be personal; obedience, personal; worship, a spiritual act; repentance, an interior exercise; peace, the heart's contentment with itself. Christ came to be a mediator, not between the race and its Sovereign, but between the soul and its Author. He came to bless the world, by blessing, in the first instance, this and that one of those who make up the world. To regard the establishment of a universal religion as the immediate end of Christ's labors is to overlook the means which he used for this end. As a house is built by adding stone to stone and timber to timber, so the spiritual temple, of which he is at once foundation and dome, the beginning and the end, approaches its completion only as the number of disciples increases who compose that "building in the Lord."

Equally plain is it that Christ came to rescue man from a state of great want and peril. Whatever we may think of the soul's condition, he thought it a condition that called for help. He represented the Father as having sent him to befriend the soul in its exigency. He regarded man as suffering under the evil of sin; which he treated as an internal malady, that, if not cured, would be fatal. Nothing can be more distinct than his own words: "I am not come to call the righteous, but sinners, to repentance." "What shall a man give in exchange for his soul?" he asked with an emphasis alike solemn and tender. "What shall it profit a man, if he gain the whole world, and lose his own soul?" The most startling and searching question, this, that was ever put before a man to answer, be he king or beggar, — a question that, in its very form, dishonors all outward differences. The whole world, with its pomp, wealth, rank, pleasure, is as nothing in comparison with a human soul. Christ saw the soul hastening to ruin, already involved in ruin: this fact was enough for him. Sin was destroying man: that was enough to awaken his sympathy. He entered into no discussion respecting the origin of human sinfulness. We find in the Evangelists nothing about "native depravity," or any theory in explanation of the state to which man had reduced himself. He was a sinner, on the broad road to destruction: the naked truth needed nothing to increase its fearful meaning. Christ sought to afford relief. "The Son of man is come," he said, "to save that which was lost." The sheep perishing among the bleak and barren mountains must be brought back to the fold, where it will be cared for, no matter by what tempted to wander off. The prodigal son must be induced to return to his Father's arms, let what may have moved him to leave the home of plenty and peace.

This is the interpretation which I put on Christ's mission, ministry, gospel, cross, purpose, and work. As I read those pages of evangelic narrative and apostolic commentary, one truth seems to me as clear as if it were written on the sky in letters of light; namely, that "Christ Jesus came into the world to save sinners." There were social disorders enough in his day. Galilee was a miserably misgoverned province; Jerusalem was full of intrigue, faction, and profligacy. But Jesus undertook no political revolution, organized no social reform, let the external evils of city and country alone; while he addressed himself to the spiritual darkness and corruption of which the souls of men were the seats. Repentance was the key-note of his preaching; mercy for sinful man was the revelation which he sealed in his own blood. Christ lived and died that he might become "the author of eternal salvation unto all them that obey him." The "Saviour!" That is the title which, above all others, belongs to him. Yes, above all others; for Messiah, Son of God, Mediator, and the many other titles which describe his various relations to heaven or to earth, pour their significance into this, as that which at once needs and explains them all.

And mark, I pray you, my hearers, that this is a title which Christ bears now, in reference to his present influence. Sin is still the universal disease; in all of us a taint that must be eradicated before we can possess a pure and noble character. Whatever Christ came to be to the men of his time, he should be to us. Whatever his religion offered to them as needed by them, it offers to us as needed by us. Whatever his cross revealed or sealed to them, it reveals or seals to us. His blood was "shed for many for the remission of sins." That word "many" takes in all generations and all people. Christ "our Saviour;" that is proper language for us to use. How suitable! let them say, who, by his instruction and persuasion, have been brought out of the bondage of sinful habits, and are conscious of a liberty enjoyed only by those whom he has made sons and heirs of God.

We may abridge the meaning of salvation, not only by giving it a merely historical value, but by unduly limiting its moral import. The familiar use of the word is an example of this error. Salvation is the name commonly given to the initial state of the believer, instead of covering, as it should, his whole experience, from the first act of faith to the last moment of earthly consciousness. The sinner we hear spoken of as "saved," when snatched from the ruin on the brink of which he was standing. But the soul needs to be saved, or delivered from its perils and infirmities, as long as it continues to sin. Until the mind ceases to make an evil choice, or the heart to cherish a wrong desire, the work of salvation is not finished. The converted man will be all the time getting more salvation, — that is, more deliverance from false judgments, wrong tempers, and sinful tendencies; and only in another world, where he shall begin a sinless life, will he experience full salvation. Salvation means much more than an escape from either outward or inward suffering. It means security, moral integrity, spiritual wholeness. The word, therefore, instead of expressing only the effect of Christ's influence in the earlier stages of spiritual growth, describes his connection with the soul through the whole of its present discipline; and, more than any other term, indicates the extent of the soul's obligation to him. . . .

It may be asked *how* Christ becomes the author of such an experience. Different replies would be given. — replies that might seem to invalidate, if not contradict, one another. From one quarter the inquirer might be told that Christ's teaching leads the soul out of its blindness into the light of the Divine countenance, which is equivalent to the communication of a new life; from another quarter, that it is the character; or from a third, that it is the death of Christ, which touches dormant sensibilities and rouses a dull conscience. Some may say that it is a doctrine concerning the person of Christ or the Divine nature which conceals within its mysteries the quickening and comforting resources of truth, to be enjoyed only by those who accept the doctrine as a symbolic expression of Christianity.

For us, my friends, it is sufficient to know Christ as the channel and manifestation of a Divine influence, by which the believer is so instructed, animated, enriched, and fortified, that he becomes conscious of a new experience working in him to disclose unknown capacities of life, and through this inward change spreading a new aspect over life as it lies around him. To one who has observed the effect of any fresh and important truth, scientific or practical, in giving a direction to the thoughts and an impulse to the character, it will not appear difficult of explanation that the truths which Christ has revealed respecting the Divine Being, the immortality of man, the moral exposures and spiritual relations in which man is immersed, and the means of recovery from imminent peril, should act as forces to inspire and sustain a consciousness as different from that of which either worldliness or morality is the type as heaven from earth. Let any one entirely and heartily believe all that the New Testament teaches in regard to the mission, office, and gospel of Jesus, he shall "obtain the end of his faith, even the salvation of his soul," with as absolute certainty as the introduction of the physical agencies of heat and electricity will work a change in any material substance. The depths of human consciousness shall be sounded, the heights of a divine experience shall be scaled, the soul shall become a mirror of the universe, and the universe shall be an ever unfolding testimony concerning Him of whose prolific will it is the result. . . .

We are saved by faith in Christ. I say, faith in Christ: not simply in his religion, which will follow, of course. The gospel consists partly in the fact that a special arrangement was made by God, through the mission and mediation of His Son, for the salvation of sinners. This conclusive proof of the Divine love gives to the religion of Christ the character of a "gospel," or good tidings, grateful intelligence. The miraculously attested mission of Christ is not merely the support of the gospel, but an intimate portion of it. We are saved by faith in Christ, because we receive the truth communicated by him as alike authoritative and gracious ; because we follow his counsel, trusting in its heavenly character ; because we commit ourselves to him as Teacher and Master, Guide and Friend ; because, in obedience to his instruction, we adopt new habits of thought, feeling, and action ; and because, through gratitude for the love shown in and by him, we are led to the most poignant sense of our own sinfulness towards that Being whom we have neglected or affronted, while He has exhibited such a tender interest in us. In other words, we are saved by being brought to repentance and to a new life. Our hearts are humbled, cleansed, changed. We are turned from sin to righteousness.

But, since much remains to be done, Christianity continues to exert an influence the effect of which is seen in the improvement, or, to use the Scriptural and more expressive word, in the "sanctification" of the believer. In our modern forms of speech, Christ becomes the author, first of conversion or of awakening, according as the soul had sunk into depravity or into moral lethargy ; and then of progress, as its quickened and directed energies seek the perfection for which it was made ; the whole experience of change and of growth constituting what has been styled " the Christian consciousness," — a phrase exposed to the charge of mysticism, yet capable of being used in a true and admirable sense. To produce this consciousness was the purpose of Christ's entrance into the world, of his departure from it by a violent death, of his reappearance among men after his crucifixion, and of the various agencies which he set in operation through the truth which he announced, the cross on which he suffered, and the kingdom which he established. It is this consciousness which makes one a Christian ; which verifies the words of Christ,

"He that believeth in me, though he were dead, yet shall he live;" which explains his language, "I am the vine, ye are the branches;" which secures for the soul peace on earth, and entitles it to the anticipation of a glorious immortality. This consciousness is "salvation by faith;" this is personal religion; this is the soul's witness to itself that it has become a partaker of Divine holiness.

Now this, I repeat, is the essential thing in an interpretation and use of the gospel, — that it be regarded and be received as the author of a spiritual experience, by which the believer shall translate the symbolic language of Heaven into personal facts; for all truth is but symbol till it is made personal. Christ must reign within us. His title is "Prince of Life;" and only when his right to this title is confirmed by the submission of our souls is his appellation of "Saviour" made to express a reality. Christ's "mediatorial" work, on its earthly side, is this redemptive work, or his success in raising human souls into a new consciousness. The "atonement" which he accomplishes consists in his reconciliation of our hearts and wills to the will of God. Whichever of the many statements that describe his relations to man we may prefer as most accurate or most nearly exhaustive, the idea is presented of an *interior life*, of which he is the occasion.

And this idea harmonizes with that teaching of our Lord, which has been thought to constitute one of its peculiar features, if not the most peculiar. Christ spoke of feelings, motives, principles, habits of thought, rather than of overt acts. The beatitudes are a compend of his religion. What are they but formulas of the soul? "Blessed are the pure in heart," "the poor in spirit," "the meek," "they who hunger and thirst after righteousness." The commandments which he pronounced chief of all enjoined love to God and love to man, dispositions, states of the heart, habits of the interior life. Do the Epistles of the New Testament offer us an exposition of Christianity different from this? Nowhere. Paul and James agree with one another, and both with Christ. Paul says, Not ritual service nor conventional piety, but religious sentiment, penetrating and filling the soul, is needful; which some persons having understood as a depreciation of external religion, James corrects their error (not Paul's error: he had made no mistake, and James does not charge him with any) by showing that the proof of inward conviction and sensibility is the discharge of positive duties. Peter holds a similar doctrine about godliness. John insists on love, a prevailing state of the soul, as at once the evidence and the security of Christian discipleship. From Matthew to Jude, the instruction is uniform. Not what we do in itself, but what we are (and what we do as the sign of what we are) is important.

The revelations of the gospel lead us to the same conclusion. Its two most distinctive revelations are conveyed to us through the Christian doctrines respecting mercy and the Spirit. I mean not to undervalue its annunciation of "the Father," or its assurance of immortality; and yet I say, that in its exhibition of the Divine mercy, and in its promise of the Divine Spirit, it has pronounced its own character with the most emphasis. For, to sinful man, what is immortality but the menace of a fearful retribution, unless it be joined with forgiveness, which mercy alone can bestow? and of what avail is a knowledge of God as our Father, if it do not establish a nearness between our souls and him, of which we find both the statement and the method in the doctrine of the Spirit? As man's great need is pardon, so his great privilege is recipiency. Christ, in his gospel, explains the privilege and relieves the need; but, you observe, one is a want, the other a capacity, of the soul. In its most profound disclosures of truth, Christianity, therefore, addresses the innermost nature of man.

If we turn now to those exercises which indicate man's rank in the scale of being, we shall obtain an independent testimony to this value and office of the gospel. In these days, when so much is said of the dignity of human nature, and when precision either of language or of thought is so little studied, it may not be improper to ask in what this dignity consists; and the true answer, I apprehend, we shall find to be this,

— that man is most distinguished by his ability of spiritual communion; which is but another name for that faculty of faith which it is the purpose of the Gospel to call into exercise. Man's greatness does not lie in his intellect; for conscience is greater : and yet conscience is not his highest endowment. Above that, or below it, as a deeper treasure, is the ability, which he alone of the creatures on earth possesses, of contemplating and loving God.   To know God is more than to know right; to love God, more than to choose right.   Faith is man's noblest faculty, — or function ; call it which you please. But mark you, my hearers, one and all, it is a function of the *soul,* which the scholar possesses by no stronger right than the ploughboy.   I am tired of this incessant adulation of man, as if he were great in himself.   He is great in God; and without God, as the inspiration and end of his being, he is the poorest wreck that was ever tossed on the waves of existence.   Now what says Christianity, what says Christ, to this human being ?   They say, " Awake, thou fool, and slow of heart ! and know " (not thyself, it was heathen counsel and heathen flattery which said this, and no more), — " know thy God, that thou mayst know thyself; know thy weakness, that thou mayst know thy strength " (for the Christian paradox, my friends, is the solution of life's mystery, — ' when I am weak, then am I strong ') ; " live by faith now, here, in this mortal life, that thou mayst live for ever."   And it is when man listens to such voices as these, and bows himself in prayer, and makes the Eternal One his trust and his portion, that he is great; greater than La Place calculating the problems of the physical universe, or Goethe in the majesty of his genius : ay, the little child, to whom is promised the kingdom of heaven, rivalling, in the unconscious glory with which his spirit is clad, the seraphim that walk the starry floor of the skies.

Once more : let me call your attention to the fact that the best part of literature is that part which nourishes the soul. The most precious books in our libraries are those which describe or aid the soul's growth.   Devotional writings meet a want felt by all classes, just as the Psalms of David enjoy an immortal youth. The volumes that retain their popularity through generations have the salt of divine truth in them. The soul is the same in every age: it has the same sins and infirmities and struggles now which it had in Luther's day and in St. Augustine's; and the books that are dear to the heart of humanity treat of the secret experience which is made up of those struggles and infirmities and sins. The soul, too, that has found peace, loves to read of the Father's grace, and the Saviour's friendship, and the Holy Spirit's consolation. Bunyan's allegory has had fifty readers where Milton's epic has found one. Baxter's " Saint's Rest;" Doddridge's " Rise and Progress of Religion in the Soul " (happiest of titles); Thomas à Kempis's " Imitation of Christ;" Scougal's " Life of God in the Soul of Man " (title more felicitous even than Doddridge's), — it is such books as these that *last ;* books in which the soul finds its unspoken confessions written down, and its secret necessities anticipated. The only religion that can survive social changes, and never be outgrown by intellectual culture, is a religion that shall recognize these necessities and respond to these confessions; such a religion as we find in the New Testament, — the religion of him who came into the world to save sinners.

There is, doubtless, danger of bestowing a disproportionate attention on the spiritual element in character. Man's tendency is always to an excess in one direction, that must be balanced by defect in another direction. But a danger should make us watchful, not drive us to disown that in regard to which extravagance is the only possible mistake. The probability of running into error is not greater here than in any other case where one form of the religious experience is allowed to engross our interest. Doctrinal religion, if not qualified by other elements, becomes dogmatism and bigotry; ceremonial religion is apt to degenerate into routine and hypocrisy; practical religion, if disjoined from piety, tends to self-conceit or intellectual scepticism; and spiritual religion may end in mysticism. But the last is not the greatest evil of the four. The mystics of different ages have not been the worst Christians. It would not harm us, if we were more fond of meditation and the offices of the closet. It would not make us less practical to be more devout, nor less sound in faith to be more ardent in feeling.

The truth is, that a natural reaction has carried many persons towards an opposite extreme from that which they wished to avoid. In the weariness which some persons have felt under a continual inculcation of doctrinal ideas, they have given tnemselves up to what they style practical religion; forgetting that religious truth is the only solid basis of practical religion. We are building on the sand, when we build character on any thing less substantial than faith in spiritual realities. The proclivity to an exclusively practical use of the gospel has introduced a style of illustrative instruction, to the neglect — at least, the comparative neglect — of far-reaching principles. To cite but a single example: because it has seemed to us a common fault in the pulpit, while preaching against sin, to keep silence about actual sins, have we not become reprovers and assailants of sin in detail, as if that were enough; plucking this leaf, breaking down that twig, or lopping off a branch, but not laying the axe to the root? The only way to extirpate sin from the character is to remove the love of sin from the heart. The right method is to attack *sin*, rather than sins; the vice of the soul, rather than its manifestations. Sin does not lie in the action, but in the motive. The corrupt heart must be changed. A change of heart, — admirable phrase! never was there a better one, — "a change of heart" will bring about a change of life. Implant the love of God in the soul, and the sinner will renounce his evildoing. Ingraft the believer into the true vine, and he will bring forth good fruit.

I am not urging a return to opinions or methods which were wisely forsaken by our fathers. I have no love for the bondage or the "bread" of Egypt. It was a noble service which the men of fifty and forty years ago rendered to New England, and to us their children, when they said, "We will believe what the Bible teaches, and no more and no less." In grateful recollection, let us hail them, this day, as consistent advocates and successful champions of the truth which we prize more than un-counted gold. But our regard for their honored memories need not impose silence on our lips in respect to unforeseen tendencies or results of the movement which received its impulse from them. If religion has become among us too much a visible uprightness, and too little an inward experience, let us say so; in God's name, let us say so; in our fealty to Christ, let us say so; for our soul's sake, let us say so; for our children's sake, and the sake of those who may accept our construction of the gospel, let us say so. And therefore I do say, that morality without piety, good-ness without faith, practical Christianity, as it is sometimes called, without spiritual Christianity interpenetrating and sustaining it, is like a tree the heart of which has perished; or a fairly bound volume, whose pages afford no instruction. Religion enters into life or becomes practical, by first passing into the consciousness, and thence infusing itself into the conduct. Personal goodness, without this interior spring and support, is a shell, a color, a disguise, not a substantial and permanent reality. If you would have honest, kind, and generous neighbors, persuade them to take Christ into their hearts as their Lord and Saviour. If you would be thorough and consistent in goodness yourself, embrace him with a hearty faith. The soul shapes the life. The Chris-tian soul subdues speech and behavior into manifestations of itself. When we care not for what we seem, but for what we are, we make the appearance a true picture of the inward life. It is the soul that must experience the power of the gospel as a Divine gift and a Divine influence. It is an unseen experience that must prove our estimation of the Saviour in whom we believe. It is the *soul* that must be saved; and saved by its spiritual, Christian, Divine, let me style it — for it is sympathy with the infinite excellence of God — its Divine consciousness. The external blessings of Christianity are just occasions of thank-fulness; but what are they in comparison with the light, the strength, the peace, the comfort, the hope, the joy, of which it makes the soul the possessor?

We hear much in these days of the social reforms which are

needed, and which Christian men are carrying on. So far as they are conducted in a Christian spirit, and with a reliance on Christian truth, success attend them ! Let them have our sympathies, our efforts, and our prayers. But the removal of social abuses is not the object for you or me, or any man, to adopt as his end in life. The "end of our faith" is "the salvation of our souls." Inward reformation is the work which we must first undertake. This we can accomplish, each one for and in himself. The individual can correct the abuses of his own life, can eradicate the errors of his own heart, can make his own consciousness a proof of the efficacy of the gospel. God bless all honest philanthropists ! — they are servants of the Lord Jesus and friends of their kind. But the Lord Jesus offers salvation to the world by offering it to the individual. In ourselves must the Divine grace be felt, renewing, sanctifying, saving us.

Holiness, — it once was a more common word in Christian discourse and Christian conversation than now. *Holy* men and women, — why, we regard them with somewhat the same distant admiration with which we look back on the saints or martyrs of other times. Here and there we see one — a godly man, a saintly woman — standing in society like spiritual eminences that rise above the clouds of our familiar experience and enjoy the clear sunshine of God's presence. But why, tell me, I pray you, explain to yourselves, if you can, my friends, why every one of us should not aspire to the same enjoyment of celestial realities. " Be ye holy even as your Father in heaven is holy," said Jesus to the same persons to whom he delivered his instruction respecting the forgiveness of injuries and the distribution of alms. Away with the notion, which multitudes cherish, that only a few are called to be saints ! Lend no countenance to this half-gospel. Every one, every one, should be a partaker of that life through which man has his fellowship with the Eternal Father and the sinless Son.

My friends, hear the words of Christ, " *Whosoever* — whosoever drinketh of the water that I shall give him shall never thirst ; but the water that I shall give him shall be in him a fountain springing up into everlasting life." Has your experience been a confirmation of those words? Have you ever thought that the " whoso ever" includes you? Have you still unsatisfied wants, a restless heart, an impatient will? Do you know what distress or discontent is of which you say nothing because you but half understand it, that thirst of the soul which can be slaked only in the water of Christian salvation, that longing after peace, that dim outline of satisfaction which mocks the feeling of which it is the shadow, — do you know this? Then take into your innermost being the influences of which Christ is the symbol and the source, — drink, drink freely, abundantly, continually, of the water that He shall give you, and you will find the relief, the rest, the satisfaction which you want.

1862.

THE DOCTRINAL BASIS OF CHRISTIANITY.

1 Tim. iv. 6: "*A good minister of Jesus Christ, nourished up in the words of faith and of good doctrine, whereunto thou hast attained.*"

Doctrinal preaching is the exposition of positive spiritual truths. It differs, therefore, from what is usually called practical preaching, or an enforcement of the preceptive parts of religion; though, under a more correct appreciation, doctrinal preaching bears the same relation to practical as the planting of the tree to the culture of fruit. It differs also from sentimental preaching, or a weak dilution of truth in pretty phrases. It differs from rhetorical preaching, or an exhibition of electroplated ware for solid silver. It differs from all preaching but gospel preaching: which indeed it is, pre-eminently and exclusively ; for its purpose is to unfold the glad news of redemption and life which the Son of God brought from the bosom of Infinite Love. It is such preaching as we find in those discourses of Jesus, which John, the most doctrinal of the Evangelists, has given us. It is such a style of preaching as both the Acts and the Epistles show that Paul adopted, and such as he recommended to Tim-

othy in his description of "a good minister of Jesus Christ," as
one "nourished up in the words of faith and of good doctrine."

A restoration of doctrinal Christianity to its rightful place, in
the preparations of the minister for his pulpit, is the great reform
which the exigencies and the obligations of our position in the
Christian Church require us to adopt. This want our political
troubles, instead of overshadowing or putting in abeyance, make
more distinct and immediate; for, whether we desire to gain a
higher atmosphere of thought in which our souls may find relief
from the burthen that weighs on them, or to draw from the gospel the counsel and strength which shall fit us to bear our part
in the offices of the hour, there never has been a time, in
human history, when the vital doctrines of the gospel had a
larger opportunity to prove their value. And as in past ages
and as now, so through future time the disinthralment of
society from error, as well as the deliverance of the soul from
sin, must be the work of those agencies which faith in Christ
shall put in motion : not a faith in the letter of his history,
which alone sets nothing in motion; but faith in him as the
Teacher, Redeemer, and Lord, whose words must be accepted as
the quickening forces of humanity.

What are the doctrines of Christianity? Without yet specify-
ing them, our general answer would be, They are the truths
which Christianity makes prominent and essential, — prominent
in the place they hold, and essential in the influence they exert.
They are the great spiritual revelations of the Gospel. Theoretically, they constitute the substance of the Gospel; experimen-
tally, they denote its effect. They are worthy, therefore, of being
described in terms which believers have been fond of using. They
are the "doctrines of grace," or declarations setting forth the character and conditions of the Divine favor; "doctrines of the cross,"
or truths of which the cross of Christ is at once the symbol and the
assurance; "doctrines of salvation," or indications of the method
by which man may be rescued from the peril into which sin has
cast him. These are appropriate and excellent terms to use in
this connection. Perverted as they have been to designate

statements that make salvation a mystery, the cross a means of extricating the Supreme Being from a dilemma, and grace the title of immoral partiality, we have been inclined to let them fall into neglect. Would it not be better to reinstate them in the possession of their true meaning? In the interpretation which we give to the Gospel, they find their just value; and we, of all Christians in the world, have a right to use them.

It is a peculiarity of the Gospel, that it offers no systematic exposition of truth. Christ did not aim at making men profound theologians. Theology as a science lies scattered through the Bible very much as the precious stones in the breastplate of the Jewish high-priest were once scattered among the treasures of nature. Brought together, and set each in its place, they represent and reflect the Divine Will; yet the arrangement is artificial and provisional. The everlasting truths which Jesus delivered dropped from his lips, one might say on the first perusal, incidentally, as if without either plan or forethought; although a closer examination will discover a pertinency which connects the occasion with the speech, and causes the former to become a means of elucidating the latter. Even Paul, scholar and dialectician as he was, never attempts to reduce Christianity to a system: it is his commentators who have introduced scientific analysis into the Epistle to the Romans.

In any attempt which we make to define the truths of our religion, we should be guided by two rules, which have been strangely overlooked. One of these rules obliges us to seek the Christian doctrines among the *plain instructions* of Christ. They are not matters of inference, but of revelation; not the background of obscure hints, but the substance of positive instruction. A doctrine which cannot be presented in Christ's words is not a part of his Gospel. Essential truth was not left to be ingeniously deduced from what he taught: still less is it a reconciliation of opposite statements which he made; for one of these suppositions imputes to him an erroneous, and the other an insufficient, discharge of the office with which he was intrusted when he was sent to "bear witness to the truth."

The other condition of successful inquiry after Christian doctrine limits us to such truths as contain a *spiritual efficacy*, by which the character may be quickened and purified. For the object of Christ's ministry was, not to supply the believer with intellectual furniture, but to endow the soul with the energies of religious life. A revelation that should not touch the conscience nor mould the will did not fall within the purpose of his mission. His silence on many questions which men are eager to propound may be explained by this fact. How little, for example, do we know of the future world, beyond the momentous disclosures of immortality and judgment! Thousands confess their disappointment and impatience at this silence by the delight they take in fictitious description. Yet is it not plain that it would have helped us but little, in our present struggle with evil, to have been told all that we desire to know about the nature of angels or the employments of beatified spirits? and is it not probable that therefore we are taught no more? The Gospel was not given to satisfy an unprofitable curiosity, however natural or innocent. The end of faith is a spiritual consciousness. " Sanctify them by thy truth," was the prayer of Jesus.

The two conditions which we have now laid down enable us to discriminate between the Divine and the human, the true and the conjectural. They justify us in resisting any attempt to impose on our belief statements which multitudes accept. We provide, not an ingenious yet inadequate defence, but a fair and full protection of our incredulity, when we demand of the advocates of the doctrine of the Trinity, that they present, at least, one form of that doctrine in the words of Christ; or when we challenge the believers in natural depravity to show how such a dogma can give impulse or aid to a soul seeking, or needing redemption. For the sake of discrimination, we urge the importance of considering the method and design, as well as the contents, of Christ's instruction. It is not a proclivity towards unbelief, but a desire for right belief, that induces us to reject popular creeds and open the way to a sound faith. Under the countenance of a Scriptural example, we " take away the first, that we may establish the last."

Such a use of religious truths as it should be the object of the ministry to encourage might require an entire reconstruction of Christian theology. The corner-stone of the theological systems, which different sections of the Church have erected as citadels of faith, has been some attribute of the Divine Nature, — the sovereignty, for example, or the goodness of God; and the apex has been found either in the glory of God, or in the ultimate well-being of his universe. Using these as the initial and final statements, it became necessary to adjust all intermediate truths with a reference to such boundaries; and Christian doctrines have, in the main, been formulas meant to express the mysteries of the Divine government. With equal reverence and gratitude, let us take up the privilege of maintaining that the Gospel does not enter on so fruitless a task. It treats of matters more nearly level with the human consciousness. Its corner-stone is human want; its apex, everlasting life. A correct understanding of the Gospel would compel us, therefore, if bent upon framing its truths into a system, to adopt a different " scheme of divinity " from any which is, or ever has been, popular. Taking our position, not in the skies, but on the earth, we interpret Christianity as the law and the inspiration of a healthful consciousness. The first duty of the Christian minister, after having himself " attained unto the words of faith and of sound doctrine," is to lay this interpretation of the Gospel before his people in the plainest, yet most persuasive, terms which he can borrow from his own interior life.

Under such an interpretation, what will be the constituent members of doctrinal Christianity? By way of illustration rather than enumeration, let me give a partial answer to this inquiry.

In the front rank of Christian truths, foremost in the noble company, I find a doctrine concerning mediation. It is a doctrine of wide significance. It involves a view of the relations which exist between God and man, and of the place which Christ holds in the midst of these relations. It presents God as at once righteous and merciful; " just, and the justifier of him who believeth in Jesus;" sinned against, yet patient with the transgressor; forsaken by them who live only through his watchful care, still yearning after their repentant submission, and ready to forgive those whose hearts are broken in contrite grief; "commending his love to us, in that, while we were sinners, Christ died for us." It presents man as lying in a state of moral ruin, yet capable of moral renovation; weak, wilful, corrupt, self-betrayed, lost, yet stung by conscience and weary in heart; with powers and affections estranged from God, but restless in their departure from him. It presents Christ as the instrument chosen to bring men back to obedience; the Messenger, whom Divine Grace qualified for a work which no other being was competent to execute; the Instructor and Saviour of the human race, the pledge of mercy, the channel of truth, the inspirer of hope, the reconciling agency between the soul and its Maker, the "Sent" of God, the "Mediator."

What a breadth of truth is covered by this doctrine! What depths of experience, what heights of aspiration, does it disclose! In what a clear light does it set the fact of the atonement, which men have so sadly misused, first by calling it a doctrine, and then by torturing and overlaying it; till the "atonement" of the Church has resembled the "atonement" of the New Testament as little as engravings that you may have seen of the temple at Jerusalem, in which the principles of art and the traditions of history are treated with equal scorn, resemble the original structure. The atonement is the great central fact of the believer's life, for which his previous experience has been a mournful preparation, but of which his subsequent experience is a joyful result, — the conquest of the human will by the Divine love, and the seal of the Saviour's mediatorial work. Let not any man add unto it what does not belong to it, lest God "add unto him the plagues" of a darkened mind and diseased conscience; let no man take away from it any part of its meaning, lest God "take away his part out of the book of life."

The next doctrine in order of importance, — for a just arrangement of Christian truths must be founded on their relative spiritual value, — is a doctrine respecting the sons of God. Like that of which we have just spoken, this also has a large range of meaning. Like that, it involves a revelation concerning God and Christ and man. It exhibits God in the relation of a Father; for, if there be " sons of God," he must have granted to some of his creatures the privilege of calling him " Father." But to whom? Not to the whole world, except as they may choose to put themselves in a filial relation. The more I study the New Testament, the more am I inclined to restrict the revelation of " the Father." Christ makes him known, under this title, to such as through faith become children of God. To those whom he addressed as " the light of the world " and " the salt of the earth," or to the representatives of his future Church, Jesus gave permission to say, " Our Father, who art in heaven." Practically, at least, the paternal character of God can be a revelation only to those who have entered into spiritual union with Christ. " If ye had known me," were his words, " ye should have known my Father also." To those who are sons, the Gospel unfolds the parental attributes of the Divine Mind; and the Infinite One, clothed with majesty and girded with power, becomes the most tender and intimate of personal friends.

Look, now, on the other side of this relation. Frail and sinful man becomes a child of God. " Hast made us unto our God kings and priests " is the language in which the saints celebrate the praises of the Redeemer, under the Oriental imagery of the Apocalypse; but it is a nearer, and therefore a more glorious, relation to hold, which we claim as sons. " The spirit of adoption " which we have " received " lifts us, if we may so speak, out of the arms of a Providence fearful, if faithful, to lay us on the bosom of a heavenly grace; while it informs us of the design of that Providence in chastening us, even that we may become " partakers " of the holiness which constitutes the essential quality of the Divine Nature. This doctrine of sonship includes yet more; for it instructs us concerning Him who was the " well-beloved Son," and who is " not ashamed to call them who are sanctified, brethren," since he also was " sanctified and sent into the world " by the Father. On this ground, as you remember, he rested his justification in calling himself "the Son of God." If men, instead of seeking for the import of this title among inscrutable mysteries of an antecedent state of being, had accepted the definition which lies on the very surface of the Gospel, how much angry debate and how much secret distress would have been avoided!

One other example let me give of the contents of doctrinal Christianity. Distinct and bright on the pages of the New Testament stands the doctrine of eternal life. Here, again, we throw open to the believer a boundless field of experience. No word is entitled to bear a greater weight of meaning than this monosyllabic "life;" yet, till Christ raised it into a true appreciation, how little did it signify! Even now, in lands on which the light of the Gospel has not fallen, in Pagan or Mohammedan countries, how little value is set upon human life! Christ augmented the force of the term immeasurably, both by showing what life might be made here, and by announcing its continuance hereafter. As a present possession, life becomes invaluable, when seen to be, internally, a consciousness of spiritual relations; and, externally, a discharge of duties, which, however mean to a worldly eye, are glorified by their connection with character. Nothing now is ignoble, except that which conscience brands as unworthy. Whatever it is right for a man to do, in princely apparel or in peasant's dress, is honorable and holy work. At one blow did this interpretation of life strike down the artificial barriers and false judgments of society. Understood as the pursuit of excellence or as the normal growth of the soul, life is an equal privilege, and therefore an equal trust, for all. Royalty is but the pressure of a heavier obligation, while slavery is a denial of personal rights; selfishness is suicide; and love the fulness of satisfaction. Under the influence of such ideas, regeneration, the new birth, is relieved of all technical or dogmatic obscurity, and appears in its true character, as the entrance of a human soul into a consciousness of its own powers and destinies. The Saviour's words, "Except a man be born again, he cannot enter into the kingdom of

Heaven," become the statement of a law as intelligible as it is inevitable.

Still Christianity does not stop, in its explanation of "life," at the boundary of our present state of being. By carrying forward the term into an unseen world, and there investing it with imperishable associations, that it may return into our use as a symbol of immortality, the Gospel has made it the most comprehensive of the terms of human speech. While the revelation of immortality is justly regarded as one of the peculiar features of the Gospel, the form in which this revelation is made is not less worthy of notice. It is not a naked annunciation of another state of being, but a continual recognition of the indestructible qualities of the life which Christ has quickened in the soul, and which is one and the same through all stages of existence. " Whosoever liveth and believeth in me shall never die," is his promise of immortality to man.

If Christianity had paused at this point, however, it would have failed to add the sanction which is needed for the support of a struggling virtue, or the warning which may deter the sinner from fatal perseverance in the course he has chosen. There is one other doctrine of our religion, which I may not leave unnoticed, — the doctrine of retribution; which unfolds the influence of each moment on the next moment, of each period of our mortal existence on the subsequent periods, and of the whole of this life on an endless futurity. If there be any thing positive in the Gospel, it is the declaration that man is living under a judgment, which never relaxes its vigilance, nor suspends its retributive function; a judgment, for the rectitude and constancy of which the Divine attributes are a security, and the nature of which Christ has set forth, now in the unequivocal terms in which its principles are announced, and now by the terrific images in which its effects are described. Having the same foundation and the same altitude, this doctrine, and that which we last considered, stand as the pillars on which the portals of eternity are hung; through which, as faith forces them open, light from the sovereign throne streams out, and falls on every act of our mortal being.

I may not try your patience by any further description of the doctrinal basis on which Christianity would raise the fabric of character. Under these four titles, we have indicated the most important portion of the contents of the Gospel; for the value of the truths which it delivers is not numerical, but moral. It is not by quantity, but by quality, that we estimate the water of which " he who drinketh shall never thirst again." In avoiding the usual titles, as well as the usual arrangement, of the Christian doctrines, I cannot expect an instant concurrence from all minds. Yet the order to which I have given preference is recommended by its parallelism with the purposes which Christ came to effect. The mistake of theologians of almost every school has been to take their standpoint outside these purposes, and construct their system from a position at which the Christian truths do not appear in their natural relations. Christ did not come upon earth to unfold a theology of the universe, or to solve the problems which vex a student, and which lie as far behind human want as above human intelligence; but to meet the actual condition of humanity, with remedies and aids suited to this end. We shall be in the best situation for tracing the internal economy of his religion, if we place ourselves where he stood when he cried, " Repent; for the kingdom of Heaven is at hand." You observe that the Gospel did not begin with a doctrine about the mode of the Divine being, or the origin of human sinfulness; but with a recognition of the fact that man was a sinner, and a promise that God would draw the penitent soul into union with himself. Here should our exposition of Christianity begin, — in the mediatorial work of reconciliation between a miserable sinner and a gracious God; and thence, through personal verification of the doctrines of sonship, eternal life, and spiritual judgment, pass to the final cry of the believer, " Thanks be to God, who giveth us the victory."

Through personal verification; that is, through such an acquaintance of the soul with these doctrines as shall render them elements of its consciousness, and conditions of its history. Not only the nature, but the influence, of Christian truth must be understood, if we would see it restored to its rightful position, either in the regards of men or in the offices of the pulpit. This influence is neither mechanical nor intellectual nor ethical, but spiritual and experimental. Religious truth may be received either historically, when it is deposited in the memory; or intellectually, when it is lodged in the understanding; or spiritually, when it is embraced by the soul. In the first case, words alone are held by an act of faith; in the second case, ideas; in the third, vital forces, of which words are signs in the memory, and ideas in the understanding, but signs which, whether in word or in idea, are useful only as they induce the soul to entertain such forces within its own life. The excellence of preaching depends on its fidelity in rendering assistance to the soul in its acquisition of this benefit; in other words, a good sermon is that which brings the truth into connection with the innermost consciousness of the hearer. A sermon that shall simply repeat or coldly expound the truths of the Gospel may not be worthless; but such sermons alone, though preached through all the Sundays of all the years of the longest ministry that ever turned a pulpit from its legitimate uses, would not secure one soul as the seal of that life-long ministry. No, never; although the preacher should have learned all that Aristotle could teach him of logic, or Cicero of eloquence. Doctrinal Christianity must be so used by the speaker that it shall strike upon the spiritual nature of the hearer. Religion addresses itself to the religious faculties and sensibilities, not to the critical understanding or the captious taste. If these choose to lend it their support by entering into its service, so much more easy will it be for religion to transform the sinner into a saint; but, competent to effect this transformation without their aid, by too great reliance on their support, it destroys its own ability. The aim of the preacher, and the aim of a good minister in his private intercourse with the members of his congregation, should be to implant truth in the conscience and heart, and in the deeper sanctity of that province of our nature where the exercises of spiritual communion are conducted, and the soul vindicates its right to appropriate to itself the apostle's words, "Our fellowship is with the Father, and with His Son Jesus Christ."

Let it ever be borne in mind that we can apprehend the character or value of Christianity only as we take it into our consciousness.   Experience alone will enable us to understand the offices of Christ or the privileges of discipleship.   Not more true is it that only a mother can know a mother's love, than that none but a soul which has found peace can know "the peace that passeth understanding."   "Our Father, who art in heaven," is an empty phrase to him who has not a filial heart; but to him who has become as a little child, oh, what inexhaustible treasures of grace are thrown open by such a revelation of God!   "The blood of Jesus Christ his Son cleanseth us from all sin;" what is this declaration but diplomatic cipher, Egyptian hieroglyphics, an algebraic unknown quantity, to one who has not been washed in that blood? but, to him who has felt its purifying and strengthening influence, the words denote an operation which no wealth could procure, and for which no gratitude is an equivalent.   "No man," we are told, "could learn the new song that was sung before the throne, but the hundred and forty and four thousand who were redeemed from the earth."

1846.

THE LARGENESS OF CHRISTIANITY.

MATT. vii. 28: "*And it came to pass, when Jesus had ended these sayings, the people were astonished at his doctrine.*"

WE all of us suffer greatly from our familiarity with the Christian religion.   We suffer just as a person suffers from living too near any magnificent scenery.   He does not appreciate it as it deserves.   He does not study it.   He does not think about it.   Its grandeur is lost upon him.   It is to him no more than the ordinary scenes of nature, because he has been familiar with it all his life: while others will travel hundreds of miles to see these wonders of creation, and go away never to forget them, he passes them every day without feeling their power to fill the soul with admiration or undefined rapture. Just as one dwelling within the sound of Niagara, or under the shadow of the Alps, may have never been conscious of any emotion which thrilled his breast at the sublime spectacle that had been before his eyes from childhood. So we regard Christianity without any perception of its extraordinary character. Familiarity dulls the vision and steels the heart. They who heard Jesus when the Divine words, which thenceforth became an imperishable part of the world's moral atmosphere, were first spoken, were differently affected. They were surprised, amazed, rapt in wonder or in reverence, they felt the sublimity of such teaching. Even the common people, the rude peasantry of Galilee, the wild populace of Jerusalem, even they were astonished at his doctrine.

Christianity is full of *great* truths. It contains no others. All that it says is large, comprehensive, boundless. It discourses of what is higher than heaven, deeper than hell, broader than the creation, more stable than the pillars of the world or the laws of the stellar spheres. It speaks reverently, earnestly, calmly, and with what a wonderful plainness and clearness of speech, of God, the All in All, the Eternal, the Immutable. It speaks distinctly and solemnly, yet with how tender a voice, of the soul, the child and heir of God, immortal in its nature, free in its relations, with responsibilities binding it to the present and the future, the near and the remote, and with destinies which even faith cannot measure. It speaks of duty, whose seed is power, whose germination is choice, whose fruit is strength; of repentance, which is the soul's conquest of itself, and of progress, which is the soul's conquest of every thing without itself; of faith, which is the apprehension of the invisible and the enjoyment of the spiritual; of love, the condition of growth and satisfaction for all moral beings; of eternal life, as the inheritance of man, the experience which includes, explains, and harmonizes all the mysteries of his condition. With such themes as these it is conversant. And of these it treats not in labored or pompous strains, as if it were ever struggling against limitations which it could not surmount; but simply and easily, as if it knew the ground which it was treading, and had walked with the angels where human feet have never trodden.

Christianity has but *few* truths. We may not have noticed this peculiarity of our religion. Men have tried to multiply its truths. They have summoned a host of propositions from the charnel-house of a decayed superstition, and have tried to make them appear as Christian statements. They have made long creeds and longer catechisms, and cumbrous bodies of divinity, and massive and complex systems of theology, and pronounced them Christian. But Christianity disowns them all. They bear as little of the form as they breathe of the spirit of Christianity. Christianity has few truths, because what it has are so large and mean so much. Where each idea is a rich mine, an inexhaustible fountain, a fathomless ocean of instruction, there need not be many ideas. It is only when men talk of small things that they must use many words; that which suggests and quickens thought is better than that which circumscribes it. The larger the ideas which religion offers to the contemplation of its disciples, the less will be their number. The truths which the Christian faith presents to our examination, and our use also, are so important and so vast, that they must necessarily be few. They fill the soul, satisfy, task, expand it to the utmost. Christianity brings a few great principles into the light of practical relations. More would be a hinderance rather than a help in the way of life. Men want principles of large and various application, not a load of diffuse specification.

Hence arises the *silence* of Christianity on many points which awaken our curiosity, and interest earnest as well as anxious or imaginative minds. How little does it disclose of another world! Not half nor a tenth part of what many persons would like to know, — of what we should all, perhaps, like to know. Yet it has revealed the essential truths; immortality, retribution, society, distinction, — these points are established. How immense is their importance! how significant are they as facts of futurity! Questions occur in connection with our *present* interests on which we might be glad to hear the decisions of Christianity; but it is silent, or on these matters seems to say to conflicting opinions, in the words of Jesus, "Who made me a judge or a divider over you?" Political questions, economical questions, philanthropic questions, scientific questions, questions which agitate the community and perplex the student, it passes over in silence. Why? Because it presents truths of a wider bearing than we have yet thought of imputing to them; which will be found by and by to penetrate and solve all these questions. Take it up as a thing to be committed to memory, and Christianity is a child's lesson. Take it up as a thing to be pondered and searched and seen through and used, and the greatest of philosophers may spend his life upon it, and but have begun to enter into its comprehensiveness.

If the correctness of these remarks be allowed, a distinction which has sometimes been thought to exist, must fall to the ground. There is nothing in Christianity that is not of perpetual authority and universal interest. All is permanent, nothing is transient; the costume in which the truths are presented may be borrowed from the age in which they were delivered, but the truths themselves are unchangeable. The mere form of expression is not Christianity. What a man wears is not the man himself. Even in statuary Washington is one and the same, whether the artist represent him in the military or the civil garb of his own time, or in the classical dress of antiquity. With yet more justice might a similar identity have been attributed to the real Washington, let him have put on what apparel he might. The literary clothing of the Gospel is not the Gospel: that is fixed; the same yesterday, to-day, and for ever. Its truths, ideas, principles, which constitute its character, essence, substance, — these pass not away, change not, but abide immutable, immortal.

The bearing which this view of our religion has upon the question of our Lord's inspiration is important. It seems to me to go far towards establishing his claim to be considered a

specially illuminated messenger of the Divine mind. Such a grasp
of great truths as he exhibited is not to be resolved into an extraordinary insight or a peculiar genius for religion. There was
something more, something higher: there was a breadth of
vision which marked not the great man, but the prophet in the
largest sense of the word; the seer, who could look all round
the horizon and take in the measure of the world, who could see
through things into their essence and life. These sayings of
Jesus are not the guesses of a transcendental speculation, nor the
utterances of a meditative reason. They have a loftiness as well
as a purity which does not belong to the productions of human
wisdom. They seem instinct with divinity. They *are* divine.
Whence did he obtain the ability to proclaim truths which bear
such evident marks of a heavenly origin? Let us hear his own
reply: "I have not spoken of myself, but the Father who sent
me, He gave me a commandment what I should say and what I
should speak."

Nor is it the character of these sayings alone which renders
them so remarkable: the *manner* is not less worthy of notice nor
less difficult of explanation on any other supposition than that of
his elevation by means of supernatural influence above the common exercises of the human mind. It was this which first
impressed the people of Judea: they "were astonished at his
doctrine, for he taught them as one having authority, and not as
the Scribes." There was a distinct and calm delivery of truth
that was new to them. In form how positive, as of one who
knew that he was announcing what could never be overthrown,
yet how free from all arrogance or self-complacency, or even
from the delight which attends the discovery of truth! Here is
neither the rapture of the Grecian, who, in his joy at the result
of his labors, rushed forth exclaiming, "I have found it!" nor
the more quiet but not less deep satisfaction of Newton at the
close of his great work, nor the exultation of Milton, as he poured
out his burning soul, in the thought that he was writing for
other times. Yet these were great men, — men of genius; but
their manner as different from that of the teacher who came out

from Nazareth, as their gifts to the world were inferior to his. Even Shakespeare, who, more than any other, discovers the highest order of genius in the absence of all self-consciousness in his larger compositions, betrays the same weakness, if such it should be called, in his sonnets. I use these comparisons to show how entirely alone Jesus stands, as a teacher. He is unlike others, above them, beyond them, as if he came from another region of being.

And what makes this feature in his character still more remarkable is a difference which we trace between his annunciation of the truths which he brought from heaven and his allusions to his own experience. In the latter case we perceive emotion, sensibility, just the feeling which marks him as acting for himself, the very feeling which, on the supposition that he had mounted on the wings of his own intelligence to a higher sphere of thought, would have been seen in his annunciation of his discoveries. How touching are his notices of his own condition, as it was either felt or foreseen by him! "The Son of man hath not where to lay his head." "Take, eat; this do in remembrance of me." "If I am lifted up, I will draw all men unto me." But when he delivers the instructions which constituted his message to mankind, there is either the calmness of an almost automatic utterance, or the joy which was felt at being the instrument to convey such precious truth to the world. "Father, I thank thee that thou hast hid these things from the wise and prudent, and hast revealed them unto babes." Observe with what a perfect ease, beyond all study and all art, he speaks on subjects of the most sublime character, on providence, and judgment, and all the heights and depths of spiritual experience. It is wonderful, it is unparalleled, it is inexplicable, except on one admission, — this tranquillity of the bosom of Jesus, in the possession and expression of such thoughts.

If we would perceive yet more clearly the superiority of the Christian religion to all other forms of faith, and of Christ to all other teachers, we need only compare him with others who have been eminent as instructors of their race, or his Gospel with other systems of belief. We will leave the ancient world, Pagan philosophy or Jewish wisdom, and come to later times. In all the teaching of great men, who have founded communities or gathered sects, or left the impress of their own minds on society, you find something which is not great. The trivial and mean are bound up with the grand and beautiful. The proportions of the building are not preserved. The noble entrance leads to an unfinished interior, or the humble gateway does not correspond to the spacious court into which it opens. A massive pillar rests on a slight foundation, or the solid base supports no column: weakness and strength are joined together. Imperfection mars the whole work. There is something in every one's discourse which you wish, for his sake, could be omitted. Great writers cannot get away from their own littleness. Calvin must dogmatize, and Luther must rail, and Swedenborg must abound with idle conceits. But he who spake as never man spake is always consistent, always great. There is nothing little, either in him or his religion, nothing which you would wish to efface. This young man of Galilee, as he seems, who was born in obscurity and cradled in fear, whose education was a simple mother's care, who had no books and no masters, never sat at Gamaliel's feet, nor listened to Grecian sages or Egyptian priests, this plain humble Nazarene speaks words which not only pierce the heart of humanity, and at which the ages tremble, but says nothing which is poor, false, or narrow. All is great, and all is harmonious. Explain this, Unbelief. Solve this intellectual problem, this moral wonder. Listen to the Son of Mary, ye men of this generation, as if now for the first time the sound of his instruction had reached your ears, and see if you must not pronounce the teaching and the teacher Divine.

Furthermore, the fact should not be passed without notice that Christianity, sublime as are the truths which it offers to human use, is suited to the various wants of man, and enters into all the details of life. It accommodates itself to exigencies of condition, and regulates the pettiest affairs of the interior or exterior being. But this, instead of lessening its claims to our admiration, augments them; for only truths of the widest reach and noblest kind could connect themselves with all the relations and affairs of human life. It is here, as in the material world: a few elements admit of unlimited combination and application. In this respect they bear witness to the source whence they came: the primary truths of the Gospel, the ideas which lie at its foundation and compose its structure, are those in which all men may find the counsel, encouragement, rebuke, or assistance, which they need. The man on the throne, and the man in the common ranks of society, the scholar and the rustic, the richest and the poorest, the well and the sick, both sexes, and all ages, may find in the revelations of Christianity, few as they are, what shall be sufficient for their diverse moral necessities. Such sufficiency could belong only to truths of the largest scope. Because Christ taught great principles, he became the instructor of all conditions of human existence. Go from east to west, travel the earth over, and you will find no people and no individual to whom the sayings of Jesus may not bring peace, strength, and joy. The light of the one orb of day fills all the dwellings of a land, and every corner of every dwelling with its blessed radiance. So can the Gospel fill all the hearts in the land, and every chamber and nook of each heart.

The characteristic of our religion on which we are remarking, if properly understood, will be a security against two tendencies which have always prevailed, and still prevail with perhaps undiminished force, in the church. One is in the direction of exclusiveness. How is the narrow and bitter spirit of intolerance abashed — or rather, if it were capable of feeling shame, how would it be abashed — before the largeness of Christianity, — a worm crawling in the dust and trying to ape greatness in the presence of a seraph whose flight is through the heavens! A close creed, a harsh judgment, and a self-sufficient bigotry, are the component parts of exclusiveness, and they are as foreign from the mind of Christ, or the genius of his religion, as light from darkness.

The other tendency is towards formalism. It may be an honest and conscientious formalism, a reverence for the methods

in which piety expresses itself, a reliance on ways and means as
of equal importance with that to which they lead, an extravagant
use of the outward, though to the inevitable neglect of the inward, part of religion. I speak now only of *such* an error; not of
a false regard to the forms of worship, put on from unworthy motives. What sterner rebuke could be administered than to place
the Gospel of Matthew or John on the altar of many a church
named after him whose teaching the Evangelist has recorded?
See what a factitious importance has been ascribed to points
of mere form or ceremony, — how men have magnified the little
and overlooked the grand; have quarrelled about trifles, instead
of agreeing upon that before which the rise or fall of empires
seems small. Oh, how is more than half the controversy of our
times stripped of all interest and value, when brought into connection with the sayings of Christ! The man who can read the
Sermon on the Mount, or the conversation with the woman of
Samaria, or the final discourses of our Lord with his disciples
and go away to talk about the ritual of a church, as if its details
were of moment, — to say the best of him, and we might say
what would be more harsh and not less true, — cannot have
much of the usual susceptibility to moral influence which we
find in human nature. The sincere formalist can be but an
imperfect — may I not say, but a poor? — Christian. He has not
apprehended the greatness of the Christian truths. He does not
understand the Gospel in its vital characteristic. And every
church which prides itself or troubles itself about ceremonies
and canons and ecclesiastical practices has departed from the
grand peculiarity of the religion which Jesus taught.

Christianity is large. It is meant to expand, not to contract,
the mind. The soul beneath its influence grows large. Its
truths are reflections of the infinite attributes of God, and they
communicate something of His nature to the believer. My
hearers, study to have a Christianity in your own hearts, which
shall be all-embracing, all-vivifying. Let the glorious distinction of our faith stand out before the eyes of men. Let the
greatness of Jesus be seen, *his* great mind, *his* great heart, *his*

great life; of Jesus, whose sayings were full of power, because they meant more than tongue had ever uttered before, whose actions were his words translated into reality, and whose sufferings were his teachings seen through the medium of disaster, still grand and glorious, — teachings which have never yet found adequate expression in any language or character but his own.

1849.

GREAT PRINCIPLES IN SMALL MATTERS.

LUKE xvi. 10: *"He that is faithful in that which is least is faithful also in much : and he that is unjust in the least is unjust also in much."*

ONE of the most remarkable peculiarities of our religion is its connection of the sublimest truths with the most common details of life. The revelation of the Christian faith, how grand! the duties of the Christian life, how simple! It is as if one should plant his feet upon the earth while his head was among the stars. And yet we are not affected by any sense of incongruity as we notice this union of the loftiest truth with the most familiar experience. It never occurs to us that it is an unnatural connection; it never seems to us awkward or ludicrous : we are neither surprised nor perplexed by it. Still it is very remarkable, and strongly indicative of the Divine origin which we ascribe to Christianity.

In the life of Jesus, that best commentary upon his religion, we find the same union of great principles with the incidents of daily life. It is the character of Jesus that gives grandeur to the situations in which he is placed, not the situations that make the character appear extraordinary. He never sought to draw attention to himself by an unusual manner of life; he affected no dignity, studied no arts of impression, and in his outward relations exhibited no desire to be unlike the men among whom he lived. With singular emphasis may it be said, that he was found

in fashion as a man. If any one had come to Judea to seek
Christ, where would he have found him? Let us suppose that
the Roman Emperor, having heard of his name and the sensation
he was producing, had sent some one to inquire into the nature
or ground of his pretensions, would he have found him, like the
Grecian philosopher, walking in the groves of some academy
dedicated to contemplation? or like the Jewish Rabbi, in some
chamber of the temple, with scholars sitting at his feet? would
he have been led through many apartments to the interior of a
palace, and been received in the midst of wealth and splendor?
or have been conducted to Christ's presence through armed hosts
and all the equipment of a military array? No. If they had
looked for him in any unusual place or amidst circumstances
suited to captivate admiration by the external associations
with which they invested his person, their search would have
ended in disappointment. Three times, as we read, was Jesus
the object of such a curiosity, and where was he then found?
Once, when the Eastern sages inquired after the child whose star
had guided them to the city of David, they were obliged to turn
their feet towards the little village of Bethlehem, where he lay
in a manger. Once, when the messengers of the Sanhedrim
joined the crowds that thronged about the great Teacher, they
found him pronouncing his sublime lessons of faith and duty to
the multitudes that had congregated within the courts of the
temple, amidst the bustle and traffic and conversation that grew
out of the recurrence of one of the national festivals. And once,
when the disciples of John came with questions suggested by
their own and their master's doubts, they found him in Galilee
surrounded by the sick, the poor, and the miserable, whom his
Divine word was restoring to comfort and health. As we read
the history of our Lord, from the carpenter's house at Nazareth
or the marriage feast in Cana, to the trial in Pilate's hall or the
crucifixion on Calvary, we observe the connection of supernatural power and a spotless excellence with the habits and
scenes of ordinary life. In his person the Gospel journeyed and
tarried, toiled and rested, with men in their usual course of life's

engagements. "He keepeth company with publicans and sinners," said his enemies.

In this respect our Lord was the type of his religion, and in him was seen the pattern of a Christian life. Every thing was easy and natural, yet holy and Divine. The largest truths filled the smallest occasions, the sublimest principles penetrated the most familiar movements, even as the warmth of the great orb of day enters the vessels of the least flower, and its influence reaches to the growth that springs up in the gloomiest cavern. Now the Christian must reflect the character of his Master, and show that he understands his religion by the union which his life shall exhibit of great principles with common acts. He must carry the truths,

> "Whose height,
> Whose depth unfathomed, no man knows,"

into the relations and scenes which compose his daily life. They must control and sanctify every movement; and yet every movement must be simple, easy, made as it were unconsciously. Just as a man pursues his business or a woman attends to her domestic concerns, without thinking what are the purposes that determine action in the one case or the other. These domestic affairs, this worldly business, must not be neglected, but they must be Christianized, spiritualized, beatified. Christianity is a religion for the earth and the world, for home and society, a religion which the statesman, the merchant, and the day-laborer, the rich man, the poor man, the sick man, the mother, the girl, the child, must all feel in its continually restraining, moulding, and quickening influence, as they fulfil the engagements of their several positions. Christianity did not build the convent. Her structure is a cheerful and well-ordered home ; the school-house is of her rearing as much as the Church. She frequents the market-place and walks in the streets with a bright and gentle face. Every-day life is the scene in which she exhibits her triumph over the hostile influences of sense and sin. In the midst of the world she makes those who follow her counsels unworldly.

How? By bringing great principles into connection with little matters. By making the trader as scrupulous in regard to the least dishonesty as he would be concerning a great fraud, through the principle of integrity which Christian faith implants in his breast. By preventing the mechanic from gaining circuitously that which he would be ashamed to secure by direct means, through the conviction it establishes within him that there is an intrinsic right and wrong in conduct, which the mere form of proceeding cannot change. By keeping the farmer in strict habits of self-control, through the presence in his mind of the thought that nothing is hidden from God. By rendering us sincere, gentle, and disinterested in our domestic offices, through the sentiment of love which it infuses into the heart. By leading us to care for all human want through the benevolent sympathies which it awakens and preserves fresh within us. By restoring the authority of conscience in all questions that can arise respecting what should be done or left undone. By connecting a recognition of a law emanating from the highest source in the universe with the most casual occurrences. By giving to the whole of life a sacredness through the associations which it forms between present conduct and future experience. Christianity does not send a man away from what is pleasant or trite that he may seek out some new situation in which to manifest the forms of faith, but it tells him to do right and be a Christian just here and now. The flagrant sin it rebukes, and so does it condemn the least transgression. It knows of no venial offence, and it pays little regard to the distinctions which human laws are obliged to admit. Evil speaking is wicked, whether it break forth in malediction, or expend its force in petty calumnies. Passion is sinful, whether it lead to murder or to the suppression of kindness. Desire, if freely indulged, is as criminal as gratification. The whole heart is brought under the influence of religious truth through the principle of faith ; the whole life, through the principle of obedience.

Such is the general action of Christianity. Let me now present one or two illustrations of the connection which it establishes between the grandest truths and the most familiar circumstances. The truth that there is a God, — let us take this, the primary truth, the largest truth, the sublimest, the most sacred of all truths. Who can embrace its extent ; who fathom its meaning ? Newton stood abashed before its greatness ; the angels do not comprehend its full import. God, — the name we give to the Infinite One, the Heavenly Father, the Omniscient Judge, the Holy and the Everlasting. This name, and all that it suggests to a devout mind, Christianity associates with the most familiar part of our experience; with all we see, enjoy, suffer, *do*. For it teaches us that God is the author of every thing, and His providence the life of all life ; that the flight of the bird or the fall of the raindrop is an evidence of His power; that every pulsation of our heart proclaims His care ; that each thought which darts through our minds declares how much we are indebted to Him. There is nothing beautiful without God, from the tint on the violet's leaf to the holiness that adorns the spirit. There is nothing grand in nature or in character without Him. There is no happiness which does not flow (through how many channels !) from Him, the primal Source. There is no sorrow with which His love is not connected as its origin or its consolation. There is no act that we can perform, nor purpose that we can meditate, that can be separated from Him who has spread the law of duty over our whole existence.

Duty let us take, then, as our second illustration. The idea of duty our religion binds in with all our mental and physical experience. For, in revealing the moral character of our present life, the responsibleness under which we are placed in the midst of the circumstances that surround us, the obligation to make every thing subservient to the growth and perfection of character, it compels the true disciple, the man who believes with a steady faith, to recognize a law that touches on every relation and act of his being. He can do nothing so small that it has not a moral value. He can hide himself in no solitude so deep, that obligation will not follow him or spring up at his side. He may shut out the world from his private apartment,

32

and bury himself within its seclusion; yet from every side of that apartment may be seen the word from whose force he has endeavored to escape, shining upon him in letters of supernatural light, — that fearful word *ought*, — not more fearful in its positive than in its interrogative form, — *ought* he to live in such retirement? or, if he may leave all the common scenes of exposure, what *ought* he to do in his privacy? Capacity and opportunity only change the character of duty: no effort or choice of ours can destroy it. It is omnipresent; it is immortal; it is supreme : for it is the will and voice of God. Nothing stands on neutral ground, midway between right and wrong. There is no such neutral ground. As reasonably might we speak of a region of space between our earth and the sun where the force of attraction ceases. The moral universe is held together by the law of duty, penetrating every part and every moment, as truly as the material creation is held together by the law which keeps worlds and stars from plunging into ruin.

We all lie within the embrace of the great principle of moral responsibleness, and out of its prolific energy springs another grand truth which accommodates itself to the most trivial offices of our being. We are fellow-creatures, who owe one another disinterested kindness. The sentiment of *love* Christianity blends with all the intercourse of life. It tells us that we live in and for one another, — the rich for the poor, and the poor for the rich ; the man of thoughtful study for the man of active pursuits, and the latter for the former. The African for the American, and the American for the African ; for it makes neighborhood a synonyme for humanity, and the world the sphere over which our generous sympathies should be extended. "Love," that is another word of vast significance, as large even as the name of the Infinite, for God is love. Put a Christian interpretation on the word, take it out of the limitations within which romance and poetry, to say nothing of our selfishness, endeavor to confine it, make it mean all that Christ meant by it when he said, "Thou shalt love thy neighbor as thyself," all that the apostle meant when he said, "Love is the fulfilling of the law," — how does it spread itself over all human interests, all human affairs! A Christian must love the man whom he meets in the street, stranger though he be; the beggar who comes to his door, squalid and sinful; the individual with whom he transacts his business, be he who he may. And in the exercise of love, conscious of the feelings which an unselfish justice and a ready sympathy shall beget, he will deal with his fellow-man of whatever class, and on whatever occasion, as with a brother, — one whom he must benefit if he can, whom he must never injure, never neglect.

For his fellow-man shares with him the world which the Creator has appointed for the education of the human race, and the immortality which the Creator has bestowed on every one of that race; and the world must not be made sad, nor immortality be made an occasion of dread, instead of a subject of rejoicing, by man's inhumanity or unfaithfulness to man.

Let this truth of *immortality* suggest one more illustration of what we have said concerning the union of the highest subject of thought with the most ordinary portions of experience. Christianity instructs us to regard the future as a development and consequence of the present. Man not only will live again, but his life hereafter will be shaped and colored by his life here. The law of retribution, twin companion of the law of duty, follows us wherever we go. Our right or wrong conduct involves issues running on through an unmeasured futurity. The little drops that fall upon the bosom of the Mississippi, each no bigger than a child's tear, swell its current, till it pours its volume of waters in majesty and blessing into the ocean. The pebble that obtains a release from its position in the dam which holds those waters in check offers an entrance to the stream, which creates a wider and wider opening, till the whole structure falls before the violence of the current, that now spreads devastation over a compact city. From the acorn grows the oak, from the oak the forest; and, on the other hand, from the seed which the wind lets fall on a grassy field springs up the weed, of the weed a pernicious vegetation, and the field is given over to its ugly and unprofitable growth. So in the moral world. So in the field of individual experience, the least act well performed on the one hand, the slightest departure from right doing on the other, may beget results that shall spread themselves over years and ages. Time is the beginning of eternity, and each moment in time sends out threads that bind it to the remotest period of eternity.

Now in all this connection of the great with the small, the highest principles with the lowest departments of life, the largest truth with the least act, let us notice the perfect wisdom of God.

Life is made up of *particulars.* There are few great occasions in any one's life. Most of our experience must be common, familiar, ordinary ; and if religious truths influenced only the extraordinary moments that fall into our experience, it would be with us as it would be with the earth, did the sun-light rest on the tops of the mountains, but left the plains and valleys which constitute the greater part of its surface in darkness. Few persons can make themselves remarkable by what they shall accomplish or undertake. Most of us must occupy situations of no more than usual interest or importance. But few can be rulers or missionaries. A world full of distinguished people would be a very uncomfortable, perhaps it would not be a habitable, world. We do not want a world made up of such men as Howard or Herschel, men great in science or great in philanthropy. Let every one be great in goodness, — but that is a grandeur which may be acquired in the humblest discharge of duty. And this is the truth so precious which Christ brought forth to human view, — that in the humblest employment we may build up a perfect character by fidelity to the circumstances in which Providence has placed us, and obedience to those Divine principles which the gospel of Christ makes the guide and staff of life.

Again, our *enjoyments* come not from unusual events. Novelty imparts a zest to delight; but constant novelty would weary the heart, as a succession of rich viands soon offends or vitiates the taste. Our *familiar* joys are our best joys, — those which fill our homes with cheerfulness, and make daily life pleasant. We do not stop to analyze our satisfaction ; and it is

well that we do not, for we should then act like children who
tear their pretty toys in pieces to learn how they are made: but,
if we did, we should find they arise out of our usual relations,
out of the necessary dependence and labor of life, out of what
God has spread in profusion around us, and what we are continually, though unconsciously, converting into the material of
happiness, even as our lungs convert the air they breathe into the
nourishment of our being. Is it not agreeable to our own judgment of what a wise Father would arrange, that the great principles by which we must be controlled should connect themselves
with the little rills that fertilize the heart, rather than with the
torrents that may sometimes pour themselves over our consciousness with a force of joy almost too great for us to bear?

Yet again, our heavy *sorrows* do not come with every hour, or
cloud every sunrise. Storms do not compose the years, nor does
the east wind prevail through the greater number of the months.
The storms have their use, and the east wind accomplishes a
beneficent end; and so do out great afflictions render us a service for which they are needed. But our frequent trials are
light trials: they are the little annoyances of every moment, that
require patience towards man as well as faith towards God.
Now what so proper, or so needful, as that we should bring the
eternal laws of the moral world, the elements of religion, into
connection with these details of experience, that so we may be
steadfast, immovable, always abounding in the work of the
Lord? The crimes of men are not so numerous as their vices ;
their vices are not so numerous as their foibles. The foible
grows into the vice; the vice ripens into the crime. And so,
because we neglect the germ, the fruit is bitter and noxious.
Let us begin with truth and duty and God, let us make Christ
the ruler of conscience and the pattern of life in little things,
and we shall both frame and cement an excellence which shall
deprive the trials that now disturb our peace of all power, like
walls of stone upon which poisoned arrows fall harmless.

We may now perceive both the justice and the extent of the
law of which our text is the expression, " He that is faithful

in that which is least is faithful also in much, and he that is un-just in the least is unjust also in much ; " a law inseparable from the rectitude of the Divine Providence, and conducive to the wel-fare of man. I will but add two brief remarks, which are sug-gested as of most practical value. First, in regard to ourselves. Let it be our object to establish Christian habits. Our habits constitute our character. Let them be pervaded and moulded by the religion of Christ. Let our faith become habitual, our piety habitual, our benevolence habitual. Let duty become a habit. Then shall we be safe ; then will life be pleasant and holy.

Secondly, in regard to our children. Let us implant in them right principles. They must form their own habits, but we can fix their principles. Out of the latter will arise the former. Let us establish in their hearts the great principles of piety and duty, and they will be prepared to meet the temptations and bear the responsibilities of life.

With good habits growing out of right principles in ourselves, and right principles growing up into good habits in our children, why should we not be as happy as in this life of vicissitude man can ever be? We shall have nothing to fear on this side the grave, since we shall be prepared for all change in outward condition by the inward stability we shall maintain. Nor shall we have reason to dread what we may encounter hereafter ; since, having been faithful in that which is least, as it arose under the various relations of life, we shall receive the approbation of Him whose welcome voice shall pronounce the sentence : " Well done, good and faithful servant : thou hast been faithful over a few things, I will make thee ruler over many things : enter thou into the joy of thy Lord."

1858.

" LIFE."

THE doctrine of " Life," though it has not received from Christian men the attention to which from its place in the Gos-pel it is entitled, is really the heart of the Gospel, the innermost of what may justly be styled the doctrines of grace. " I am come," said Jesus, "that they might have life, and that they might have it more abundantly." How could he have described the design of his mission in plainer words? Abundance of life, — growth, force, satisfaction, — all that enters into our idea of a vigorous vitality, — this is the ultimate purpose of the Divine economy in Christ. And that life the Christian realizes through a faith which enables him to appropriate the Saviour's words to his own use, while a work of assimilation to his Master is going on within him. Blessed dependence of the believer on Him in whom are such treasures of heavenly grace, that, though the world should through uncounted generations live upon him, his ability to meet the demands of their souls would be as great as at the first! He only will be slow to accept this statement who is unable to see in spiritual truth an infinite capacity of reproduction; of which Jesus having the control, the miracle of the loaves becomes the type of a Divine work perpetually renewed, and thousands are fed, and countless thousands will be fed, so long as there are any that need.

I have beheld many of the fairest works of the Creative Hand, I have admired, too, the productions of human skill; but never, never among the works of man or God, have I seen that which enkindled such admiration or delight as the result of the combined agencies of Divine and human will in the character of one who, through a living union with Christ, had translated " the beauty of holiness " from a figure of speech to a visible and unfading reality.

What a grand spectacle is a true life, — severe in its rectitude, sublime in its purpose, beneficent in its action; a life devoted to God, though spent among men; a life sincere and therefore fresh, laborious and therefore useful, above low aims and mean arts; wise in its faith, generous in its ardor, sweet in its spirit, devout in its aspiration! How do the honors and praises and pleasures of the world fade into dimness before the splendor of a righteousness like this! What a depth of Divine philosophy was there in that saying, commonplace as it may seem to us who have heard it read from our childhood, " A man's life consisteth not in the abundance of the things which he possesseth " ! Now can we understand that oft recurring language of the New Testament, which portrays the believer's privilege in terms which the wildest enthusiasm seems to have borrowed from the boldest rhetoric, — men and women caught up from obscurity and constituted " kings and priests unto God," sinners lifted from the dust and called to have their " fellowship with the Father and the Son," the poor assured that all things are theirs, the miserable filled with a peace such as the world can neither give nor take away, the friendless made " heirs of God and joint-heirs with Christ." What a legacy to Christendom was language like this! What a burthen of blessing for us to have received! And when I think that we owe this " inheritance of the saints," into which we enter through faith, to Him who died that we might live, I am eager to join in the Apocalyptic ascription of glory and dominion " unto him that loved us, and has washed us from our sins in his own blood."

My friends, as I read the religious history of past times or of our own, it devolves on us, and those who agree with us in religious belief, rather than on any other portion of the Church, to proclaim the truth which has formed the subject of our remarks. By the concurrence of all other denominations in upholding some dogma or practice, some specific confession or experience, as the test of Christian discipleship, it has fallen to us to vindicate the supremacy of Christ's glorious doctrine of Life. In the articles of organization adopted not long ago by a Unitarian Society in one of the Western States of the American Union, occurs the statement, that " believing salvation rests, not on superficial observance of rites, nor on intellectual assent to creeds, nor on any arbitrary decree, but, under the grace of God, on the rightness of the ruling affection, on humble faithfulness of life, and integral goodness of character," its members desired to " go forth and live the Christian life, not as a form, but as a principle, with a warmer philanthropy, a holier consecration, a deeper piety, a more united front, than they had yet shown, in the fear and affection of God, in the faith and love of Christ." That was language worthy of the men from whom it came, worthy of the doctrine which they and we hold to be "the truth as it is in Jesus." It is on such a confession as this that we must build the hope of visible growth or denominational force. That a sect may acquire stability or exert a control over opinion, it must rest on an affirmative basis. A negative position can preserve it from decay only so long as it shall be quickened by a spirit of antagonism, which after a time, thank God, must lose its energy. Antagonism is an active, but not a lifegiving principle. The soul can be nourished on it no more than the body can thrive on the stimulus of strong drink. For the support of a denomination, it must likewise have something more positive than love of freedom ; for, noble as is the vindication of the soul's right to be taught by Christ himself, freedom is but the removal of obstacles to the enjoyment of that right. In its essence it is denial, or the negation of restraint; and therefore to build up a denomination with the cement of liberty is like laying masonry with quicksilver, — the parts will not cohere. It is the office of each sect to represent some truth of which it is the discoverer or the guardian. Its place in the Church can be accounted for in no other way; and, unless it be loyal to the truth of which it is the representative, it must perish.

Now I say that the truth which distinguishes our religious body is that of which our text is the concise yet sufficient expression; which other portions of the Church, indeed, have not always failed to recognize as a part of the gospel, — how could they, when it was so plain? — but which they have treated with comparative neglect. It is our office to rescue it from such neglect. I claim for it priority and sovereignty. At once doctrine and commandment, it covers the whole of faith and the whole of duty. Men have done well to lay stress on the atonement, for without it the soul is lost; but the atonement is only the initial experience, of which life is the continuance and consummation. They have done well to warn the sinner that his ways are the ways of death; but the great evil of that death is that it is the absence of life. They have done well to turn the thought of the believer on a future world, that he might not be seduced by the temptations of the present ; but it is a higher view of heaven to regard it as the expansion of that elementary life of which the soul may become conscious here, than to represent it as distant, remote, intangible. Continuous life, ever more vigorous, ever more abundant, this is the promise of Christ to his disciples. Under a just interpretation of this promise, the world becomes a scene of spiritual education. Our common employments, reflecting the radiance of heaven, are changed into saintly offices, as the windows of our houses are turned into sheets of gold by the western light. Religion, disowning.nothing that is necessary or beautiful, recognizes the worth of familiar sympathies and social pleasures. As this house, dedicated to the worship of God, receives the ornament of these graceful vines and brilliant flowers as in harmony with its sacred character, so may the consecrated life be adorned with the fair and rich courtesies of neighborhood and brotherly kindness. Our whole life, outward and inward, may be " hidden with Christ in God," because it shall all — all, from meanest toil to holiest prayer — be that living sacrifice, of which Christ is both the author and the type.

As I think of the power which resides in this truth to lay hold on the consciences and hearts of men, I long to see, not here and there one, but many who shall take it up and make themselves benefactors of the people, by saying unto them, In the name of Christ the Lord, I command you to *live.* That which you now call life is not worthy of the name. What a mean and wearisome thing it is ; what a burthen and a curse you make of your existence ! It is not *life* to bury one's self in worldliness or to drown one's self in pleasure. Man of business, I tell you to pour a new vitality into your affairs, — the vitali·y of faith, which shall render success inevitable, however small your pecuniary gain. Care-worn woman, bright-eyed girl, I tell you to infuse into your plans for the day and the year the spirit of immortality, that you may neither now nor hereafter pine over inevitable disappointment. Theologian, ritualist, formalist, cast away your traditions, your ceremonies, your conventional morals, your ascetic piety, and accept now, now, the life everlasting.

Oh for the men who shall preach " Christ the life of the world," with a zeal ready to cry out, Woe is me, if I preach not the living gospel! O God! raise thou up another Wesley, another Luther, another Paul, with the gospel of life in their hearts and on their tongues, to send it through the land, across the sea, around the earth! O Christ! inspire thou another John with thine own temper, that his words, like those of thine apostle, may be full of persuasion, declaring that " God so loved us, that He sent His only begotten Son into the world, that we might live through him."

" That we might live through him." Bear these words in your remembrance, believer, wherever you go: they shall be your defence and your solace. Repeat them in the ears of your fellow-men: the weary heart of society will listen and rejoice. Pronounce them where sin gathers its votaries, and the dead shall start into life. Inscribe them on the tomb, and our burial-places shall be known as the gateways of immortality.

1849–1850.

IMPORTANCE OF OPINIONS AS THE BASIS OF A RELIGIOUS LIFE.

EVERY man has a theology of his own. He may not know it ; he may not know the meaning of the word ; but what then ? Every man has his theory of health, though he may never have heard of physiology or dietetics. He believes that he must eat and sleep and work, or that he must avoid this or that indulgence, if he would be well, and he practises accordingly ; yet, were you to ask him what hygienic treatment he pursued, he might stare at you in amazement. It has been said that words are things; but people often get the things without the words they are called by. "What can a poor woman," it is asked, "who must work all the day to earn bread for her children, and at night perhaps can only with much painstaking read a chapter in her Bible, know of the science of theology? What does she need to know of it? Is she not the better without it?" Of theology as a science she knows nothing, and needs to know nothing; but of that which constitutes the substance of theology she knows a great deal. Of the principles which regul te the transmission of caloric from her scanty fire through the atmosphere to her limbs, or determine the fitness of one sort of garment rather than another to protect her against the winter's cold, she is profoundly ignorant; but with the great facts and relations that exist between the fuel she consumes, the clothing she wears, and her own physical condition, she is entirely conversant. So are the great spiritual facts and relations, which are best ascertained through experience, familiar to her, although she be a stranger to the reasonings that might explain, or the principles that underlie, those facts and relations. Take away her knowledge of these, her *heart-knowledge* of them, and you leave her to a destitution of which her former poverty was not even a type, a wretchedness of which she had had no conception before, because you take from her her knowledge of God's providence and will, her faith in God, her theology.

No, it may be said hers is what you have called it, *heart-knowledge*, while theology belongs to the mind. In the first instance, certainly; and the lowly Christian of whom we have spoken received it into her heart through her mind. The difference between her and the man who has legitimated his conclusions by reasoning and study is simply this, — that the ideas which she has received pass at once into her heart, and there become sentiments and habits, and as such, rather than as ideas, are entertained by her, while with him they remain long, perhaps always, among the furniture of his mind, and are there examined as mental conceptions. He is a theologian, she is not; but she has a theology as well as he, and with her as well as with him its foundation is truth apprehended by the intellect. Ideas are essential to religion, — its basis, its groundwork, its fountain.

There is a kind of discourse on this subject, which — I would say with all possible respect for those who use it — appears to me to be either void of meaning or full of mischief. Religion is sentiment, we are told, and not doctrine; love, and not belief; spiritual experience, and not intellectual discrimination. Now what sentiment is there which does not have its origin in thought, what love that does not flow from a belief concerning the object of the affection, what inward experience that can be disjoined from all intellectual activity? The instinctive love of the parent recognizes truths respecting her child which determine the character and intensity of her affection; the love of the child, the moment it passes beyond a mere animal clinging to the care that nourishes it, contemplates certain realities on which its little mind passes judgment. Our moral sentiments do not disown their dependence on the mind. That is the background on which they are formed, as truly as the figures on the painter's canvas derive their life from what he puts behind them. Our aspirations after purity and bliss, after heaven and God, spring out of our ideas concerning God and heaven and holiness and happiness. The seraph's rapture is the fire of an intellectual conception. A religion of mere sentiment, like the watery appearances of the desert, will be found neither to afford refreshment nor to have any substance. A purely æsthetic piety, like the gorgeousness of the clouds, neither gives warmth nor promises permanence; it is not worth talking about, in prose or in poetry.

Again, we are told that religion is life and not dogma, obedience and not faith; and we assent to the remark, when interpreted as common sense and experience should teach us to receive it. The life is the essential thing; but what consistency or practical worth will there be in a life which is not governed by fixed rules or proper motives? and what are rules or motives but the conclusions at which the mind arrives in its inquiries

after duty? Obedience is what God requires; but how shall
we become obedient, if we remain in ignorance alike of the
Being whom we should obey and the service we should render?
and how can such ignorance be removed, except by implanting
in the mind certain notions respecting God and His law? In
the last analysis, the religious life must be reduced to a practical
use of certain convictions which the mind accepts. They may
be many or few, they may be correct or incorrect; but on their
character and strength will depend the growth, stability, and
reality of the religious life. . . .

But the sharp discrimination of religious ideas, it is said, opens
the door to sectarianism with all its evils. Better to live in some
indistinctness of thought than to covet a precision of faith that
will only separate us from our Christian brethren. Not so, I
say. It is not better to dwell in a mist than in a clear atmosphere, even if we must go a little distance from our neighbors
to get the blue sky. If the possession of a well-formed belief
separate us from others in some of the conclusions we may
adopt, it unites us to them through the respect and confidence
which are mutually entertained by those who know that each
has been faithful in his inquiries, and values his faith because it
is the result of honest investigation. Of all foolish notions, I
know of none more idle than the error, which some people
defend, that Christians will come nearer to one another when
they cease from an attempt to construct for themselves a precise
and positive faith. How do men that live in darkness find out
that they are near one another, except as they may jostle, or by
their cries affright, one another? It is only when each one
knows where he stands and where others stand that they can
really measure the distance between them; and then it will
probably be found to be less than they had supposed. But this
dread of sectarianism which almost makes monomaniacs of some
persons, it is only an example of the vagueness of thought in
which they delight. . . . I believe in sectarianism as a legitimate consequence of an earnest faith. What a man esteems to
be the gospel is his gospel; and what he values as God's most

precious gift he should be anxious to communicate to others. This is sectarianism, — warm and practical attachment to a cer tain interpretation of the Christian records, in which an indi vidual agrees with some persons, and differs from others. Of this sectarianism I wish the country and the world were full. Let a man speak and act as if he prized what he receives as Divine truth. Let him desire for others a participation with himself in its comforts and hopes. Let him expend generous and vigorous effort in diffusing around him, through the land, over the world, the doctrines which he associates with the being of a God and the mediation of Christ. Let him join heart and hand with those who accept the same doctrines ; and while he loves all who love the Lord Jesus Christ in sincerity, let his action be most strenuous, his connection most close, with those with whom he can act most freely, and yet most cordially. Such a secta rianism as this I should rejoice to see on every side. It would make us all better Christians. It would fill the earth with the knowledge of the Lord, and carry out the spirit of the prayer which we learned in our childhood, — " Thy kingdom come," — and of that other prayer which was uttered amidst the sympa thies of the last night of the Saviour's ministry, — " I in them, and thou in me, that they may be made perfect in one."

For such a sectarianism does not produce bitterness or strife ; but, on the contrary, nourishes a spirit of candor and Christian brotherhood. It may sound paradoxical, but I believe it is unde niably true, that an enlightened sectarianism is the root from which must spring a true charity ; because an enlightened secta rianism, being founded on an intelligent acquaintance with both the principles and the grounds of the belief which it cherishes, and also with the principles and grounds of the various forms of belief around it, cannot be betrayed into injustice through igno rance, nor be led into a passionate defence of its own positions by a consciousness of inability to maintain them by calm and clear argument. And, further still, it allows and respects in others the rights which it exercises itself, and thinks all the better of a theological opponent for his open and resolute vindication of his own faith. Bigots are generally men or narrow habits of thought, of little study, and very imperfect theological education. A man whose conclusions are the result of careful investigation will seldom be irritated by the remarks of others, and will never deny to them the privilege of independent thought. Uncharitableness and persecution have arisen, not from men's holding definite opinions on religious subjects, but from their attempting to impose those opinions on others, or from their maintaining that others must be in sinful and fatal error, because they differ from them. It is the claim of infallibility, not the sincerity of personal conviction, that has filled the Church with discord, and made both Catholic and Protestant inquisitors. The Church will be full of love when liberty of thought is allowed and accuracy of thought is made an object of desire. Every man should be Orthodox in his own estimation, and every one should let his fellow-Christians call themselves Orthodox too. It is not taking the name ourselves that makes the trouble, but the denying of the name to others.

"Ah, but then there will be sects!" Yes, there will be, and there always have been. There were sects in the first age of our religion, and there will be sects to its last age. And if by sects you mean companies of believers holding different views of truth, then there will be sects in heaven. And I thank God for it; for then there may be improvements, — growth in knowledge and growth in love. What can be more absurd than to suppose that finite minds shall ever apprehend all the facts of the spiritual universe alike. Why, that is to clothe them with the attributes of Omniscience. Paul and Peter did not think just alike when they were engaged in preaching the Gospel on earth, nor do I believe that their spiritual perceptions are now precisely alike. I hope heaven is not a monotone of thought.

Let us strive, then, to have clear and settled opinions in religion. Away with that wretched habit of indecision and instability in regard to Christian doctrines, which saps the very life of the soul. Disown it, discard it. It deprives us of the comfort and benefit of faith. It prevents our being believers, and it hinders us from becoming inquirers. It is fatal to a healthy development of the religious nature. It is the modern Anti-Christ. The vice of the present day in many neighborhoods is not scepticism, but doctrinal indifference, and that is unfaithfulness to our own souls and ingratitude to God, who has given us the truth which those souls need, but which some among us appear unwilling to accept. I do not ask men to believe as I believe, but I implore them to have a belief of their own, whether it be like mine or not. I can respect a whole-souled Catholic, but I can only pity a half-Protestant. I can see something to admire in genuine and hearty Calvinism, but I can only condemn and deplore equivocal Unitarianism. Be something, for the truth's sake, and for the sake of your own honor and your own hope. Be a Trinitarian or a Unitarian. You cannot be both, you cannot be neither. See which you are. Believe in the natural depravity of man and the vicarious atonement of Christ, or disbelieve them. You cannot hold to both. No man can serve two masters, and no man can hold two opposite opinions. Do you say you have no opinions? Then you are much to be pitied. Do you say you wish to have none? Then you are much to be censured. Do you say you are a Christian and that is all you wish to be, then we rejoice with you that you are something. But to be a Christian is more than to take the name or to believe in the divinity of Christ's mission. " He that heareth these sayings of mine," are his words, — " he that heareth these sayings of mine, and doeth them, I will liken him unto a wise man, who built his house upon a rock." We must keep his sayings ; and, that we may keep them in any profitable or practical sense, we must understand them. That is what he means by " hearing" them, — discovering their import and accepting them as true. Without faith we cannot please God. And without faith we cannot obey Christ. Personal religion has no solid or durable basis, except in spiritual convictions ; and these convictions are the soul's private property, its well-digested belief, its interpretation of Divine truth, its religious opinions.

WHAT UNITARIANS BELIEVE.

1845.

I SPEAK not with any authority except such as belongs to honest private conviction, and a somewhat large acquaintance with the opinions entertained by other Unitarian believers here and elsewhere. They have no accepted creed which I may quote, no formularies of faith nor symbolical books which they recognize as containing the only accredited exposition of their views, and no ecclesiastical body from which such an exposition might emanate. The right and duty of personal inquiry, which are the elementary principles of their religious state, preclude any attempt to utter other than private persuasions or the impressions which a wide and careful observation may have given. Such observation will lead any one to a knowledge of certain great doctrines which are held in common by Unitarians in America and in Europe, and will show that they accord in respect to the grounds of their belief, and in their dissent from many popular representations of the Gospel.

What are the truths of Unitarian Christianity? What do Unitarians believe?

We believe in God, as the Supreme, Perfect, and Infinite Being, Lord of heaven and earth, Author of all life, Source of every blessing, Searcher of hearts, and Judge of men. We believe in His universal, constant, and righteous providence, through which alone the frame-work of the creation and the processes of animate or inanimate existence are sustained. We believe in His moral government, which He exercises over all beings endowed with intellectual or moral capacities, and which, as it is rightfully exercised, so is inflexibly administered. We believe in His paternal character, in which He has been pleased to reveal Himself to our admiration and love; a character which never shows Him to us as weakly indulgent or capriciously tender, but as always consistent with His own perfections while full of parental regard towards men. We believe in the requisitions of duty which He has promulgated, by which are laid upon us the obligations of outward and inward righteousness, and it is made incumbent on us to cultivate purity, devotion, disinterestedness, and the harmonious expansion of our nature, that the result may be an excellence which shall redound to the glory of God. We believe in His mercy, which enables Him, without impairing the integrity of His government or subverting the original conditions of His favor, to forgive the penitent sinner and admit the renewed soul to an inheritance of eternal life. We believe in His revelations, which He has made by those of old times who spake as they were moved by the Holy Spirit, — Moses and the Divinely inspired teachers of the Jewish people, and in a later age by Jesus Christ, the Son of His love and the Messenger of His grace. We believe that God is one in every sense in which the term can be applied to Him, — one in nature, in person, in character, in revelation ; and therefore we are Unitarians.

We believe that Jesus was the Christ, — the Anointed and Sent of God, whose truth he proclaimed, whose authority he represented, whose love he unfolded ; and therefore we are Christians. We believe that Jesus Christ came on a special mission to our world, — to instruct the ignorant, to save the sinful, and to give assurance of immortality to those who were subject to death ; that such a Teacher and Redeemer was needed ; that he spake as never man spake, lived as never man lived, and died as never man died. We read the history of his life with mingled admiration and gratitude. We are moved by his cross to exercises of faith, penitence, and hope. We rejoice in his resurrection, and celebrate him as Head of his Church, the authoritative Expounder of the Divine will, the faultless Pattern of the Christian character, the Manifestation and Pledge of the true life.

We believe that man is a free and responsible being, capable of rising to successive heights of virtue, or of falling into deeper and deeper degradation ; that sin is his ruin, and faith in spiritual and eternal realities the means of his salvation ; that if he sin, it is through choice or negligence, but that in working out his own salvation he needs the Divine assistance. We believe that man in his individual person is from early childhood, through the force of appetite, the disadvantage of ignorance, and the strength of temptation, liable to moral corruption ; that social life is in many of its forms artificial, and in many of its influences injurious; and that both the individual and society must be regenerated by the action of Christian truth.

We believe that all life, private and public, all human powers and relations, all thought, feeling, and activity, should be brought under the control of religious principle and be pervaded by Christian sentiment. We believe that piety is the only sure foundation of morality, and morality the needed evidence of piety. We believe that " perfection from weakness through progress " is the law of life for man ; and that this law can be kept only where an humble heart is joined with a resolute mind and an earnest faith. We believe that men should love and serve one another, while all love the Heavenly Father, and follow the Lord Jesus to a common glory.

We believe in human immortality and a righteous retribution after death; when they who have lived in obedience or have reconciled themselves to God through sincere repentance shall enter upon a nobler fruition of life, while they who have been disobedient and impenitent shall realize the consequences of their folly in shame and suffering.

We believe in the Scriptures of the Old and New Testaments, as containing the authentic records of God's wonderful and gracious ways, seen in the history of His ancient people, and in the miraculous works and Divine teachings of Jesus and his Apostles, and to these Scriptures we appeal as the decisive authority upon questions of faith or duty, interpreting them in the devout exercise of that reason through which alone we are capable of receiving a communication from Heaven.

We believe in the Christian Church, as a consequence of the labors and sufferings by which Christ has gathered unto himself, out of many nations and communions, "a peculiar people," embracing his Gospel and cherishing his˙ spirit, — the Church on earth, with its ministry, its ordinances and its responsibilities, the anticipation and promise of the Church in heaven.

Such are the prominent truths of Unitarian Christianity, I conceive, as held by those who adopt this name as the designation of their faith, and who, however they may disagree on questions of inferior moment, would probably concur in this exhibition of the articles of their belief.

1849.

There is a Unitarian theology. It includes our faith in God, in Christ, in man ; in the moral character and the final issues of the present life; in the Father whom we worship, in the Son whom we honor, in the Holy Spirit which we receive; in our own capacity, and frailty; in the vileness and peril of sin; in the Gospel as a Divine gift; in progress as the law of man's being, and in perfection as its end ; in spiritual renovation, and spiritual experience; in love as the great principle of sanctification, and in eternal life as its consequence and reward. I would not be guilty of the presumption of forming a creed for others but is there one of us, brethren, that would hesitate to acknowledge these as articles of his belief? They constitute the framework of our theology. They include the revealed, fundamental, vital truths of religion.

Where is your Unitarian theology? it is said. In the Bible, we reply. In our hearts, again we reply. And I would add, Here, in the doctrines of which I have now given the briefest statement. The existence, perfection, and unity of God, the universality and tenderness of His providence, the integrity of His government, the Divine authority of Jesus of Nazareth, the perpetual obligation of obedience, the efficacy of repentance, the exercise of mercy as sealed to the believer in the blood of the cross, the certainty of retribution, the promise of immortality, — are these empty words or disconnected phrases? Is there no substance nor consistency in these forms of thought? We have a theology, — a definite, compact theology. Besides its reason-ableness and its Scriptural origin, in both which respects we claim for our faith the superiority over other forms of belief, it has the other three marks by which we distinguish a sound and true theology from that which is false : it is positive, con-sistent, and efficacious.

A *positive* theology. It consists in affirmation, not in denial. "The Unitarians have only a negative faith," say religious jour-nalists and Christian preachers all over the country ; and the people believe them. And yet a more palpable falsehood never came from the pen or tongue of mortal man ! Our theology at this very moment is better settled than that of half the Protestant sects about us. On every one of the great points of religious interest, our conceptions are not less distinct, and are much more uniform, than those which we find in other denominations. And a *consistent* as well as a positive theology. Its truths do not contradict one another, but have the essential characteristic of a science, — that they support and depend upon one another. Around the central fact of man's being, our great truths of Divine beneficence, mercy, and judgment, and all the associated doctrines of Christian faith, arrange themselves by a law, I will not say, of moral crystallization, but of spiritual attraction. But most of all do I value our theological tenets for their *spiritual quality and efficacy.* Their moral power is their glory. They place truths before the soul in an attitude which compels its submission ; truths which quicken and invigorate the con-science, warm and cleanse the heart, at once control and sustain the will. They are " the power of God, and the wisdom of God unto salvation to every one that believeth."

But again, if any one ask what are its truths, the answer may be that they are the truths on which the various bodies of Christians concur. They are *the common Christianity of all sects.* By our positive views of doctrine, we are brought into sympathy with the universal Church. Where, then, is our pecu-liar theology ? Why, just here. The peculiarity of our belief consists in our making the Christianity of all denominations the true exposition of the Gospel. It is painful to remark how slow men are in perceiving that our elevation of the current opinions of the Church into the place of essential truths of religion, and our refusal to allow any other opinions to share this distinction, may constitute as decisive a peculiarity as any novelty of statement or vehemence of expression. It is peculiar to us, it distinguishes us, that we make the catholic belief the true belief. If we alone maintain the sufficiency of this belief, what can more distinctly mark us than this very fact? The substantial difference between us and other Christians, I conceive, lies not so much in diversity of opinion upon certain questions of dogmatic theology as in the recognition by us of the right of every sincere follower of Jesus to the name and hope of a Christian, to whatever denomination he may belong, while others require the exercise or expression of faith in certain tenets peculiar to themselves. We of course prefer our own interpretation of Scripture, and wish that every one might see with us that it is the proper interpretation; we consider many of the errors that prevail around us pernicious. But we do not think that any one, whose heart is searched and his life controlled by the great truths which the various Christian bodies accept, can be in fatal error. The essential theology, therefore, according to us, is found in all these bodies; and this essential theology being, as I have said, that which remains after we have thrown away what gives a special character to the symbols of these several bodies, our peculiarity consists in making the common faith of the Church the essential faith of the believer.

This seems to members of other communions a very meagre faith, — nothing but what every Christian believes! Once concurrence with those who constituted the household of the saints was regarded as a just ground of satisfaction; but now, unless one add something to the common inheritance, he is thought to have " denied the faith " and to be " worse than an infidel." It is made of little account to adore the incomprehensible greatness of God, unless one also believes in a certain mode of the Divine existence; to prostrate one's self in gratitude before the cross of the Redeemer, unless he accept a particular explanation of the efficacy of his death; to tremble under the sense of moral responsibleness and the consciousness of sin, unless he admit that we are wholly ruined, and incapable of ourselves to take a step towards a holy life! How is it possible to put greater dishonor on the fundamental truths of religion, than to pronounce them, not only logically incomplete, but morally inadequate? . . .

Attempts have been made again and again to take our love of freedom as the basis of union: but it is too broad a basis; it occupies too much ground for the superstructure. Some of us prefer the title of Liberal Christians to any other designation, because it expresses our candor, and especially our attachment to the great, miscalled Protestant, principle of the right of private judgment. But it is not the name by which we may best be described; it does not define, does not limit us enough. If love of religious liberty be the ground of our denominational union, then Christians of every denomination may belong to us; for there are many in every church who prize their own freedom as dearly, and are as prompt to respect the rights of others, as we. Nay, men of no Christian denomination may belong to us; for the love of mental freedom may burn in the breasts of those who have not entered into visible connection with any body of believers. Nay, further, free-thinkers of every name and every class, men who stand in antagonism to every thing but liberty, may belong to us; for they may all be actuated by a sincere regard for the rights of thought and of conscience. Now I have no objection to a union of all sorts of men on this basis. It may have its advantages and its pleasures, but the union which we need is of a different kind. Our sympathy and co-operation must have a basis of doctrinal agreement. I care little for the name we may take or be known by; perhaps it was an unwise choice which, in its result, has doomed us to be called, if we are called by any distinctive appellation, Unitarians. But that our union, our existence as a body acting together in mutual confidence and for certain great purposes, must rest on our theological persuasions, appears to me just as clear as that the union of the States which compose our republic must rest, not on the common love of civil liberty which animates the hearts of the people, nor on any circumstances of geographical position or historical association, but on the principles, the integrity, and the authority of that Constitution which the people of these United States have agreed to take as the expression and security of their political connection.

1871.

NOT in any spirit of arrogance or injustice to other denominations are these views presented, but rather in the exercise of that same right and the discharge of that same duty which we would accord to all other sects; believing that every Christian body, large or small, has a right, and is bound, to promulgate its opinions, to make them, if possible, intelligible to the community, and to circulate them as widely as possible, with the hope of bringing others to entertain the same belief with themselves. Each denomination, of course, thinks that it holds the truth, or it has no right to exist. I do not conceive that there is any impertinence in such assumption. On the contrary, it seems to me that an individual who does not believe that he holds more nearly the exact truth as it is in Christ than those who differ from him should retire at once to his closet, open his Bible, and ask God to teach him what is truth. We undertake to expound the way of God, as we think, more perfectly — that is, with a nearer approach to a full and just statement of religious truth — than other denominations. This is all we propose to do. Not to assail them; surely not to misrepresent them, nor to discourage them, if it were possible to throw discouragement upon their labors.

OBJECTIONS ANSWERED: A COMMON FAITH.

But, in any such attempt, we meet at once with an objection which I wish for a moment to consider. It is said that Unitarians do not agree among themselves, and therefore that they

cannot give any common statement of their faith.   Is it in fact
fatally true of our body that we are so disintegrated that we are
not bound together by any sympathies of faith?   Is it, indeed,
more true of us, if we would look beneath the surface, and go
behind verbal confessions, than of other religious bodies, who,
(God help their consciences!), accepting a common phraseology,
put very different interpretations upon the same words?   Is
there not a substantial agreement among Unitarians?   Are there
not certain great fundamental truths which they universally, or,
at least, generally, accept?   Are there not points of difference
between themselves and other religious bodies which may be
properly and intelligently stated?   The Boston Board of Trade
once passed through a very warm discussion in regard to a certain subject which had been brought before them.   They differed,—differed earnestly, as honest, intelligent men should differ.
But, if I should thence infer that there were not certain great
underlying principles in regard to trade and business on which
the Board of Trade concurred, I should make a sad mistake.
So we may come and give you what is the prevalent doctrine
amongst us; and, if any one dissents from it, allow him not only
the right of dissent, but the opportunity, if we may, of expressing that dissent.

THE RIGHT OF PRIVATE JUDGMENT.

But the objection is pressed still further.   It is said, "You
Unitarians cannot agree upon any common statement of belief,
because you allow the right of private judgment.   You say that
every man may and must decide for himself; that he must read
the Bible with his own eyes, draw thence his own conclusions,
frame them into his own creed, if he is willing to have a creed,
and then he must stand by that, whether others will concur with
him or rebuke him."   Yes, we do stand on the right and duty
of private judgment; a right which we will not attempt to evade,
a duty which we shall not, I hope, neglect; granting it to every
one else, while we claim it and exercise it for ourselves.   And
in doing this we but follow noble examples.   We are Protes-

tants of the Protestants, as truly as Paul was " a Hebrew of the Hebrews." And from this principle of private judgment, of Christian liberty, — the corner-stone, we are willing to admit, of all real Christian faith and all true Christian action, — from this principle our fathers drew, and we still draw, attachment to that form of ecclesiastical organization which alone we accept for our churches. We are *Congregationalists* to the very last drop of our hearts' blood. We will let no hierarchy ; we will let no church, though it write *Infallible* over its doors; we will let no pope, though his church choose to write *Infallibility* on his brow ; we will let no company of fellow-men, let them be ever so venerable or honorable, honest or wise; we will let no association of churches, however sincere or earnest, — come within the walls of any of our congregations and say what shall be believed or what shall be done there. Every church stands on its own immunities, its own privileges, and its own responsibilities. That is Congregationalism, and we are Congregationalists ; not we alone, but other bodies with us larger still. But no religious body in New England or elsewhere can be called more strictly a Congregationalist body than we.

THE VALUE OF FAITH.

But there is still another objection which we must meet. We are told that we care very little about faith. " Unitarians," it is said, " talk about goodness ; hope to be saved by their own good works, their own good temper ; " or, when the charge is more mildly brought, it is said we exaggerate the importance of righteousness, and therefore underrate the necessity of faith. With all modesty, and yet with all firmness, such as belongs to the subject, would I deny this allegation. I say we do not undervalue faith, but we hold it to be essential to a religious experience and to a happy life. Now there are two kinds of faith, and we believe in the necessity of both kinds. There is a faith of the mind, an intellectual faith, which receives certain truths, and endeavors to extract from them their meaning, lays up that meaning among the stores of mental learning, and there leaves it. Now, that kind of faith, though it be called barren, is yet needful, for there can be no other faith without it. That is the root. If you plant a root in the ground, and cover it up, and prevent its springing up and spreading out and bringing forth fruit, you may say it is of no use; but the root must be in the ground, or there will be no tree, no foliage, and no fruit. So ideas must be lodged in the mind, — religious ideas, — and they are the roots of character. But we are sometimes reminded that religious sentiment lies at the basis of religious life. It does sometimes; but it is not a safe reliance, friends. In the common course of events, religious sentiment may carry one forward toward perfection; but in the strain and stress of life, and when doubts come up and questions arise on this side and on that, we must have thought, and thought must grasp ideas, and those ideas must be religious ideas, and religious ideas make up one kind of faith.

But there is another kind of faith. To return again to our comparison: the root must appear before the branch, and must bring forth whatever is its characteristic product; and so faith must bring forth its own kind of excellence. Christian faith must produce Christian graces. The faith of the Gospel being planted in the soul must then quicken all the energies of the soul and cause them to expand; that is, to ripen, and to yield the fruits of salvation and life. If the faith of the mind does not thus become the faith of the heart, the intelligence, the will, it may be called, as it was by the Apostle, a "dead" faith. Sensible men will say it is an absurdity. We must invest our religious ideas in character, in life, and then they will not only be safe, but they will be profitable.

We believe, then, in the importance of faith, and we show you its twofold nature. We stand where Paul stood, when he said that "a man is justified by faith," — that is, made acceptable before God, and led by the Divine goodness toward righteousness, in consequence of his belief in, and use of, the great Christian ideas; and we stand where James stood, when he said that the mere mental reception of such ideas was insufficient, and that we must show their reality and their power in good works.

So do we, as we hope, repel one and another charge, or answer one and another question; and having thus endeavored in a few, but I hope sufficient, words, to make out our sense of the need of faith, and also to indicate its nature, it remains only that I should attempt to show you the context of Christian faith or Christian doctrine, as held by Unitarians.

In our atlases, you know, there will be an introductory map; it may be a map of the world, in which great countries will occupy but a little space; it may be a map of the United States, in which the several States will seem to offer but little for the eye to study; and that introductory map may be little consulted, not nearly so much as one of those which are meant to represent a smaller territory; and yet only from such a general map can you get an idea of the relative proportions or of the actual internal relations of the different countries: and so if I, by the remarks which I shall go on to offer, may show you the true relations of our belief, though it will be but by touching here and there, I may possibly afford something of advantage.

UNITARIAN BELIEF IN GOD.

Taking up, then, the inquiry, "What do Unitarians believe?" we first are led to speak, both from the importance and the magnitude of the subject, concerning their faith in God. Unitarians are *Theists*. I emphasize the word, because I would distinguish it from other words. "Does any one doubt that we believe in God?" it may be asked. I fear that some do. But, whether others entertain any doubt upon that question or not, we not only entertain no doubt ourselves, but we put the strongest emphasis on our belief in God. We are not Deists, because, by a rather singular use of the term, "Deism" conveys only a negative idea. It presents the thought that whoever may be called a Deist denies the Christian revelation, and does not make prominent the fact that he believes in God. And yet "Deist" and "Theist" are perfectly synonymous terms, one derived from the Latin, the other from the Greek. We are not Deists, because we believe, as I shall have occasion to say, in Divine Revelation.   We are not Pantheists, because we believe in the Divine personality.   We do not believe in any form of Pantheism which clouds that central truth of the personal God, the Deity, incomprehensible in His personal being, and yet having an intelligence and consciousness and activity of His own towards all His creatures, towards all His works, so that they, springing from Him, depend upon Him, live in Him, while He lives in and through them; yet He and they are not God, but He alone.   And we believe concerning this God that He is not only infinite in His attributes, sovereign in His sway, and perfect in His moral disposition and activity, but that He stands to us in the relation of a father, so that we may call Him, and ought to call Him, " Our Father," exercising towards us parental inclinations and desires, claiming from us filial tempers and filial obedience.   And this is our great exhibition of the Divine character, — that it is parental.   Other denominations may accept the same view, but we think that we hold it forth with a distinctness that is seldom found in other religious bodies, and that we ought to take it to our own hearts with a faith, a gratitude, and a joy beyond words to express.

It follows from this, our belief concerning God, that we are Unitarians, because we believe not only that God is our Father, but that the Father, and the Father alone, is God.   We repudiate the word " Deism," because it has come to have, not a double, but a single and a negative, meaning.   We accept the word " Unitarian," because it has a double meaning, both positive and negative.   Positive, because it affirms the simple and absolute unity of the Supreme Being; and negative, because it excludes any other being from a participation in the Divine nature.   We think we are not rising beyond the reach of human thought when we thus speak of God.   If God exists in a threefold personality, it is something which we cannot understand, and therefore cannot believe: we can only repeat the words.   If He be any other than a single being in His personality and in His consciousness, we have more than one God, — which the whole Christian world would reject as a folly; and therefore, while we do not attempt to pry into the mysteries of that infinite and eternal nature, we yet say that, while God has been pleased to reveal Himself to man, — at least, is pleased to have man stand in certain relations of knowledge, faith, and duty towards Him, — we can only accept this for our definition of the Divine Being, that He is One in all senses in which unity can be predicated of an intelligent and conscious nature.

BELIEF IN REVELATION AND THE BIBLE.

It follows also from our idea of God as a Father, and our belief in Him as the only primal source of truth or spiritual influence, that we accept revelation, because this Being, who is possessed of infinite attributes, can communicate knowledge or influence of one kind or another to His creatures, and a Father will be disposed to influence His children by instruction and by whatever methods He may see fit to use for drawing them to Himself. God reveals Himself in various ways, mediate and immediate. Nature is a revelation of its Author. The clouds as well as the sunshine, the flower that breathes its odor and dies, the tree that stands for centuries, every form of animal life, every aspect of being, is a revelation of the Creator; and science, as it goes deeper in its researches, as it rectifies its own errors, as it comes into closer intercourse with the physical universe, obtains new testimony concerning the being, the agency, the wisdom, and the goodness of God. Human life, personal experience, social history, are all methods which God uses to reveal Himself; and he who will listen to the voices within himself, or will read the page of history with an open eye, will find much that will help him, if not to understand God, at least to trust in Him, and to commit his ways into the hands of a most faithful Creator.

But there are also special and exceptional revelations of the Divine nature. Instead of repudiating such as absurd or impossible, we say they are not only possible, in consequence of the possession of infinite resources by the Supreme Being, but they are probable, in consequence of the interest which He feels in His intelligent creatures, whom He will be ready to instruct when they fall into depths of ignorance, whom He will be ready to help when they ask Him to bestow His assistance; and therefore a special revelation, or an occasional revelation, interposing itself in the affairs of this world, at one time and another, is not improbable, but is the most likely thing, if we will deduce probability from the character of God.

Such a revelation can be transmitted only through tradition or through writing. We believe that we have one book which contains a record of facts, — special revelations. That book is *the* book, — the Bible. We believe, therefore, in the Scriptures. We plant our faith in the Scriptures. We do not desire to reduce their authority. We hold them to be precious beyond all price or comparison. But we do not affirm that the Scriptures were written at one time, or by one hand, or that their contents are of equal authority. We believe that they contain much besides the records of Divine revelation; and therefore we hold it to be our duty to search those Scriptures, not only that we may find what they contain of the truth of God, but that we may discriminate between what is of divine and what is of human origin. Instead of treating the Scriptures irreverently, when we thus endeavor to determine the comparative value of different parts, we hold that we pay them the most sincere and humble and grateful respect. And if in an epistle, — which generally, or with that single exception, we think was written by an apostle, — we find a passage which we believe from the most correct edition of the text, from the most careful research, and the most candid inquiry, was not a product of the apostolic inspiration or of the apostolic dictation, we say that we reverence the Bible and that we stand up for its truth and its authority, when we refuse to let that passage be read in our churches or in our homes as a part of the Divine Revelation.

Therefore, we not only believe in special revelations, but we value the memorial by which such revelations have in past times been transmitted to our age, and will go on through all the ages of the future.

BELIEF IN CHRIST.

From which it follows that we are Christians. Not only Theists and Unitarians, but believers in Jesus Christ, because we are believers in the Christian Scriptures, in their general strain of narrative and instruction. Jesus Christ is the central figure always presented to the student of the New Testament. Abstract, if it be possible, from the New Testament all mention of Jesus Christ, and you leave nothing but worthless threads; — I had almost said, you leave not a thread for the eye to scan. Eliminate the mission, the mystery, and the work of Christ from the Christian Scriptures, and the Christian Scriptures are not worth binding nor buying nor reading nor having.

We believe in Christ. That is, we believe that in the course of ages, centuries past, One stood upon the earth who spoke in the name of Almighty God, the Heavenly Father, and taught men how to be good and wise and happy; taught them how to turn from evil ways to ways of purity and peace. We differ about questions that may afterward arise about Christ. There are questions that we do not think it is necessary for us to determine; but the great truth of the special mission, and the concurrent truth of a full inspiration, and the subsequent truth of an ultimate authority connected with Christ, we hold, and therefore we are Christians.

BELIEF IN MAN'S SIN AND CHRIST'S ATONEMENT.

And being thus believers in Jesus Christ as the messenger of God and the mediator between God and man, we are led at once to inquire and to learn the relations which exist between him and mankind, or between him and the individual man; which is simply saying that we are led next and necessarily to certain views of human nature and human condition. We are led to believe in man as he was regarded by Christ, who, representing the Divine wisdom, could not have mistaken man's state. And now, applying this test, using this glass by which to look at human nature, what do we find? We find that man, in the

34

New Testament, whether in the teachings of Christ, in the commentaries on or explanations of those teachings by his apostles, is regarded as a sinner. The first thought that comes to the reader of the New Testament concerning mankind, when he opens this portion of the Bible, is that man sinned, — has sinned, does sin, and probably will sin; for the first word of the Saviour was, "Repent ye!" and the word of his forerunner was the same, "Repent!" and the "baptism of repentance" was preached in Judea at the beginning, and the Gospel of Salvation was glad tidings of deliverance from the dominion of sin. And there I might almost say Christianity stops in one direction; in another, as we shall see, it pursues its blessed course. But it does not go, as I think, into the inquiry concerning the origin of human sinfulness or the constituents of human nature. Christianity and Christ deal with facts. The *fact* of sin; the *fact* of human need; the *fact* of human exposure; the *fact* of human peril. All these facts Christianity accepts at once. They were patent and could not be denied. And because they were not only patent but universal, and not only undeniable but involved wretchedness for the race, Christ came and lived and died.

Now, without meaning to complain of what is called Orthodoxy, or the popular religion, we do maintain that Orthodoxy goes beyond Scripture, and tries to explain what Scripture, if it does not leave untouched, touches with a very light hand. Orthodoxy undertakes to explain, for instance, the origin of sin. It may tell you it is hereditary; it may tell you it is not only ancestral, but that it may be traced back beyond the Deluge to the Garden of Eden; or it may give you some other explanation. Christianity simply says, Man is a sinner, and must be saved. So in regard to the Atonement, as it is called: the Orthodox faith not only accepts the Atonement and tries to explain it, not only says that Christ is reconciling man to God and that forgiveness is announced to us, but undertakes to show the ground of that forgiveness in the Divine Mind. Now we think we show more humility when we let such questions stand by themselves for the Divine Mind to answer. Will God forgive the sinner? is the question;

and that question — thanks be to the Divine mercy ! — is answered in the Gospel of Christ.

We believe, therefore, in points of faith which it is said, unjustly, that we reject. For instance, as I have just now named, we believe in the Atonement. No body of Christians in the wide-spread church that takes the name of Christ believes in the Atonement more thoroughly, more heartily, more gratefully than we. It is the essential thing in the Gospel, — this reconciliation of rebel man, of the hard heart, of the impenitent soul, or of the suffering and aching spirit, conscious of its needs, to the Heavenly Father. That is the Atonement of the New Testament, and we believe in it as we believe in God himself.

We believe in the Cross of Christ. We believe in Him who died, " the just for the unjust, that he might bring us to God ; " who suffered the agony of crucifixion, that he might not only bear witness to his own fidelity and finish the work which was given him to do, but that he might address such persuasions to the cold heart, to the conscience of man, to his moral sensibilities and sympathies, that he would wake from the sleep of evil, from the death of sin, and rise in Christ to a new life. We believe in the efficacy of the Cross.

BELIEF IN REGENERATION AND RETRIBUTION.

We believe in regeneration. What is regeneration ? Observe Christ's doctrine concerning regeneration, when he talked to Nicodemus : that a man must become a new creature, must be " new-born." Can it be better explained than by the Apostle, when he says : " that ye put off concerning the former conversation the old man, which is corrupt according to the deceitful lusts ; and be renewed in the spirit of your mind ; and that ye put on the new man," — being " born again," says Christ, — " which after God is created in righteousness and true holiness " ? We believe in regeneration. We believe in that change. We believe that change must take place with the sinner, or he must suffer the penalty of his transgression, and go down to ruin. And therefore we believe in retribution. We believe that every sin has its penalty bound to it by the eternal decree of Omnipotence and by the eternal law of love. We believe that sin must be punished, because God loves the sinner, — not his sin, but the sinner; and therefore, as he loved the world when it was "dead in trespasses and sins," and sent His dear Son to die for it, so God loves the sinner in his impenitence and unbelief, and will put him to trouble, to suffering, to anguish, here or hereafter, until the sinner shall have been impelled to pour out his soul in penitent confession, and accept mercy. And if the sinner will not do it, then God's punishment must follow him.

BELIEF IN THE HOLY SPIRIT AND IN PRAYER.

These, then, are our general views concerning man, concerning human condition, human wants, and human relief, through Christ and God. And therefore it follows, from our statements thus far, that we believe in spiritual life ; because we hold that the sinner, brought to repentance, renewed in the temper of his mind, becomes a new being, becomes now a child of God, realizes within himself a consciousness to which he was a stranger before, the vital element of which consciousness is spirit ; and that spirit comes partly from the depths of his own being which have been hidden hitherto, because covered up by selfishness or unbelief, and partly comes from the Infinite Spirit Himself, God sending down His assistance to those who need it. And that is our doctrine of the Holy Spirit. We believe in the Holy Spirit. We not only believe in a holy spirit which every man may have and exercise, under the influence of Christ's teachings and character, but we believe in the Holy Spirit as an effusion from the high heavens, coming down so gently, yet with such mighty power, to enter into the human soul, to refresh it, and encourage it, and comfort it, and fill it with the hope of heaven. This is our doctrine of the Holy Spirit. Not that it is a personality separate from the Father, but that it is His own life, expressing itself in an influence which comes forth, and comes forth intentionally, to those who personally ask for it, or do not ask for it.

We believe, therefore, in prayer, as the dictate of human

nature : not only as the cry of the human heart when it cries, as did the Psalmist, " for the living God," but as the aspiration of the soul, when, taught and encouraged by Christ, it lifts up though it be but the faintest desire above the atmosphere of earth into the skies. And, as it rises, it gets more force, and becomes a mighty appeal and enters into the bosom of the Eternal Father, to move Him, shall I say? — why not say it? — to move Him to send down His spirit of truth and mercy.

And, thus believing in the spiritual life, as created by faith and renewed by the spirit, you can understand, dear friends, — to return for a moment to a point in the earlier part of our remarks, — how the value of faith depends not so much on its quantity as on its quality. A man may believe a great many things, and yet hold them with such faith that they shall be of very little value or service to him ; he may believe a very few things with such an earnest and appropriating faith, make them elements of character, make them virtual inspirations, make them a law also unto himself, that they transform him into an angel upon earth. It is not quantity, but quality. A few grains of gold are worth more than many pounds of iron.

BELIEF IN RIGHTEOUSNESS AND LOVE.

And, once more, it follows from all this, and follows particularly from our last statement, that we believe in the spirit and life as affecting and pervading the soul, determining its exercise, guiding the will, making the inner man to be after the image of God, as it was originally formed, and is now restored by Christ. We believe also in outward righteousness, in personal character, exhibiting and vindicating itself in the various relations of social existence. We believe that this spiritual life, if it be genuine, will not and cannot shut itself up in the recesses of one's own thought and feeling. We believe it must go forth to do good ; that, without making any display of itself, without coveting admiration or praise, it will involuntarily, spontaneously, continually, offer itself for imitation, to incite others to good deeds, and to the relief of those who are in the way of transgression, or folly, or suffering, whatever it may be. And thus the Christian will be, and must be, a philanthropist; and any Christian who is not a practical and active philanthropist is but half a Christian : he is not a follower of Jesus who " went about doing good; " not a Christian after the pattern of the Apostle, who said that we must "do good to all as we have opportunity, especially," indeed, " to those who are of the household of faith," and therefore nearest to us, most within our reach, but also to all who are not Christian, who are not good men, according to the standard set forth in that glorious parable of the good Samaritan.

And so, friends, not only doing good in the world, but trying to be good, — that is, all pressing on toward perfection, and yet all feeling that we are beset and encompassed by innumerable temptations and have not yet reached the goal, — becomes the test of Christian faith, becomes the expression of the life of Christ in God that belongs to us.

" LIFE AND LOVE," THE UNITARIAN MOTTO.

And therefore, finally, there are two words which we love, which we repeat, and which become each a motto that we would never forget nor disobey, — LIFE and LOVE. Both of these are principles of Christianity. No man has really LIFE in him until in his own consciousness he has, to some extent, interpreted the words of Jesus : " I am come that they might have life, and that they might have it more abundantly." No man has realized the fulness of his own existence until he has opened his soul to the Divine instruction which comes through the Gospel, and has made himself familiar with the highest and best in his nature, which he can reach only when he is really a *living* man, in the best sense of that noble word " man," until he has made his manhood to be rich with the spirit of Christ, until he has brought it to express itself in all its proportions and in all its relations. And no one is a thorough Christian, no one has a right to regard himself, no matter what others may say of him, as a thorough believer, until he has learned by tender sympathies, by gentle moods of feeling, by a broad charity, and by an active benevolence, what that mighty word Love imports, that word, — I had almost said, the largest and most suggestive of all words, but I am reminded that I have spoken one still larger, — yet that word Love, which we carry up to the throne of God, and there, when we would best acquaint ourselves with the unseen, the everlasting, the ever-glorious, we say, *He* is Love. We, then, taking the word to ourselves, pressing it into our hearts, making it, as it were, the impulse that governs us and yet withal restrains us, can claim to be disciples of Christ.

So, then, friends, I have run over, I hope, sufficiently, perhaps at too much length, the points of our faith which seem to belong together, and to follow one after another, by an almost, if not absolutely, necessary sequence. It is said that Calvinism is the most logical form of doctrine ever devised; for, if you assume its premises, you can but go on, step by step, to its conclusions. There is some truth in this remark. Happily, its premises are false. But I conceive that we have a faith which is not fragmentary and disjointed, but the parts of which fit into each other with admirable symmetry; nay, more, that the different articles of belief follow upon one another by an almost inevitable law of deduction. And thus we are brought, from our faith in God, with which we began, to communion with God, with which we end. Believing in Him, whom the creation compels us to honor as its Author, we at last arrive at Him who is Perfect Love. Are we *Infidels*, then? Should that name ever be flung against us? Are we not *Believers*, emphatically? Are we not, also, as a body of believers, agreed upon these great points of doctrine? And, though we be a small denomination, have we not a faith in which we may rejoice and be glad?

THE MINISTER AND HIS BUSINESS.

1839.

THE pulpit is the spot on which *conviction* must plant itself, and speak in the tones of a calmness too deep to be passionate, too earnest to be mechanical, of themes which beginning with

the soul of man spread themselves out through the infinite relations of God and eternity.　On such themes a man should speak,
if he open his mouth upon them, with reverence and with solicitude, but also from acquaintance, — an acquaintance so intimate
that it has become a part of his habitual consciousness.　My first
advice to the young minister would be, Preach what you believe,
and nothing else.　Go just as far in your sermon as you have gone
in your faith; where the one stops let the other stop.　Better reiterate one idea fifty times, if each time it come from your inmost
conviction, than utter fifty ideas which have only taken up their
summer residence in your mind.

All ministers were not made for the same kind of work.
Each holds the ministry according as he has received mercy.
One loves study, another action; one is of a logical turn of mind,
another feels the truth which he cannot reason out; one will
touch and subdue his hearers on Sunday, another's powers of
persuasion must be exercised in private; one does best when he
writes, another will effect more in one extemporaneous address
than in twenty written discourses.　Now what can be more
absurd than to place all these different capacities of usefulness
upon one Procrustes' bed, and stretch and lop till they are all
brought to what is considered the standard of ministerial service!
In following his own tastes, the individual must doubtless be
careful that he do not destroy the symmetry of his own character by allowing too much indulgence to a particular inclination,
as well as considerate of the usages which time has hallowed,
and around which, if their general adoption be not an argument
in their favor, of more or less weight as the case may be, the
reverence and attachment of the community may have closely
entwined themselves.

I have known so much needless suffering to be endured by
ministers, and so much unjust comparison to be instituted by the
people, that I am the more anxious to expose the error of imag-
ining that there is only one road of professional success; that
what one person does well another can and ought to do equally

well. Hence the impatience of a congregation when they hear a better preacher than their own, forgetful of the influence which he exerts in private; or, on the other hand, when they learn that another pastor visits more than theirs, unmindful of the greater attention which the latter bestows upon his sermons. Hence, too, the unnatural and unprofitable struggle of the clergyman to imitate first this and then that clerical brother, whose success seems to be a rebuke of his own indolence. We cannot all be alike. Our success must lie in different lines of usefulness. It is through variety of endowments, and therefore of exercises, that the Church must be benefited. " As every man hath received the gift," says the apostle, "even so minister the same one to another, as good stewards of the manifold " — mark the word! — " the *manifold* grace of God."

1840.

Enter not the pulpit with any other than the highest purposes. Prepare your mind for the services of the hour by prayer and meditation. Come not hither to give entertainment, to win applause, or to discharge a professional task. That you may clear your conscience in this matter, let me direct you to the end which you must keep in view, and the means which you must use for this end. The end which you must contemplate in all your ministrations here, is the culture of the human soul. To the soul must you address yourself, — to the spiritual and immortal nature of man. Preach to the *souls* of your hearers, preach with the single view of making them partakers of a Divine life. In every one of the congregation, under whatever outward appearance, behold the elements of a perfection which you must help him to understand and unfold, and do not account yourself to have done any thing as you ought, unless you have at least tried to make him a better man. Come hither Sunday after Sunday with just the same purpose, — to aid these people in freeing, exalting, sanctifying, perfecting themselves. Fear not that by incessant contemplation you will exhaust the vitality of this purpose. The more you ponder the great idea which must ever be uppermost in your mind, the more sublime, comprehensive, inexhaustible will it seem to you.   Penetrate the meaning of the common words of religious instruction, — least understood because most used, — *man, duty, God.*   The soul, I repeat, — comprehend its nature, condition, destiny ; capable of an exaltation which mocks the power of language ; sunk often into a state of the most pitiable debasement, and still more often wrapped in a lethargy whose fatal slumber you must dissolve ; with an endless progress before it, whose character the influences it shall here acknowledge must affect, and may for ever determine.   To save this soul from ruin, to redeem it from thraldom, to bring it to God, to prepare it for heaven, is your work ; and if you set before yourself any other design than this, I say to you, my brother, you are not fit for the ministry.   Go elsewhere and get your bread.   Go elsewhere, and work for money, for honor, for fame.   But take not another step beyond the threshold of the sacred office.

The instrument which you must use in affecting the souls of men is Christian truth.   You are ordained to be a *Christian* minister.   Preach, therefore, Christianity.   Preach not philosophy, preach not the maxims of a conventional morality, preach not human folly or human wisdom ; preach Christianity, preach Christ, — Christ, the Son of God and the Saviour of men, — Christ crucified, yet risen, — Christ the sufferer, but the Master, — Christ the image of God and the model for man.   Make the New Testament your text-book ; not as do some, merely for the sake of getting a text, but that you may draw thence your doctrine and persuasion.   Make Jesus your study and the source of your inspiration.   Come to this people with his religion on your tongue and in your heart.

Preach plainly, with the aim of being understood, and not as if this were the last thing you cared about.   Utter the truth, be it popular or unpopular, let it strike where it may, wound though it shall.   Be honest.   Preach nothing which you do not believe.

Give forth your own convictions. Be as little of the parrot as of the hypocrite. Say what you think. Preach the Christianity which you find in the Bible, — not what some one else, or all others, have said is there. The very first requisite in a minister is integrity of soul. Let your sermons, and oh, for conscience' and for the altar's sake, let your prayers, be the expression of your own mind. Borrow nothing from another for the sake of filling up or filling out. Make all that you repeat your own by the concurrence and sympathy of your own mind, before you let it pass your lips. If it were possible, I would say, let your discourse be as close a copy of your convictions as if the light of truth, like the action of the sun on the material surface, could transfer thither each line and point. Dread every form and degree of dishonesty.

1842.

The end of preaching is not to communicate new views of truth, but to awaken attention to old views; not to feed the mind, but to quicken it; not to educate the intellect, so much as to direct the conscience and soften and elevate the heart. The end of preaching is effect. Some persons are afraid of this word in this connection. Preaching for effect, they conceive, must proceed from an equivocal motive and tend to a doubtful result. Still I repeat, that preaching should aim at effect, and that the best preaching is effectual preaching. If a man rises in a pulpit and reads or recites a beautiful piece of composition, which sends away the hearers with their tongues loud in praise of his scholarship or his eloquence, but with their hearts bare of all impression, I do not call that preaching. It may be beautiful, it may be eloquent, it may be very good in its proper place, but it is not preaching. He *preaches* who makes people feel and act, who leads them to examine themselves and to live as Christian men should live. Whitefield preached, when he drew all Dr. Franklin's money out of his pocket, and when he made a vast congregation tremble and weep; and yet I suppose that, if a critic should review a volume of Whitefield's sermons, he would pronounce it a poor book. I do not mean to say that tears or raptures are evidence of good preaching, or that the pulpit should aim at producing excitement; but I maintain that moral impression and spiritual life are the results at which it should look, and with which alone it should be satisfied.

And now I ask, how can there be such preaching, except it come from the soul? How can a minister *affect* others, and so produce the *effect* he should desire, if he be not in earnest, and most heartily in earnest? What is the secret of his power over an audience? What is the channel through which his soul flows into their souls? Sympathy, — sympathy established between them and him by his utterance. But now mark: the state of mind to be awakened in them is a religious state, — a state of strong interest in religion. If their minds be in such a state, there can be sympathy between them and him only when his mind is in a similar state; that is, a state of strong religious interest, a state of spiritual activity and fervor.

I hold it therefore to be absolutely indispensable to good preaching that the minister write and deliver his sermon from a soul burning with religious conviction; that he write and deliver it almost as if he could not help writing and delivering it, as if he realized the force of the Apostle's declaration, — "A necessity is laid upon me; yea, woe is unto me, if I preach not the gospel." Call this love of souls zeal, fanaticism, by whatever good or bad name you please: it matters not how it is called or how described, if it only be found in the preacher. But among us the minister is not required to preach once or twice a year, when a special interest warms his bosom, but Sunday after Sunday, year after year, till he stops because he can preach no longer. Here is our young friend, going to stand up in this pulpit on the next Lord's day to preach the everlasting gospel to this people, and from that day to his death there may never a week pass in which he will not be called to the same service, except as regard to his physical frame shall provide for him occasional rest. How can he come every week into this place with a sermon, — not a written something, but a *sermon,* —

and preach — not speak to inattentive hearers, but *preach* — to his fellow-men, on whose spirits the cloud and the burden of sin have fallen as he has felt them fall on his own spirit, and who like himself are heirs of immortality, — how shall he preach to them · every Sunday, unless his whole soul be in his ministry? It cannot be, it cannot be. He may gain admiration, he may be loaded with praise, he may be idolized, — and show only that he has great talents or fine personal gifts; but he cannot come to this people, in his weekly ministrations, " in the fulness of the blessing of the gospel of Christ," unless he has caught that spirit of devotedness which carried Christ to crucifixion, that he might "draw all men unto himself," and which prompted Paul to "become all things to all men, that he might by all means save some."

The minister's life is not a life free from trial. Rather is it a life of peculiar trial. If any one enter it in the hope of finding a couch of ease and a path of roses, he will be bitterly disappointed. I have read of clerical sinecures and of " luxurious parsons," but I thank God this is not the country for such men or such things. Here, if no one else works, the minister must; and work, often, till both body and mind cry out for repose. *This*, however, can hardly be called a trial. It is not the work, but the feeling that he works to little purpose, which tries his spirit. Week after week — and happy will he be if it should not be year after year — he must labor in the pulpit and out of the pulpit, by day and by night, in his study and among his people, and see little fruit of his labor. I conceive that there is no other employment in which men engage that yields so little visible result as the ministry of our established churches. In the early days of a congregation, or at certain periods in its subsequent history, the minister may have undeniable, or even abundant evidence, that his exertions are blessed in the improvement of his people. But in the general course of his services he will have more occasion to adopt the Prophet's exclamation, — " Who hath believed our report, and to whom is the arm of the Lord revealed?" Discouragement will track his steps and weigh down his heart. His efforts will seem to be without reward, his prayers without answer. If some seed fall on good ground, much the greater part will be devoured by the fowls of the air, be choked by thorns, or be scattered on a stony soil where it will not take root. Complaint, too, will arise where he had hoped to find support. He may be misunderstood and misrepresented, the sympathy that was expressed at the commencement of his course grow cold, new voices and new ways be preferred to his familiar voice and trite methods of discourse or action, and he whose usefulness was prophesied in terms which no probable result could have satisfied be condemned for loss of interest or want of force.

Besides exposure to the caprice of opinion and the difficulties that grow out of the inaptitude of people to receive religious impression, from which it is possible that the minister may be saved, there is one cause of distress which he cannot but feel, and must feel the more keenly the nearer his appreciation of the responsibilities of his office approaches the truth. He feels how inadequate are his powers to the task he has undertaken. That task in its length and breadth, its height and depth, stands before him, and fills the whole scene of his earthly existence, like a gigantic mountain occupying the whole field of vision before a traveller, and seeming to mock his purpose of advancing on his journey. The sense of inadequacy — the most painful conviction that can enter the mind — comes upon him, and well will it be with him if it do not take him captive and lead him to the brink of despair. It is the work of the Lord which he has chosen: who among the sons of men is equal to the performance of this work? The conversion of the sinful; the instruction of the well-disposed, many of them older, all perhaps better, than himself; the maintenance of the Christian cause against error, vice, and irreligion; the prosecution of that enterprise whose corner-stone was laid in the tomb of Jesus; the spread of that religion whose entrance into the world was celebrated by angels in the songs of heaven, — these are the things to be done, and who is sufficient for these things? May not, must not, the Christian minister tremble, when the conception of all that needs to be done, and all that ought to be done by one who would "follow Christ in the regeneration," comes to his mind as the measure of his own duty?

Under the pressure of these various grounds of anxiety, troubled and disheartened, the minister must be sustained by a resolute devotion to his work, or it will be too much for his strength. Unless he

> "Hath given
> Himself, his powers, his hopes, his *life*,
> To the great cause of truth and Heaven,"

he will faint and grow weary. He must have married his heart to it with the solemn words, "What God hath joined together let not man put asunder;" and then, loving it as the chosen of his heart, he will not suffer any thing to disturb his satisfaction in the choice which he has made. This *love* of the ministry, this adherence to it for its own sake, will enable a man to bear and to do what without such a principle of attachment would drive him from it, or make him go through its wearisome offices like a prisoner through his appointed tasks. We have all seen what love will do, — how it will nerve the delicate frame of woman as with iron firmness, and give strength before which obstacles that appear insuperable vanish like mists before a mighty wind. It has converted the sick-chamber into a paradise, and filled the dungeon with joy. It has made toils that wore out the body seem light as dreams, and led men to brave dangers as they would take a pleasant walk. So will it pour fortitude and energy into the heart of the Christian minister amidst all his trials. Let him only love his profession, and neither the experience of disappointment nor the contemplation of duty will check "the current of his strong resolve." It was this which enabled Paul to say, "I will very gladly spend and be spent for you; though the more abundantly I love you, the less I be loved." And it is this which, in the bosom of the humblest follower of the Apostle now, will support him under all difficulties, — nay, will carry him triumphantly over them all.

For so laboring, in faithful love, he will be successful. Here, then, I am brought to my last argument in favor of the devotedness which is my theme, — that it will secure the ends of the ministry. Who have been successful in this department of labor? Devoted men. Who have been powerful preachers? Devoted men. Who have been useful pastors? Devoted men. Who have infused their own spirit into the generation about them, and imprinted their own image upon the generation after them? Devoted men. In all ages and in all lands a devoted ministry has been a successful ministry. From that wedlock of which I have spoken, between the heart and the aim of the life, have been born efficiency and success. He who by assiduous culture brings one vine in the vineyard of the Lord to bear fruit, illustrates the value of such culture, as well as he who from a more fertile spot gathers more or heavier clusters. From every walk of ministerial service arise the witnesses to the efficacy of laborious zeal. Hail! ye champions of duty, ye teachers of a holy truth! We welcome you with the message you bear to our hearts, — never to despond, and never to be idle. From you we learn the conditions of success, and the rewards of fidelity; for on your lives was stamped the character of devotedness, and the scenes of your industry bore evidence of usefulness.

The question may be asked, whether we mean to teach that all ministers should exhibit similar absorption in their professional duties. I will not presume to speak in condemnation of those (if any there be) who do not; but I certainly mean to indicate this as the standard of ministerial fidelity. I know not at what lower point to place it. Our doctrine simply is, that a minister who would do his duty must devote all his faculties and resources to his ministry. "What!" you may say, "his whole time and strength?" Yes, I answer; with that due qualification of such language which common sense will supply. I do not mean that he must go without sleep, or that he may neglect his family, or that he need relinquish all intercourse with society except that which springs out of his pastoral relation, or that he may not inform himself of the literature of his times; but that his office must ever be uppermost in his thoughts and deepest in his heart, — that he must not entangle himself with cares that shall hinder him in the discharge of its functions, nor covet pleasures, social or mental, that would divert his interest from the great purpose of his life. I confess I do not understand how one who "takes heed to his ministry to fulfil it" can attend to any thing else, except as an incidental and subsidiary part of his life. How one can satisfy his conscience in uniting politcal service with the pastoral office, or in dividing his time between the duties of the pulpit and the studies of classical antiquity, as if the latter were, to say the least, as dear to his heart as the former, is a problem that I am unable to solve. Such combinations remind me of the image described by Daniel, which had "feet part of iron and part of clay," — good therefore neither for speed nor for strength. It has often been said, with an appearance of pride and delight, that the scholars of both Old and New England have been found among her clergy. But this seems to me equivocal praise : the clergyman has too much to do in his peculiar vocation to permit him to be earning the laurels of scholarship. If he crave literary distinction, I fear that he undervalues ministerial service.

"But may not the minister seek relaxation, nor cultivate the pleasures of taste and fancy? May he not enjoy the refreshment of society, nor bestow any attention upon the occurrences of the world about him?" Certainly, I repeat, I would advance no such extravagant doctrine. Let him keep up an acquaintance with mankind, with books, with life in its changing aspects. But let him make every thing auxiliary to the one great purpose of his own life. Let him find texts in men, and sermons in the world. When he is not preaching, let him gather up materials which he may use in the pulpit; when he is not conversing on the soul's wants and destinies, let him be increasing his ability to discourse on these themes. Often must he say to the fascinations of leisure and pleasure, "I am doing a great work, so that I cannot come down: why should the work cease,

35

whilst I leave it and come down to you?" And when he seems to be most free from his professional occupations, he must be preparing himself for renewed diligence. The ministry must be to him the storehouse into which he brings all the thoughts, facts, experience, that he collects abroad, and to the supply of which he makes home, friends, books, society, nature, providence, — all he sees, all he hears, all he does, — tributary.

1850.

I know how much may be said about extravagance and enthusiasm. God help us! I wish we had some enthusiasm! It would do us good. We have been so afraid of it that we are like invalids shut up in their close apartments, till a breath of fresh air fills them with nervous apprehension. Conventional propriety and classic purity are very well in their place, and the Apostle tells us to let our moderation be known unto all men, — a very easy maxim, by the way, to observe, according to the sense which many persons put upon it; but I remember that he, too, wrote that it is good to be zealously affected *always* in a good thing, and I doubt if our times need account that a stale truth. The example of men on every side address a lesson to us to which we should do well to take heed. Look at the habits of farmer, of merchant, of lawyer, physician, man of science, artist, politician. Look at the mountebank, who will undergo harder training and suffer more privation to excel in his art than men are willing to endure for conscience' sake and for Christ. Look where you will, and let society in all its departments of action teach us what choice and devotedness are. The martyrdoms of our age are all on the side of the world. And they put *him* to shame who holds the ministry to be a place for self-indulgence, or for any thing but strenuous endeavor and whole-hearted service.

I know, again, it is said the minister needs intervals of rest, and that numberless examples attest the bad effects of an incessant devotion to professional labor. I answer that few ministers — very few, very few indeed — have been injured by too hard work. It was not their industry, but their irregularity, which disabled almost every one of those who have been driven to a premature relinquishment of their tasks. If you could call from the grave the thousands of the clergy who have gone down thither with broken constitutions, you would find them ready to confess that through a disregard of the laws of health in the way in which they did their work, and not through the amount of work, they brought their usefulness to an end; which, with harder work differently arranged, might have been postponed for years. There are no pages of biography more mournful than those which record the violation of physical laws by Christian ministers. Charge not their wilful mistakes upon too exclusive an aim.

The discourse may be written or unwritten, but it must have been prepared. A purely extemporaneous service is what, if possible, should never dishonor the pulpit. It is a mistake, I conceive, to prescribe a particular method or time of writing sermons. Each mind has its own habits of composition, and to put it into those of another mind may be like making David exchange his sling for armor, which encumbers him at every step. I doubt much, for instance, the wisdom of that common piece of advice, which I suppose every young minister has heard, and almost every one has neglected since the days when Christian preaching began, — not to defer writing till the close of the week. With all respect for those who, age after age, have repeated this counsel to so little good purpose, I question whether the proper form in which it should be given is not this, — Do not defer your preparation for the pulpit till the last day of the week. Now of this preparation the writing of the discourse is with many the very least part; and it may be doubted whether the mental and moral excitement which a limited period of time begets is not an aid in the construction of sentences intended for a popular audience. Such sermons as Butler's or Barrows' or Jeremy Taylor's, laden with thought or sparkling with beauty, like all elaborate composition, require more time to fit them to pass from the workshop of the mind to the place of public criticism, but such sermons would not be the best for a congregation to hear every Sunday; and Buckminster, that seraph of the pulpit, as one of our own number has so beautifully styled him, wrote some of his most effective discourses after the twilight had faded on Saturday evening. What needs to be insisted on, is the early and large preparation which the mind should make for the pulpit, whether the hands take up the pen at the commencement or the close of the week. One of the most eminent preachers of New England, the champion of Trinitarian Congregationalism, now as venerable in years as he has been abundant in labors, once told me that he wrote his sermons when walking through the streets of Boston. Never, O preacher, — am I tempted to say, — never let your thought be off from your sermon. Let the whole week qualify you to give instruction on the Lord's day. Be your own audience and your own preacher the week through.

1856.

The position in which you stand towards your minister requires you not only to regard him with respect and affection, but to give expression to these feelings on every suitable opportunity. Let me indicate one or two mistakes which you should avoid. There are several ways of treating a minister that are admirably suited to diminish his usefulness. He may be neglected, like a family Bible, which has been bought because it makes a respectable appearance in a drawing-room, and is left to the care of the maid, whose office it is to dust the furniture. Under this sort of treatment, a minister, being a man, and therefore more or less affected by sympathy, is very apt to become discouraged; and let me tell you, my friends, that, if you wish to put an end to his exertions for your good, you need only poison his heart with discouragement. It is as sure as strychnine, if it be a little slower in its action. He may, again, be flattered and petted, met every Monday morning with compliments on his sermons, and pampered the week through with attentions, like a distinguished visitor or a pet animal. Being a man, and therefore susceptible of injury from such unwholesome nutriment, he will lose the humility and disinterestedness which may have been the strength of his character; and, if he should sink into a mere practitioner of routine, whom will the people have to blame but themselves? Sometimes the minister is treated with a punctilious civility, the remnant of that consideration in which the clergy were held when the children trembled and their parents put on propriety, because the minister was approaching the house. Such civility neither expresses nor wins confidence.

Yet other ministers are watched and scrutinized and criticised, like Franklin's statue or the Mechanics' Exhibition, their defects exaggerated, imaginary faults imputed, and their claims to estimation discussed with more than an amateur's zeal or a trader's coolness. Such a practice excludes a just appreciation of the ministry, and is a sign of a deficient spirituality among the people. A minister is neither a merchantable commodity nor a work of art; but a man whose business it is to preach the Gospel in public and in private, and whose desire it should be to make his fellow-men partakers of the grace of God through Jesus Christ. Let him pursue his work according to his ability, without invidious comparison or intrusive superintendence. Each one can do the most good by a diligent use of his own gifts. The custom of measuring ministers with one another, as horses are compared together on a race-ground, is as injurious as it is contemptible. Be just to your minister, remembering that, if he be a man, he cannot be faultless, and, if he be a Christian, he cannot be useless. Let him do his work in his own way, and begin to complain of him only when you find that he is not doing it. Give him large liberty. If he is a wise man, he will not abuse it; but if he is a good man he will need it.

Encourage your minister by a prompt sympathy in every good purpose in which he may seek your co-operation. Encourage him by frank intercourse and a cordial welcome to your homes. Let him understand this night that he has an open entrance to your hearts, which will never be closed till he has betrayed your confidence. Do not dishearten him by a polite exterior, which says, in as decorous a manner as behavior can say it, "Sir, you are paid for *preaching*, — mind your own business." My friends, your minister will neglect his business most shamefully, if he do not offer you his assistance in the warfare which your souls must carry on with doubt and temptation. He does not come here simply to preach. Oh that worst heresy of Protestantism! would that the Spirit of the Lord might cast it out for ever! He comes to guide your tottering steps to Christ, to help your burdened souls on their way to God; and how can he do it, if he have no acquaintance with the history of your souls? Brethren, brethren, your minister has a right to be your friend; and, if you do not mean to make him such, do not make him your minister.

1858.

In too many of our congregations there is an impatience of any other than "practical preaching." I know not what the taste or demand of this people may be; but this I know, that, the more your preaching shall resemble that to which the multitude listened as they stood around the Galilean hill, the more practical will it be in tone and effect. And of this also may I remind you, that all good living must have a basis of belief on which to rest. The Christian righteousness grows out of the root of divine truth; and the farmer might as well expect to gather fruit from the fence with which he encloses his field as the Christian minister to make good men by delivering mere moral discourses. We must be believers if we would be saints. Therefore, do not withhold clear or sufficient dogmatic instruction. Enable your people to explain and justify to themselves their own faith; and upon this foundation rear a superstructure of practical counsel, that shall have the commandments of the Lord as its framework.

You need not leave Christ in order to expose the sins of the day. The most timely preaching is a reproduction of the Saviour's words in connection with present circumstances; as it

is the same light that shone on the palm-groves and olive-trees
of Judea which gives its rich shades to our American foliage.
In respect to this style of sermon, let me caution you against an
error into which both ministers and congregations sometimes
fall. There is a great difference between preaching *to* the times
and preaching *at* the times; the same difference that there is
between persuading a man and provoking him. I doubt if **we**
do the world much good by making it angry.

That you may justly discharge the functions of the ministerial
office, let me address to you the advice which Paul sent to
Timothy : " Give thyself wholly to these things." It is advice
which, like a two-edged sword, strikes down indulgence on this
side and on that, — the indulgence of sloth and the indulgence
of taste. " Give thyself *wholly ;* " that is plain and decisive language. Wholly. Keep back nothing. Devote all your energies, physical and mental, to this work. Do your best; do your
utmost. Justify the application to yourself of that title, better
than any ever worn by dignitary or prelate, — " a *workman* that
needeth not to be ashamed." There are no cardinals nor
bishops, thank God, under our Congregational polity ; but God
be thanked that there is not one of us who may not be a "workman." And the work is worthy of all the strength we can bring
to it. It needs all our ability and all our industry. It requires
all the force and all the skill and all the culture and all the zeal
we can lend to it. It demands men who will work in sight and
out of sight, in their pulpits and in their studies. Of all the
exhibitions that wound a Christian sensibility, what exceeds the
spectacle of a man standing before immortal fellow-men, and
talking to them of sin and judgment and eternity, as a nurse
would sing her lullabies to a baby ? Of all the unworthy uses
of a social position, what goes farther than his who reclines on
the respect and confidence of his people, — like an invalid on his
couch, — getting the reward, indeed, of his indolence in chronic
infirmities of the mind ? My friend, be you a student. Read,
think, write, for your own improvement, that your " profiting

may appear to all." This is not an age of the world in which
a minister may have an easy time. He has no right to it; and,
if he had, the world would not let him enjoy it. Men are
wanted of clear and vigorous minds, well trained and well
stored, to encounter the keen scepticism and to overthrow the
manful worldliness of the times. Never was there a period in
the history of the Church when a union of knowledge and fervor
was more important in the expounders of the Gospel.

"Give thyself wholly to *these* things;" a plain hint that other
things must be left to other men. You will find enough to do
in your own vocation,—various as well as constant employment.
Content yourself with being a good minister. Do not let circumstances tempt you to dilute your consecration to this service
with worldly engagement of any sort. Do not covet occupation,
still less distinction, in any other walk of life. It may be advan-
tageous to the health of both body and mind that you should
handle the spade or the plane, just as it will increase your relish
and digestion of spiritual truth to take up often a lighter kind of
study. But use all these exercises not only as subordinate, but
as subsidiary, to your professional usefulness. Have one purpose in life, — to make your people ripe for heaven. Be not
diverted from this purpose by opportunity or solicitation. Exercise your rights as a citizen, but leave political action to those
who have time for it. If the town should propose to send you
to the Legislature or to Congress, tell them you really cannot
afford to go; for it will cost you what neither three hundred nor
three thousand dollars a session would repay. Even the interests of education must not obtain too great a share of your time.
Do not be ambitious to serve on the School Committee. It certainly may be a question, whether the New England practice of
putting this task on the clergymen of the town be altogether
wise or just. By those who faithfully perform what is imposed
on them, I know it is often found to be a serious diversion of
time from other more strictly appropriate labors. A less close
and responsible connection with the schools has become a privi-

lege which they have a right to claim, in view of the multiplied
professional requisitions to which they are subject on the one
hand, and of the greatly augmented demands which our progressive system of education makes upon its friends, on the other
hand.

The one word which best describes the spirit of a minister's
life is *consecration.* You belong not to yourself, but to the
Lord. You are his servant, for whom you must live, even as
he, your Master, lives in you. I charge you not to make your
removal to this place the occasion of any loss of diligence.
Rather " stir thou up the gift of God," which was committed to
thee at thy induction into the office of a Christian pastor. Do
not exult in the thought that you have a desk full of sermons
ready for use. If I might utter a word of strictly private counsel, I would suggest to you, my friend, the propriety of putting
those manuscripts under lock and key, and then forgetting where
you have put the key. You ought to be able to write better
sermons now than you wrote when you were a younger man.
But it requires a great deal of courage and conscience to sit
down before sixteen pages of blank paper, when, by opening a
drawer at one's right hand, he can substitute for them just that
number of well-written pages, which none of his congregation
have ever seen.

A single-hearted dedication of yourself to the true ends of the
ministry will secure you in the enjoyment of an independence,
without which your efficiency must be crippled. This independence is endangered, not only by assault from abroad, but by an
involuntary deference arising out of the admiration we feel for
those who are successful in an enterprise like our own. Be not
eager to resemble any one of your contemporaries; since a man's
strength always lies in what belongs to him as his own, not in
what he has borrowed. Be true to your own nature. God has
made us to differ, and each one must excel in his own way.
Peculiarities may be both innocent and helpful, if they be
natural; but, if acquired, they are a weight and an offence. Be

neither a servile copyist nor an ambitious rival. Men love honesty everywhere, but most of all in the pulpit. A mocking-bird astonishes us, but we soon grow weary of astonishment; while the bobolink of our woods never tires us with his note, nor the robbin, nor even the sparrow. Peril to one's truthfulness comes in part from the constraint under which many persons are put by social opinion: they are afraid to differ from those whom they respect or love. It is a subtle influence, which, when resisted, sometimes produces a disagreeable bluntness or obstinacy, either of which is a detriment to a minister's usefulness. The only effectual means of protection against this influence lies in that unconscious superiority which is seen in one so entirely engaged in his work that the thought of others' judgment does not find room to lodge in his mind. Real independence belongs to him who thinks least about it. The rights of the pulpit are most likely to be maintained by one who never speaks of them, because he feels no anxiety lest they should be invaded. I have never yet seen reason to believe that the people of New England wish to listen to one whom they have robbed of the power of free speech; and I cannot doubt that he who is least jealous of an interference with his own privileges will have least occasion for their defence.

In the details of your ministry, distinct from the prominent function of preaching, let the same purpose control, the same spirit animate you, as in the exercise of that function. In the conference-room and the Sunday school, with the Bible class and the social meeting, in your pastoral visits and in your interviews with the sick and the bereaved, seek one result as the goal of your various yet concurrent efforts; to wit, the redemption of human souls from the tyranny and ruin of sin. Everywhere keep in mind the two great facts of the Christian life, — birth and growth, the beginning and the progress; in the New Testament language, regeneration and sanctification. Be not satisfied with promoting good neighborhood and preventing social disorder. It is only an incident of our religion that it acts as the world's police. Its visible effects are the consequence of an inward operation: the consciousness, that innermost retreat of our personality, is the seat of its power. To implant Christian sentiments in the heart is the surest way to produce an exhibition of the social virtues. The relations which men sustain to God are immeasurably more important than those which they hold to one another. The destinies of immortality who shall think of comparing with the success or misfortune that may attend on any worldly enterprise? Now it is your business to present these primary relations and final destinies in such terms as shall arrest attention, compel belief, inspire a sense of duty, and create an experience of the peace which "passeth all understanding." Not I, not we who are assembled in sympathy with your own hope, but the providence of God and the cross of Christ charge you not to evade or imperil the high commission which you bear as one who in Christ's name should beseech men to be reconciled to God. Hark! my brother. Hear you not the smothered cries of want and ignorance and fear, entreating you to come to their rescue? Hear you not the voice of Jesus, saying from the midst of his toil and his death, "Fill ye up" what remaineth of the agencies of mercy? Hear you not the command of God, to "spend and be spent" for the salvation of those whom you may guide from the paths of destruction to the city of refuge? Bear you every thing, and brave every thing, rather than the remembrance of a superficial or perfunctory service at the altar on which the Lamb of God was offered a voluntary sacrifice "for the sins of the people."

In your private character, be you "an example to the believers." In these days, when the old reverence for the clergy has given way to a captious or indignant criticism, there is more need than ever that the minister of religion should be a man of blameless life. His influence hangs on his character. If men respect him for his integrity and consistency, they will give heed to what he says; if they do not, he becomes to them a mere clerical demagogue. Do not be afraid of showing the quality of your mind. Let it be seen that you are "a man of God."

Because you should not sink the man in the minister, you need not sink the minister in the man. Lay aside gown and bands if you please, the white cravat and the black coat (though they are not without their use through the force of association), but do not lay aside the seriousness, the dignity, the prudence, or the meekness, which become a servant of Jesus Christ, while engaged in his household. If they be nothing but the livery which shows who is your Master, that livery you are bound to wear. Before men, be you without reproach; and, if possible, before God. Keep a pure conscience and a clean heart in His sight who seeth what is within us. "Take heed to yourself," for the ministry has its peculiar temptations. Beware of the influence of praise on the simplicity of your character, and beware of the tendency of habit to sink into routine. Freshen your piety by constant prayer. Invigorate your faith by continual obedience. Illustrate your teaching by your own example. There may seem to be little difference between a minister who rejoices in his work, and one who goes through its duties mechanically; and yet it is the difference between freedom and bondage. In the same train of cars which bore some of your friends to unite in the satisfactions of this hour were a company of prisoners, handcuffed, and forced to travel through the sweet summer morning, with all nature smiling around them. Yet their hearts received no pleasurable excitement from the motion or the scenery. They went as they were carried, because circumstances were stronger than they. I think I have seen some ministers who wore the handcuffs of habit, and moved along the road of life with a dull unconcern, prisoners of a condition stronger than their own will. Let your heart be in your ministry, and let it bear you every day nearer to heaven.

1860.

The very first condition of happiness or success with a minister is that he be *full of faith*. It is not with a mind beset by doubts, or entangled in the meshes of a subtle philosophy, that you should take on yourself the instruction of this people. You do not come to set before them speculations, conjectures, idle fancies. They have not invited you hither that you may have an opportunity of ascertaining by study and observation whether there is any truth in religion. They have not asked you to come among them for your sake, but for theirs. They expect you to explain and urge the great religious facts as you unfold to their view the positive duties of life. To a minister, faith is what capital is to the merchant, or genius to the artist: it is what he must work from and work with.

In pursuing your ministry, have a definite aim, and adhere to it. Know what you are trying to do. Every one who succeeds in life has a purpose, which he keeps steadily in view. Labor expended without an object is thrown away. Now and then one, in clambering a hill with a vacant mind, may put his hand on a shrub whose roots, laid bare by the seizure, shall tell him that he is walking over beds of golden ore ; but that is a rare experience, and still more rarely does it benefit the discoverer. The man who arrives at an end worth reaching sets out for that end. Your aim is the same with his whose ministry began in the wilderness and ended on the cross. You wish to save men from sin and lead them to God. This is the purpose for which you will labor and live. It is too great a purpose to be lightly undertaken, too solemn a purpose to be carelessly entertained. Let this purpose govern and animate you. Your sermons will then have meaning and effect, your conversation point and value, your life significance and weight. It has been said that sermons are sometimes written because on Sunday the preacher is expected to keep the people awake or asleep for half an hour. Sermons of this sort are made from the dictionary, not from a human brain or a human heart. Eschew such preaching, as the most barefaced insult to man and the grossest abuse of Divine forbearance. Preach thought, preach sense, preach God's truth and Christ's love and man's duty and the soul's need and the world's peril, the great salvation and the glorious hope that have come through the Gospel ; and preach with all your might, for the sake of bringing men into the kingdom of heaven.

In maintaining your professional loyalty, you will of course be brought into occasional, if not frequent, collision with opinions and practices around you ; and will be obliged to vindicate your independence of conventional restrictions and social influences, by an example which may conflict with the standard of the times. Yet in this community, and I believe in every Christian community, a minister is respected for his integrity of life, even though it rebuke the ways of society. The people do not complain of a preacher for illustrating the excellence and practicability of his own instructions. And therefore there is perhaps as much need to caution him against running into the error of a false independence as to remind him that he must not let his conduct out of the pulpit bring the sincerity of his public discourse under suspicion. There is a parade of clerical manliness, which is only the disguise of conscious weakness ; as there is an affectation of liberty, which betrays a want of sound judgment. Let me charge you to be simple and true. Eccentricity is not freedom : it is only an exchange of *masters,* custom for self-will. Do not exhibit or cherish any reluctance to appear as a minister. Why, in the name of honor or honesty, should you not be known as what you are? The lawyer, the merchant, the mechanic, is not afraid to be seen with the lawyer's brief or the merchant's ledger or the mechanic's tool in his hand, or to be heard using language which indicates his employment. Why should the minister wish to hide the badges of his office ? Just be simple and true, and think nothing about the judgment of others on your appearance. Then you will make the best impression, and save yourself a world of trouble.

Occasions, however, will continually arise on which you must maintain more or less of a professional character. Not only in the days of sickness and mourning, when you will be called, or be led by your own sympathies, into the homes of your people, but in your usual visits at their houses, you should endeavor to leave a ministerial blessing. I do not mean to suggest that you should carry a grave face over every threshold, or make your whole conversation to bear on religious subjects; for this would be as foolish as it would be difficult, alike unnatural and useless. But I do charge you to take the purpose of your ministry as a guide and prompter in seizing on every opportunity for addressing spiritual counsel to those who will welcome, if they do not expect it. One of the hardest practical questions which comes before us, my brother, concerns the character of our parochial intercourse. It may be made stiff and repulsive; and it may degenerate into idle gossip or worldly friendship. Avoid both extremes. Have a spirit of faithfulness in your breast, and you will not fall into any serious mistake. I once heard a brother say — he said it modestly, when it was a proper remark — that, as he stood on the doorstep waiting for admission into the house of a family belonging to his congregation, he prayed for wisdom to make his visit profitable to them. It opened a glimpse into the secret history of a life which I longed to imitate.

You will meet with discouragements and disappointments in your ministry. You would meet with them in any ministry on earth. They belong to the experience of man, which always includes the trials that brace the character and mature the judgment. The friend who will express to you our Christian fellowship will speak words of cheer and hope. I charge you not to yield to early or later difficulties, that may sometimes make your feet weary as you tread the path of conscientious service. Do not forsake your work as soon as it loses its pleasant novelty, — obeying the fashion of the times rather than the voice of duty or the dictates of discretion. An humble, faithful, wise minister will seldom take or give — never take, seldom give — offence that will *last.* Be sincere and diligent, modest yet courageous, cheerful though earnest, a hard worker, a firm believer, a cordial friend, a good man, and you will not be unsuccessful. I charge you, my brother, to "make full proof of your ministry." What more need I say? Make full proof of your ministry from this night, on and through, to the end.

1847.

LIFE IN DEATH.

ACCORDING to the Christian revelation, and according to the example of Christ, we *live* when we are true to ourselves as moral, spiritual, immortal beings; when we are penetrated by a sense of God, the Infinite Life of the universe; when we look out of the shadows of a passing hour into the realities of the Divine law and the Divine love; when the objects of faith are interwoven with our consciousness by the threads of spiritual sympathy, and our present toil becomes the promise and security of our future glory. To live, in the sense which the Gospel adopts, is to cherish high aims and pure purposes; to feel that we have souls and to treat them worthily; to use the flesh as the instrument of the spirit, and the world as the means of reaching an elevation above its cares and follies. He *lives*, who understands what he should live for. He *lives*, who is quickened and filled with the Divine spirit of truth.

To one who has realized such a life, what we call death ceases to have the character usually ascribed to it. It is a circumstance in the course of his experience, not the end of his being; a circumstance connected with momentous consequences, but not the terrific fact which fills so many minds with dread. To die is to pass into a more intense consciousness of life, — to lay aside the incumbrance of the flesh, which impaired the force of that consciousness here, and to become more sensible, through spiritual affinities and an actual participation, of the divine element which pervades all nature. Death is the entrance to a higher and fuller life.

Under this view, the time and manner of the soul's departure from its present " tabernacle " are seen to be of but little importance. In the haste of our grief at the death of a friend, we may speak of it as premature, and so it may appear to a judgment guided by mortal associations. But, if the event itself be only a circumstance in the progress of an immortal nature towards perfection, it cannot with propriety be styled premature. He who has died has in fact surmounted a great obstruction in his way to glory, — an obstruction which interrupted his full experience of life; how can the removal of such an obstruction ever take place too soon? We speak of sudden death as a calamity. But to whom? Not to him who is prepared for the change: to him no more a calamity than any other sudden access of happiness. Nor to those who remain behind is it an unmitigated calamity; since they, through the strength of their love overpowering the sense of bereavement, may participate in the joy of him who has risen from the confinement of his earthly abode to the mansions whose walls embrace the universe and rest on eternal foundations. He has gained what he was continually seeking, — less constraint and more enjoyment in the use of his faculties. He was pressing on, and God stretched out His hand and helped him forward.

1866.

WELL DONE, GOOD AND FAITHFUL SERVANT!

WHEN I was able to collect my thoughts after hearing of his removal, the knowledge of which came to most of us like the lightning's blinding flash, the one word that seemed to me to be the central point in my recollection of him was faithful, — *faithful*. It would yield its place to no other word; no other word would fill its place. He had been a faithful minister, a faithful man; faithful in public and in private; faithful in his home; faithful in his pastoral relations, as so many aching hearts attest; faithful in his delivery of the message with which he was intrusted for the congregation when he met them here; faithful in the closet, since only in communion with God could he have acquired that purity and solidity of character which came under our notice; faithful according to that which had been committed to him, — whether ten talents or two it matters not, so long as the encouragement stands ample for our imitation.

I lingered over the word. I. could not resist the fascination and the authority with which it held me. At last I released myself from this monotone of thought, only to be caught within the grasp of another word that appeared not less to belong to him, — "done." It held me as I repeated the sentence so appropriate in this new connection, — "Well done, good and faithful servant!" It seemed to me to separate itself from the rest of the line, and to stand in its own absolute meaning. *Done,* — finished, — the work ended, — the time arrived for us to give him up, — the earthly life completed as well as closed, — was this its meaning? The more I thought, the more ready was I to accept it in this sense. Why not? It does not lessen our faith in another life, to believe that this had rounded its circle. We borrow fresh assurance of immortality from such a truth. To die when earth has no more work to demand of us is to enter on our heavenly progress at the right moment. He of whom I am speaking once added, after quoting from the lips of another the expression, "He has passed on," "Passed on! Beautiful thought! He has not stopped, he has not ceased to be ; he has passed on, in faith and duty and love, to higher labors and undefiled reward." Shall not we say the same of the friend whose mortal vestment alone is waiting for its burial? Yet, before I follow the spirit to its new abode, I must tarry a little longer near this sign of the past, — *done.* Had he not finished his work? Had not the earthly life reached its natural limit? Ignorantly indeed, but truly, he was the prophet of his own departure. He did not know, when he delivered back into your hands the ministry which you had placed in his hands, that he could have retained it but a few weeks longer. He had asked for a little longer period of co-operation with you in behalf of the interests which were nearest to his heart. "Let me serve you whenever I can, till strength and life fail." How characteristic the wish! How like his whole course the request conveyed in those words! Work; with you; always. But he had lived out his appointed term. The unseen messenger of the Divine love touched the thread which was just ready to break, and the released spirit "passed on," — passed up, passed into the blissful recompense of the faithful.

Not here, where he pointed the mourner to heaven ; nor there, whence he lifted the eye of faith to the spiritual mansions; nor in any place, nor at any time, — let us speak of him as *dead.* It is a sad and cold word. Alive, *alive,* more conscious of life than he could be while with us; with undimmed sight and renewed strength; welcomed by those who had gone before him, surrounded by the holy and happy ones in whose society the intimacies of earth are not forgotten, though the sympathies of the soul be quickened; gazing on that face, radiant with light, which he loved to study as he saw it through the gloom of crucifixion, or prostrate in the rapture of adoration before Him who is at once hidden and revealed by the ineffable glory; drinking in with delight the knowledge which on every side invites his enjoyment, or moving in rapid flight to execute the errands of Divine grace on which he is sent through realms of being that have never passed across the astronomer's field of vision, or bending in fond ministries of influence over those whom he has left to bear a little longer life's toil and peril, — so will we think of him. And, as our thoughts climb up to the blessed experience of which he is now a partaker, our ears shall be unsealed, and the echo of that salutation which greeted him when he passed through the flaming gates into the celestial abodes shall fall like heavenly music on our spirits, — " Well done, good and faithful servant! enter thou into the joy of thy Lord."

APPENDIX.

PRINTED SERMONS, ADDRESSES, AND ESSAYS.

(Most of these printed in pamphlets.)

Of Religious Doctrine, Feeling, and Life.

1830. The Defect of the Times : in. the " Unitarian Advocate."
Personal Interest in Religion : in the " Unitarian Advocate."
The New Birth : in the " Unitarian Advocate."
Unitarian Christianity Suited to Make Men Holy : Sermon
at the Ordination of Rev. A. B. Muzzey, at Framingham.
The Doctrine of Divine Influence : in the " Unitarian Advo-
cate."
Sufferings and Death of Children Consistent with the Divine
Goodness : in Rev. Francis Parkman's " Offering of Sym-
pathy."

1831. Divine Providence : in the " Unitarian Advocate."
Necessity and Sufficiency of Religion : in the " Liberal
Preacher," and reprinted in the " Monthly Religious
Magazine," November, 1871.
A Sermon on Religion for Children.
Revivals : American Unitarian Association Tract, No. 50.
Repentance : in the " Unitarian Advocate."

1832. The Claims of Religion on the Female Sex : in the " Liberal
Preacher."
The Demoniacs of the New Testament : from the " Scrip-
tural Interpreter."

1833. Unitarianism Not a Negative System : Sermon at the Dedication of the Independent Congregational Church in
Ipswich. American Unitarian Association Tract, No. 94.

1834. A New Year's Wish for the Children of my Society.

1835. To the Children of the Federal Street Society.

1836 A Life of Prayer : in the " Liberal Preacher."

1836. Religious Consolation : A volume of selections edited by E. S. G., with an Introduction on Christian Faith. Second edition, 1854.

1839 Atonement. A. U. A. Tract, No. 149.

1840. Unitarian Christianity, What it Is, and What it Is Not : Sermon at the Installation of Rev. John Parkman, at Dover, N.H.

The Spring : A Sermon for Children.

1842. Righteousness the Central Principle of Christianity and the True Basis of the Unitarian Denomination : A Sermon delivered before the Unitarian Convention at Worcester. American Unitarian Association Tract, No 184.

1843. The Value of Natural Religion : The Dudleian Lecture at Harvard College. From the " Christian Examiner."

1845. Mr. Parker and his Views : from the " Christian Examiner."

The Faith of the Unitarian Christian Explained, Justified, and Distinguished : Sermon at the Dedication of the Unitarian Church in Montreal, Canada. American Unitarian Association Tract, No. 220.

1846–1847. Ten Lectures on the Scriptures. In the " Christian World " and the " Sunday Telegraph," Dec. to April.

1847. The Essential in Christianity : A. U. A. Tract, No. 241.

1848. To the Children of the Congregation.

Trust in God : in " Sermons on Christian Communion," edited by J. R. Sullivan.

1849. The Nature and Importance of our Theology : An Address read before the Ministerial Conference in Boston. From the " Christian Examiner."

1856. The Unitarian Belief : from the " Quarterly Journal of the American Unitarian Association."

1859. The Soul's Salvation through Faith in Christ : Sermon at the Ordination of Rév. J. C. Kimball, at Beverly.

1862. The Doctrinal Basis of Christianity to be Preached : Sermon at the Ordination of Rev. James DeNormandie, at Portsmouth, N.H.

1864. Loyalty to Christ : Sermon at the Installation of Rev. A. P. Putnam, at Brooklyn, N.Y.

1868. Christ's Gracious Invitation and Promise : A Sermon preached at the Boston Theatre. In the " Christian Register," January 18.

1871. The Belief of Unitarians : Introductory Sermon of a Course on Unitarian Doctrines delivered in Boston. From the " Christian Register," March 4, 1871.

Of the Ministry.

1833. The Christian Ministry : Sermon at the Ordination of Rev.
A. P. Peabody, at Portsmouth, N.H.

1835. Address to the Society at the Installation of Rev. W. P.
Lunt, at Quincy.

1840. Charge at the Ordination of Rev. George E. Ellis, at
Charlestown.

1842. A Devoted Ministry : Sermon at the Ordination of Rev.
J. I. T. Coolidge over the Purchase Street Congregational
Church in Boston.

Charge at the Ordination of Rev. Amos Smith over the
New North Church in Boston.

1846. Address to the People at the Installation of Rev. David
Fosdick at Hollis Street Church in Boston.

1848. The Relation of the Pulpit to Future Ages: A Sermon
preached before the Massachusetts Convention of Congregational Ministers. From the " Christian Examiner."

1853. Charge at the Installation of Rev. Rufus Ellis over the First
Church in Boston.

1855. Address to the People at the Installation of Rev. Charles
Lowe over the North Church in Salem.

1856. Address to the People at the Installation of Rev. E. E. Hale
over the South Congregational Church in Boston.

1858. Charge at the Installation of Rev. G. Reynolds, at Concord.

1867. Address at the Semi-Centennial Celebration of the Cambridge Divinity School.

Of Philanthropy and Education.

1831. Address delivered before the Boston Sunday School Society
on the Fiftieth Anniversary of the Sunday School Institution.

1846. The Temperance Cause : A Discourse delivered before the
Boston Young Men's Total Abstinence Society.

1848. The Object, Subjects, and Methods of the Ministry at
Large : A Discourse delivered before the Benevolent
Fraternity of Churches.

1849. Sermon before the Fatherless and Widows' Society.

1850. Education the Means of Giving Woman her Proper Position
in Society : An Address delivered before the Graduates
and Members of the West Newton State Normal School.

1852. The Spirit of Reform : A Fast Day Sermon. From the " Boston Evening Transcript."

1853. Domestic Discipline : A Fast Day Sermon. In the " Boston Evening Transcript."

1857. Dissipation : A Sermon.

The Influence of Woman : A Sermon. (Not published.)

Antioch College : in the " Quarterly Journal of the American Unitarian Association."

1860. Address delivered before the Sunday School Convention at Fitchburg.

1863. The Benevolent Fraternity of Churches : A Discourse delivered in the Arlington Street Church. Also printed with the " Twenty-Ninth Annual Report of the Boston Fraternity of Churches."

Of the Nation.

1830. Importance of a Just Moral Sentiment in the People of the United States : A Thanksgiving Day Discourse.

1835. The Times : in the " Knickerbocker Magazine."

1842. The Religion of Politics : the Annual Election Sermon.

1845. Peace, Not War : A Sermon preached December 14.

1850. Our Help is in God : A Sermon preached February 24, the Fugitive Slave Bill being under discussion.

Thanksgiving for the Union : A Thanksgiving Day Sermon.

1854. Relation of the North to Slavery : A Sermon preached June 11, after the rendition of Burns.

1856. The State of the Country : A Sermon preached June 8, after Brooks's assault on Charles Sumner.

1860. A Sober Word for the Hour : A Thanksgiving Day Sermon, on the eve of war.

1863. Repentance amidst Deliverance ; Mobs : Two Sermons preached July 12 and July 19, after Gettysburg and the New York riots.

On Special Occasions.

1840. The Arrival of the " Britannia."

1851. The Railroad Jubilee : in the " Boston Evening Transcript."

1858. The Atlantic Telegraph.

1860. The Prince's Visit.

1868. The National Commercial Convention.

Memorials of Friends.

1842. Address at the Funeral of Rev. W. E. Channing, D.D., and Sermon delivered in the Federal Street Meeting-house on the Sunday after the Death of Dr. Channing : with Notes. The former also printed as American Unitarian Association Tract, No. 187.

1847. A Good Old Age : A Sermon memorial of Hon. John Davis, LL.D.

Discourse delivered at the Funeral of Rev. W. B. O. Peabody, D.D., in Springfield.

The Good Judge : A Sermon memorial of Hon. Artemas Ward, LL.D.

1852. The Faithful Man : A Sermon memorial of Thomas Tarbell, Esq.

1853. The Useful Man : A Sermon preached at the Funeral of Hon. Charles Paine in Northfield, Vt.

1854. Discourse delivered at the Funeral of Rev. Alex. Young, D.D., Pastor of the New South Church, Boston.

1859. Sermon preached in the First Independent Church in Baltimore, on the Sunday after the Death of Rev. Geo. W. Burnap, D.D.

The Physician : A Sermon memorial of Marshall S. Perry, M.D.

1861. Religion Conducive to Prosperity in this Life : A Sermon memorial of Hon. Nathan Appleton.

1864. The Discipline of the Hour : A Sermon memorial of Mrs. S. L. Torrey. (Not published.)

Discourse occasioned by the Death of the Hon. Josiah Quincy.

Discourse delivered in the Church of the First Parish in Dedham on the Sunday after the Death of Rev. Alvan Lamson, D.D.

1866. Address at the Funeral of Rev. Edward B. Hall, D.D., Pastor of First Congregational Society in Providence, R.I.

1867. An Address at the Commemorative Service held on the Twenty-fifth Anniversary of Dr. Channing's Death in Arlington Street Church.

1869. Death in its Purpose and Effect : A Discourse in memory of Robert Waterston. (Not published.)

1871. Discourse in Memory of Mr. Robert B. Storer.

The Christian Scholar : A Memorial of Mr. George Ticknor. In " Old and New," May, 1871.

Of his Church and Himself.

1839. Hymns and Exercises for the Federal Street Sunday School: arranged by E. S. G.

1860. A Memorial of the Federal Street Meeting-house : A Discourse preached on the last Sunday morning of its use for Public Worship, March 13, 1859, by the Minister of the Congregation ; and Addresses delivered in the afternoon of that day by others ; with an Appendix.

1862. Positive Faith : A Discourse preached at the Dedication of the Church in Arlington Street, Dec. 11, 1861 : with an Appendix.

Services for Arlington Street Church.

1864. Sermon preached at the Close of the Fortieth Year of his Ministry, July 3, 1864.

1870. The Old and the New : A Sermon preached Jan. 2, 1870.

MAGAZINE ARTICLES

NOT INCLUDED IN THE PREVIOUS LIST.

(Editorial Articles, save the five starred.)

In the " Scriptural Interpreter."

1831. Vol. I.　The Temptation of Jesus Christ.

The Brevity of the Gospels.

1832. Vol. II.　The Excellences and Defects of the Old Testament. (Two articles.)

The Lord's Prayer.

The Sermon on the Mount.

1833. Vol. III. The Use of the Bible in the Instruction of Children.

First Principles of Scriptural Interpretation : A Lecture delivered before the Sunday School Society. (Two articles.)

The Appearance of the Angels to the Shepherds.

1834. Vol. IV. On the Domestic Reading of the Scriptures.

Familiar Letters on the Old Testament. (Five articles.)

The Mosaic and the Christian Dispensations Compared. (Two articles.)

1835. Vol. V. On Inspiration.

Besides many shorter pieces, — aids in interpreting the Bible.

In the " Monthly Miscellany of Religion and Letters."

1839. Vol. I.   * Aggregate Meeting of Unitarians in London.
1840. Vol. II.   Editorial Notice.
                The Close of the Year.
                Claims of the Bible on our Perusal.
       Vol. III.   Life and Character of the late Dr. Tuckerman.
                The Church and the World.
1841. Vol. IV.   Common School Education.
                Death of President Harrison.
                The Example of Christ.
       Vol. V.   Manchester College Lectures.
                Christ an Example.
                Thrush's ' Last Thoughts ' on War.
                Recent Deaths in England.
                The Paternal Government of God.
1842. Vol. VI.   To Our Readers.
                Grounds of Religious Belief.
1843. Vol. VIII.   Where does the New Year Find us?
                English Sermons on Dr. Channing's Death.
                (Three articles.)
       Vol. IX.   Dogmatism.
                Disruption of the Scottish Church.
                The late Thomas Thrush of England.
                The Ministry at Large.
                The late Rev. Henry Ware, Jr.
Besides many short pieces in the department of " Intelligence."

In the " Monthly Religious Magazine."

1844. Vol. I.   Personal and Social Reform.
                The Presidential Election.
                Spiritual Kindred;
                Prison Discipline.
1845. Vol. II.   * Practical Preaching.
1847. Vol. IV.   * The Anniversary Week.
1862. Vol. XXVIII. * The Bicentenary of the English Non-
                Conformists : A Discourse delivered in
                Boston, Aug. 31, 1862.

In the " Christian Examiner."

1825.	Vol. II.	* Erroneous Views of Death.
1844.	Vol. XXXVI.	Editorial Notice by A. L. & E. S. G.
		What is Christianity?
		Present Position of Unitarianism.
	Vol. XXXVII.	Present Position of Unitarianism.
		Sketches of the Reformers.
1845.	Vol. XXXVIII.	The Church.
	Vol. XXXIX.	Harvard College — Sectarianism.
1846.	Vol. XL.	The Unitarian Denomination.
	Vol. XLI.	The Cause of Peace.
		Greenwood's Miscellaneous Writings.
1847.	Vol. XLIII.	Religious Aspect of the Time.
1848.	Vol. XLIV.	The Mexican War.
		Whitwell's Translation of Romans.
1849.	Vol. XLVI.	Kentish's Notes on Scripture.
		The Unitarian Meetings.

Besides short pieces in the department of " Intelligence."